The Baby Boom

AMERICANS BORN 1946 to 1964

6th EDITION

The American Generations Series

BY CHERYL RUSSELL

New Strategist Publications, Inc.
Ithaca, New York

New Strategist Publications, Inc.
P.O. Box 242, Ithaca, New York 14851
800/848-0842; 607/273-0913
www.newstrategist.com

ISBN 978-1-935114-17-8

Printed in the United States of America

Table of Contents

Chapter 5. Income

Chapter 6. Labor Force

Chapter 7. Living Arrangements

Chapter 8. Population

Chapter 9. Spending

Chapter 10. Time Use

Chapter 11. Wealth

Tables

Chapter 4. Housing

Chapter 5. Income

Chapter 6. Labor Force

Chapter 7. Living Arrangements

Chapter 8. Population

Chapter 9. Spending

Chapter 10. Time Use

Chapter 11. Wealth

Illustrations

Chapter 1. Attitudes

Chapter 2. Education

Chapter 3. Health

Chapter 4. Housing

Chapter 5. Income

Introduction

The mood of the nation—its problems and concerns, hopes and fears—are influenced by the age structure of the population. For more than 50 years, the Baby-Boom generation has been one of the most important—if not *the* most important—factors shaping the age structure. The enormous size of the Baby-Boom generation ensures that when it sneezes the nation catches a cold. Today, the United States has pneumonia, suffering through the worst economic downturn in at least a generation. The decline of the housing and stock markets has decimated the net worth of Boomers, millions of whom are on the brink of retirement. The sixth edition of *The Baby Boom: Americans Born 1946 to 1964* is your strategic guide to the changing socioeconomic status of the most important generation of Americans.

The oldest Boomers have crossed the threshold into old age, turning 62 in 2008 and becoming eligible for early Social Security benefits. Few have saved much money, and those who managed to save are watching their wealth disappear as housing and stock values decline. The priorities of Baby Boomers are changing—and fast. *The Baby Boom: Americans Born 1946 to 1964* details the status of the Baby-Boom generation today and reveals the direction in which their new priorities may steer the nation in the future.

It is not easy to study the nation's 76 million Boomers. Few government surveys focus solely on the generation, and the ages of Boomers usually do not fit neatly into traditional five- or ten-year age categories. In 2009, for example, Boomers span the ages from 45 to 63. To analyze the socioeconomic status of Boomers, most of the tables in this book must approximate the Baby-Boom generation. Single-year-of-age data are shown when they are available, but five-year age groups are most common. If five-year age categories are shown, Boomers are included in the 45-to-49 age group at the younger end through the 60-to-64 age group at the older end. In a few tables, data are available only for 10-year or even broader age groups, which forces a more general analysis of trends among the middle aged.

Whether Boomer age groups are exact or approximate, however, the results are clear. Although many Boomers are in their peak earning and spending years, they are experiencing economic setbacks that began well before the current recession. The oldest Boomers are now empty-nesters and some are retirees. Many are postponing retirement, and their greater labor force participation is boosting the incomes of 55-to-64-year-olds. It looks like the Golden Years of the Baby-Boom generation are going to be busy. *The Baby Boom: Americans Born 1946 to 1964* is your guide to the dynamic and unfolding story of the fate of the Baby-Boom generation and the future of the nation itself.

How to use this book

The Baby Boom: Americans Born 1946 to 1964 is designed for easy use. It is divided into 11 chapters, organized alphabetically: Attitudes, Education, Health, Housing, Income, Labor Force, Living Arrangements, Population, Spending, Time Use, and Wealth.

The sixth edition of *The Baby Boom* includes the latest data on the changing demographics of homeownership, based on the Census Bureau's 2008 Housing Vacancies and Homeownership Survey. In the Health chapter, you will find up-to-date statistics on health insurance coverage, as well as new data on the use of alternative medicine. The Income chapter, with statistics from the 2008 Current Population Survey, reveals the struggle of so many Americans to stay afloat. *The Baby Boom* presents labor force data for 2008, which includes the government's labor force projections that show rising labor force participation among older Boomers. It contains new data on the health of the population, which includes updated estimates of the overweight and obese. The Census Bureau's latest population projections are also included in the book, which show the enormous growth of the older population already in progress. *The Baby Boom* also presents estimates of household wealth from the Federal Reserve Board's 2007 Survey of Consumer Finances, which reveal the financial status of households just as the housing bubble burst and the recession began. New to this edition is an Attitudes chapter with data from the 2008 General Social Survey that compare and contrast the perspectives of the generations.

Most of the tables in *The Baby Boom* are based on data collected by the federal government, in particular the Census Bureau, the Bureau of Labor Statistics, the National Center for Education Statistics, the National Center for Health Statistics, and the Federal Reserve Board. The federal government is the best source of up-to-date, reliable information on the changing characteristics of Americans. By having *The Baby Boom* on your bookshelf, you can get the answers to your questions faster than you can online. Even better, visit www.newstrategist.com and download the PDF version of *The Baby Boom*, which includes links to an Excel version of every table in the book, which will enable you to do your own analyses, put together a PowerPoint presentation, etc.

Each chapter of *The Baby Boom* includes the demographic and lifestyle data most important to researchers. Within each chapter, most of the tables are based on data collected by the federal government, but they are not simply reproductions of government spreadsheets—as is the case in many reference books. Instead, each table is compiled and created by New Strategist's editors with calculations designed to reveal the trends. The task of extracting and processing raw data from the government's web sites to create a single table can require hours of effort. New Strategist has done the work for you, with each table telling a story about Boomers—a story explained by the accompanying text and chart, which analyze the data and highlight future trends. If you need more information than the tables and text provide, you can plumb the original source listed at the bottom of each table.

The book contains a comprehensive list of tables to help you locate the information you need. For a more detailed search, see the index at the back of the book. Also at the back of the book is the glossary, which defines the terms and describes the many surveys referenced in the tables and text.

Although more than half of Americans are now younger than the youngest Boomer, the Baby Boom continues to be the most influential of all the generations. With *The Baby Boom: Americans Born 1946 to 1964* in your hands, you have a guide not only to Boomers but to the likely course of our nation as well.

CHAPTER

1

Attitudes

■ Older Americans are the most trusting. Forty-one percent of older Americans say most people can be trusted. In contrast, only 24 percent of Millennials say others can be trusted.

■ Generation Xers are least satisfied with their finances, with 36 percent saying they are not at all satisfied.

■ Boomers are most likely to say that their pay has not kept pace with inflation. Forty-five percent of Boomers feel like they are falling behind.

■ Older Americans are by far most likely to think they are much better off than their parents were at the same age (45 percent). Generation Xers are least likely to agree (24 percent).

■ The percentage of people who think two children is ideal ranges from a high of 55 percent among Baby Boomers to a low of 41 percent among Millennials. A larger 44 percent of Millennials think three or more children is ideal.

■ While only 40 percent of older Americans believe in evolution, the share climbs to 48 percent among Boomers, to 52 percent among Gen Xers, and to 62 percent among Millennials.

■ The 52 percent majority of Millennials sees nothing wrong with sexual relations between adults of the same sex. Support shrinks to 45 percent among Gen Xers, 34 percent among Boomers, and to a mere 19 percent among older Americans.

Older Americans Are the Happiest

Most of the married are very happily married.

When asked how happy they are, only about one in three Americans say they are very happy. The 54 percent majority reports feeling only pretty happy. Older people are happier than middle-aged or younger adults. Forty percent of older Americans say they are very happy compared with 31 percent of Baby Boomers and Generation Xers and just 27 percent of Millennials.

The 62 percent majority of married Americans say they are very happily married. Here, too, older Americans are the happiest group, with 67 of them saying they are very happily married. Only 60 percent of Boomers say the same.

Americans are almost evenly split on whether life is exciting (47 percent) or pretty routine (48 percent). Variations by generation are small, but Generation X is slightly more likely than others to find life exciting.

Few believe most people can be trusted. Only 32 percent of the public says that most people can be trusted, down from 37 percent who felt that way 10 years earlier. Younger generations are far less trusting than older Americans, as only 24 percent of Millennials believe most people can be trusted compared with 41 percent of people aged 63 or older.

■ Younger generations of Americans are struggling with a deteriorating economy, which reduces their happiness and increases their distrust.

Few Millennials trust others

(percent of people aged 18 or older who think most people can be trusted, by generation, 2008)

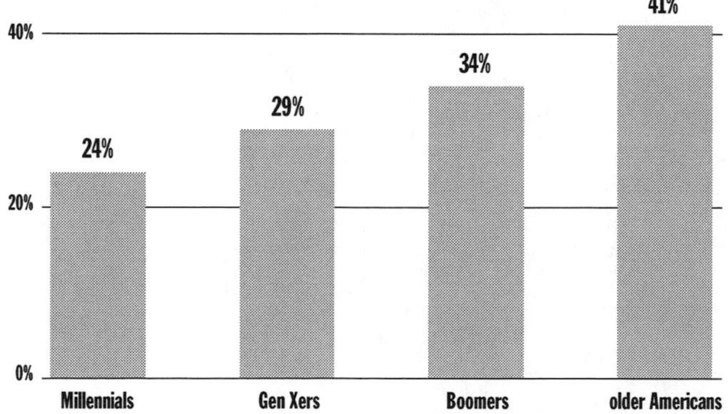

Table 1.1 General Happiness, 2008

"Taken all together, how would you say things are these days—would you say that you are very happy, pretty happy, or not too happy?"

(percent of people aged 18 or older responding by generation, 2008)

	very happy	pretty happy	not too happy
Total people	**31.7%**	**54.4%**	**13.9%**
Millennial generation (aged 18 to 31)	27.4	55.8	16.8
Generation X (aged 32 to 43)	31.0	57.0	12.0
Baby Boom (aged 44 to 62)	30.8	55.6	13.6
Older Americans (aged 63 or older)	39.7	47.2	13.1

Source: Survey Documentation and Analysis, Computer-assisted Survey Methods Program, University of California, Berkeley, General Social Surveys, 1972-2008 Cumulative Data Files, Internet site http://sda.berkeley.edu/cgi-bin32/hsda?harcsda+gss08; calculations by New Strategist

Table 1.2 Happiness of Marriage, 2008

"Taking all things together, how would you describe your marriage?"

(percent of currently married people aged 18 or older responding by generation, 2008)

	very happy	pretty happy	not too happy
Total married people	**62.1%**	**35.3%**	**2.6%**
Millennial generation (aged 18 to 31)	63.7	35.1	1.1
Generation X (aged 32 to 43)	61.5	35.7	2.7
Baby Boom (aged 44 to 62)	60.0	36.7	3.3
Older Americans (aged 63 or older)	66.6	31.7	1.7

Source: Survey Documentation and Analysis, Computer-assisted Survey Methods Program, University of California, Berkeley, General Social Surveys, 1972-2008 Cumulative Data Files, Internet site http://sda.berkeley.edu/cgi-bin32/hsda?harcsda+gss08; calculations by New Strategist

Table 1.3 Is Life Exciting, Routine, or Dull, 2008

"In general, do you find life exciting, pretty routine, or dull?"

(percent of people aged 18 or older responding by generation, 2008)

	exciting	pretty routine	dull
Total people	**47.2%**	**48.1%**	**3.8%**
Millennial generation (aged 18 to 31)	47.4	48.5	3.8
Generation X (aged 32 to 43)	48.6	46.5	3.1
Baby Boom (aged 44 to 62)	46.7	49.0	3.9
Older Americans (aged 63 or older)	46.4	47.7	4.4

Note: Numbers will not sum to total because "don't know" is not shown.
Source: Survey Documentation and Analysis, Computer-assisted Survey Methods Program, University of California, Berkeley, General Social Surveys, 1972-2008 Cumulative Data Files, Internet site http://sda.berkeley.edu/cgi-bin32/hsda?harcsda+gss08; calculations by New Strategist

Table 1.4 Trust in Others, 2008

"Generally speaking, would you say that most people can be trusted or that you can't be too careful in life?"

(percent of people aged 18 or older responding by generation, 2008)

	can trust	cannot trust	depends
Total people	**31.9%**	**63.9%**	**4.3%**
Millennial generation (aged 18 to 31)	24.5	71.1	4.4
Generation X (aged 32 to 43)	29.3	66.7	4.1
Baby Boom (aged 44 to 62)	34.3	61.5	4.2
Older Americans (aged 63 or older)	40.5	55.4	4.1

Source: Survey Documentation and Analysis, Computer-assisted Survey Methods Program, University of California, Berkeley, General Social Surveys, 1972-2008 Cumulative Data Files, Internet site http://sda.berkeley.edu/cgi-bin32/hsda?harcsda+gss08; calculations by New Strategist

Belief in Hard Work Is Strong among Younger Generations

Generation Xers are most likely to own a business.

How do people get ahead? Two-thirds of Americans say it is by hard work. Only 12 percent believe luck alone gets people ahead. Generation Xers (71 percent) and Millennials (70 percent) believe most strongly in hard work to get ahead, whereas Boomers (63 percent) give the least credence to hard work.

Millennials are most likely to live in the same city as they did when they were 16 years old, in part because they have had less time to move than older generations. Boomers are less likely than Gen Xers or older Americans to live in a different state than they did at age 16.

The likelihood of owning a business is greatest among Generation Xers (18 percent) and Boomers (15 percent). Only 8 percent of Millennials own a business, and the share among older Americans is an even smaller 6 percent.

■ The belief in luck as the most important way to get ahead is strongest among older Americans.

Business ownership peaks in middle age

(percent of people aged 18 or older who currently own and help manage a business, by generation, 2008)

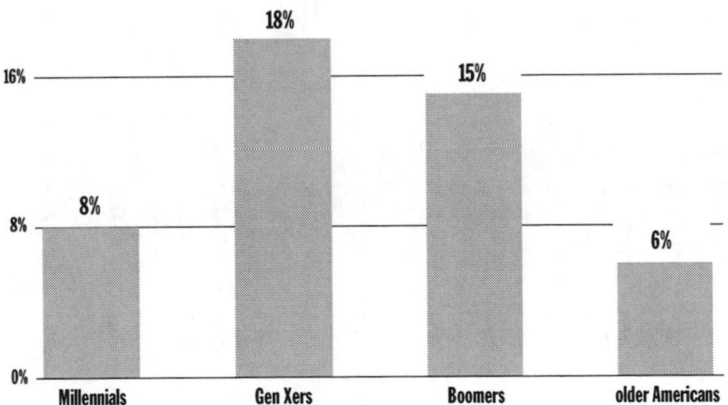

Table 1.5 How People Get Ahead, 2008

"Some people say that people get ahead by their own hard work; others say that lucky breaks or help from other people are more important. Which do you think is most important?"

(percent of people aged 18 or older responding by generation, 2008)

	hard work	both equally	luck
Total people	**67.1%**	**20.8%**	**12.1%**
Millennial generation (aged 18 to 31)	70.2	18.0	11.8
Generation X (aged 32 to 43)	70.7	20.5	8.9
Baby Boom (aged 44 to 62)	63.4	23.7	12.9
Older Americans (aged 63 or older)	66.2	19.2	14.7

Source: Survey Documentation and Analysis, Computer-assisted Survey Methods Program, University of California, Berkeley, General Social Surveys, 1972-2008 Cumulative Data Files, Internet site http://sda.berkeley.edu/cgi-bin32/hsda?harcsda+gss08; calculations by New Strategist

Table 1.6 Geographic Mobility Since Age 16, 2008

"When you were 16 years old, were you living in this same (city/town/county)?"

(percent of people aged 18 or older responding by generation, 2008)

	same city	same state different city	different state
Total people	**40.0%**	**23.2%**	**36.8%**
Millennial generation (aged 18 to 31)	55.4	16.6	28.0
Generation X (aged 32 to 43)	34.1	22.9	43.0
Baby Boom (aged 44 to 62)	37.0	27.1	35.9
Older Americans (aged 63 or older)	32.9	24.5	42.6

Source: Survey Documentation and Analysis, Computer-assisted Survey Methods Program, University of California, Berkeley, General Social Surveys, 1972-2008 Cumulative Data Files, Internet site http://sda.berkeley.edu/cgi-bin32/hsda?harcsda+gss08; calculations by New Strategist

Table 1.7 Business Ownership, 2008

"Are you, alone or with others, currently the owner of a business you help manage, including self-employment or selling any goods or services to others?"

(percent of people aged 18 or older responding by generation, 2008)

	yes	no
Total people	**12.6%**	**87.4%**
Millennial generation (aged 18 to 31)	8.4	91.6
Generation X (aged 32 to 43)	18.1	81.9
Baby Boom (aged 44 to 62)	15.4	84.6
Older Americans (aged 63 or older)	5.8	94.2

Source: Survey Documentation and Analysis, Computer-assisted Survey Methods Program, University of California, Berkeley, General Social Surveys, 1972-2008 Cumulative Data Files, Internet site http://sda.berkeley.edu/cgi-bin32/hsda?harcsda+gss08; calculations by New Strategist

More than One-Third of Gen Xers Are Dissatisfied with Their Finances

Many say that their pay has not kept up with the cost of living.

Few Americans identify with the lower class, but even fewer think they are in the upper class. The 89 percent majority of every generation sees itself as either working class or middle class, but the distribution varies greatly. Whereas Millennials, Xers, and Boomers are more likely to call themselves working class than middle class, the opposite is true for older Americans. The highest share of self-identified lower-class people occurs among Millennials (8 percent). Older Americans are most likely to describe themselves as upper class (5 percent).

A 47 percent plurality of Americans believes their family income is average, while not quite one-third says they make less than average. Baby Boomers are most likely to say they have above average incomes, and they may well be right since they are in their peak earning years.

The share of people who are satisfied with their financial situation stood at 29 percent in 2008, down slightly from the 31 percent of 1998. In parallel, those more or less satisfied with their finances have declined from 44 to 42 percent. Satisfaction with personal finances is greatest among older Americans, only 20 percent of whom are not at all satisfied. The dissatisfied share peaks among Generation Xers at 36 percent, as they juggle college loans, mortgages, and the expenses of growing families.

When asked whether the pay at their current job has kept pace with the cost of living, Boomers are by far most likely to say it has not. The Millennial generation has the largest share of people who say their pay has just about kept pace with inflation. In each generation about one in four say their pay has risen faster than the cost of living.

■ Financial backsliding was common among working Americans even before the current economic disruptions.

Many Boomers and younger adults are dissatisfied with their financial situation

(percent of people aged 18 or older who say they are not at all satisfied with their financial situation, by generation, 2008)

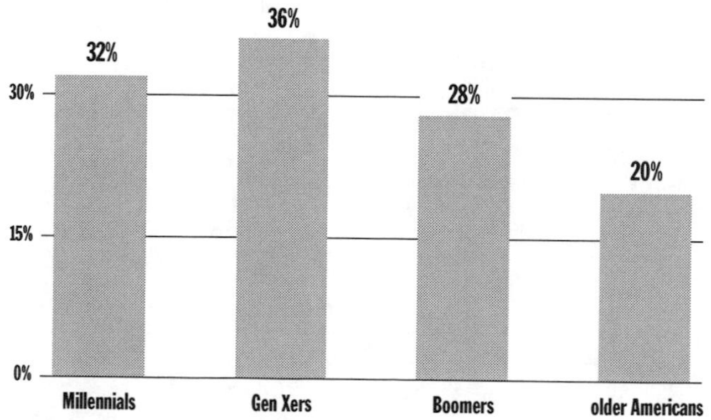

Table 1.8 Social Class Membership, 2008

"If you were asked to use one of four names for your social class, which would you say you belong in: the lower class, the working class, the middle class, or the upper class?"

(percent of people aged 18 or older responding by generation, 2008)

	lower	working	middle	upper
Total people	**7.3%**	**45.7%**	**43.4%**	**3.6%**
Millennial generation (aged 18 to 31)	8.1	49.4	40.1	2.5
Generation X (aged 32 to 43)	6.7	50.5	38.6	4.2
Baby Boom (aged 44 to 62)	7.3	45.5	43.7	3.5
Older Americans (aged 63 or older)	6.6	35.3	53.2	4.8

Source: Survey Documentation and Analysis, Computer-assisted Survey Methods Program, University of California, Berkeley, General Social Surveys, 1972-2008 Cumulative Data Files, Internet site http://sda.berkeley.edu/cgi-bin32/hsda?harcsda+gss08; calculations by New Strategist

Table 1.9 Family Income Relative to Others, 2008

"Compared with American families in general, would you say your family income is far below average, below average, average, above average, or far above average?"

(percent of people aged 18 or older responding by generation, 2008)

	far below average	below average	average	above average	far above average
Total people	**6.3%**	**25.2%**	**46.7%**	**19.8%**	**2.0%**
Millennial generation (aged 18 to 31)	6.6	26.8	49.4	16.5	0.7
Generation X (aged 32 to 43)	7.8	25.5	43.9	20.7	2.2
Baby Boom (aged 44 to 62)	5.6	22.8	46.2	22.4	3.1
Older Americans (aged 63 or older)	5.0	27.8	47.9	17.9	1.4

Source: Survey Documentation and Analysis, Computer-assisted Survey Methods Program, University of California, Berkeley, General Social Surveys, 1972-2008 Cumulative Data Files, Internet site http://sda.berkeley.edu/cgi-bin32/hsda?harcsda+gss08; calculations by New Strategist

Table 1.10 Satisfaction with Financial Situation, 2008

"So far as you and your family are concerned, would you say that you are pretty well satisfied with your present financial situation, more or less satisfied, or not satisfied at all?"

(percent of people aged 18 or older responding by generation, 2008)

	satisfied	more or less satisfied	not at all sarisfied
Total people	**28.9%**	**41.7%**	**29.4%**
Millennial generation (aged 18 to 31)	24.8	43.7	31.5
Generation X (aged 32 to 43)	20.5	43.7	35.7
Baby Boom (aged 44 to 62)	27.3	44.2	28.4
Older Americans (aged 63 or older)	48.0	31.6	20.4

Source: Survey Documentation and Analysis, Computer-assisted Survey Methods Program, University of California, Berkeley, General Social Surveys, 1972-2008 Cumulative Data Files, Internet site http://sda.berkeley.edu/cgi-bin32/hsda?harcsda+gss08; calculations by New Strategist

Table 1.11 How Has Pay Changed, 2008

"Thinking about your current employer, how much has your pay changed on your current job since you began? Would you say . . . "

(percent of employed people aged 18 to 62 responding by generation, 2008)

	my pay has gone up more than the cost of living	my pay has stayed about the same as the cost of living	my pay has not kept up with the cost of living
Total people	**23.5%**	**35.6%**	**40.9%**
Millennial generation (aged 18 to 31)	22.7	41.9	35.3
Generation X (aged 32 to 43)	24.9	37.7	37.4
Baby Boom (aged 44 to 62)	22.9	32.3	44.8

Source: Survey Documentation and Analysis, Computer-assisted Survey Methods Program, University of California, Berkeley, General Social Surveys, 1972-2008 Cumulative Data Files, Internet site http://sda.berkeley.edu/cgi-bin32/hsda?harcsda+gss08; calculations by New Strategist

The American Standard of Living May Be Falling

Fewer Americans believe they are better off than their parents.

When comparing their own standard of living now with that of their parents when they were the same age, 63 percent of respondents say they are better off. The figure was 66 percent 10 years earlier. Older Americans are by far most likely to think they are much better off than their parents were at the same age (45 percent). Generation Xers are least likely to agree (24 percent).

When asked whether they think they have a good chance to improve their standard of living, 59 percent of Americans agree. This is down sharply from the 74 percent of a decade earlier. Not surprisingly, younger people—with most of their life ahead of them—are more hopeful than older Americans. Seventy-two percent of Millennials, but only 47 percent of older Americans, believe that their standard of living will improve.

Sixty percent of respondents believe their children will have a better standard of living when they reach the respondent's present age. The share is 67 percent among Millennials, 61 percent among Xers, 57 percent among Boomers, and 53 percent among older Americans. One in four Boomers and older Americans predict their children will be worse off, but fewer Xers (16 percent) and Millennials (13 percent) agree.

■ The Americans who now have the least are most likely to believe things will be better in the future.

Most still believe children will be better off

(percent of people aged 18 or older with children who think their children's standard of living will be somewhat or much better than theirs is now, by generation, 2008)

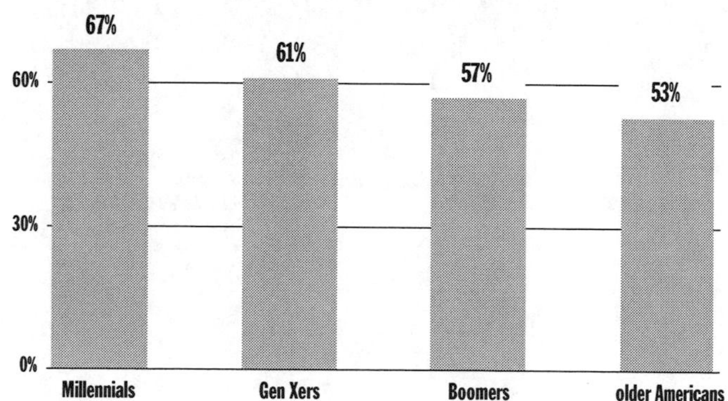

Table 1.12 Parents' Standard of Living, 2008

"Compared to your parents when they were the age you are now, do you think your own standard of living now is much better, somewhat better, about the same, somewhat worse, or much worse than theirs was?"

(percent of people aged 18 or older responding by generation, 2008)

	much better	somewhat better	about the same	somewhat worse	much worse
Total people	**31.6%**	**31.1%**	**21.1%**	**11.5%**	**4.6%**
Millennial generation (aged 18 to 31)	32.9	32.6	20.3	10.5	3.7
Generation X (aged 32 to 43)	24.1	31.6	22.0	16.3	6.1
Baby Boom (aged 44 to 62)	28.9	31.4	22.3	12.4	5.1
Older Americans (aged 63 or older)	45.1	27.9	19.1	5.2	2.7

Source: Survey Documentation and Analysis, Computer-assisted Survey Methods Program, University of California, Berkeley, General Social Surveys, 1972-2008 Cumulative Data Files, Internet site http://sda.berkeley.edu/cgi-bin32/hsda?harcsda+gss08; calculations by New Strategist

Table 1.13 Standard of Living Will Improve, 2008

"The way things are in America, people like me and my family have a good chance of improving our standard of living. Do you agree or disagree?"

(percent of people aged 18 or older responding by generation, 2008)

	strongly agree	agree	neither	disagree	strongly disagree
Total people	**14.7%**	**44.7%**	**13.9%**	**22.9%**	**3.8%**
Millennial generation (aged 18 to 31)	19.6	52.2	11.3	14.0	2.9
Generation X (aged 32 to 43)	15.2	44.7	13.7	21.7	4.6
Baby Boom (aged 44 to 62)	12.0	44.9	11.8	27.9	3.4
Older Americans (aged 63 or older)	13.2	33.6	22.3	26.0	4.9

Source: Survey Documentation and Analysis, Computer-assisted Survey Methods Program, University of California, Berkeley, General Social Surveys, 1972-2008 Cumulative Data Files, Internet site http://sda.berkeley.edu/cgi-bin32/hsda?harcsda+gss08; calculations by New Strategist

Table 1.14 Children's Standard of Living, 2008

"When your children are at the age you are now, do you think their standard of living will be much better, somewhat better, about the same, somewhat worse, or much worse than yours is now?"

(percent of people aged 18 or older with children responding by generation, 2008)

	much better	somewhat better	about the same	somewhat worse	much worse
Total people with children	**30.7%**	**29.2%**	**20.0%**	**14.3%**	**5.8%**
Millennial generation (aged 18 to 31)	40.1	27.0	19.3	8.0	5.5
Generation X (aged 32 to 43)	25.5	36.0	22.9	12.4	3.6
Baby Boom (aged 44 to 62)	27.7	29.5	18.4	17.7	6.5
Older Americans (aged 63 or older)	30.3	23.2	21.3	17.5	7.6

Source: Survey Documentation and Analysis, Computer-assisted Survey Methods Program, University of California, Berkeley, General Social Surveys, 1972-2008 Cumulative Data Files, Internet site http://sda.berkeley.edu/cgi-bin32/hsda?harcsda+gss08; calculations by New Strategist

Two Children Are Most Popular

Many Millennials think three children is the ideal number, however.

Across generations a plurality of Americans thinks that two is the ideal number of children. Boomers, who are finished with their childbearing, are most enthusiastic about two—55 percent say two children is ideal and only 29 percent think three or more is best. In contrast, only 41 percent of Millennials think two is ideal and a larger 44 percent say three or more is best. Millennials are more likely than the oldest Americans—who gave birth to the Baby Boom generation—to think three or more children is ideal.

Regardless of their number, most children are subject to a good, hard spanking when they misbehave. Seventy-one percent of Americans believe children sometimes must be spanked, with little difference by generation.

The 52 percent majority of older Americans believes it is better for everyone involved if the man is the achiever outside the home and the woman takes care of the home and family. Only about one-third of the younger generations agree. A similar gap exists with regard to working mothers. Among Boomers and younger generations, about three out of four think a working mother can have just as warm and secure a relationship with her children as a mother who does not work. Only 62 percent of older Americans agree.

Support for the view that government should help people who are sick and in need is strongest among Millennials and declines with age. Twenty-one percent of older Americans—the only age group that is covered by government-provided health insurance—believe people should help themselves. Only 12 percent of Millennials agree.

■ The generation gap in attitudes between Boomers and their parents is greater than the gap between Boomers and their children.

Few among the younger generations think traditional sex roles are best

(percent of people aged 18 or older who think traditional sex roles are best, by generation, 2008)

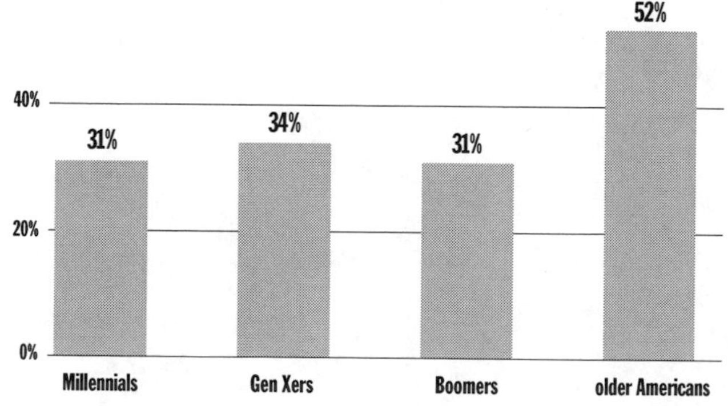

Table 1.15 Ideal Number of Children, 2008

"What do you think is the ideal number of children for a family to have?"

(percent of people aged 18 or older responding by generation, 2008)

	none	one	two	three	four or more	as many as want
Total people	**1.0%**	**2.5%**	**47.7%**	**26.6%**	**10.1%**	**12.1%**
Millennial generation (aged 18 to 31)	0.7	3.9	40.6	34.3	10.1	10.4
Generation X (aged 32 to 43)	0.0	2.5	44.4	29.3	12.0	11.9
Baby Boom (aged 44 to 62)	1.5	1.6	55.2	19.2	9.4	13.2
Older Americans (aged 63 or older)	1.4	2.5	45.5	28.3	9.6	12.6

Source: Survey Documentation and Analysis, Computer-assisted Survey Methods Program, University of California, Berkeley, General Social Surveys, 1972-2008 Cumulative Data Files, Internet site http://sda.berkeley.edu/cgi-bin32/hsda?harcsda+gss08; calculations by New Strategist

Table 1.16 Spanking Children, 2008

"Do you strongly agree, agree, disagree, or strongly disagree that it is sometimes necessary to discipline a child with a good, hard, spanking?"

(percent of people aged 18 or older responding by generation, 2008)

	strongly agree	agree	disagree	strongly disagree
Total people	**24.7%**	**46.2%**	**23.1%**	**6.0%**
Millennial generation (aged 18 to 31)	29.8	41.0	23.0	6.2
Generation X (aged 32 to 43)	19.9	52.3	22.6	5.2
Baby Boom (aged 44 to 62)	24.7	46.1	22.7	6.5
Older Americans (aged 63 or older)	22.9	46.1	25.2	5.7

Source: Survey Documentation and Analysis, Computer-assisted Survey Methods Program, University of California, Berkeley, General Social Surveys, 1972-2008 Cumulative Data Files, Internet site http://sda.berkeley.edu/cgi-bin32/hsda?harcsda+gss08; calculations by New Strategist

Table 1.17 Better for Man to Work, Woman to Tend Home, 2008

"It is much better for everyone involved if the man is the achiever outside the home and the woman takes care of the home and family."

(percent of people aged 18 or older responding by generation, 2008)

	strongly agree	agree	disagree	strongly disagree
Total people	**8.2%**	**27.0%**	**47.2%**	**17.5%**
Millennial generation (aged 18 to 31)	7.3	24.0	44.5	24.2
Generation X (aged 32 to 43)	8.4	25.2	47.8	18.6
Baby Boom (aged 44 to 62)	7.5	24.0	50.7	17.8
Older Americans (aged 63 or older)	11.3	40.5	42.6	5.5

Source: Survey Documentation and Analysis, Computer-assisted Survey Methods Program, University of California, Berkeley, General Social Surveys, 1972-2008 Cumulative Data Files, Internet site http://sda.berkeley.edu/cgi-bin32/hsda?harcsda+gss08; calculations by New Strategist

Table 1.18 Working Mother's Relationship with Children, 2008

"Do you strongly agree, agree, disagree, or strongly disagree with the statement: A working mother can establish just as warm and secure a relationship with her children as a mother who does not work."

(percent of people aged 18 or older responding by generation, 2008)

	strongly agree	agree	disagree	strongly disagree
Total people	**26.3%**	**46.0%**	**22.2%**	**5.4%**
Millennial generation (aged 18 to 31)	26.0	46.1	22.5	5.4
Generation X (aged 32 to 43)	31.4	44.5	20.9	3.2
Baby Boom (aged 44 to 62)	26.3	49.0	19.0	5.6
Older Americans (aged 63 or older)	20.7	41.4	29.9	7.9

Source: Survey Documentation and Analysis, Computer-assisted Survey Methods Program, University of California, Berkeley, General Social Surveys, 1972-2008 Cumulative Data Files, Internet site http://sda.berkeley.edu/cgi-bin32/hsda?harcsda+gss08; calculations by New Strategist

Table 1.19 Should Government Help the Sick, 2008

"Some people think that it is the responsibility of the government in Washington to see to it that people have help in paying for doctors and hospital bills; they are at point 1. Others think that these matters are not the responsibility of the federal government and that people should take care of these things themselves; they are at point 5. Where would you place yourself on this scale?"

(percent of people aged 18 or older responding by generation, 2008)

	1 government should help	2	3 agree with both	4	5 people should help themselves
Total people	**34.9%**	**18.7%**	**30.0%**	**9.3%**	**7.1%**
Millennial generation (aged 18 to 31)	39.0	23.1	25.9	5.2	6.8
Generation X (aged 32 to 43)	35.0	19.8	30.7	9.4	5.1
Baby Boom (aged 44 to 62)	35.2	18.5	28.0	11.4	7.0
Older Americans (aged 63 or older)	28.7	11.2	39.1	10.0	11.0

Source: Survey Documentation and Analysis, Computer-assisted Survey Methods Program, University of California, Berkeley, General Social Surveys, 1972-2008 Cumulative Data Files, Internet site http://sda.berkeley.edu/cgi-bin32/hsda?harcsda+gss08; calculations by New Strategist

Religious Diversity Is on the Rise

Share of Protestants dwindles with each successive generation.

Asked whether science makes our way of life change too fast, the 52 percent majority of Americans disagrees with the statement. Each successive generation is a little surer than the previous one. While 51 percent of older Americans think things change too fast, only 45 percent of Millennials hold that opinion.

Americans are almost equally divided between those who believe in evolution (51 percent) and those who do not (49 percent), but there are large differences by generation. While only 40 percent of older Americans believe in evolution, the share climbs to 48 percent among Boomers, to 52 percent among Gen Xers, and to 62 percent among Millennials.

Among older Americans, 60 percent are Protestants. Among Baby Boomers, the figure is 58 percent. Yet only 39 percent of Generation Xers and Millennials call themselves Protestant. Conversely, the share of people with no religious preference climbs from a mere 7 percent among older Americans to a substantial 27 percent among Millennials. Older Americans are twice as likely as members of younger generations to describe themselves as very religious and they are more likely to see the Bible as the word of God.

The majority of Americans disapproves of the Supreme Court decision barring local governments from requiring religious readings in public schools. While the slight majority of Millennials and nearly half the Generation Xers support the decision, only 36 percent of Baby Boomers and just 31 percent of older Americans back the Supreme Court's decision.

■ Along with the growing racial and ethnic diversity of the American, religious preferences are also growing more diverse.

Younger generations are less Protestant

(percent of people aged 18 or older whose religious preference is Protestant, by generation, 2008)

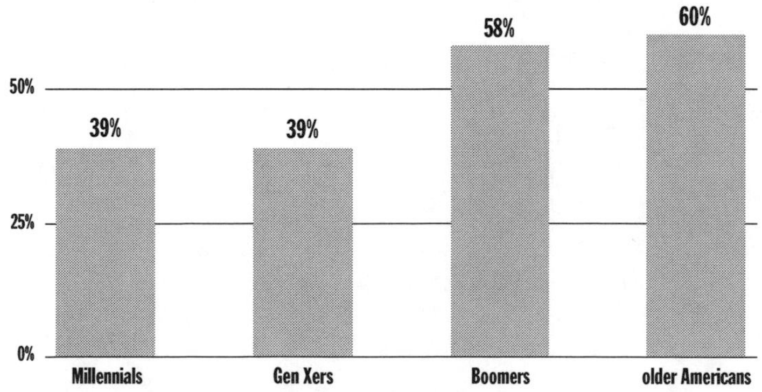

Table 1.20 Attitude toward Science, 2008

"Do you strongly agree, agree, disagree, or strongly disagree with the statement: Science makes our way of life change too fast."

(percent of people aged 18 or older responding by generation, 2008)

	strongly agree	agree	disagree	strongly disagree
Total people	**9.0%**	**38.8%**	**43.9%**	**8.3%**
Millennial generation (aged 18 to 31)	8.3	36.3	46.1	9.3
Generation X (aged 32 to 43)	8.4	39.4	44.9	7.3
Baby Boom (aged 44 to 62)	10.3	38.0	42.2	9.4
Older Americans (aged 63 or older)	7.6	43.4	43.4	5.7

Source: Survey Documentation and Analysis, Computer-assisted Survey Methods Program, University of California, Berkeley, General Social Surveys, 1972-2008 Cumulative Data Files, Internet site http://sda.berkeley.edu/cgi-bin32/hsda?harcsda+gss08; calculations by New Strategist

Table 1.21 Attitude toward Evolution, 2008

"True or false: Human beings, as we know them today, developed from earlier species of animals."

(percent of people aged 18 or older responding by generation, 2008)

	true	false
Total people	**50.9%**	**49.1%**
Millennial generation (aged 18 to 31)	62.1	37.9
Generation X (aged 32 to 43)	51.8	48.2
Baby Boom (aged 44 to 62)	47.8	52.2
Older Americans (aged 63 or older)	39.8	60.2

Source: Survey Documentation and Analysis, Computer-assisted Survey Methods Program, University of California, Berkeley, General Social Surveys, 1972-2008 Cumulative Data Files, Internet site http://sda.berkeley.edu/cgi-bin32/hsda?harcsda+gss08; calculations by New Strategist

Table 1.22 Religious Preference, 2008

"What is your religious preference?"

(percent of people aged 18 or older responding by generation, 2008)

	Protestant	Catholic	Jewish	none
Total people	**49.8%**	**25.1%**	**1.7%**	**16.8%**
Millennial generation (aged 18 to 31)	39.0	26.3	1.2	27.1
Generation X (aged 32 to 43)	39.1	28.1	2.9	18.9
Baby Boom (aged 44 to 62)	58.4	21.1	0.9	13.6
Older Americans (aged 63 or older)	60.1	27.3	2.6	7.2

Note: Figures will not sum to 100 percent because "other religion" is not shown.
Source: Survey Documentation and Analysis, Computer-assisted Survey Methods Program, University of California, Berkeley, General Social Surveys, 1972-2008 Cumulative Data Files, Internet site http://sda.berkeley.edu/cgi-bin32/hsda?harcsda+gss08; calculations by New Strategist

Table 1.23 Degree of Religiosity, 2008

"To what extent do you consider yourself a religious person?"

(percent of people aged 18 or older responding by generation, 2008)

	very religious	moderately relgious	slightly religious	not religious
Total people	**18.2%**	**42.2%**	**23.4%**	**16.2%**
Millennial generation (aged 18 to 31)	12.1	33.1	28.1	26.7
Generation X (aged 32 to 43)	13.8	40.6	25.7	19.9
Baby Boom (aged 44 to 62)	20.1	45.9	22.1	11.9
Older Americans (aged 63 or older)	27.7	48.6	17.4	6.3

Source: Survey Documentation and Analysis, Computer-assisted Survey Methods Program, University of California, Berkeley, General Social Surveys, 1972-2008 Cumulative Data Files, Internet site http://sda.berkeley.edu/cgi-bin32/hsda?harcsda+gss08; calculations by New Strategist

Table 1.24 Belief in the Bible, 2008

"Which of these statements comes closest to describing your feelings about the Bible? 1) The Bible is the actual word of God and is to be taken literally, word for word; 2) The Bible is the inspired word of God but not everything in it should be taken literally, word for word; 3) The Bible is an ancient book of fables, legends, history, and moral precepts recorded by men."

(percent of people aged 18 or older responding by generation, 2008)

	word of God	inspired word	book of fables	other
Total people	**32.0%**	**47.0%**	**19.6%**	**1.4%**
Millennial generation (aged 18 to 31)	27.5	50.3	21.0	1.3
Generation X (aged 32 to 43)	30.8	46.3	20.3	2.6
Baby Boom (aged 44 to 62)	33.6	44.9	20.6	1.0
Older Americans (aged 63 or older)	36.0	48.1	15.0	1.0

Source: Survey Documentation and Analysis, Computer-assisted Survey Methods Program, University of California, Berkeley, General Social Surveys, 1972-2008 Cumulative Data Files, Internet site http://sda.berkeley.edu/cgi-bin32/hsda?harcsda+gss08; calculations by New Strategist

Table 1.25 Bible in the Public Schools, 2008

"The United States Supreme Court has ruled that no state or local government may require the reading of the Lord's Prayer or Bible verses in public schools. What are your views on this? Do you approve or disapprove of the court ruling?"

(percent of people aged 18 or older responding by generation, 2008)

	approve	disapprove
Total people	**41.8%**	**58.2%**
Millennial generation (aged 18 to 31)	52.8	47.2
Generation X (aged 32 to 43)	48.0	52.0
Baby Boom (aged 44 to 62)	36.2	63.8
Older Americans (aged 63 or older)	30.7	69.3

Source: Survey Documentation and Analysis, Computer-assisted Survey Methods Program, University of California, Berkeley, General Social Surveys, 1972-2008 Cumulative Data Files, Internet site http://sda.berkeley.edu/cgi-bin32/hsda?harcsda+gss08; calculations by New Strategist

Growing Tolerance of Sexual Behavior

Americans are growing more accepting of premarital sex and homosexuality.

The share of Americans who believe that premarital sex is not wrong at all grew from 43 percent in 1998 to 55 percent in 2008. While the majority of Boomers and younger generations see nothing wrong with premarital sex, the share is just 38 percent among older Americans.

When it comes to sexual relations between adults of the same sex, the trend of growing tolerance is apparent as well. Each successive generation is less likely to condemn homosexuality. The 52 percent majority of Millennials sees nothing wrong with same-sex sexual relations, but support dwindles to 45 percent among Xers, 34 percent among Boomers, and a mere 19 percent among older Americans.

■ Acceptance of gays and lesbians will grow as tolerant Millennials replace older, less tolerant generations in the population.

Most Millennials see nothing wrong with gays and lesbians

(percent of people aged 18 or older who see nothing wrong with sexual relations between two adults of the same sex, by generation, 2008)

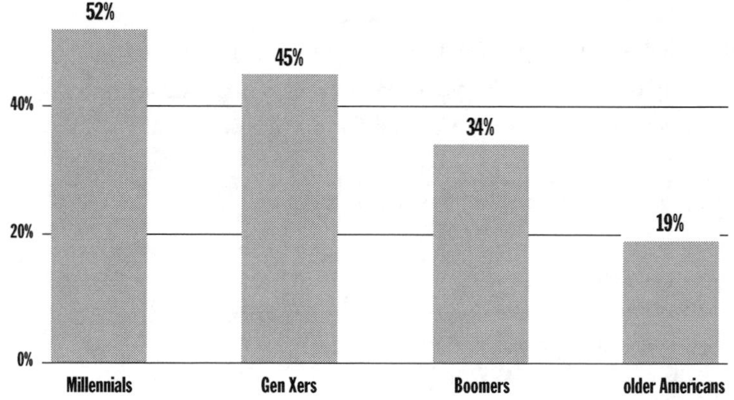

Table 1.26 Premarital Sex, 2008

"If a man and woman have sex relations before marriage, do you think it is always wrong, almost always wrong, wrong only sometimes, or not wrong at all?"

(percent of people aged 18 or older responding by generation, 2008)

	always wrong	almost always wrong	sometimes wrong	not wrong at all
Total people	**22.6%**	**7.2%**	**15.4%**	**54.8%**
Millennial generation (aged 18 to 31)	17.5	6.9	15.8	59.8
Generation X (aged 32 to 43)	21.0	4.9	17.7	56.5
Baby Boom (aged 44 to 62)	23.0	6.5	12.4	58.1
Older Americans (aged 63 or older)	31.0	11.7	18.9	38.4

Source: Survey Documentation and Analysis, Computer-assisted Survey Methods Program, University of California, Berkeley, General Social Surveys, 1972-2008 Cumulative Data Files, Internet site http://sda.berkeley.edu/cgi-bin32/hsda?harcsda+gss08; calculations by New Strategist

Table 1.27 Homosexual Relations, 2008

"What about sexual relations between two adults of the same sex?"

(percent of people aged 18 or older responding by generation, 2008)

	always wrong	almost always wrong	sometimes wrong	not wrong at all
Total people	**52.4%**	**3.1%**	**6.7%**	**37.8%**
Millennial generation (aged 18 to 31)	41.4	1.8	5.3	51.5
Generation X (aged 32 to 43)	47.0	4.3	3.9	44.8
Baby Boom (aged 44 to 62)	53.0	3.3	10.0	33.8
Older Americans (aged 63 or older)	72.6	2.8	5.4	19.2

Source: Survey Documentation and Analysis, Computer-assisted Survey Methods Program, University of California, Berkeley, General Social Surveys, 1972-2008 Cumulative Data Files, Internet site http://sda.berkeley.edu/cgi-bin32/hsda?harcsda+gss08; calculations by New Strategist

Television News Is Most Important

The Internet has jumped into the number two position.

Nearly half of Americans get most of their news from television, 22 percent from the Internet, and 20 percent from the newspaper. Together these three news outlets are the main source of news for 90 percent of the public. But there are big differences by generation. Millennials are far more likely than any other generation to depend on the Internet. Thirty-eight percent of Millennials say the Internet is their most important source of news versus 30 percent of Gen Xers, 15 percent of Boomers and just 5 percent of older Americans. The Millennial attachment to the Internet is so strong that it has boosted the Internet into second place as a news source.

When asked about their political leanings, Americans like to point to the moderate middle (39 percent). A slightly smaller 36 percent say they are conservative, and 26 percent identify themselves as liberal. Millennials are twice as likely as older Americans to hold liberal views. The share of self-described conservatives drops with each successive generation, from 45 percent among older Americans to 28 percent among Millennials. In fact, a larger share of Millennials is liberal than conservative—the only generation in which liberals outnumber conservatives.

■ Millennials depend more on the Internet than on television for the news.

News sources differ dramatically by generation

(percent of people aged 18 or older who turn to each source for the news, by generation, 2008)

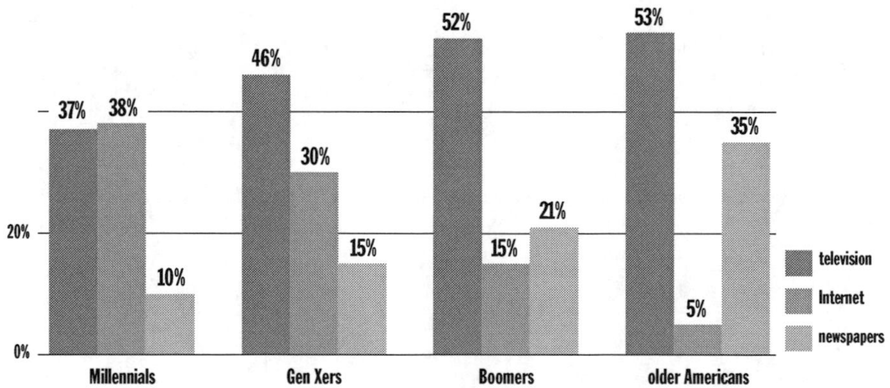

Table 1.28 Main Source of Information about Events in the News, 2008

"We are interested in how people get information about events in the news. Where do you get most of your information about current news events?"

(percent of people aged 18 or older responding by generation, 2008)

	television	Internet	newspapers	radio	family, friends and colleagues	books, magazines, other
Total people	**47.5%**	**22.0%**	**19.6%**	**6.1%**	**2.8%**	**2.0%**
Millennial generation (aged 18 to 31)	36.8	38.3	9.8	8.4	5.9	0.8
Generation X (aged 32 to 43)	46.3	30.0	15.2	3.1	3.1	2.3
Baby Boom (aged 44 to 62)	52.4	14.8	21.5	7.6	1.5	2.2
Older Americans (aged 63 or older)	53.1	5.0	34.5	3.5	1.0	2.9

Source: Survey Documentation and Analysis, Computer-assisted Survey Methods Program, University of California, Berkeley, General Social Surveys, 1972-2008 Cumulative Data Files, Internet site http://sda.berkeley.edu/cgi-bin32/hsda?harcsda+gss08; calculations by New Strategist

Table 1.29 Political Leanings, 2008

"We hear a lot of talk these days about liberals and conservatives. On a seven-point scale from extremely liberal (1) to extremely conservative (7), where would you place yourself?"

(percent of people aged 18 or older responding by generation, 2008)

	1 extremely liberal	2 liberal	3 slightly liberal	4 moderate	5 slightly conservative	6 conservative	7 extremely conservative
Total people	**2.9%**	**12.2%**	**10.6%**	**38.6%**	**15.1%**	**16.7%**	**3.9%**
Millennial generation (aged 18 to 31)	3.0	16.1	15.3	37.6	13.9	12.2	2.0
Generation X (aged 32 to 43)	3.7	12.9	11.1	39.4	15.6	12.3	5.0
Baby Boom (aged 44 to 62)	2.1	11.1	10.2	38.4	15.9	18.1	4.1
Older Americans (aged 63 or older)	3.2	8.8	4.8	38.4	14.8	25.4	4.6

Source: Survey Documentation and Analysis, Computer-assisted Survey Methods Program, University of California, Berkeley, General Social Surveys, 1972-2008 Cumulative Data Files, Internet site http://sda.berkeley.edu/cgi-bin32/hsda?harcsda+gss08; calculations by New Strategist

Millennials and Gen Xers Are at Odds over Death Penalty

Overall opposition to capital punishment is growing.

Opposition to capital punishment is growing. In 1998, 27 percent of the public opposed the death penalty for persons convicted of murder. In 2008, the figure had increased to 32 percent. In a generational pattern rarely seen, support for the death penalty is strongest among Generation X (71 percent) and weakest among Millennials (63 percent).

The vast majority of Americans favors requiring a permit for gun ownership, and there is little variation by generation. Generation Xers are slightly more likely to favor gun permits than the other generations.

Support for legal abortion under certain circumstances is overwhelming. Nine out of 10 Americans approve of abortion if the women's health is in serious danger, and three-quarters if the pregnancy is the result of rape or there is a chance of serious defect in the baby. Economic and lifestyle reasons garner substantially lower approval ratings of 40 to 44 percent. Generally, there are only small differences in opinion by generation, but there are exceptions. Millennials are sharply less likely than the other generations to allow abortion because of a serious defect in the baby, for example. Boomers are much more accepting than other generations of abortion because a woman does not want more children. Older Americans are more likely than younger generations to want to outlaw abortion for economic and lifestyle reasons, but not for health reasons.

The two-thirds majority of Americans favor the right of the terminally ill to die with a doctor's assistance, but support for this measure has fallen slightly over the last decade. Support is strongest among Boomers, who are at an age when they may well see a terminally ill parent suffer, but it is weakest among older Americans themselves.

■ The generation gap between Boomers and older Americans is readily apparent on the issue of abortion for economic or lifestyle reasons.

Most do not favor allowing abortions for any reason

(percent of people aged 18 or older who favor legal abortion for any reason, by generation, 2008)

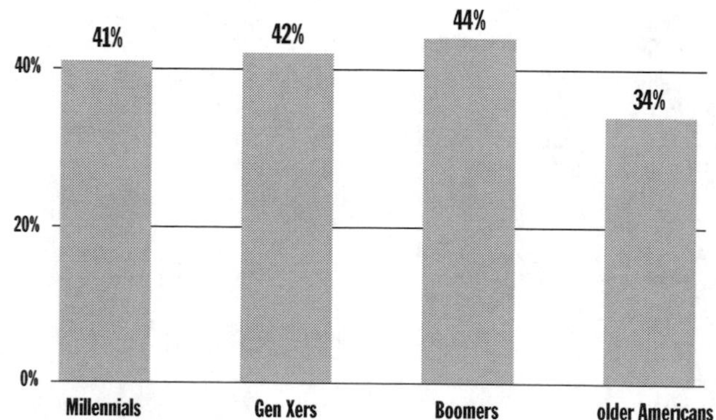

Table 1.30 Favor or Oppose Death Penalty for Murder, 2008

"Do you favor or oppose the death penalty for persons convicted of murder?"

(percent of people aged 18 or older responding by generation, 2008)

	favor	oppose
Total people	**67.6%**	**32.4%**
Millennial generation (aged 18 to 31)	62.8	37.2
Generation X (aged 32 to 43)	71.0	29.0
Baby Boom (aged 44 to 62)	68.0	32.0
Older Americans (aged 63 or older)	69.5	30.5

Source: Survey Documentation and Analysis, Computer-assisted Survey Methods Program, University of California, Berkeley, General Social Surveys, 1972-2008 Cumulative Data Files, Internet site http://sda.berkeley.edu/cgi-bin32/hsda?harcsda+gss08; calculations by New Strategist

Table 1.31 Favor or Oppose Gun Permits, 2008

"Would you favor or oppose a law which would require a person to obtain a police permit before he or she could buy a gun?"

(percent of people aged 18 or older responding by generation, 2008)

	favor	oppose
Total people	**79.1%**	**20.9%**
Millennial generation (aged 18 to 31)	78.3	21.7
Generation X (aged 32 to 43)	81.1	18.8
Baby Boom (aged 44 to 62)	78.4	21.6
Older Americans (aged 63 or older)	78.7	21.3

Source: Survey Documentation and Analysis, Computer-assisted Survey Methods Program, University of California, Berkeley, General Social Surveys, 1972-2008 Cumulative Data Files, Internet site http://sda.berkeley.edu/cgi-bin32/hsda?harcsda+gss08; calculations by New Strategist

Table 1.32 Support for Legal Abortion by Reason, 2008

"Please tell me whether or not you think it should be possible for a pregnant woman to obtain a legal abortion if . . . "

(percent of people aged 18 or older responding yes by generation, 2008)

	her health is seriously endangered	pregnancy is the result of a rape	there is a serious defect in the baby	she cannot afford more children	she does not want more childen	she is single and does not want to marry the man	she wants it for any reason
Total people	**88.6%**	**75.6%**	**73.7%**	**42.3%**	**43.7%**	**40.3%**	**41.2%**
Millennial generation (aged 18 to 31)	85.5	75.8	64.1	43.9	41.5	38.8	41.2
Generation X (aged 32 to 43)	90.6	76.8	75.6	39.4	41.9	40.3	41.8
Baby Boom (aged 44 to 62)	90.4	74.6	78.1	46.2	50.0	43.3	44.5
Older Americans (aged 63 or older)	86.6	75.4	75.2	35.2	35.4	35.1	33.6

Source: Survey Documentation and Analysis, Computer-assisted Survey Methods Program, University of California, Berkeley, General Social Surveys, 1972-2008 Cumulative Data Files, Internet site http://sda.berkeley.edu/cgi-bin32/hsda?harcsda+gss08; calculations by New Strategist

Table 1.33 Doctor-Assisted Suicide, 2008

"When a person has a disease that cannot be cured, do you think doctors should be allowed by law to end the patient's life by some painless means if the patient and his family request it?"

(percent of people aged 18 or older responding by generation, 2008)

	yes	no
Total people	**66.2%**	**33.8%**
Millennial generation (aged 18 to 31)	63.7	36.3
Generation X (aged 32 to 43)	66.1	33.9
Baby Boom (aged 44 to 62)	69.9	30.1
Older Americans (aged 63 or older)	61.1	38.9

Source: Survey Documentation and Analysis, Computer-assisted Survey Methods Program, University of California, Berkeley, General Social Surveys, 1972-2008 Cumulative Data Files, Internet site http://sda.berkeley.edu/cgi-bin32/hsda?harcsda+gss08; calculations by New Strategist

CHAPTER
2

Education

■ The Baby-Boom generation was the first to go to college in significant numbers. Overall, the 58 percent majority of Boomers have college experience and 29 percent have at least a bachelor's degree.

■ Men aged 55 to 64—an age group now almost entirely filled with the oldest Boomers—are among the most highly educated of all Americans. More than one-third has at least a bachelor's degree, and 15 percent have an advanced degree.

■ Women aged 45 to 64 are less educated than their male counterparts. Among people aged 55 to 59, for example, 29 percent of women and 34 percent of men have a college degree.

■ Asians are by far the best-educated Boomers. More than half of Asian men and 44 percent of Asian women aged 45 to 64 have a bachelor's degree or more education.

■ Almost one-third of people aged 45 to 64 took work-related courses in 2005, and one in five participated in personal interest courses.

Boomers Rank Second in Educational Attainment

Generation X is the most highly educated generation.

The percentage of Americans with a college degree peaks in early middle age. One reason for the middle-aged peak is that it takes many people more than four years to complete their bachelor's degree.

Thirty-three percent of Generation Xers have a college degree, the highest level of education among the generations. Boomers are not far behind, at 30 percent. Thirty-two percent of people aged 25 to 34 (most of whom are Millennials) are college graduates, a figure that may rise as they get older. Among Americans aged 65 or older, only 20 percent are college graduates.

■ The women of Generation X are better educated than Boomer women, pushing the percentage of Generation Xers with a college degree above that of Boomers.

The 35-to-44 age group has the highest level of educational attainment

(percent of people aged 25 or older with a bachelor's degree, by age, 2008)

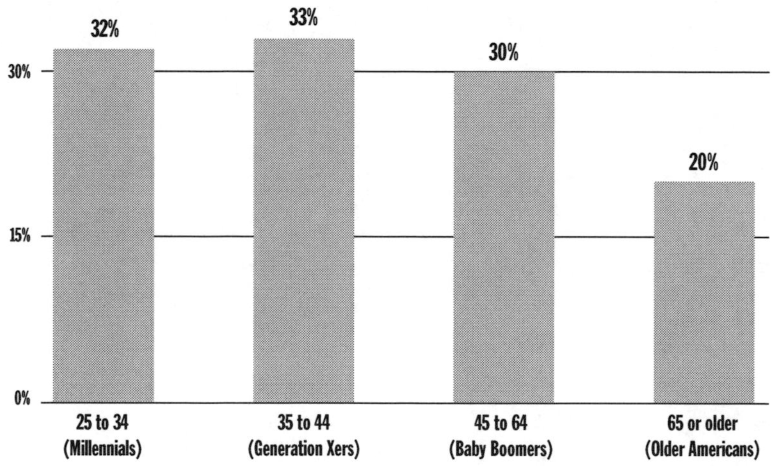

Table 2.1 Educational Attainment by Generation, 2008

(number and percent distribution of people aged 25 or older by highest level of education by generation, 2008; numbers in thousands)

	total 25 or older	Millennials (25 to 34)	Generation X (35 to 44)	Boomers (45 to 64)	older Americans (65 or older)
Total people	**196,305**	**40,146**	**42,132**	**77,237**	**36,790**
Not a high school graduate	26,340	4,768	4,792	8,474	8,306
High school graduate	61,183	11,297	12,040	24,290	13,559
Some college, no degree	33,812	7,396	7,199	13,694	5,523
Associate's degree	17,182	3,717	4,158	7,429	1,877
Bachelor's degree	37,559	9,421	9,204	14,527	4,407
Master's degree	14,765	2,792	3,506	6,337	2,129
Professional degree	2,991	490	693	1,356	453
Doctoral degree	2,472	267	538	1,132	536
High school graduate or more	169,964	35,380	37,338	68,765	28,484
Some college or more	108,781	24,083	25,298	44,475	14,925
Associate's degree or more	74,969	16,687	18,099	30,781	9,402
Bachelor's degree or more	57,787	12,970	13,941	23,352	7,525
Total people	**100.0%**	**100.0%**	**100.0%**	**100.0%**	**100.0%**
Not a high school graduate	13.4	11.9	11.4	11.0	22.6
High school graduate	31.2	28.1	28.6	31.4	36.9
Some college, no degree	17.2	18.4	17.1	17.7	15.0
Associate's degree	8.8	9.3	9.9	9.6	5.1
Bachelor's degree	19.1	23.5	21.8	18.8	12.0
Master's degree	7.5	7.0	8.3	8.2	5.8
Professional degree	1.5	1.2	1.6	1.8	1.2
Doctoral degree	1.3	0.7	1.3	1.5	1.5
High school graduate or more	86.6	88.1	88.6	89.0	77.4
Some college or more	55.4	60.0	60.0	57.6	40.6
Associate's degree or more	38.2	41.6	43.0	39.9	25.6
Bachelor's degree or more	29.4	32.3	33.1	30.2	20.5

Source: Bureau of the Census, Educational Attainment in the United States: 2008, detailed tables, Internet site http://www.census.gov/population/www/socdemo/education/cps2008.html; calculations by New Strategist

Most Boomers Have Been to College

Three out of 10 are college graduates.

The Baby-Boom generation was the first to go to college in significant numbers. Overall, the 58 percent majority have been to college—18 percent have college experience but no degree, 10 percent have an associate's degree, 19 percent have a bachelor's degree, and 11 percent have a graduate degree.

Until recently, the oldest Boomer men were better educated than any other Americans. Thirty-five percent of men aged 60 to 64 have a college degree, thanks to draft deferments offered to college students during the Vietnam War. Boomer women are significantly less likely than Boomer men to have a college degree, lowering the overall educational attainment of the Baby-Boom generation. In the past few years, the educational attainment of Boomer men has been eclipsed by the women of Generation X. Thirty-seven percent of women aged 35 to 39 have a bachelor's degree or more education.

■ Because most Boomers have college experience, they are eager to see their children go to college as well.

More than half the Baby-Boom generation has college experience

(percent distribution of people aged 45 to 64 by educational attainment, 2008)

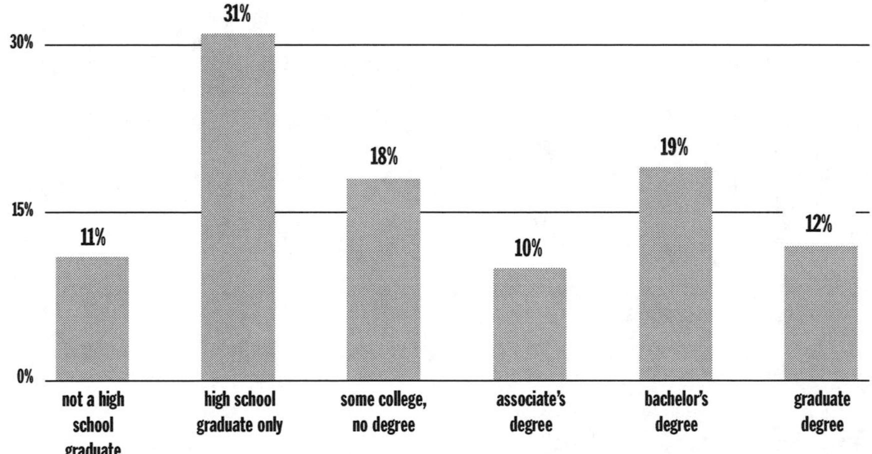

Table 2.2 Educational Attainment of Baby Boomers, 2008

(number and percent distribution of people aged 25 or older, aged 45 to 64, and aged 45 to 64 in five-year age groups, by highest level of education, 2008; numbers in thousands)

		aged 45 to 64				
	total 25 or older	total	45 to 49	50 to 54	55 to 59	60 to 64
Total people	**196,305**	**77,237**	**22,701**	**21,234**	**18,371**	**14,931**
Not a high school graduate	26,340	8,474	2,500	2,237	1,936	1,801
High school graduate	61183	24,290	7,297	6,772	5,589	4,632
Some college, no degree	33,812	13,694	4,021	3,661	3,302	2,710
Associate's degree	17,182	7,429	2,278	2,185	1,744	1,222
Bachelor's degree	37,559	14,527	4,380	4,051	3,462	2,634
Master's degree	14,765	6,337	1,592	1,689	1,679	1,377
Professional degree	2,991	1,356	349	395	344	268
Doctoral degree	2,472	1,132	282	245	316	289
High school graduate or more	169,964	68,765	20,199	18,998	16,436	13,132
Some college or more	108,781	44,475	12,902	12,226	10,847	8,500
Associate's degree or more	74,969	30,781	8,881	8,565	7,545	5,790
Bachelor's degree or more	57,787	23,352	6,603	6,380	5,801	4,568
Total people	**100.0%**	**100.0%**	**100.0%**	**100.0%**	**100.0%**	**100.0%**
Not a high school graduate	13.4	11.0	11.0	10.5	10.5	12.1
High school graduate	31.2	31.4	32.1	31.9	30.4	31.0
Some college, no degree	17.2	17.7	17.7	17.2	18.0	18.2
Associate's degree	8.8	9.6	10.0	10.3	9.5	8.2
Bachelor's degree	19.1	18.8	19.3	19.1	18.8	17.6
Master's degree	7.5	8.2	7.0	8.0	9.1	9.2
Professional degree	1.5	1.8	1.5	1.9	1.9	1.8
Doctoral degree	1.3	1.5	1.2	1.2	1.7	1.9
High school graduate or more	86.6	89.0	89.0	89.5	89.5	88.0
Some college or more	55.4	57.6	56.8	57.6	59.0	56.9
Associate's degree or more	38.2	39.9	39.1	40.3	41.1	38.8
Bachelor's degree or more	29.4	30.2	29.1	30.0	31.6	30.6

Source: Bureau of the Census, Educational Attainment in the United States: 2008, detailed tables, Internet site http://www .census.gov/population/www/socdemo/education/cps2008.html; calculations by New Strategist

Boomer Men Are among the Best Educated

More than one-third of men aged 55 to 64 have a bachelor's degree.

Men aged 55 to 64—an age group now almost entirely filled with the oldest Boomers—are among the most highly educated of all Americans. More than one-third has a college diploma, and nearly 15 percent have an advanced degree. Behind this high level of education is the Vietnam War. To avoid being drafted during the 1960s and early 1970s, many young men opted for college deferments. Most of those men are now in their late fifties and early sixties.

When the war ended, so did the incentive to stay in school. Consequently, younger Boomer men are less educated than their older counterparts. Still, more than half of men aged 45 to 54 have college experience and 29 percent have at least a bachelor's degree.

■ The high educational attainment of Baby-Boom men transformed American society, driving the demand for technology and creating the service economy.

Men aged 60 to 64 are the best educated

(percent of men aged 45 to 64 with a bachelor's degree, 2008)

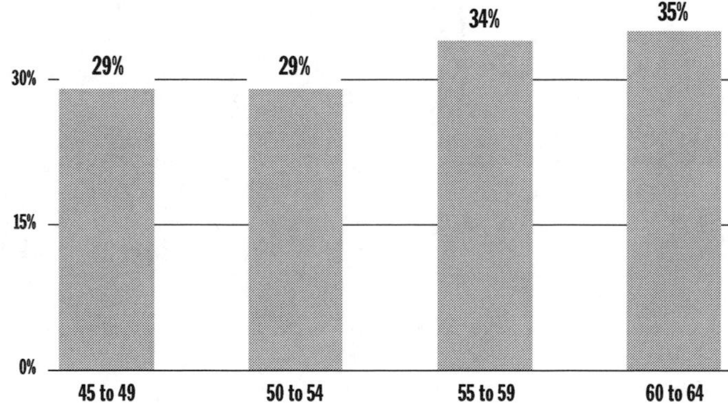

Table 2.3 Educational Attainment of Baby-Boom Men, 2008

(number and percent distribution of men aged 25 or older and aged 45 to 64 in five-year age groups, by highest level of education, 2008; numbers in thousands)

		aged 45 to 64				
	total 25 or older	total	45 to 49	50 to 54	55 to 59	60 to 64
Total men	**94,470**	**37,618**	**11,165**	**10,374**	**8,929**	**7,150**
Not a high school graduate	13,298	4,406	1,393	1,184	1,003	826
High school graduate	29,491	11,698	3,796	3,438	2,462	2,002
Some college, no degree	15,810	6,424	1,803	1,751	1,609	1,261
Associate's degree	7,436	3,266	942	957	791	576
Bachelor's degree	18,042	7,147	2,034	1,931	1,784	1,398
Master's degree	6,886	3,013	789	691	830	703
Professional degree	1,877	910	214	266	244	186
Doctoral degree	1,628	756	196	155	206	199
High school graduate or more	81,170	33,214	9,774	9,189	7,926	6,325
Some college or more	51,679	21,516	5,978	5,751	5,464	4,323
Associate's degree or more	35,869	15,092	4,175	4,000	3,855	3,062
Bachelor's degree or more	28,433	11,826	3,233	3,043	3,064	2,486
Total men	**100.0%**	**100.0%**	**100.0%**	**100.0%**	**100.0%**	**100.0%**
Not a high school graduate	14.1	11.7	12.5	11.4	11.2	11.6
High school graduate	31.2	31.1	34.0	33.1	27.6	28.0
Some college, no degree	16.7	17.1	16.1	16.9	18.0	17.6
Associate's degree	7.9	8.7	8.4	9.2	8.9	8.1
Bachelor's degree	19.1	19.0	18.2	18.6	20.0	19.6
Master's degree	7.3	8.0	7.1	6.7	9.3	9.8
Professional degree	2.0	2.4	1.9	2.6	2.7	2.6
Doctoral degree	1.7	2.0	1.8	1.5	2.3	2.8
High school graduate or more	85.9	88.3	87.5	88.6	88.8	88.5
Some college or more	54.7	57.2	53.5	55.4	61.2	60.5
Associate's degree or more	38.0	40.1	37.4	38.6	43.2	42.8
Bachelor's degree or more	30.1	31.4	29.0	29.3	34.3	34.8

Source: Bureau of the Census, Educational Attainment in the United States: 2008, detailed tables, Internet site http://www.census.gov/population/www/socdemo/education/cps2008.html; calculations by New Strategist

Most Boomer Women Have Been to College

More than one in four has a bachelor's degree.

Unlike their male counterparts, Boomer women did not have the threat of being drafted and sent to Vietnam as an incentive to keep them in college. Consequently, women aged 45 to 64 are less educated than their male counterparts. Among people aged 55 to 59, for example, 29 percent of women and 34 percent of men have a bachelor's degree.

Baby-Boom women are much more educated than older generations of women, however. Twenty-nine percent of Baby-Boom women have a bachelor's degree compared with just 16 percent of women aged 65 or older. Gen X women have the highest level of educational attainment in the nation. Thirty-seven percent of women aged 35 to 39 have a bachelor's degree.

■ Because people marry those with similar educational backgrounds, college-educated Boomers tend to be married to one another. With earnings closely linked to education, those couples are now the most affluent in the nation.

Among Boomer women, those aged 50 to 54 are the best educated

(percent of women aged 45 to 64 with a bachelor's degree, 2008)

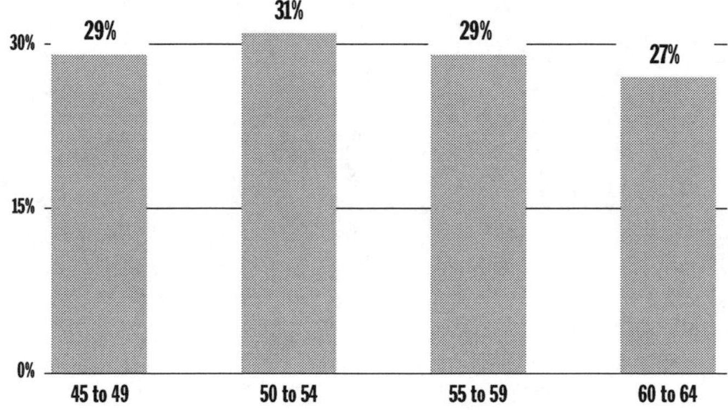

Table 2.4 Educational Attainment of Baby-Boom Women, 2008

(number and percent distribution of women aged 25 or older and aged 45 to 64 in five-year age groups, by highest level of education, 2008; numbers in thousands)

		aged 45 to 64				
	total 25 or older	total	45 to 49	50 to 54	55 to 59	60 to 64
Total women	**101,835**	**39,619**	**11,536**	**10,860**	**9,442**	**7,781**
Not a high school graduate	13,042	4,069	1,110	1,052	932	975
High school graduate	31,692	12,590	3,501	3,333	3,126	2,630
Some college, no degree	18,002	7,270	2,219	1,909	1,693	1,449
Associate's degree	9,746	4,164	1,337	1,228	953	646
Bachelor's degree	19,517	7,380	2,346	2,120	1,678	1,236
Master's degree	7,879	3,324	803	998	849	674
Professional degree	1,114	447	136	129	100	82
Doctoral degree	844	376	86	90	110	90
High school graduate or more	88,794	35,551	10,428	9,807	8,509	6,807
Some college or more	57,102	22,961	6,927	6,474	5,383	4,177
Associate's degree or more	39,100	15,691	4,708	4,565	3,690	2,728
Bachelor's degree or more	29,354	11,527	3,371	3,337	2,737	2,082
Total women	**100.0%**	**100.0%**	**100.0%**	**100.0%**	**100.0%**	**100.0%**
Not a high school graduate	12.8	10.3	9.6	9.7	9.9	12.5
High school graduate	31.1	31.8	30.3	30.7	33.1	33.8
Some college, no degree	17.7	18.3	19.2	17.6	17.9	18.6
Associate's degree	9.6	10.5	11.6	11.3	10.1	8.3
Bachelor's degree	19.2	18.6	20.3	19.5	17.8	15.9
Master's degree	7.7	8.4	7.0	9.2	9.0	8.7
Professional degree	1.1	1.1	1.2	1.2	1.1	1.1
Doctoral degree	0.8	0.9	0.7	0.8	1.2	1.2
High school graduate or more	87.2	89.7	90.4	90.3	90.1	87.5
Some college or more	56.1	58.0	60.0	59.6	57.0	53.7
Associate's degree or more	38.4	39.6	40.8	42.0	39.1	35.1
Bachelor's degree or more	28.8	29.1	29.2	30.7	29.0	26.8

Source: Bureau of the Census, Educational Attainment in the United States: 2008, detailed tables, Internet site http://www.census.gov/population/www/socdemo/education/cps2008.html; calculations by New Strategist

Among Boomer Men, Asians Are the Best Educated

Hispanics are the least educated.

Asians are by far the best-educated Baby-Boom men. Seventy percent of Asian men aged 45 to 64 have some college experience and more than half have a bachelor's degree. Among non-Hispanic white men, the figures are 61 and 35 percent, respectively.

Black men are less educated than Asian or non-Hispanic white men, but the great majority (83 percent) are high school graduates and 47 percent have college experience. Only 19 percent have a bachelor's degree, however.

Hispanic men are by far the least educated. Only 62 percent of Hispanic men of the Baby-Boom generation are high school graduates. Just 33 percent have college experience, and 14 percent have a bachelor's degree. One reason for the low educational level of Hispanics is that many are immigrants from countries that offer little educational opportunity.

■ Educational attainment is directly linked to income. The gap in the education of men by race and Hispanic origin translates into occupational and income differences.

More than half of Asian Baby-Boom men have a bachelor's degree

(percent of men aged 45 to 64 with a bachelor's degree, 2008)

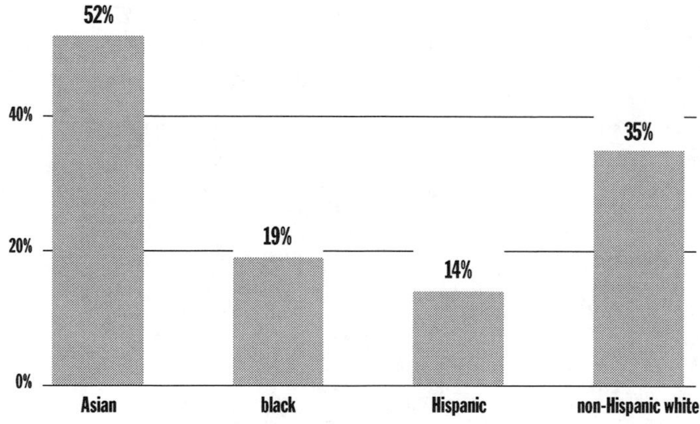

Table 2.5 Educational Attainment of Baby-Boom Men by Race and Hispanic Origin, 2008

(number and percent distribution of men aged 45 to 64 by educational attainment, race, and Hispanic origin, 2008; numbers in thousands)

	total	Asian	black	Hispanic	non-Hispanic white
Total men aged 45 to 64	**37,618**	**1,538**	**3,930**	**3,820**	**27,957**
Not a high school graduate	4,406	155	662	1,470	2,078
High school graduate	11,698	301	1,420	1,103	8,747
Some college, no degree	6,424	172	761	503	4,914
Associate's degree	3,266	106	350	201	2,555
Bachelor's degree	7,147	459	484	332	5,830
Master's degree	3,013	194	178	150	2,466
Professional degree	910	73	36	56	735
Doctoral degree	756	76	38	9	634
High school graduate or more	33,214	1,381	3,267	2,354	25,881
Some college or more	21,516	1,080	1,847	1,251	17,134
Associate's degree or more	15,092	908	1,086	748	12,220
Bachelor's degree or more	11,826	802	736	547	9,665
Total men aged 45 to 64	**100.0%**	**100.0%**	**100.0%**	**100.0%**	**100.0%**
Not a high school graduate	11.7	10.1	16.8	38.5	7.4
High school graduate	31.1	19.6	36.1	28.9	31.3
Some college, no degree	17.1	11.2	19.4	13.2	17.6
Associate's degree	8.7	6.9	8.9	5.3	9.1
Bachelor's degree	19.0	29.8	12.3	8.7	20.9
Master's degree	8.0	12.6	4.5	3.9	8.8
Professional degree	2.4	4.7	0.9	1.5	2.6
Doctoral degree	2.0	4.9	1.0	0.2	2.3
High school graduate or more	88.3	89.8	83.1	61.6	92.6
Some college or more	57.2	70.2	47.0	32.7	61.3
Associate's degree or more	40.1	59.0	27.6	19.6	43.7
Bachelor's degree or more	31.4	52.1	18.7	14.3	34.6

Note: Asians and blacks are those who identify themselves as being of the race alone and those who identify themselves as being of the race in combination with other races. Non-Hispanic whites are those who identify themselves as being white alone and not Hispanic. Numbers do not add to total because not all races are shown and Hispanics may be of any race.
Source: Bureau of the Census, Educational Attainment in the United States: 2008, detailed tables, Internet site http://www.census.gov/population/www/socdemo/education/cps2008.html; calculations by New Strategist

Among Boomer Women, Hispanics Lag in Education

Asian women have the highest level of education.

Among women aged 45 to 64 in 2008, Asians are by far the best educated. Fully 62 percent have college experience and 44 percent have a bachelor's degree. Interestingly, however, Asian women are less likely to have a high school diploma than non-Hispanic white women. The explanation lies in the socioeconomic differences within the Asian-American community itself, with some being immigrants from countries with little educational opportunity such as Vietnam.

Sixty-two percent of non-Hispanic white women of the Baby-Boom generation have college experience, while 32 percent have a bachelor's degree. Among black women in the age group, the figures are a smaller 51 and 20 percent, respectively. Hispanics are the least educated. Only 62 percent have a high school diploma and just 13 percent have a bachelor's degree.

■ With earnings directly linked to education, Asian women should reap the biggest rewards in the job market thanks to their high level of educational attainment.

Among Boomer women, Asians are the best educated

(percent of women aged 45 to 64 with a bachelor's degree, 2008)

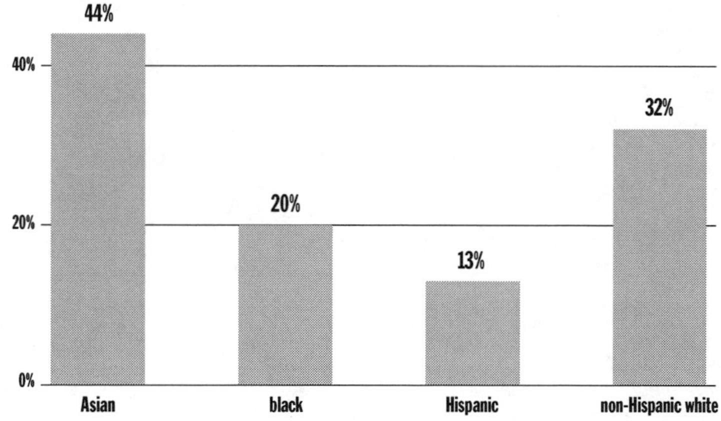

Table 2.6 Educational Attainment of Baby-Boom Women by Race and Hispanic Origin, 2008

(number and percent distribution of women aged 45 to 64 by educational attainment, race, and Hispanic origin, 2008; numbers in thousands)

	total	Asian	black	Hispanic	non-Hispanic white
Total women aged 45 to 64	**39,619**	**1,783**	**4,817**	**3,860**	**28,783**
Not a high school graduate	4,069	244	664	1,460	1,659
High school graduate	12,590	430	1,709	1,087	9,229
Some college, no degree	7,270	177	1,001	542	5,454
Associate's degree	4,164	144	457	265	3,256
Bachelor's degree	7,380	576	670	339	5,755
Master's degree	3,324	152	256	130	2,771
Professional degree	447	35	26	29	355
Doctoral degree	376	27	32	9	301
High school graduate or more	35,551	1,541	4,151	2,401	27,121
Some college or more	22,961	1,111	2,442	1,314	17,892
Associate's degree or more	15,691	934	1,441	772	12,438
Bachelor's degree or more	11,527	790	984	507	9,182
Total women aged 45 to 64	**100.0%**	**100.0%**	**100.0%**	**100.0%**	**100.0%**
Not a high school graduate	10.3	13.7	13.8	37.8	5.8
High school graduate	31.8	24.1	35.5	28.2	32.1
Some college, no degree	18.3	9.9	20.8	14.0	18.9
Associate's degree	10.5	8.1	9.5	6.9	11.3
Bachelor's degree	18.6	32.3	13.9	8.8	20.0
Master's degree	8.4	8.5	5.3	3.4	9.6
Professional degree	1.1	2.0	0.5	0.8	1.2
Doctoral degree	0.9	1.5	0.7	0.2	1.0
High school graduate or more	89.7	86.4	86.2	62.2	94.2
Some college or more	58.0	62.3	50.7	34.0	62.2
Associate's degree or more	39.6	52.4	29.9	20.0	43.2
Bachelor's degree or more	29.1	44.3	20.4	13.1	31.9

Note: Asians and blacks are those who identify themselves as being of the race alone and those who identify themselves as being of the race in combination with other races. Non-Hispanic whites are those who identify themselves as being white alone and not Hispanic. Numbers do not add to total because not all races are shown and Hispanics may be of any race.
Source: Bureau of the Census, Educational Attainment in the United States: 2008, detailed tables, Internet site http://www.census.gov/population/www/socdemo/education/cps2008.html; calculations by New Strategist

Few Boomers Are Still in School

The number of Boomers in school surpasses 1 million, however.

Just 1.7 percent of people aged 45 to 64 were enrolled in school in 2007. (Boomers were aged 43 to 61 in that year.) Although the proportion is small, the numbers add up because the generation is so large. In 2007, 1.3 million people aged 45 to 64 were in school.

Among Boomers in school, women outnumber men by more than 2 to 1. While 1.1 percent of men aged 45 to 64 are in school, the proportion is 2.3 percent among women in the age group.

■ As the economic downturn boosts unemployment, the percentage of Boomers who are in school may rise.

Women outnumber men in school

(number of people aged 45 to 64 enrolled in school, by sex, 2007)

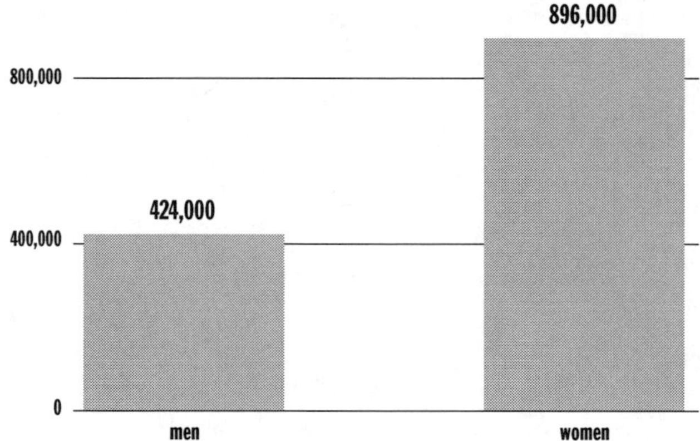

Table 2.7 School Enrollment by Sex and Age, 2007

(total number of people aged 3 or older, and number and percent enrolled in school by sex and age, 2007; numbers in thousands)

		enrolled	
	total	number	percent
Total people	**285,410**	**75,967**	**26.6%**
Under age 45	172,382	74,583	43.3
Aged 45 to 64	76,586	1,321	1.7
Aged 45 to 49	22,675	602	2.7
Aged 50 to 54	21,036	468	2.2
Aged 55 to 59	18,250	168	0.9
Aged 60 to 64	14,625	83	0.6
Aged 65 or older	36,443	60	0.2
Total females	**145,806**	**38,398**	**26.3**
Under age 45	85,635	37,466	43.8
Aged 45 to 64	39,363	896	2.3
Aged 45 to 49	11,542	399	3.5
Aged 50 to 54	10,770	311	2.9
Aged 55 to 59	9,446	127	1.3
Aged 60 to 64	7,605	59	0.8
Aged 65 or older	20,808	32	0.2
Total males	**139,603**	**37,569**	**26.9**
Under age 45	86,746	37,116	42.8
Aged 45 to 64	37,223	424	1.1
Aged 45 to 49	11,133	203	1.8
Aged 50 to 54	10,266	156	1.5
Aged 55 to 59	8,804	41	0.5
Aged 60 to 64	7,020	24	0.3
Aged 65 or older	15,635	27	0.2

Source: Bureau of the Census, School Enrollment--Social and Economic Characteristics of Students: October 2007, Internet site http://www.census.gov/population/www/socdemo/school/cps2007.html; calculations by New Strategist

Nearly 1.2 Million Boomers Are Still in College

They account for only 5 percent of undergraduates.

The number of older college students may be growing as Boomers age, but their share among all students remains small. Less than 5 percent of people enrolled in institutions of higher education in 2007 were aged 45 to 64. The Boomer share of those attending graduate school, however, was a larger 15 percent.

There is a clear distinction between younger and older Boomers. People aged 45 to 54 who are enrolled in institutions of higher education are more likely to be undergraduates, while their 55-to-64-year-old counterparts are more likely to be pursuing graduate studies.

■ Because highly educated people are the ones most likely to seek even more education, Boomers will continue to enroll in college even as they age into their sixties.

Boomers account for 15 percent of graduate students

(students aged 45 to 64 as a percentage of total students, by level of study, 2007)

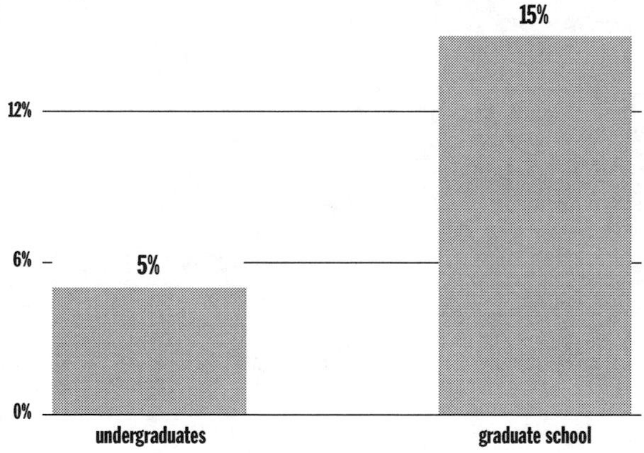

Table 2.8 College Students by Age and Enrollment Level, 2007

(number and percent distribution of people aged 15 or older enrolled in institutions of higher education by age and level of enrollment, 2007; numbers in thousands)

	total	undergraduate	graduate school
Total enrolled	**17,956**	**14,365**	**3,591**
Under age 45	16,706	13,680	3,026
Aged 45 to 64	1,199	656	543
Aged 45 to 49	549	313	236
Aged 50 to 54	417	237	180
Aged 55 to 59	156	72	84
Aged 60 to 64	77	34	43
Aged 65 or older	50	27	23
PERCENT DISTRIBUTION AGE			
Total enrolled	**100.0%**	**100.0%**	**100.0%**
Under age 45	93.0	95.2	84.3
Aged 45 to 64	6.7	4.6	15.1
Aged 45 to 49	3.1	2.2	6.6
Aged 50 to 54	2.3	1.6	5.0
Aged 55 to 59	0.9	0.5	2.3
Aged 60 to 64	0.4	0.2	1.2
Aged 65 or older	0.3	0.2	0.6
PERCENT DISTRIBUTION LEVEL OF ENROLLMENT			
Total enrolled	**100.0%**	**80.0%**	**20.0%**
Under age 45	100.0	81.9	18.1
Aged 45 to 64	100.0	54.7	45.3
Aged 45 to 49	100.0	57.0	43.0
Aged 50 to 54	100.0	56.8	43.2
Aged 55 to 59	100.0	46.2	53.8
Aged 60 to 64	100.0	44.2	55.8
Aged 65 or older	100.0	54.0	46.0

Source: Bureau of the Census, School Enrollment--Social and Economic Characteristics of Students: October 2007, Internet site http://www.census.gov/population/www/socdemo/school/cps2007.html; calculations by New Strategist

Many Adults Participate in Education for Job-Related Reasons

Life-long learning is becoming a necessity for job security.

As job security dwindles, many workers are turning to the educational system to try to stay on track. Overall, 27 percent of Americans aged 16 or older participated in work-related adult education during 2005 (the latest available data), while another 21 percent took personal interest courses and 5 percent were enrolled in part-time degree or diploma programs.

The share of Americans involved in work-related adult education rises from 32 percent among the youngest Generation Xers to its peaks of over 36 percent among the youngest Baby Boomers. Participation in personal interest courses declines slightly with age, as does participation in part-time degree or diploma programs.

■ Many Americans who participate in work-related education are retraining themselves to compete in the increasingly global economy.

Work-related training peaks in the 45-to-54 age group

(percent of workers who participated in work-related adult education activities, by age, 2005)

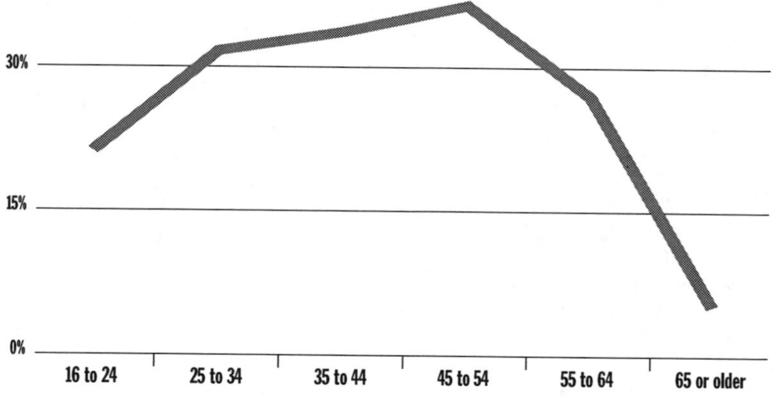

Table 2.9 Participation in Adult Education by Age, 2005

(percent of people aged 16 or older who participate in formal adult education activities, by age and type of adult education activity, 2005)

	total	percent participating in any activity	work-related courses	personal interest courses	part-time degree or diploma programs
Total people	**100.0%**	**44.4%**	**26.9%**	**21.4%**	**5.0%**
Aged 16 to 24	100.0	52.9	21.2	26.6	11.4
Aged 25 to 34	100.0	52.2	31.7	22.1	8.7
Aged 35 to 44	100.0	48.7	33.7	22.1	5.3
Aged 45 to 54	100.0	47.9	36.5	19.7	3.8
Aged 55 to 64	100.0	40.3	27.0	20.7	1.5
Aged 65 or older	100.0	22.9	5.2	18.8	0.3

Source: National Center for Education Statistics, The Condition of Education, Participation in Adult Education, Indicator 10 (2007), Internet site http://nces.ed.gov/programs/coe/2007/section1/indicator10.asp; calculations by New Strategist

CHAPTER

3

Health

■ The percentage of Americans reporting "excellent" or "very good" health declines from 54 percent in the 45-to-54 age group to 49 percent in the 55-to-64 age group as chronic conditions become common.

■ Most Baby Boomers are overweight. The average Boomer man weighs nearly 200 pounds. The average Boomer woman weighs more than 170 pounds.

■ Among all Americans, 15.3 percent do not have health insurance. The figure ranges from 12 to 15 percent among 45-to-64-year-olds.

■ Thirty-three percent of Americans aged 45 to 64 have experienced joint pain lasting longer than three months, making it the most common health condition in the age group.

■ Sixty-six percent of people aged 45 to 64 have taken at least one prescription drug in the past month, and 34 percent have taken three or more.

■ Heart disease and cancer are the two leading causes of death in the United States. Among 45-to-64-year-olds, however, cancer is the number-one cause of death.

Most 45-to-54-Year-Olds Feel Excellent or Very Good

The proportion falls below 50 percent in the 55-to-64 age group, however.

Overall, the 55 percent majority of Americans aged 18 or older say their health is "excellent" or "very good." The figure peaks at 63 percent in the 25-to-34 age group, then declines with age. The percentage of Americans who report excellent or very good health falls substantially within the 45-to-64 age group, from 54 percent among 45-to-54-year-olds to just 49 percent among 55-to-64-year-olds. Behind the decline is the rise of chronic conditions as people age.

Fewer than half of people aged 65 or older report that their health is excellent or very good. Nevertheless, the proportion saying they are in poor health remains below 8 percent, regardless of age. Among people aged 65 or older, the proportion saying their health is excellent or very good (38 percent) surpasses the proportion saying their health is only "fair" or "poor" (25 percent).

■ Medical advances that allow people to manage chronic conditions should boost the proportions of people reporting excellent or very good health in the years ahead.

Nearly half of 55-to-64-year-olds say their health is excellent or very good

(percent of people aged 18 or older who say their health is excellent or very good, by age, 2008)

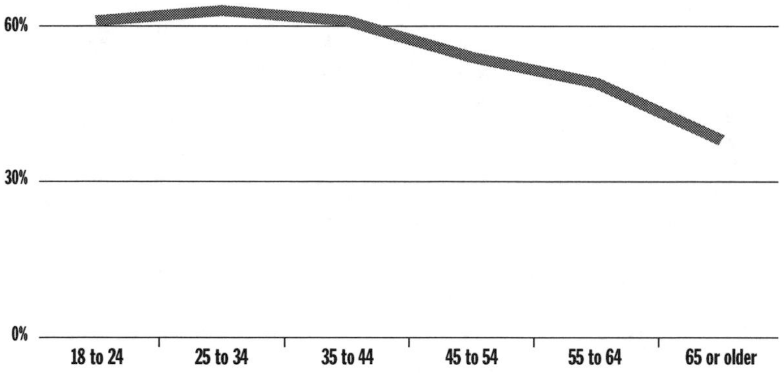

Table 3.1 Health Status by Age, 2008

(percent distribution of people aged 18 or older by self-reported health status, by age, 2008)

	total	excellent	very good	good	fair	poor
Total people	**100.0%**	**20.1%**	**34.9%**	**30.0%**	**10.6%**	**3.8%**
Aged 18 to 24	100.0	25.1	35.7	29.7	6.6	1.0
Aged 25 to 34	100.0	24.8	38.1	28.9	7.3	1.4
Aged 35 to 44	100.0	23.7	37.2	28.3	8.0	2.1
Aged 45 to 54	100.0	19.6	34.5	29.1	10.3	4.2
Aged 55 to 64	100.0	17.3	31.5	30.3	13.8	5.6
Aged 65 or older	100.0	11.4	26.7	34.1	18.0	7.4

Source: Centers for Disease Control and Prevention, Behavioral Risk Factor Surveillance System Prevalence Data, 2008, Internet site http://apps.nccd.cdc.gov/brfss/

Weight Problems Are the Norm for Boomers

Most men and women are overweight.

Americans have a weight problem, and Boomers are no exception. The average Boomer man weighs nearly 200 pounds. The average Boomer woman weighs more than 170 pounds. Nearly 80 percent of Boomer men and 67 to 70 percent of Boomer women are overweight, and more than one-third are obese.

Although many people say they exercise, only 31 percent of adults participate in regular leisure-time physical activity, according to government data. The figure ranges from a high of 38 percent among 18-to-24-year-olds to a low of 17 percent among people aged 75 or older. Among 45-to-64-year-olds, only 27 to 31 percent participate in regular leisure-time physical activity.

■ Most Baby Boomers lack the willpower to eat less or exercise more—fueling a diet and weight loss industry that never lacks for customers.

Middle-aged Americans weigh more than they should

(percent distribution of people aged 45 to 54 by weight status, by sex, 2003–06)

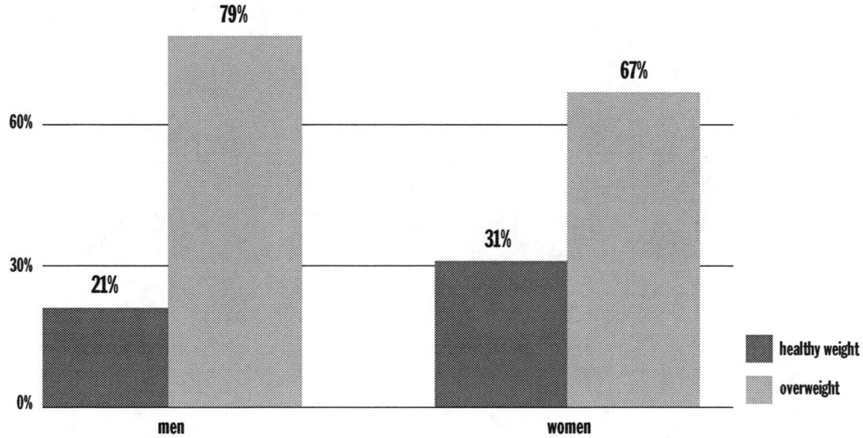

Table 3.2 Average Measured Weight by Age and Sex, 2003–06

(average weight in pounds of people aged 20 or older by age and sex, 2003–06)

	men	women
Total aged 20 or older	**194.7**	**164.7**
Aged 20 to 29	188.3	155.9
Aged 30 to 39	194.1	164.7
Aged 40 to 49	202.3	171.3
Aged 50 to 59	198.8	172.1
Aged 60 to 69	198.3	170.5
Aged 70 to 79	187.4	155.6
Aged 80 or older	168.1	142.2

Note: Data are based on measured weight of a sample of the civilian noninstitutionalized population.
Source: National Center for Health Statistics, Anthropometric Reference Data for Children and Adults: United States, 2003–2006, National Health Statistics Reports, Number 10, 2008, Internet site http://www.cdc.gov/nchs/products/pubs/pubd/nhsr/nhsr.htm; calculations by New Strategist

Table 3.3 Weight Status by Sex and Age, 2003–06

(percent distribution of people aged 20 or older by weight status, sex, and age, 2003–06)

			overweight	
	total	healthy weight	total	obese
TOTAL PEOPLE	**100.0%**	**31.4%**	**66.9%**	**34.1%**
Total men	**100.0**	**26.1**	**72.6**	**33.1**
Aged 20 to 34	100.0	35.9	61.6	26.2
Aged 35 to 44	100.0	24.1	75.2	37.0
Aged 45 to 54	100.0	20.8	78.5	34.6
Aged 55 to 64	100.0	19.3	79.7	39.3
Aged 65 to 74	100.0	21.2	78.0	33.0
Aged 75 or older	100.0	33.1	65.8	24.0
Total women	**100.0**	**36.6**	**61.2**	**35.2**
Aged 20 to 34	100.0	45.1	50.9	28.4
Aged 35 to 44	100.0	37.6	60.7	36.1
Aged 45 to 54	100.0	31.1	67.3	40.0
Aged 55 to 64	100.0	29.5	69.6	41.0
Aged 65 to 74	100.0	28.5	70.5	36.4
Aged 75 or older	100.0	35.4	62.6	24.2

Note: Data are based on measured height and weight of a sample of the civilian noninstitutionalized population. Overweight is defined as a body mass index of 25 or higher. Obesity is defined as a body mass index of 30 or higher. Body mass index is calculated by dividing weight in kilograms by height in meters squared. Percentages do not add to total because "underweight" is not shown.
Source: National Center for Health Statistics, Health, United States, 2008, Internet site http://www.cdc.gov/nchs/hus.htm

Table 3.4 Leisure-Time Physical Activity Level by Sex and Age, 2006

(percent distribution of people aged 18 or older by leisure-time physical activity level, by sex and age, 2006)

	total	physically inactive	at least some physical activity	regular physical activity
TOTAL PEOPLE	**100.0%**	**39.5%**	**29.6%**	**30.9%**
Aged 18 to 24	100.0	34.8	27.1	38.1
Aged 25 to 44	100.0	35.0	31.6	33.4
Aged 45 to 54	100.0	38.2	30.7	31.1
Aged 55 to 64	100.0	41.9	30.9	27.2
Aged 65 to 74	100.0	48.0	25.8	26.2
Aged 75 or older	100.0	59.6	23.1	17.3
Total men	**100.0**	**38.5**	**27.4**	**33.1**
Aged 18 to 44	100.0	34.2	28.8	36.9
Aged 45 to 54	100.0	39.0	28.4	32.7
Aged 55 to 64	100.0	41.1	30.6	28.2
Aged 65 to 74	100.0	46.9	25.0	28.2
Aged 75 or older	100.0	52.1	26.6	21.4
Total women	**100.0**	**40.3**	**30.7**	**29.0**
Aged 18 to 44	100.0	35.6	32.0	32.4
Aged 45 to 54	100.0	37.5	33.0	29.5
Aged 55 to 64	100.0	42.6	31.1	26.3
Aged 65 to 74	100.0	49.0	26.5	24.5
Aged 75 or older	100.0	64.4	20.8	14.7

Note: "Physically inactive" are those with no sessions of light-to-moderate or vigorous leisure-time physical activity of at least 10 minutes duration during past week. "At least some physical activity" includes those with at least one light-to-moderate or vigorous leisure-time physical activity of at least 10 minutes duration during past week, but who did not meet the definition for regular leisure-time activity. "Regular physical activity" includes those who did three or more sessions per week of vigorous activity lasting at least 20 minutes or five or more sessions per week of light-to-moderate activity lasting at least 30 minutes.
Source: National Center for Health Statistics, Health, United States, 2008, Internet site http://www.cdc.gov/nchs/hus.htm

More than 20 Percent of 45-to-54-Year-Olds Smoke Cigarettes

Fewer 55-to-64-year-olds are smokers.

The percentage of Americans who smoke cigarettes has declined sharply from what it was a few decades ago. Nevertheless, a substantial 18 percent of people aged 18 or older were current smokers in 2008. Among people aged 45 to 54, about 21 percent smoke cigarettes. The figure is a smaller 16 percent among 55-to-64-year-olds. A substantial number of adults say they are former smokers, including 25 to 35 percent of 45-to-64-year-olds.

Drinking is much more popular than smoking. Overall, 54 percent of people aged 18 or older have had an alcoholic beverage in the past month. The proportion peaks at 61 percent in the broad 25-to-44 age group. Among 45-to-64-year-olds, 53 to 58 percent have had an alcoholic beverage in the past 30 days.

Although many Boomers have experience with illicit drugs, particularly marijuana, few continue to use them. Only 2 to 7 percent of people aged 45 to 64 have used illicit drugs in the past month. But most people between the ages of 19 and 59 have used illicit drugs at some point in their lives. Most 45-to-54-year-olds have used marijuana in the past, although only 4 to 5 percent have used it in the past month.

■ As Boomers age and health concerns become increasingly important, the proportion who smoke or drink will decline.

Many Boomers are former smokers

(percent distribution of people aged 45 to 54 by cigarette smoking status, 2008)

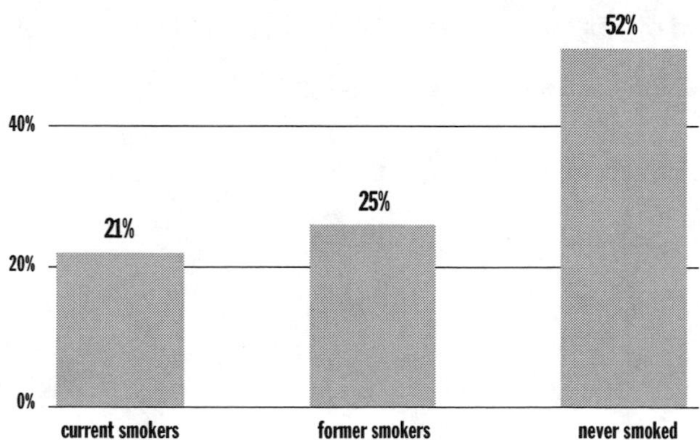

Table 3.5 Cigarette Smoking Status by Age, 2008

(percent distribution of people aged 18 or older by age and cigarette smoking status, 2008)

	total	current smokers			former smoker	never smoked
		total	smoke every day	smoke some days		
Total people	**100.0%**	**18.2%**	**13.4%**	**4.8%**	**25.2%**	**55.3%**
Aged 18 to 24	100.0	23.0	15.8	7.2	7.2	70.0
Aged 25 to 34	100.0	23.5	16.8	6.7	17.6	58.4
Aged 35 to 44	100.0	20.0	14.9	5.1	18.7	60.6
Aged 45 to 54	100.0	20.5	16.0	4.5	25.2	52.4
Aged 55 to 64	100.0	16.4	12.4	4.0	35.0	46.6
Aged 65 or older	100.0	8.0	6.0	2.0	42.9	48.8

Source: Centers for Disease Control and Prevention, Behavioral Risk Factor Surveillance System Prevalence Data, 2008, Internet site http://apps.nccd.cdc.gov/brfss/index.asp; calculations by New Strategist

Table 3.6 Alcohol Use by Age, 2008

(percent distribution of people aged 18 or older by whether they have had at least one drink of alcohol within the past 30 days, by age, 2008)

	total	yes	no
Total people	**100.0%**	**54.4%**	**45.5%**
Aged 18 to 24	100.0	49.9	50.0
Aged 25 to 34	100.0	60.5	39.4
Aged 35 to 44	100.0	60.5	39.4
Aged 45 to 54	100.0	58.4	41.5
Aged 55 to 64	100.0	53.4	46.5
Aged 65 or older	100.0	40.6	59.3

Source: Centers for Disease Control and Prevention, Behavioral Risk Factor Surveillance System Prevalence Data, 2008, Internet site http://apps.nccd.cdc.gov/brfss/index.asp

Table 3.7 Illicit Drug Use by People Aged 12 or Older, 2007

(percent of people aged 12 or older who ever used any illicit drug, who used an illicit drug in the past year, and who used an illicit drug in the past month, by age, 2007)

	ever used	used in past year	used in past month
Total people	**46.1%**	**14.4%**	**8.0%**
Aged 12	9.9	5.4	2.7
Aged 13	16.4	10.2	4.0
Aged 14	21.4	14.7	6.7
Aged 15	29.0	21.4	11.0
Aged 16	37.6	28.6	14.8
Aged 17	41.5	30.8	17.4
Aged 18	46.9	34.8	20.7
Aged 19	53.3	36.6	22.3
Aged 20	57.1	36.6	22.0
Aged 21	60.3	37.6	23.1
Aged 22	59.6	32.8	20.0
Aged 23	62.7	31.6	17.5
Aged 24	62.1	28.7	16.1
Aged 25	60.1	25.4	15.4
Aged 26 to 29	57.8	23.0	12.8
Aged 30 to 34	55.5	16.9	9.4
Aged 35 to 39	56.1	13.9	7.3
Aged 40 to 44	58.6	13.1	7.0
Aged 45 to 49	61.0	11.9	7.2
Aged 50 to 54	58.9	10.6	5.7
Aged 55 to 59	51.6	8.0	4.1
Aged 60 to 64	35.0	4.4	1.9
Aged 65 or older	10.7	1.0	0.7

Note: Illicit drugs include marijuana, hashish, cocaine (including crack), heroin, hallucinogens, inhalants, or any prescription-type psychotherapeutic used nonmedically.
Source: SAMHSA, Office of Applied Studies, National Survey on Drug Use and Health, 2007, Internet site http://www.oas.samhsa.gov/nsduh/2k7nsduh/2k7Results.pdf

Table 3.8 Marijuana Use by People Aged 12 or Older, 2007

(percent of people aged 12 or older who ever used marijuana, who used marijuana in the past year, and who used marijuana in the past month, by age, 2007)

	ever used	used in past year	used in past month
Total people	**40.6%**	**10.1%**	**5.8%**
Aged 12	1.3	1.0	0.6
Aged 13	4.1	2.9	1.3
Aged 14	9.9	7.8	3.7
Aged 15	17.9	14.4	7.6
Aged 16	27.5	21.8	11.4
Aged 17	34.9	25.8	14.9
Aged 18	39.5	28.3	17.1
Aged 19	46.8	31.4	18.9
Aged 20	50.8	31.5	19.2
Aged 21	53.8	31.0	18.9
Aged 22	53.1	27.4	16.7
Aged 23	57.0	25.1	14.6
Aged 24	55.2	23.0	12.7
Aged 25	52.8	20.3	12.5
Aged 26 to 29	52.0	17.4	9.8
Aged 30 to 34	48.8	11.1	6.3
Aged 35 to 39	49.8	8.9	5.4
Aged 40 to 44	53.5	8.0	4.5
Aged 45 to 49	56.9	7.9	4.9
Aged 50 to 54	54.8	6.7	3.8
Aged 55 to 59	46.2	4.4	2.1
Aged 60 to 64	29.6	1.9	0.6
Aged 65 or older	8.4	0.3	0.2

Source: SAMHSA, Office of Applied Studies, National Survey on Drug Use and Health, 2007, Internet site http://oas.samhsa .gov/NSDUH/2k7NSDUH/tabs/Sect1peTabs1to46.htm#Tab1.1A

Many Middle-Aged Americans Lack Health Insurance

More than 10 million of the nation's uninsured are aged 45 to 64.

Among all Americans, 46 million lacked health insurance in 2007—or 15 percent of the population. The figure ranges from12 to 15 percent among 45-to-64-year-olds.

Fifty-nine percent of the population has private, employment-based health insurance, but many of those with employment-based coverage get their insurance through a spouse rather than their own job. Only about half of 45-to-64-year-olds have health insurance coverage through their own employment. Eight to 10 percent of 45-to-64-year-olds buy private health insurance on their own. Twelve to 20 percent have government health insurance.

Not surprisingly, health care expenses rise with age. Median health care expenses for people aged 40 or older exceed $1,000 annually. Only 20 percent of those expenses are paid for out-of-pocket. Private insurance covers the largest share. Among 40-to-59-year-olds, private insurance pays for 55 to 58 percent of annual medical bills.

■ Look for a renewed entrepreneurial spirit among Boomers as they sign up for Medicare and are free to pursue their dreams once health insurance is no longer an issue.

Many Americans do not have health insurance coverage

(percent of people aged 18 or older without health insurance, by age, 2007)

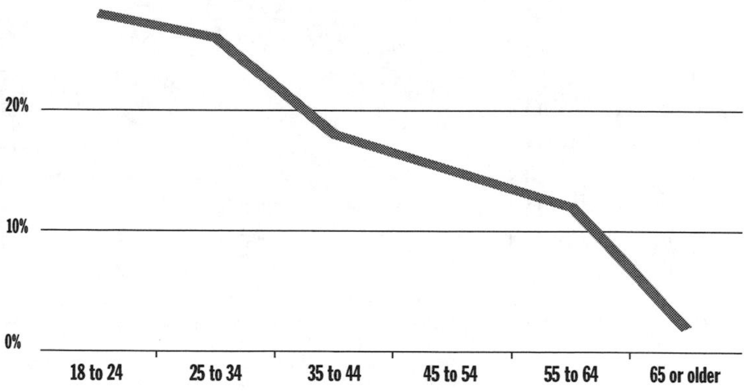

Table 3.9 Health Insurance Coverage by Age, 2007

(number and percent distribution of people by age and health insurance coverage status, 2007; numbers in thousands)

		with health insurance			
	total	total	private	government	not covered
Total people	**299,106**	**253,449**	**201,991**	**83,031**	**45,657**
Under age 65	262,316	217,345	180,785	48,567	44,971
Under age 18	74,403	66,254	47,750	23,041	8,149
Aged 18 to 24	28,398	20,407	17,074	4,428	7,991
Aged 25 to 34	40,146	29,817	26,430	4,539	10,329
Aged 35 to 44	42,132	34,415	31,067	4,546	7,717
Aged 45 to 54	43,935	37,161	33,350	5,363	6,774
Aged 55 to 64	33,302	29,291	25,114	6,651	4,011
Aged 65 or older	36,790	36,103	21,206	34,464	686
PERCENT DISTRIBUTION BY COVERAGE STATUS					
Total people	**100.0%**	**84.7%**	**67.5%**	**27.8%**	**15.3%**
Under age 65	100.0	82.9	68.9	18.5	17.1
Under age 18	100.0	89.0	64.2	31.0	11.0
Aged 18 to 24	100.0	71.9	60.1	15.6	28.1
Aged 25 to 34	100.0	74.3	65.8	11.3	25.7
Aged 35 to 44	100.0	81.7	73.7	10.8	18.3
Aged 45 to 54	100.0	84.6	75.9	12.2	15.4
Aged 55 to 64	100.0	88.0	75.4	20.0	12.0
Aged 65 or older	100.0	98.1	57.6	93.7	1.9
PERCENT DISTRIBUTION BY AGE					
Total people	**100.0%**	**100.0%**	**100.0%**	**100.0%**	**100.0%**
Under age 65	87.7	85.8	89.5	58.5	98.5
Under age 18	24.9	26.1	23.6	27.7	17.8
Aged 18 to 24	9.5	8.1	8.5	5.3	17.5
Aged 25 to 34	13.4	11.8	13.1	5.5	22.6
Aged 35 to 44	14.1	13.6	15.4	5.5	16.9
Aged 45 to 54	14.7	14.7	16.5	6.5	14.8
Aged 55 to 64	11.1	11.6	12.4	8.0	8.8
Aged 65 or older	12.3	14.2	10.5	41.5	1.5

Note: Numbers may not add to total because some people have more than one type of health insurance coverage.
Source: Bureau of the Census, Health Insurance, Table HI01, Internet site http://pubdb3.census.gov/macro/032008/health/toc .htm; calculations by New Strategist

Table 3.10 Private Health Insurance Coverage by Age, 2007

(number and percent distribution of people by age and private health insurance coverage status, 2007; numbers in thousands)

		with private health insurance			
			employment based		
	total	total	total	own	direct purchase
Total people	**299,106**	**201,991**	**177,446**	**93,774**	**26,673**
Under age 65	262,316	180,785	164,888	84,332	17,127
Under age 18	74,403	47,750	44,252	227	3,930
Aged 18 to 24	28,398	17,074	13,747	5,386	1,635
Aged 25 to 34	40,146	26,430	24,505	19,005	2,347
Aged 35 to 44	42,132	31,067	29,009	20,616	2,687
Aged 45 to 54	43,935	33,350	30,805	22,486	3,292
Aged 55 to 64	33,302	25,114	22,569	16,612	3,237
Aged 65 or older	36,790	21,206	12,558	9,442	9,546
PERCENT DISTRIBUTION BY COVERAGE STATUS					
Total people	**100.0%**	**67.5%**	**59.3%**	**31.4%**	**8.9%**
Under age 65	100.0	68.9	62.9	32.1	6.5
Under age 18	100.0	64.2	59.5	0.3	5.3
Aged 18 to 24	100.0	60.1	48.4	19.0	5.8
Aged 25 to 34	100.0	65.8	61.0	47.3	5.8
Aged 35 to 44	100.0	73.7	68.9	48.9	6.4
Aged 45 to 54	100.0	75.9	70.1	51.2	7.5
Aged 55 to 64	100.0	75.4	67.8	49.9	9.7
Aged 65 or older	100.0	57.6	34.1	25.7	25.9
PERCENT DISTRIBUTION BY AGE					
Total people	**100.0%**	**100.0%**	**100.0%**	**100.0%**	**100.0%**
Under age 65	87.7	89.5	92.9	89.9	64.2
Under age 18	24.9	23.6	24.9	0.2	14.7
Aged 18 to 24	9.5	8.5	7.7	5.7	6.1
Aged 25 to 34	13.4	13.1	13.8	20.3	8.8
Aged 35 to 44	14.1	15.4	16.3	22.0	10.1
Aged 45 to 54	14.7	16.5	17.4	24.0	12.3
Aged 55 to 64	11.1	12.4	12.7	17.7	12.1
Aged 65 or older	12.3	10.5	7.1	10.1	35.8

Note: Numbers may not add to total because some people have more than one type of health insurance coverage.
Source: Bureau of the Census, Health Insurance, Table HI01, Internet site http://pubdb3.census.gov/macro/032008/health/toc .htm; calculations by New Strategist

Table 3.11 Government Health Insurance Coverage by Age, 2007

(number and percent distribution of people by age and government health insurance coverage status, 2007; numbers in thousands)

		with government health insurance			
	total	total	Medicaid	Medicare	military
Total people	**299,106**	**83,031**	**39,554**	**41,375**	**10,955**
Under age 65	262,316	48,567	36,291	7,097	8,351
Under age 18	74,403	23,041	20,899	518	2,101
Aged 18 to 24	28,398	4,428	3,563	180	823
Aged 25 to 34	40,146	4,539	3,237	501	1,047
Aged 35 to 44	42,132	4,546	3,027	924	1,016
Aged 45 to 54	43,935	5,363	3,103	1,795	1,285
Aged 55 to 64	33,302	6,651	2,462	3,179	2,079
Aged 65 or older	36,790	34,464	3,263	34,278	2,604
PERCENT DISTRIBUTION BY COVERAGE STATUS					
Total people	**100.0%**	**27.8%**	**13.2%**	**13.8%**	**3.7%**
Under age 65	100.0	18.5	13.8	2.7	3.2
Under age 18	100.0	31.0	28.1	0.7	2.8
Aged 18 to 24	100.0	15.6	12.5	0.6	2.9
Aged 25 to 34	100.0	11.3	8.1	1.2	2.6
Aged 35 to 44	100.0	10.8	7.2	2.2	2.4
Aged 45 to 54	100.0	12.2	7.1	4.1	2.9
Aged 55 to 64	100.0	20.0	7.4	9.5	6.2
Aged 65 or older	100.0	93.7	8.9	93.2	7.1
PERCENT DISTRIBUTION BY AGE					
Total people	**100.0%**	**100.0%**	**100.0%**	**100.0%**	**100.0%**
Under age 65	87.7	58.5	91.8	17.2	76.2
Under age 18	24.9	27.7	52.8	1.3	19.2
Aged 18 to 24	9.5	5.3	9.0	0.4	7.5
Aged 25 to 34	13.4	5.5	8.2	1.2	9.6
Aged 35 to 44	14.1	5.5	7.7	2.2	9.3
Aged 45 to 54	14.7	6.5	7.8	4.3	11.7
Aged 55 to 64	11.1	8.0	6.2	7.7	19.0
Aged 65 or older	12.3	41.5	8.2	82.8	23.8

Note: Numbers may not add to total because some people have more than one type of health insurance coverage.
Source: Bureau of the Census, Health Insurance, Table HI01, Internet site http://pubdb3.census.gov/macro/032008/health/toc .htm; calculations by New Strategist

Table 3.12 Spending on Health Care by Age, 2006

(percent of people with health care expense, median expense per person, total expenses, and percent distribution of total expenses by source of payment, by age, 2006)

	total (thousands)	percent with expense	median expense per person	total expenses: amount (millions)	total expenses: percent distribution
Total people	**299,267**	**84.6%**	**$1,185**	**$1,033,056**	**100.0%**
Under age 18	74,106	85.4	462	98,789	9.6
Aged 18 to 29	49,243	73.5	685	79,302	7.7
Aged 30 to 39	39,719	78.5	1,017	94,457	9.1
Aged 40 to 49	44,328	83.8	1,100	129,809	12.6
Aged 50 to 59	39,458	90.0	2,220	207,157	20.1
Aged 60 to 64	14,433	91.8	2,855	90,222	8.7
Aged 65 or older	37,980	96.7	4,215	333,320	32.3

PERCENT DISTRIBUTION BY SOURCE OF PAYMENT

	total	out of pocket	private insurance	Medicare	Medicaid	other
Total people	**100.0%**	**19.0%**	**41.7%**	**23.5%**	**8.7%**	**7.1%**
Under age 18	100.0	20.5	50.7	0.5	23.7	4.6
Aged 18 to 29	100.0	24.8	46.3	0.8	20.0	8.1
Aged 30 to 39	100.0	19.5	62.3	3.0	8.3	6.8
Aged 40 to 49	100.0	20.3	55.3	6.1	10.0	8.3
Aged 50 to 59	100.0	19.6	57.6	8.9	7.0	6.9
Aged 60 to 64	100.0	22.1	52.2	10.7	7.8	7.2
Aged 65 or older	100.0	15.2	14.1	60.9	2.4	7.3

Note: "Other" insurance includes Department of Veterans Affairs (except Tricare), American Indian Health Service, state and local clinics, worker's compensation, homeowner's and automobile insurance, etc.
Source: Agency for Healthcare Research and Quality, Medical Expenditure Panel Survey, 2006, Internet site http://www.meps.ahrq.gov/mepsweb/data_stats/quick_tables_results.jsp?component=1&subcomponent=0&tableSeries=1&year=-1&SearchMethod=1&Action=Search; calculations by New Strategist

Health Problems Increase in the 45-to-64 Age Group

Chronic joint symptoms are the most common health condition among the middle aged.

Thirty-three percent of Americans aged 45 to 64 have experienced joint pain lasting longer than three months, making it the most common health condition in the age group. Hypertension follows, with 32 percent of 45-to-64-year-olds experiencing this problem. Twenty-nine percent have pain in their lower back.

The percentage of people experiencing health problems rises, sometimes steeply, in the 45-to-64 age group. Only 8 percent of 18-to-44-year-olds have hypertension, for example, versus 32 percent of those aged 45 to 64. The prevalence of arthritis rises from 7 percent among younger adults to 28 percent in the 45-to-64 age group. The prevalence of hearing problems rises from 6 percent among younger adults to 18 percent among 45-to-64-year-olds.

As Americans became more aware of the problems associated with high cholesterol over the past few decades, rates have dropped in most age groups. The same cannot be said for high blood pressure. More than 50 percent of men and women aged 55 to 64 either had high blood pressure or were taking hypertensive medication in 2003–06, a higher share than in 1988–94.

■ As the Baby-Boom generation ages into its sixties, the number of people with heart disease, arthritis, and hearing problems will rise.

The percentage of people with arthritis rises with age

(percent of people with arthritis, by age, 2007)

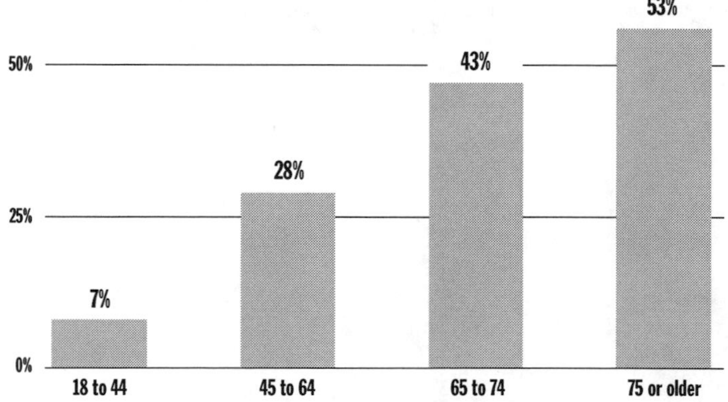

Table 3.13 Number of Adults with Health Conditions by Age, 2007

(number of people aged 18 or older with selected health conditions, by type of condition and age, 2007; numbers in thousands)

				aged 65 or older		
	total	18 to 44	45 to 64	total	65 to 74	75 or older
TOTAL PEOPLE 18 OR OLDER	**223,181**	**110,890**	**76,136**	**36,155**	**19,258**	**16,897**
Selected circulatory diseases						
Heart disease, all types	25,095	4,591	9,266	11,239	5,199	6,040
Coronary	13,674	1,041	5,091	7,542	3,571	3,971
Hypertension	52,920	9,094	24,383	19,442	9,763	9,679
Stroke	5,426	285	2,156	2,985	1,205	1,780
Selected respiratory conditions						
Emphysema	3,736	226	1,765	1,745	861	884
Asthma, ever	24,402	12,996	7,895	3,511	2,030	1,481
Asthma, still	16,177	7,996	5,476	2,704	1,591	1,113
Hay fever	16,882	7,420	7,210	2,252	1,302	950
Sinusitis	25,953	10,261	11,154	4,538	2,589	1,949
Chronic bronchitis	7,604	2,515	3,226	1,863	1,050	813
Selected types of cancer						
Any cancer	16,370	2,085	6,305	7,980	3,757	4,223
Breast cancer	2,630	178	1,028	1,424	626	798
Cervical cancer	1,011	437	417	157	92	65
Prostate cancer	2,037	0	543	1,494	651	843
Other selected diseases and conditions						
Diabetes	17,273	2,432	8,093	6,748	3,840	2,908
Ulcers	14,501	4,616	5,641	4,244	2,119	2,125
Kidney disease	3,343	759	1,226	1,359	593	766
Liver disease	2,649	749	1,374	526	368	158
Arthritis	46,429	7,810	21,428	17,192	8,322	8,870
Chronic joint symptoms	53,945	14,776	24,820	14,350	7,140	7,210
Migraines or severe headaches	27,364	16,427	9,277	1,660	1,075	585
Pain in neck	29,019	11,833	12,073	5,113	2,833	2,280
Pain in lower back	57,070	24,555	21,860	10,655	5,650	5,005
Pain in face or jaw	9,062	4,649	3,455	957	607	350
Selected sensory problems						
Hearing	33,318	6,597	13,400	13,320	5,739	7,581
Vision	22,378	7,596	9,297	5,484	2,472	3,012
Absence of all natural teeth	16,997	2,066	5,606	9,325	4,284	5,041

Note: The conditions shown are those that have ever been diagnosed by a doctor, except as noted. Hay fever, sinusitis, and chronic bronchitis have been diagnosed in the past 12 months. Kidney and liver diseases have been diagnosed in the past 12 months and exclude kidney stones, bladder infections, and incontinence. Chronic joint symptoms are shown if respondent had pain, aching, or stiffness in or around a joint (excluding back and neck) and the condition began more than three months ago. Migraines and pain in neck, lower back, face, or jaw are shown only if pain lasted a whole day or more.
Source: National Center for Health Statistics, Summary Health Statistics for U.S. Adults: National Health Interview Survey, 2007, Vital and Health Statistics, Series 10, No. 240, 2008, Internet site http://www.cdc.gov/nchs/nhis.htm

Table 3.14 Distribution of Health Conditions among Adults by Age, 2007

(percent distribution of people aged 18 or older with selected health conditions, by type of condition and age, 2007)

				aged 65 or older		
	total	18 to 44	45 to 64	total	65 to 74	75 or older
TOTAL PEOPLE 18 OR OLDER	**100.0%**	**49.7%**	**34.1%**	**16.2%**	**8.6%**	**7.6%**
Selected circulatory diseases						
Heart disease, all types	100.0	18.3	36.9	44.8	20.7	24.1
Coronary	100.0	7.6	37.2	55.2	26.1	29.0
Hypertension	100.0	17.2	46.1	36.7	18.4	18.3
Stroke	100.0	5.3	39.7	55.0	22.2	32.8
Selected respiratory conditions						
Emphysema	100.0	6.0	47.2	46.7	23.0	23.7
Asthma, ever	100.0	53.3	32.4	14.4	8.3	6.1
Asthma, still	100.0	49.4	33.9	16.7	9.8	6.9
Hay fever	100.0	44.0	42.7	13.3	7.7	5.6
Sinusitis	100.0	39.5	43.0	17.5	10.0	7.5
Chronic bronchitis	100.0	33.1	42.4	24.5	13.8	10.7
Selected types of cancer						
Any cancer	100.0	12.7	38.5	48.7	23.0	25.8
Breast cancer	100.0	6.8	39.1	54.1	23.8	30.3
Cervical cancer	100.0	43.2	41.2	15.5	9.1	6.4
Prostate cancer	100.0	0	26.7	73.3	32.0	41.4
Other selected diseases and conditions						
Diabetes	100.0	14.1	46.9	39.1	22.2	16.8
Ulcers	100.0	31.8	38.9	29.3	14.6	14.7
Kidney disease	100.0	22.7	36.7	40.7	17.7	22.9
Liver disease	100.0	28.3	51.9	19.9	13.9	6.0
Arthritis	100.0	16.8	46.2	37.0	17.9	19.1
Chronic joint symptoms	100.0	27.4	46.0	26.6	13.2	13.4
Migraines or severe headaches	100.0	60.0	33.9	6.1	3.9	2.1
Pain in neck	100.0	40.8	41.6	17.6	9.8	7.9
Pain in lower back	100.0	43.0	38.3	18.7	9.9	8.8
Pain in face or jaw	100.0	51.3	38.1	10.6	6.7	3.9
Selected sensory problems						
Hearing	100.0	19.8	40.2	40.0	17.2	22.8
Vision	100.0	33.9	41.5	24.5	11.0	13.5
Absence of all natural teeth	100.0	12.2	33.0	54.9	25.2	29.7

Note: The conditions shown are those that have ever been diagnosed by a doctor, except as noted. Hay fever, sinusitis, and chronic bronchitis have been diagnosed in the past 12 months. Kidney and liver diseases have been diagnosed in the past 12 months and exclude kidney stones, bladder infections, and incontinence. Chronic joint symptoms are shown if respondent had pain, aching, or stiffness in or around a joint (excluding back and neck) and the condition began more than three months ago. Migraines and pain in neck, lower back, face, or jaw are shown only if pain lasted a whole day or more.
Source: National Center for Health Statistics, Summary Health Statistics for U.S. Adults: National Health Interview Survey, 2007, Vital and Health Statistics, Series 10, No. 240, 2008, Internet site http://www.cdc.gov/nchs/nhis.htm; calculations by New Strategist

Table 3.15 Percent of Adults with Health Conditions by Age, 2007

(percent of people aged 18 or older with selected health conditions, by type of condition and age, 2007)

	total	18 to 44	45 to 64	65 to 74	75 or older
TOTAL PEOPLE 18 OR OLDER	**100.0%**	**100.0%**	**100.0%**	**100.0%**	**100.0%**
Selected circulatory diseases					
Heart disease, all types	11.3	4.1	12.2	27.1	35.8
Coronary	6.1	0.9	6.7	18.6	23.6
Hypertension	23.7	8.2	32.1	50.9	57.4
Stroke	2.4	0.3	2.8	6.3	10.6
Selected respiratory conditions					
Emphysema	1.7	0.2	2.3	4.5	5.2
Asthma, ever	10.9	11.7	10.4	10.6	8.8
Asthma, still	7.3	7.2	7.2	8.3	6.6
Hay fever	7.6	6.7	9.5	6.8	5.6
Sinusitis	11.6	9.3	14.7	13.5	11.6
Chronic bronchitis	3.4	2.3	4.2	5.5	4.8
Selected types of cancer					
Any cancer	7.3	1.9	8.3	19.6	25.0
Breast cancer	1.2	0.2	1.4	3.3	4.7
Cervical cancer	0.9	0.8	1.1	0.9	0.6
Prostate cancer	1.9	0	1.5	7.4	12.8
Other selected diseases and conditions					
Diabetes	7.8	2.2	10.7	20.3	17.6
Ulcers	6.5	4.2	7.4	11.0	12.6
Kidney disease	1.5	0.7	1.6	3.1	4.5
Liver disease	1.2	0.7	1.8	1.9	0.9
Arthritis	20.8	7.1	28.2	43.4	52.7
Chronic joint symptoms	24.2	13.3	32.6	37.2	42.9
Migraines or severe headaches	12.3	14.8	12.2	5.6	3.5
Pain in neck	13.0	10.7	15.9	14.7	13.5
Pain in lower back	25.6	22.2	28.7	29.4	29.7
Pain in face or jaw	4.1	4.2	4.5	3.2	2.1
Selected sensory problems					
Hearing	14.9	6.0	17.6	29.8	45.0
Vision	10.0	6.9	12.2	12.9	17.9
Absence of all natural teeth	7.6	1.9	7.4	22.4	30.1

Note: The conditions shown are those that have ever been diagnosed by a doctor, except as noted. Hay fever, sinusitis, and chronic bronchitis have been diagnosed in the past 12 months. Kidney and liver diseases have been diagnosed in the past 12 months and exclude kidney stones, bladder infections, and incontinence. Chronic joint symptoms are shown if respondent had pain, aching, or stiffness in or around a joint (excluding back and neck) and the condition began more than three months ago. Migraines and pain in neck, lower back, face, or jaw are shown only if pain lasted a whole day or more.
Source: National Center for Health Statistics, Summary Health Statistics for U.S. Adults: National Health Interview Survey, 2007, Vital and Health Statistics, Series 10, No. 240, 2008, Internet site http://www.cdc.gov/nchs/nhis.htm; calculations by New Strategist

Table 3.16 Hypertension by Sex and Age, 1988–94 and 2003–06

(percent of people aged 20 or older who have hypertension or take antihypertensive medication, by sex and age, 1988–94 and 2003–06; percentage point change, 1988–94 to 2003–06)

	2003–06	1988–94	percentage point change
TOTAL PEOPLE	**32.1%**	**24.1%**	**8.0**
Total men	**31.3**	**23.8**	**7.5**
Aged 20 to 34	9.2	7.1	2.1
Aged 35 to 44	21.1	17.1	0.0
Aged 45 to 54	36.2	29.2	7.0
Aged 55 to 64	50.2	40.6	9.6
Aged 65 to 74	64.1	54.4	9.7
Aged 75 or older	65.0	60.4	4.6
Total women	**32.9**	**24.4**	**8.5**
Aged 20 to 34	2.2	2.9	–0.7
Aged 35 to 44	12.6	11.2	1.4
Aged 45 to 54	36.2	23.9	12.3
Aged 55 to 64	54.4	42.6	11.8
Aged 65 to 74	70.8	56.2	14.6
Aged 75 or older	80.2	73.6	6.6

Note: A person is defined as having hypertension if he or she has a systolic pressure of at least 140 mmHg, diastolic pressure of at least 90 mmHg, or takes antihypertensive medication.
Source: National Center for Health Statistics, Health, United States, 2008, Internet site http://www.cdc.gov/nchs/hus.htm; calculations by New Strategist

Table 3.17 High Cholesterol by Sex and Age, 1988–94 and 2003–06

(percent of people aged 20 or older who have high serum cholesterol, by sex and age, 1988–94 and 2003–06; percentage point change, 1988–94 to 2003–06)

	2003–06	1988–94	percentage point change
TOTAL PEOPLE	**16.4%**	**19.6%**	**–3.2**
Total men	**15.2**	**17.7**	**–2.5**
Aged 20 to 34	9.5	8.2	1.3
Aged 35 to 44	20.5	19.4	1.1
Aged 45 to 54	20.8	26.6	–5.8
Aged 55 to 64	16.0	28.0	–12.0
Aged 65 to 74	10.9	21.9	–11.0
Aged 75 or older	9.6	20.4	–10.8
Total women	**17.5**	**21.3**	**–3.8**
Aged 20 to 34	10.3	7.3	3.0
Aged 35 to 44	12.7	12.3	0.4
Aged 45 to 54	19.7	26.7	–7.0
Aged 55 to 64	30.5	40.9	–10.4
Aged 65 to 74	24.2	41.3	–17.1
Aged 75 or older	18.6	38.2	–19.6

Note: High cholesterol is defined as 240 mg/dL or more.
Source: National Center for Health Statistics, Health, United States, 2008, Internet site http://www.cdc.gov/nchs/hus.htm; calculations by New Strategist

Prescription Drug Use Is Increasing

More Americans use a growing number of prescriptions.

The use of prescription drugs to treat a variety of illnesses, particularly chronic conditions, increased substantially between 1988–94 and 2001–04. The percentage of people who take at least one drug in the past month rose from 38 to 47 percent during those years. The percentage who use three or more prescription drugs in the past month climbed from 11 to 20 percent. Sixty-six percent of people aged 45 to 64 have taken at least one prescription drug in the past month, and 34 percent have taken three or more.

Regardless of age, most people have incurred a prescription drug expense during the past year, with the proportion rising from a low of 50 percent among 18-to-24-year-olds to a high of 92 percent among people aged 65 or older, according to the federal government's Medical Expenditure Panel Survey. Expenses for prescription drugs rise with age, to more than $1,300 per year for people aged 65 or older.

■ Behind the increase in the use of prescriptions is the introduction and marketing of new drugs to treat chronic health problems.

Most have prescription drug expenses

(percent of people with prescription drug expenses, by age, 2006)

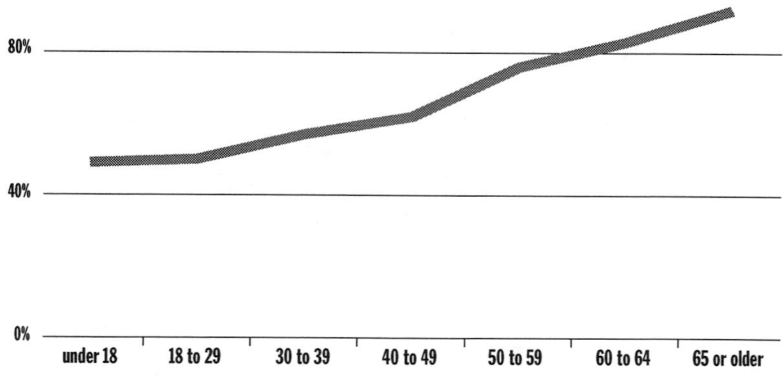

Table 3.18 Prescription Drug Use by Sex and Age, 1988–94 and 2001–04

(percent of people aged 18 or older who took at least one or three or more prescription drugs in the past month, by sex and age, 1988–94 and 2001–04; percentage point change, 1988–94 to 2001–04)

	at least one			three or more		
	2001–04	1988–94	percentage point change	2001–04	1988–94	percentage point change
TOTAL PEOPLE	**46.5%**	**37.8%**	**8.7**	**19.9%**	**11.0%**	**8.9**
Under age 18	23.9	20.5	3.4	4.0	2.4	1.6
Aged 18 to 44	37.6	31.3	6.3	10.2	5.7	4.5
Aged 45 to 64	66.2	54.8	11.4	34.2	20.0	14.2
Aged 65 or older	87.3	73.6	13.7	59.6	35.3	24.3
Total females	**52.2**	**44.6**	**7.6**	**23.3**	**13.6**	**9.7**
Under age 18	22.4	20.6	1.8	3.9	2.3	1.6
Aged 18 to 44	45.9	40.7	5.2	12.3	7.6	4.7
Aged 45 to 64	73.4	62.0	11.4	39.8	24.7	15.1
Aged 65 or older	90.1	78.3	11.8	63.8	38.2	25.6
Total males	**40.5**	**30.6**	**9.9**	**16.3**	**8.3**	**8.0**
Under age 18	25.3	20.4	4.9	4.1	2.6	1.5
Aged 18 to 44	29.2	21.5	7.7	8.0	3.6	4.4
Aged 45 to 64	58.7	47.2	11.5	28.3	15.1	13.2
Aged 65 or older	83.6	67.2	16.4	53.9	31.3	22.6

Source: National Center for Health Statistics, Health, United States, 2008, Internet site http://www.cdc.gov/nchs/hus.htm

Table 3.19 Spending on Prescription Medications by Age, 2006

(percent of people with prescription medication expense, median expense per person, total expenses, and percent distribution of total expenses by source of payment, by age, 2006)

	total (thousands)	percent with expense	median expense per person	total expenses: amount (millions)	total expenses: percent distribution
Total people	**299,267**	**62.6%**	**$364**	**$223,330**	**100.0%**
Under age 18	74,106	48.9	77	15,180	6.8
Aged 18 to 29	49,243	49.9	133	12,285	5.5
Aged 30 to 39	39,719	57.1	210	15,978	7.2
Aged 40 to 49	44,328	61.8	330	28,273	12.7
Aged 50 to 59	39,458	75.6	776	57,071	25.6
Aged 60 to 64	14,433	83.1	994	20,122	9.0
Aged 65 or older	37,980	91.7	1,367	73,422	32.9

	total	out of pocket	private insurance	Medicare	Medicaid	other
PERCENT DISTRIBUTION BY SOURCE OF PAYMENT						
Total people	**100.0%**	**34.9%**	**34.0%**	**19.9%**	**7.0%**	**4.3%**
Under age 18	100.0	26.1	47.4	0.7	24.8	0.9
Aged 18 to 29	100.0	52.5	34.2	1.5	9.5	2.3
Aged 30 to 39	100.0	37.7	44.7	4.9	10.1	2.6
Aged 40 to 49	100.0	34.1	42.5	8.6	11.2	3.6
Aged 50 to 59	100.0	32.3	48.0	9.2	7.0	3.5
Aged 60 to 64	100.0	35.6	44.0	8.4	7.2	4.8
Aged 65 or older	100.0	35.3	11.7	46.0	0.5	6.5

Note: "Other" insurance includes Department of Veterans Affairs (except Tricare), American Indian Health Service, state and local clinics, worker's compensation, homeowner's and automobile insurance, etc.
Source: Agency for Healthcare Research and Quality, Medical Expenditure Panel Survey, 2006, Internet site http://www.meps.ahrq.gov/mepsweb/data_stats/quick_tables_results.jsp?component=1&subcomponent=0&tableSeries=1&year=-1&SearchMethod=1&Action=Search; calculations by New Strategist

Millions of Middle-Aged Americans Are Disabled

Thirteen million 45-to-64-year-olds have physical difficulties.

Among Americans aged 18 or older in 2007, a substantial 33 million had one or more difficulties in physical functioning, according to a survey by the National Center for Health Statistics. The percentage of people with problems rises from a low of 5 percent among people aged 18 to 44 to a high of 37 percent among people aged 65 or older. In the 45-to-64-age group, 18 percent have physical difficulties. The most common problem is an inability to stoop, bend, or kneel, mentioned by 11 percent. More than 10 percent have difficulty standing for two hours.

People with AIDS sometimes count themselves among the nation's disabled. As of 2006, nearly 1 million people had been diagnosed with AIDS. The 59 percent majority were diagnosed between the ages of 30 and 44.

■ Although Boomers are supposed to be more health-conscious than older generations of Americans, many are already experiencing disabilities. As they age, the percentage with disabilities will rise.

Disabilities rise in middle age

(percent of people with physical difficulties, by age, 2007)

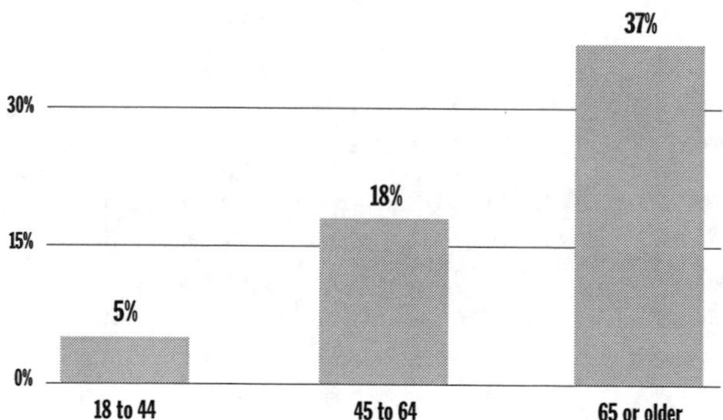

Table 3.20 Difficulties in Physical Functioning among Adults by Age, 2007

(number and percent distribution of people aged 18 or older with difficulties in physical functioning, by type of difficulty and age, 2007; numbers in thousands)

				aged 65 or older		
	total	18 to 44	45 to 64	total	65 to 74	75 or older
Total people aged 18 or older	**223,181**	**110,890**	**76,136**	**36,155**	**19,258**	**16,897**
Total with any physical difficulty	32,977	5,852	13,658	13,467	5,675	7,792
Walk quarter of a mile	16,183	2,000	6,270	7,914	3,142	4,772
Climb 10 steps without resting	12,148	1,469	4,897	5,782	2,128	3,654
Stand for two hours	19,368	2,905	7,971	8,492	3,522	4,970
Sit for two hours	7,220	1,589	3,736	1,895	912	983
Stoop, bend, or kneel	19,943	3,254	8,705	7,983	3,445	4,538
Reach over head	5,543	827	2,517	2,199	861	1,338
Grasp or handle small objects	3,667	482	1,639	1,546	608	938
Lift or carry 10 pounds	8,927	1,237	3,682	4,008	1,574	2,434
Push or pull large objects	14,068	2,333	5,798	5,936	2,465	3,471
PERCENT WITH PHYSICAL DIFFICULTY BY AGE						
Total people aged 18 or older	**100.0%**	**100.0%**	**100.0%**	**100.0%**	**100.0%**	**100.0%**
Total with any physical difficulty	14.8	5.3	17.9	37.2	29.5	46.1
Walk quarter of a mile	7.3	1.8	8.2	21.9	16.3	28.2
Climb 10 steps without resting	5.4	1.3	6.4	16.0	11.0	21.6
Stand for two hours	8.7	2.6	10.5	23.5	18.3	29.4
Sit for two hours	3.2	1.4	4.9	5.2	4.7	5.8
Stoop, bend, or kneel	8.9	2.9	11.4	22.1	17.9	26.9
Reach over head	2.5	0.7	3.3	6.1	4.5	7.9
Grasp or handle small objects	1.6	0.4	2.2	4.3	3.2	5.6
Lift or carry 10 pounds	4.0	1.1	4.8	11.1	8.2	14.4
Push or pull large objects	6.3	2.1	7.6	16.4	12.8	20.5
PERCENT DISTRIBUTION OF THOSE WITH PHYSICAL DIFFICULTIES BY AGE						
Total people aged 18 or older	**100.0%**	**49.7%**	**34.1%**	**16.2%**	**8.6%**	**7.6%**
Total with any physical difficulty	100.0	17.7	41.4	40.8	17.2	23.6
Walk quarter of a mile	100.0	12.4	38.7	48.9	19.4	29.5
Climb 10 steps without resting	100.0	12.1	40.3	47.6	17.5	30.1
Stand for two hours	100.0	15.0	41.2	43.8	18.2	25.7
Sit for two hours	100.0	22.0	51.7	26.2	12.6	13.6
Stoop, bend, or kneel	100.0	16.3	43.6	40.0	17.3	22.8
Reach over head	100.0	14.9	45.4	39.7	15.5	24.1
Grasp or handle small objects	100.0	13.1	44.7	42.2	16.6	25.6
Lift or carry 10 pounds	100.0	13.9	41.2	44.9	17.6	27.3
Push or pull large objects	100.0	16.6	41.2	42.2	17.5	24.7

Note: Respondents were classified as having difficulties if they responded "very difficult" or "can't do at all."
Source: National Center for Health Statistics, Summary Health Statistics for U.S. Adults: National Health Interview Survey, 2007, Vital and Health Statistics, Series 10, No. 240, 2008, Internet site http://www.cdc.gov/nchs/nhis.htm; calculations by New Strategist

Table 3.21 Cumulative Number of AIDS Cases by Sex and Age, through 2006

(cumulative number and percent distribution of AIDS cases by sex and age at diagnosis, through 2006)

	number	percent distribution
TOTAL CASES	**982,498**	**100.0%**
Sex		
Males aged 13 or older	783,786	79.8
Females aged 13 or older	189,566	19.3
Age		
Under age 13	9,156	0.9
Aged 13 to 14	1,078	0.1
Aged 15 to 19	5,626	0.6
Aged 20 to 24	36,225	3.7
Aged 25 to 29	117,099	11.9
Aged 30 to 34	197,530	20.1
Aged 35 to 39	213,573	21.7
Aged 40 to 44	170,531	17.4
Aged 45 to 49	107,207	10.9
Aged 50 to 54	59,907	6.1
Aged 55 to 59	32,190	3.3
Aged 60 to 64	17,303	1.8
Aged 65 or older	15,074	1.5

Source: Centers for Disease Control and Prevention, Cases of HIV/AIDS and AIDS, Internet site http://www.cdc.gov/hiv/topics/surveillance/resources/reports/2006report/table3.htm

Boomers Are Filling Physician Waiting Rooms

People aged 45 to 64 visit a doctor an average of 3.5 times a year.

In 2006, Americans visited a physician a total of 902 million times. Among the broad age groups examined by the National Center for Health Statistics, people aged 45 to 64 account for the largest share (28 percent) of physician visits.

The age group also accounts for 28 percent of visits to hospital outpatient departments and for a smaller 21 percent of visits to emergency departments. Only 8 percent of 45-to-64-year-olds spent a night in the hospital during the past year.

When people who visit a doctor or health care clinic are asked to rate the care they receive, fewer than half give it the highest rating (a 9 or 10 on a scale of 0 to 10). The proportion who rate their experience a 9 or 10 rises in the older age groups, peaking at 62 percent among Medicare recipients.

■ As the Baby-Boom generation ages, older Americans will become the dominant health care consumers, boosting demand for physicians trained in geriatric medicine.

People aged 45 to 64 see a doctor nearly four times a year

(average number of physician visits per person per year, by age, 2006)

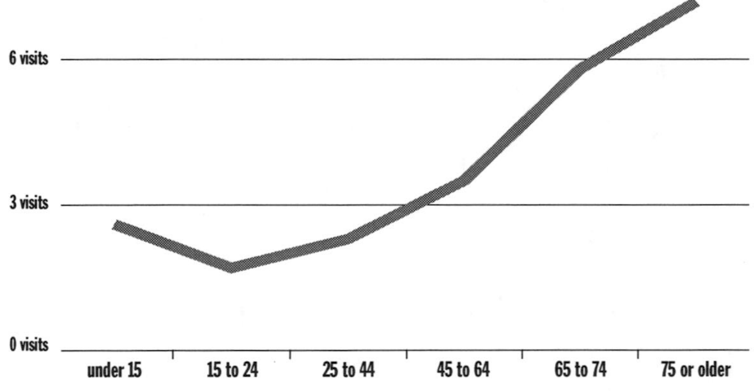

Table 3.22 Physician Office Visits by Sex and Age, 2006

(total number, percent distribution, and number of physician office visits per person per year, by sex and age, 2006; numbers in thousands)

	total	percent distribution	average visits per year
TOTAL VISITS	**901,954**	**100.0%**	**3.1**
Under age 15	157,906	17.5	2.6
Aged 15 to 24	72,411	8.0	1.7
Aged 25 to 44	185,305	20.5	2.3
Aged 45 to 64	256,494	28.4	3.5
Aged 65 to 74	108,063	12.0	5.8
Aged 75 or older	121,774	13.5	7.2
Visits by females	**533,292**	**59.1**	**3.6**
Under age 15	76,300	8.5	2.6
Aged 15 to 24	49,641	5.5	2.4
Aged 25 to 44	122,261	13.6	3.0
Aged 45 to 64	149,778	16.6	3.9
Aged 65 to 74	60,699	6.7	6.0
Aged 75 or older	74,613	8.3	7.3
Visits by males	**368,662**	**40.9**	**2.6**
Under age 15	81,607	9.0	2.6
Aged 15 to 24	22,770	2.5	1.1
Aged 25 to 44	63,044	7.0	1.6
Aged 45 to 64	106,716	11.8	3.0
Aged 65 to 74	47,364	5.3	5.5
Aged 75 or older	47,161	5.2	7.1

Source: National Center for Health Statistics, National Ambulatory Medical Care Survey: 2006 Summary, National Health Statistics Report, No. 3, 2008; Internet site http://www.cdc.gov/nchs/about/major/ahcd/adata.htm

Table 3.23 Hospital Outpatient Department Visits by Age and Reason, 2006

(number and percent distribution of visits to hospital outpatient departments by age and major reason for visit, 2006; numbers in thousands)

	total		major reason for visit						
	number	percent distribution	total	acute problem	chronic problem, routine	chronic problem, flare-up	pre- or post-surgery	preventive care	unknown
Total visits	**102,208**	**100.0%**	**100.0%**	**36.7%**	**31.1%**	**6.8%**	**4.3%**	**19.4%**	**1.7%**
Under age 15	19,864	19.4	100.0	48.9	17.6	3.7	2.0	24.8	2.8
Aged 15 to 24	12,012	11.8	100.0	38.9	16.0	4.7	3.5	34.8	2.1
Aged 25 to 44	25,104	24.6	100.0	37.3	27.2	7.0	4.3	22.6	1.5
Aged 45 to 64	28,707	28.1	100.0	32.2	41.4	8.4	5.4	11.5	1.1
Aged 65 or older	16,522	16.2	100.0	27.4	46.2	8.8	5.9	10.3	1.4

Source: National Center for Health Statistics, National Hospital Ambulatory Medical Care Survey: 2006 Outpatient Department Summary, National Health Statistics Reports, No. 4, 2008; Internet site http://www.cdc.gov/nchs/about/major/ahcd/adata.htm; calculations by New Strategist

Table 3.24 Emergency Department Visits by Age and Urgency of Problem, 2006

(number of visits to emergency rooms and percent distribution by urgency of problem, by age, 2006; numbers in thousands)

	total		percent distribution by urgency of problem						
	number	percent distribution	total	immediate	emergent	urgent	semiurgent	nonurgent	unknown
Total visits	**119,191**	**100.0%**	**100.0%**	**5.1%**	**10.8%**	**36.6%**	**22.0%**	**12.1%**	**13.4%**
Under age 15	21,876	18.4	100.0	3.1	7.8	35.0	25.6	14.6	13.9
Aged 15 to 24	19,525	16.4	100.0	4.1	8.4	34.3	24.7	14.3	14.1
Aged 25 to 44	35,034	29.4	100.0	4.3	10.1	36.4	22.7	12.9	13.6
Aged 45 to 64	25,466	21.4	100.0	5.9	12.8	37.1	20.0	11.1	13.2
Aged 65 or older	17,290	14.5	100.0	9.2	15.4	41.3	15.5	6.7	11.9

Note: "Immediate" is a visit in which the patient should be seen immediately. "Emergent" is a visit in which the patient should be seen within 1 to 14 minutes; "urgent" is a visit in which the patient should be seen within 15 to 60 minutes; "semiurgent" is a visit in which the patient should be seen within 61 to 120 minutes; "nonurgent" is a visit in which the patient should be seen within 121 minutes to 24 hours; "unknown" is a visit with no mention of immediacy or triage or the patient was dead on arrival.
Source: National Center for Health Statistics, National Hospital Ambulatory Medical Care Survey: 2006 Emergency Department Summary, National Health Statistics Reports, No. 7, 2008; Internet site http://www.cdc.gov/nchs/about/major/ahcd/adata.htm

Table 3.25 Rating of Health Care Received from Doctor's Office or Clinic, 2006

(number of people aged 18 or older visiting a doctor or health care clinic in past 12 months, and percent distribution by rating for health care received on a scale from 0 (worst) to 10 (best), by age, 2006; people in thousands)

	with health care visit		rating		
	number	percent	9 to 10	7 to 8	0 to 6
Total people	**140,898**	**100.0%**	**49.3%**	**35.8%**	**13.9%**
Aged 18 to 29	24,274	100.0	42.6	40.2	16.5
Aged 30 to 39	23,007	100.0	43.8	41.3	14.0
Aged 40 to 49	26,565	100.0	45.6	37.6	16.2
Aged 50 to 59	27,436	100.0	48.1	37.0	14.0
Aged 60 to 64	10,666	100.0	54.8	32.6	12.1
Aged 65 or older	28,951	100.0	61.9	26.1	10.2

Source: Agency for Healthcare Research and Quality, Medical Expenditure Panel Survey, 2006, Internet site http://www.meps.ahrq.gov/mepsweb/data_stats/quick_tables_results.jsp?component=1&subcomponent=0&tableSeries=3&year=-1&SearchMethod=1&Action=Search; calculations by New Strategist

Table 3.26 Number of Overnight Hospital Stays by Age, 2007

(total number of people and percent distribution by experience of an overnight hospital stay in past 12 months, by age, 2007; numbers in thousands)

	total		number of stays	
	number	percent	none	one or more
Total people	**296,905**	**100.0%**	**91.8**	**8.2**
Under age 12	48,526	100.0	92.3	7.7
Aged 12 to 17	25,200	100.0	97.5	2.5
Aged 18 to 44	110,889	100.0	93.3	6.7
Aged 45 to 64	76,110	100.0	91.8	8.2
Aged 65 or older	36,180	100.0	82.7	17.3

Source: National Center for Health Statistics, Summary Health Statistics for the U.S. Population: National Health Interview Survey, 2007, Vital and Health Statistics, Series 10, No. 238, 2008, Internet site http://www.cdc.gov/nchs/nhis.htm; calculations by New Strategist

Many Americans Turn to Alternative Medicine

People in their fifties are most likely to seek alternative therapies.

Alternative medicine is a big business. In 2007, fully 38 percent of Americans aged 18 or older used a complementary or alternative medicine or therapy, according to a study by the National Center for Health Statistics. Alternative treatments range from popular regimens such as the South Beach diet to chiropractic care, yoga, and acupuncture.

Middle-aged adults are most likely to use alternative medicine. Forty-four percent of people aged 50 to 59 used alternative medicine in 2007, with 24 percent using biologically based therapies (which include special diets) and 23 percent using mind-body therapy (which includes meditation and yoga).

■ The use of alternative medicine falls steeply with age as health problems become more severe.

The use of alternative medicine peaks in middle age

(percent of people aged 18 or older who have used alternative medicine in the past 12 months, by age, 2007)

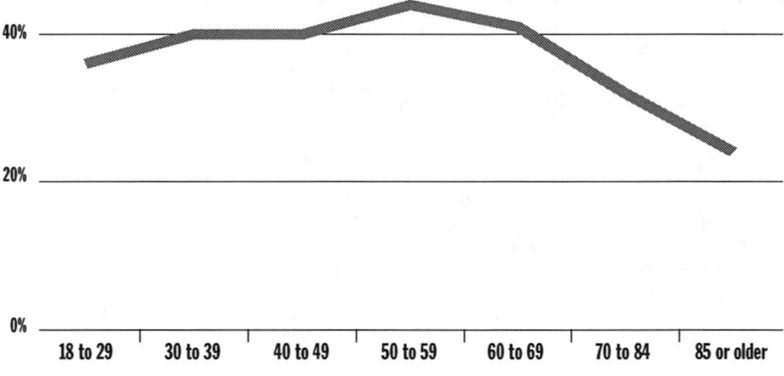

Table 3.27 Adults Who Use Complementary and Alternative Medicine by Age, 2007

(percent of people aged 18 or older who used complementary or alternative medicine in the past 12 months, by age, 2007)

	any use	biologically based therapies	mind-body therapies	alternative medical systems	manipulative and body-based therapies
Total adults	**38.3%**	**19.9%**	**19.2%**	**3.4%**	**15.2%**
Aged 18 to 29	36.3	15.9	21.3	3.2	15.1
Aged 30 to 39	39.6	19.8	19.9	3.6	17.2
Aged 40 to 49	40.1	20.4	19.7	4.6	17.4
Aged 50 to 59	44.1	24.2	22.9	4.9	17.3
Aged 60 to 69	41.0	25.4	17.3	2.8	13.8
Aged 70 to 84	32.1	19.3	11.9	1.8	9.9
Aged 85 or older	24.2	13.7	9.8	1.9	7.0

Definitions: Biologically based therapies include chelation therapy, nonvitamin, nonmineral, natural products, and diet-based therapies. Mind-body therapies include biofeedback; meditation; guided imagery; progressive relaxation; deep breathing exercises; hypnosis; yoga; tai chi; and qi gong. Alternative medical systems include acupuncture; ayurveda; homeopathic treatment; naturopathy; and traditional healers. Manipulative body-based therapies include chiropractic or osteopathic manipulation; massage; and movement therapies.

Source: National Center for Health Statistics, Complementary and Alternative Medicine Use Among Adults and Children: United States, 2007, National Health Statistics Report, No. 12, 2008; Internet site http://nccam.nih.gov/news/camstats/2007/index.htm

Causes of Death Shift in Middle Age

Accidents become less important, while heart disease climbs to second place.

Heart disease and cancer are the two leading causes of death in the United States. Among 45-to-64-year-olds, however, the order is reversed—cancer kills more than heart disease. Accidents are the third leading cause of death among 45-to-54-year-olds and fall to fourth place among 55-to-64-year-olds.

HIV infection has become a much less important cause of death because new drug treatments have slowed the progress of the disease. Still, among 45-to-54-year-olds, HIV ranks eighth as a cause of death. HIV does not make the top-10 list among 55-to-64-year-olds.

If middle age is defined as the point when people have lived half their lives, then 40-year-olds are exactly middle-aged and 50-year-olds are definitely over the hill. Men aged 50 can expect to live 28.8 more years, on average. Women aged 50 can expect to live another 32.5 years.

■ As Boomers age, preventing heart disease and cancer will become an increasingly important focus of their daily life.

Baby Boomers have lived more years than they have remaining

(years of life remaining for people at selected ages, 2006)

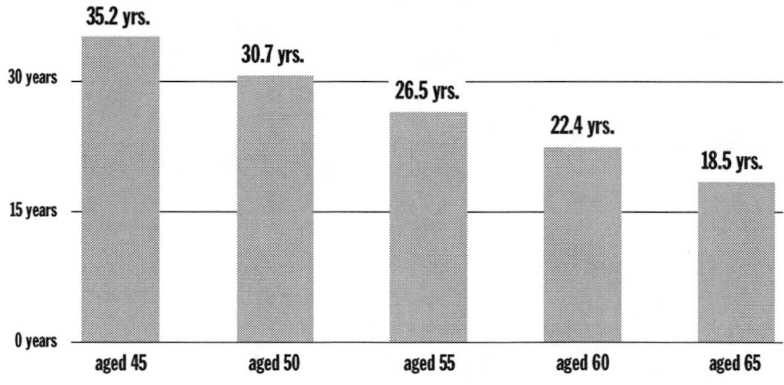

Table 3.28 Leading Causes of Death for People Aged 45 to 54, 2006

(number and percent distribution of deaths accounted for by the 10 leading causes of death for people aged 45 to 54, 2006)

	number	percent distribution
All causes	**185,031**	**100.0%**
1. Malignant neoplasms (cancer) (2)	50,334	27.2
2. Diseases of heart (1)	38,095	20.6
3. Accidents (unintentional injuries) (5)	19,675	10.6
4. Chronic liver disease and cirrhosis (12)	7,712	4.2
5. Suicide (11)	7,426	4.0
6. Cerebrovascular diseases (3)	6,341	3.4
7. Diabetes mellitus (6)	5,692	3.1
8. Human immunodeficiency virus infection	4,377	2.4
9. Chronic lower respiratory disease (4)	3,924	2.1
10. Viral hepatitis	2,911	1.6
All other causes	38,544	20.8

Note: Number in parentheses shows rank for all Americans if the cause of death is among top 15.
Source: National Center for Health Statistics, Deaths: Final Data for 2006, National Vital Statistics Reports, Vol. 57, No. 14, 2009; Internet site http://www.cdc.gov/nchs/products/nvsr.htm#vol57; calculations by New Strategist

Table 3.29 Leading Causes of Death for People Aged 55 to 64, 2006

(number and percent distribution of deaths accounted for by the 10 leading causes of death for people aged 55 to 64, 2006)

	number	percent distribution
All causes	**281,401**	**100.0%**
1. Malignant neoplasms (cancer) (2)	101,454	36.1
2. Diseases of heart (1)	65,477	23.3
3. Chronic lower respiratory disease (4)	12,375	4.4
4. Accidents (unintentional injuries) (5)	11,446	4.1
5. Diabetes mellitus (6)	11,432	4.1
6. Cerebrovascular diseases (3)	10,518	3.7
7. Chronic liver disease and cirrhosis (12)	7,217	2.6
8. Suicide (11)	4,583	1.6
9. Nephritis, nephrotic syndrome, nephrosis (9)	4,368	1.6
10. Septicemia (10)	4,032	1.4
All other causes	48,499	17.2

Note: Number in parentheses shows rank for all Americans if the cause of death is among top 15.
Source: National Center for Health Statistics, Deaths: Final Data for 2006, National Vital Statistics Reports, Vol. 57, No. 14, 2009; Internet site http://www.cdc.gov/nchs/products/nvsr.htm#vol57; calculations by New Strategist

Table 3.30 Life Expectancy by Age and Sex, 2006

(expected years of life remaining at selected ages, by sex, 2006)

	total	females	males
At birth	77.7	80.2	75.1
Aged 1	77.2	79.7	74.7
Aged 5	73.3	75.8	70.8
Aged 10	68.4	70.8	65.8
Aged 15	63.4	65.9	60.9
Aged 20	58.6	61.0	56.1
Aged 25	53.9	56.1	51.5
Aged 30	49.2	51.3	46.9
Aged 35	44.4	46.4	42.2
Aged 40	39.7	41.7	37.6
Aged 45	35.2	37.0	33.1
Aged 50	30.7	32.5	28.8
Aged 55	26.5	28.0	24.7
Aged 60	22.4	23.8	20.7
Aged 65	18.5	19.7	17.0
Aged 70	14.9	15.9	13.6
Aged 75	11.6	12.3	10.5
Aged 80	8.7	9.3	7.8
Aged 85	6.4	6.8	5.7
Aged 90	4.6	4.8	4.1
Aged 95	3.2	3.3	2.9
Aged 100	2.3	2.3	2.0

Source: National Center for Health Statistics, Deaths: Final Data for 2006, National Vital Statistics Reports, Vol. 57, No. 14, 2009; Internet site http://www.cdc.gov/nchs/products/nvsr.htm#vol57; calculations by New Strategist

CHAPTER

4

Housing

■ The homeownership rate has declined. Between 2004 and 2008, the homeownership rate fell in every age group. It showed a 2.7 percentage point decline among householders aged 45 to 49. (Boomers were aged 44 to 62 in 2008.)

■ During the past decade the Baby-Boom generation filled the 45-to-64 age group, when homeownership rates peak. Boomer demand for homes fueled the housing bubble.

■ Although married couples are most likely to own a home, most householders aged 45 or older are homeowners regardless of household type.

■ Householders aged 45 to 64 are most likely to live in single-family, detached homes. Seventy-two percent lived in this type of home in 2007.

■ The median value of the homes owned by married couples aged 45 to 64 stood at $235,723 in 2007, 23 percent above the average. Their homes probably are worth much less today.

■ The mobility rate falls steeply in middle age. Only 7 percent of people aged 45 to 64 moved between 2007 and 2008.

Homeownership Rate Has Declined

Since 2004, rate has fallen in every age group.

The homeownership rate in the United States reached a peak of 69.0 percent in 2004. Since then, the rate has fallen by 1.2 percentage points, to 67.8 percent in 2008, as the housing market collapsed. Householders aged 45 to 49 saw their homeownership rate fall by nearly 3 percentage points between 2004 and 2008.

In 2008, the overall homeownership rate was 0.4 percentage points greater than in 2000. But for the middle aged, homeownership was 1 to 2 percentage points lower in 2008 than in 2000. In contrast, the 2008 homeownership rate for householders under age 45 was slightly higher than in 2000, as it was for householders aged 60 to 64. The homeownership rate of Boomers has fallen because many purchased homes when housing prices were at their peak, and they have lost their homes in the economic downturn.

■ If the housing market stabilizes, the homeownership rate of Boomers should start to climb as they get older.

After peaking in 2004, homeownership rate has fallen sharply among householders aged 45 to 54

(homeownership rate of householders aged 45 to 64, by age, 2004 to 2008)

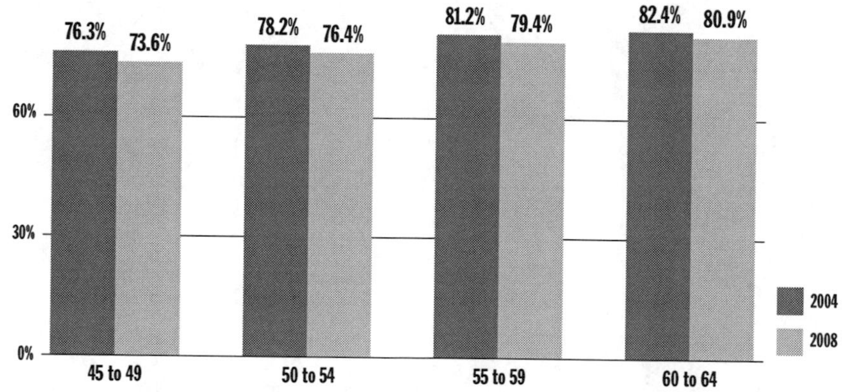

Table 4.1 Homeownership by Age of Householder, 2000 to 2008

(percentage of householders who own their home by age of householder, 2000 to 2008; percentage point change, 2004–08, and 2000–08)

				percentage point change	
	2008	2004	2000	2004–08	2000–08
Total households	**67.8%**	**69.0%**	**67.4%**	**–1.2**	**0.4**
Under age 35	41.0	43.1	40.8	–2.1	0.2
Aged 35 to 44	67.0	69.2	66.3	–2.2	0.7
Aged 45 to 49	73.6	76.3	74.7	–2.7	–1.1
Aged 50 to 54	76.4	78.2	78.5	–1.8	–2.1
Aged 55 to 59	79.4	81.2	80.4	–1.8	–1.0
Aged 60 to 64	80.9	82.4	80.3	–1.5	0.6
Aged 65 or older	80.1	81.1	80.4	–1.0	–0.3

Source: Bureau of the Census, Housing Vacancies and Homeownership Survey, Internet site http://www.census.gov/hhes/www/housing/hvs/annual08/ann08ind.html; calculations by New Strategist

Homeownership Rises with Age

At least three of four householders aged 45 or older own their home.

The housing bubble was not the only reason for the booming housing industry over the past decade. Another factor was the aging of the Baby Boom generation into the lifestage when homeownership peaks. The homeownership rate climbs steeply as people enter their thirties, forties, and fifties. During the past two decades, Boomers filled those age groups, fueling the real estate, construction, and home improvement industries. In fact, growing Boomer demand for homes helped to create the housing bubble.

Those least likely to own a home are young adults who have not yet accumulated the savings for a down payment and are not yet earning enough to qualify for a mortgage. Only 41 percent of householders under age 35 own a home. The homeownership rate peaks at more than 80 percent among Americans aged 60 or older.

■ Although the homeownership rate has receded from its peak, the pattern of homeownership—a rising rate as people age—is unchanged.

Homeowners greatly outnumber renters among 45-to-64-year-olds

(percent distribution of householders aged 45 to 64 by homeownership status and age, 2008)

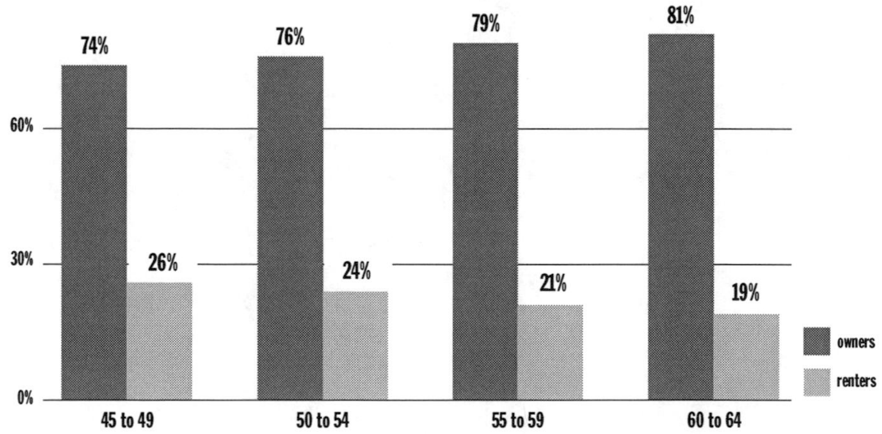

Table 4.2 Owners and Renters by Age of Householder, 2008

(number and percent distribution of householders by homeownership status, and owner and renter share of total, by age of householder, 2008; numbers in thousands)

		owners			renters		
	total	number	percent distribution	share of total	number	percent distribution	share of total
Total households	**111,409**	**75,566**	**100.0%**	**67.8%**	**35,843**	**100.0%**	**32.2%**
Under age 35	24,710	10,120	13.4	41.0	14,589	40.7	59.0
Aged 35 to 44	21,524	14,425	19.1	67.0	7,098	19.8	33.0
Aged 45 to 64	42,200	32,607	43.1	77.3	9,593	26.8	22.7
Aged 45 to 49	11,968	8,812	11.7	73.6	3,155	8.8	26.4
Aged 50 to 54	11,415	8,725	11.5	76.4	2,690	7.5	23.6
Aged 55 to 59	10,217	8,107	10.7	79.4	2,109	5.9	20.6
Aged 60 to 64	8,601	6,962	9.2	80.9	1,639	4.6	19.1
Aged 65 or older	22,976	18,414	24.4	80.1	4,562	12.7	19.9

Source: Bureau of the Census, Housing Vacancies and Homeownership Survey, Internet site http://www.census.gov/hhes/www/housing/hvs/historic/index.html; calculations by New Strategist

Married Couples Are Most Likely to Be Homeowners

Two incomes make homes more affordable.

The homeownership rate among all married couples stood at 83.4 percent in 2008, much higher than the 67.8 percent rate for all households. Among Boomer couples, the homeownership rate ranges from 87.2 percent in the 45-to-49 age group to fully 92.0 percent among couples aged 60 to 64.

Homeownership is much lower for other types of households and lowest for female-headed families, at 49.5 percent in 2008. Regardless of household type, however, most householders aged 45 or older are homeowners.

■ The lax lending standards of the housing bubble did not eliminate differences in homeownership rates by household type.

More than 90 percent of couples aged 55 or older own their home

(percent of married-couple householders who own their home, by age, 2008)

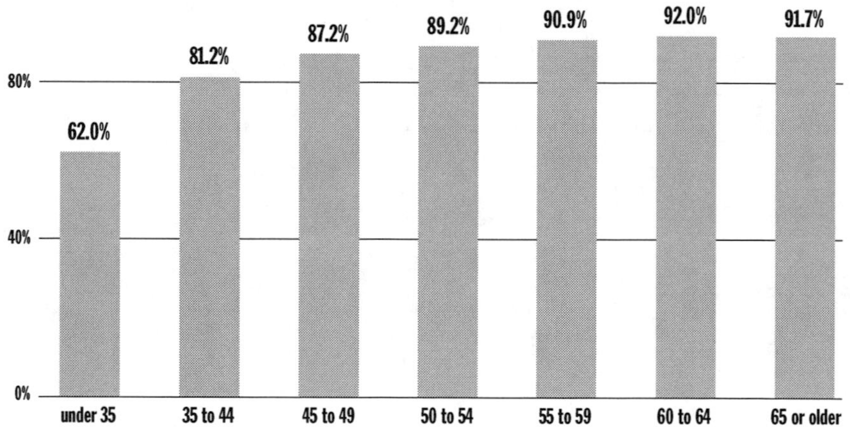

Table 4.3 Homeownership Rate by Age of Householder and Type of Household, 2008

(percent of households that own their home, by age of householder and type of household, 2008)

		family households			people living alone	
	total	married couples	female householder, no spouse present	male householder, no spouse present	females	males
Total households	**67.8%**	**83.4%**	**49.5%**	**57.6%**	**58.6%**	**50.6%**
Under age 35	41.0	62.0	26.2	42.0	22.7	28.8
Aged 35 to 44	67.0	81.2	45.2	56.5	47.5	45.6
Aged 45 to 49	73.6	87.2	58.6	67.9	52.8	51.3
Aged 50 to 54	76.4	89.2	62.3	71.3	56.7	56.5
Aged 55 to 59	79.4	90.9	66.0	76.7	64.0	59.3
Aged 60 to 64	80.9	92.0	67.7	75.2	68.0	61.2
Aged 65 or older	80.1	91.7	81.2	81.2	69.4	68.2

Source: Bureau of the Census, Housing Vacancies and Homeownership Survey, Internet site http://www.census.gov/hhes/www/housing/hvs/annual08/ann08ind.html

Most Middle-Aged Blacks and Hispanics Are Homeowners

The homeownership rate for blacks aged 45 or older exceeds 55 percent.

The homeownership rate of blacks and Hispanics is well below average. The overall homeownership rate stood at 68.3 percent for all households in 2007 (the latest data available by race, Hispanic origin, and age). Among blacks, the rate was a smaller 46.7 percent. The Hispanic rate was slightly greater at 50.5 percent.

Homeownership surpasses 50 percent among black householders beginning in the 45-to-54 age group. Among Hispanics, the rate surpasses 50 percent in the 35-to-44 age group. Homeownership peaks in the 65-or-older age group for both blacks and Hispanics.

■ Blacks are less likely than Hispanics to be homeowners because married couples head a smaller share of black households.

Most Boomers are homeowners, regardless of race or Hispanic origin

(homeownership rate of total householders and householders aged 45 to 64, by race and Hispanic origin, 2007)

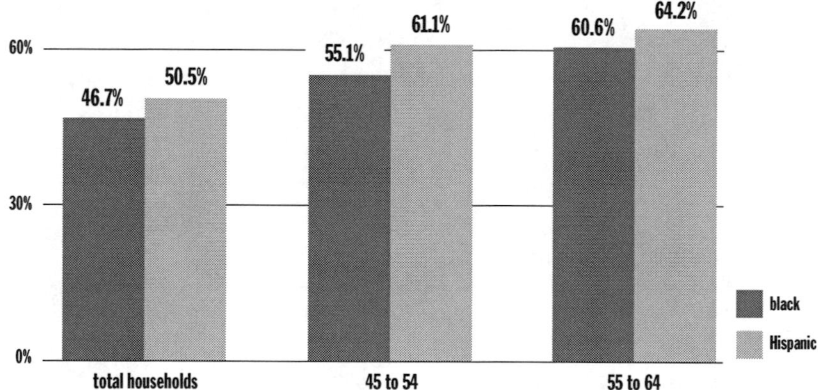

Table 4.4 Black and Hispanic Homeownership Rate by Age, 2007

(percent of total, black, and Hispanic households that own their home, by age of householder, 2007)

	total	black	Hispanic
Total households	**68.3%**	**46.7%**	**50.5%**
Under age 35	42.0	21.8	32.3
Aged 35 to 44	67.9	44.8	53.5
Aged 45 to 54	75.6	55.1	61.1
Aged 55 to 64	80.7	60.6	64.2
Aged 65 or older	79.9	65.1	65.9

Note: Blacks include only those who identify themselves as being black alone. Hispanics may be of any race.
Source: Bureau of the Census, American Housing Survey for the United States: 2007, Internet site http://www.census.gov/hhes/www/housing/ahs/ahs07/ahs07.html; calculations by New Strategist

The Middle Aged Are Most Likely to Live in Single-Family Homes

Only 16 to 17 percent of householders aged 45 to 64 live in apartments.

The majority of American households (65 percent) live in detached, single-family homes. Householders aged 45 to 64 are most likely to live in this type of home, at 72 percent. The median age of householders living in single-family detached homes is 51 years.

Apartment living is most popular among younger adults. A 46 percent minority of householders under age 35 lived in a single-family detached home in 2007, while nearly as many (42 percent) were in apartments. The median age of householders in multi-unit dwellings is just 41 years—10 years younger than the median age of those in single-family detached homes. Interestingly, however, the median age of those living in the largest apartment buildings, with 50 or more units, is a much older 57 years. Behind this figure is the movement of older adults into multi-unit retirement complexes and assisted living facilities.

Overall, 6 percent of households live in mobile homes. The proportion of mobile home householders does not vary much by age.

■ Boomers' demand for single-family detached homes helped to fuel the housing bubble over the past few years.

Most of the middle aged live in single-family homes

(percent of households living in single-family detached homes, by age of householder, 2007)

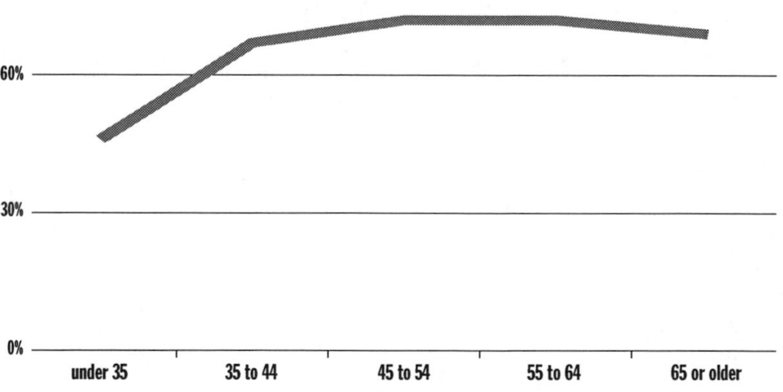

Table 4.5 Number of Units in Structure by Age of Householder, 2007

(number and percent distribution of households by age of householder and number of units in structure, 2007; numbers in thousands)

				multi-unit dwellings						
	total	one, detached	one, attached	total	2 to 4	5 to 9	10 to 19	20 to 49	50 or more	mobile homes
Total households	**110,692**	**71,435**	**6,083**	**26,256**	**8,790**	**5,258**	**4,697**	**3,645**	**3,866**	**6,919**
Under age 35	24,653	11,274	1,594	10,343	3,377	2,389	2,214	1,507	854	1,441
Aged 35 to 44	21,756	14,644	1,146	4,705	1,707	986	857	684	470	1,262
Aged 45 to 64	41,419	29,808	2,186	6,738	2,460	1,259	1,164	835	1,018	2,689
Aged 45 to 54	23,208	16,683	1,153	3,906	1,440	760	724	484	497	1,467
Aged 55 to 64	18,211	13,125	1,033	2,832	1,020	499	440	351	521	1,222
Aged 65 or older	22,865	15,710	1,157	4,470	1,246	622	461	617	1,524	1,528
Median age	49	51	48	41	41	37	37	40	57	50
PERCENT DISTRIBUTION BY AGE OF HOUSEHOLDER										
Total households	**100.0%**	**100.0%**	**100.0%**	**100.0%**	**100.0%**	**100.0%**	**100.0%**	**100.0%**	**100.0%**	**100.0%**
Under age 35	22.3	15.8	26.2	39.4	38.4	45.4	47.1	41.3	22.1	20.8
Aged 35 to 44	19.7	20.5	18.8	17.9	19.4	18.8	18.2	18.8	12.2	18.2
Aged 45 to 64	37.4	41.7	35.9	25.7	28.0	23.9	24.8	22.9	26.3	38.9
Aged 45 to 54	21.0	23.4	19.0	14.9	16.4	14.5	15.4	13.3	12.9	21.2
Aged 55 to 64	16.5	18.4	17.0	10.8	11.6	9.5	9.4	9.6	13.5	17.7
Aged 65 or older	20.7	22.0	19.0	17.0	14.2	11.8	9.8	16.9	39.4	22.1
PERCENT DISTRIBUTION BY UNITS IN STRUCTURE										
Total households	**100.0%**	**64.5%**	**5.5%**	**23.7%**	**7.9%**	**4.8%**	**4.2%**	**3.3%**	**3.5%**	**6.3%**
Under age 35	100.0	45.7	6.5	42.0	13.7	9.7	9.0	6.1	3.5	5.8
Aged 35 to 44	100.0	67.3	5.3	21.6	7.8	4.5	3.9	3.1	2.2	5.8
Aged 45 to 64	100.0	72.0	5.3	16.3	5.9	3.0	2.8	2.0	2.5	6.5
Aged 45 to 54	100.0	71.9	5.0	16.8	6.2	3.3	3.1	2.1	2.1	6.3
Aged 55 to 64	100.0	72.1	5.7	15.6	5.6	2.7	2.4	1.9	2.9	6.7
Aged 65 or older	100.0	68.7	5.1	19.5	5.4	2.7	2.0	2.7	6.7	6.7

Source: Bureau of the Census, American Housing Survey for the United States: 2007, Internet site http://www.census.gov/hhes/www/housing/ahs/ahs07/ahs07.html; calculations by New Strategist

Few Middle-Aged Householders Own New Homes

The youngest homeowners are most likely to live in a new home.

New homes are the province of the young. Overall, only 6 percent of homeowners live in a new home—one built in the past four years. The share is much greater among young homeowners, however. Thirteen percent of homeowners under age 35 live in a new home. The figure drops to 9 percent among those aged 35 to 44 and bottoms out at just 3 percent among householders aged 65 or older. Behind this pattern is the fact that older people are less likely to move and are aging in place, along with their homes.

Among renters, young adults account for the near majority (49 percent) of those in rental units built in the past four years. People aged 45 to 64 account for only 18 percent of renters in newly constructed units.

■ Despite the boom in housing construction during the past few years, the proportion of homeowners living in a new home remains modest.

Boomers account for about one-third of homeowners in new homes

(percent distribution of homeowners who live in homes built in the past four years, by age of householder, 2007)

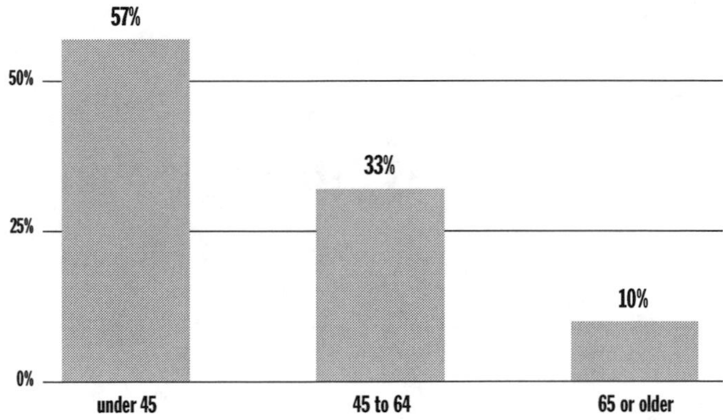

Table 4.6 Owners and Renters of New Homes by Age of Householder, 2007

(number of total occupied housing units, number and percent built in the past four years, and percent distribution of new units by housing tenure and age of householder, 2007; numbers in thousands)

		new homes		
	total	number	percent of total	percent distribution
Total households	**110,692**	**5,747**	**5.2%**	**100.0%**
Under age 35	24,653	1,860	7.5	32.4
Aged 35 to 44	21,756	1,536	7.1	26.7
Aged 45 to 64	41,419	1,739	4.2	30.3
Aged 45 to 54	23,208	1,056	4.6	18.4
Aged 55 to 64	18,211	683	3.8	11.9
Aged 65 or older	22,865	611	2.7	10.6
Total owner households	**75,647**	**4,710**	**6.2**	**100.0**
Under age 35	10,361	1,354	13.1	28.7
Aged 35 to 44	14,781	1,318	8.9	28.0
Aged 45 to 64	32,234	1,551	4.8	32.9
Aged 45 to 54	17,539	935	5.3	19.9
Aged 55 to 64	14,695	616	4.2	13.1
Aged 65 or older	18,271	487	2.7	10.3
Total renter households	**35,045**	**1,036**	**3.0**	**100.0**
Under age 35	14,291	507	3.5	48.9
Aged 35 to 44	6,975	217	3.1	20.9
Aged 45 to 64	9,185	188	2.0	18.1
Aged 45 to 54	5,669	121	2.1	11.7
Aged 55 to 64	3,516	67	1.9	6.5
Aged 65 or older	4,593	124	2.7	12.0

Source: Bureau of the Census, American Housing Survey for the United States: 2007, Internet site http://www.census.gov/hhes/www/housing/ahs/ahs07/ahs07.html; calculations by New Strategist

Housing Costs Are Highest for Homeowner Couples Aged 35 to 44

Costs are lowest for homeowners aged 65 or older.

Monthly housing costs for the average household in 2007 stood at $843, including utilities. For homeowners, median monthly housing cost was $927 including mortgages, and for renters the figure was a smaller $755.

Housing costs are highest for married-couple homeowners aged 35 to 44, not only because their homes are larger than average to make room for children but also because many are recent buyers who bought homes during the housing bubble. The median monthly housing cost for married-couple homeowners aged 35 to 44 was $1,466 in 2007—or 74 percent higher than average.

Housing costs are lowest for homeowners aged 65 or older regardless of household type. For older renters, housing costs do not decline much with age. Among married householders aged 65 or older, homeowners paid a median of $514 for housing, while renters paid a median of $814.

■ The financial advantages of homeownership grow as householders age and pay off their mortgages.

Housing costs fall after age 45

(median monthly housing costs for married-couple homeowners, by age of householder, 2007)

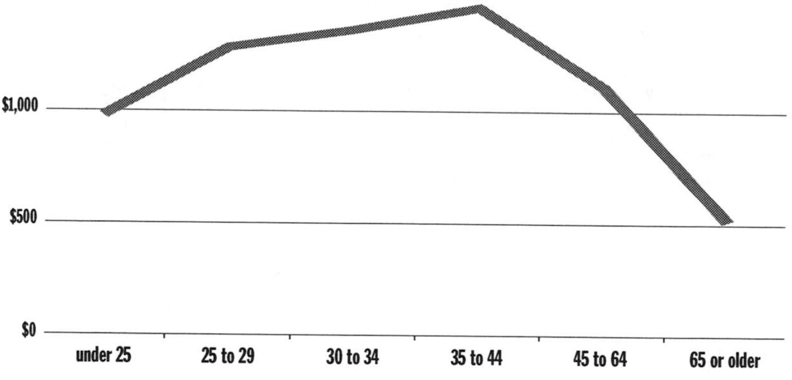

Table 4.7 Median Monthly Housing Costs by Household Type and Age of Householder, 2007

(median monthly housing costs and indexed costs by type of household, age of householder, and housing tenure, 2007)

	median monthly cost			indexed cost		
	total	owners	renters	total	owners	renters
Total households	**$843**	**$927**	**$755**	**100**	**110**	**90**
TWO-OR-MORE-PERSON HOUSEHOLDS						
Married couples	**1,026**	**1,088**	**878**	**122**	**129**	**104**
Under age 25	810	979	716	96	116	85
Aged 25 to 29	1,100	1,286	871	130	153	103
Aged 30 to 34	1,200	1,366	897	142	162	106
Aged 35 to 44	1,349	1,466	937	160	174	111
Aged 45 to 64	1,078	1,113	895	128	132	106
Aged 65 or older	536	514	814	64	61	97
Other male householder	**870**	**960**	**817**	**103**	**114**	**97**
Under age 45	903	1,131	832	107	134	99
Aged 45 to 64	877	951	782	104	113	93
Aged 65 or older	550	505	739	65	60	88
Other female householder	**801**	**867**	**773**	**95**	**103**	**92**
Under age 45	830	1,029	775	98	122	92
Aged 45 to 64	849	935	769	101	111	91
Aged 65 or older	559	496	750	66	59	89
SINGLE-PERSON HOUSEHOLDS						
Male householder	**665**	**681**	**658**	**79**	**81**	**78**
Under age 45	757	996	694	90	118	82
Aged 45 to 64	654	691	631	78	82	75
Aged 65 or older	463	426	524	55	51	62
Female householder	**585**	**523**	**640**	**69**	**62**	**76**
Under age 45	774	991	708	92	118	84
Aged 45 to 64	666	717	616	79	85	73
Aged 65 or older	425	390	528	50	46	63

Note: Housing costs include utilities, mortgages, real estate taxes, property insurance, and regime fees. The index is calculated by dividing median monthly housing costs for each household type by the median cost for total households and multiplying by 100.

Source: Bureau of the Census, American Housing Survey for the United States: 2007, Internet site http://www.census.gov/hhes/www/housing/ahs/ahs07/ahs07.html; calculations by New Strategist

Married Couples Aged 45 to 64 Own Costly Homes

The value of their homes has probably declined, however.

The median value of homes owned by married couples aged 45 to 64 stood at $235,723 in 2007—23 percent greater than the $191,471 median value of all owned homes in that year. More than one in four married couples ranging in age from 35 to 64 owned a home with a value of $400,000 or more in 2007. Many of those homes are worth far less today, however, thanks to the bursting of the housing bubble.

Among homeowning families headed by men and women without a spouse, the middle-aged also have the most valuable homes, although the properties are not as highly valued as the homes of middle-aged married couples. The median value of homes owned by female-headed family householders aged 45 to 64 stood at $172,275 in 2007, while the homes of their male counterparts were valued at a higher $182,457. Among men and women who live alone, younger homeowners have the most valuable homes, and female householders under age 65 own homes of greater value than their male counterparts.

■ Home values have been falling and are now significantly lower than the 2007 figures shown below.

Home values were close to their peak in 2007

(median value of homes owned by married couples, by age of householder, 2007)

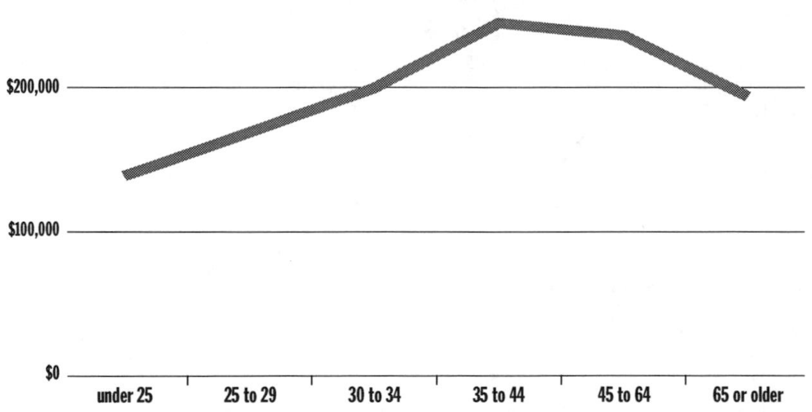

Table 4.8 Value of Owner-Occupied Homes by Type of Household and Age of Householder, 2007

(number of homeowners by value of home, median value of home, and indexed median value, by type of household and age of householder, 2007)

	number (in 000s)	under $100,000	$100,000–$149,999	$150,000–$199,999	$200,000–$299,999	$300,000–$399,999	$400,000–$499,999	$500,000–$749,999	$750,000 or more	median value of home ($)	indexed median value
Total homeowners	**75,647**	**18,779**	**11,048**	**9,643**	**13,132**	**8,060**	**4,740**	**6,234**	**4,013**	**191,471**	**100**
TWO-OR-MORE-PERSON HOUSEHOLDS											
Married couples	**46,570**	**9227**	**6,282**	**5,992**	**8,660**	**5,664**	**3,348**	**4,443**	**2,955**	**220,607**	**115**
Under age 25	540	176	122	55	66	55	17	37	11	138,617	72
Aged 25 to 29	2,133	494	438	359	415	257	72	89	10	168,736	88
Aged 30 to 34	3,456	709	500	525	739	357	234	264	128	199,431	104
Aged 35 to 44	10,245	1560	1,331	1,334	2,020	1,375	852	1,073	701	244,492	128
Aged 45 to 64	21,119	4048	2,655	2,502	3,795	2,714	1,568	2,274	1,564	235,723	123
Aged 65 or older	9,078	2242	1,237	1,216	1,625	906	605	706	541	193,584	101
Other male householder	**4,408**	**1256**	**642**	**597**	**723**	**422**	**205**	**366**	**196**	**175,616**	**92**
Under age 45	2,050	558	349	298	363	174	94	146	67	169,745	89
Aged 45 to 64	1,792	495	245	241	269	174	95	173	102	182,457	95
Aged 65 or older	565	204	48	57	91	75	16	48	27	177,446	93
Other female householder	**7,984**	**2644**	**1,323**	**925**	**1,196**	**643**	**427**	**523**	**305**	**151,366**	**79**
Under age 45	3,076	1036	609	406	403	229	138	176	78	141,246	74
Aged 45 to 64	3,349	1037	484	345	543	300	210	250	180	172,275	90
Aged 65 or older	1,558	571	230	173	250	113	79	96	46	145,242	76
SINGLE-PERSON HOUSEHOLDS											
Men living alone	**6,930**	**2321**	**1,147**	**935**	**1,007**	**563**	**318**	**403**	**235**	**149,840**	**78**
Under age 45	2,235	663	413	335	392	166	99	122	45	156,298	82
Aged 45 to 64	2,813	991	436	371	385	232	123	161	113	147,605	77
Aged 65 or older	1,882	667	299	229	229	165	96	120	77	145,811	76
Women living alone	**9,756**	**3330**	**1,653**	**1,195**	**1,547**	**768**	**442**	**499**	**322**	**146,812**	**77**
Under age 45	1,408	416	225	192	270	138	77	65	25	166,550	87
Aged 45 to 64	3,161	1035	500	453	546	246	157	146	78	155,029	81
Aged 65 or older	5,187	1880	928	550	731	384	208	288	219	138,439	72

Source: Bureau of the Census, American Housing Survey for the United States: 2007, Internet site http://www.census.gov/hhes/www/housing/ahs/ahs07/ahs07.html; calculations by New Strategist

Mobility Rate Falls Steeply in Middle Age

Most of the middle aged move for housing-related reasons.

Twelve percent of Americans aged 1 or older moved between March 2007 and March 2008, but the proportion was a smaller 7 percent among people aged 45 to 64. Within the age group, the mobility rate fell from 8 percent among 45-to-49-year-olds to just 5 percent among 62-to-64-year-olds. The majority of all movers stay within the same county. Only 13 percent of people who moved between 2007 and 2008 went to a different state.

Regardless of age, housing is the primary motivation for moving. The 43 percent plurality of movers aged 45 to 64 say housing was the main reason for the move. Family reasons ranked second as a motivation for moving, and employment ranks third. Among those who moved between 2007 and 2008 because of retirement, the 51 percent majority were aged 45 to 64.

■ Americans are moving less than they once did. Several factors are behind the decline in mobility including the collapse of the housing market, the aging of the population, and dual-income couples.

Few of the middle aged move

(percent of people who moved between March 2007 and March 2008, by age)

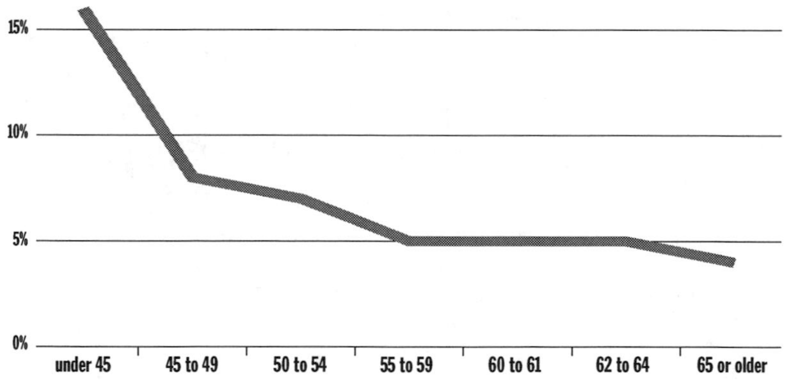

Table 4.9 Geographic Mobility by Age and Type of Move, 2007–08

(total number of people aged 1 or older, and number and percent who moved between March 2007 and March 2008, by age and type of move; numbers in thousands)

					different state			
	total	total movers	same county	different county, same state	total	same region	different region	movers from abroad
Total, aged 1 or older	**294,851**	**35,166**	**23,013**	**6,282**	**4,727**	**2,248**	**2,479**	**1,145**
Under age 45	180,825	28,922	19,144	4,989	3,803	1,820	1,983	981
Aged 45 to 64	77,237	5,513	3,103	969	701	326	375	112
Aged 45 to 49	22,701	1,723	1,169	287	215	119	96	52
Aged 50 to 54	21,234	1,462	942	275	223	93	130	22
Aged 55 to 59	18,371	1,006	605	219	166	84	82	16
Aged 60 to 61	6,941	328	184	98	36	10	26	9
Aged 62 to 64	7,990	367	203	90	61	20	41	13
Aged 65 or older	36,789	1,360	767	321	223	104	119	50
PERCENT DISTRIBUTION BY MOBILITY STATUS								
Total, aged 1 or older	**100.0%**	**11.9%**	**7.8%**	**2.1%**	**1.6%**	**0.8%**	**0.8%**	**0.4%**
Under age 45	100.0	16.0	10.6	2.8	2.1	1.0	1.1	0.5
Aged 45 to 64	100.0	7.1	4.0	1.3	0.9	0.4	0.5	0.1
Aged 45 to 49	100.0	7.6	5.1	1.3	0.9	0.5	0.4	0.2
Aged 50 to 54	100.0	6.9	4.4	1.3	1.1	0.4	0.6	0.1
Aged 55 to 59	100.0	5.5	3.3	1.2	0.9	0.5	0.4	0.1
Aged 60 to 61	100.0	4.7	2.7	1.4	0.5	0.1	0.4	0.1
Aged 62 to 64	100.0	4.6	2.5	1.1	0.8	0.3	0.5	0.2
Aged 65 or older	100.0	3.7	2.1	0.9	0.6	0.3	0.3	0.1
PERCENT DISTRIBUTION OF MOVERS BY TYPE OF MOVE								
Total, aged 1 or older	–	**100.0%**	**65.4%**	**17.9%**	**13.4%**	**6.4%**	**7.0%**	**3.3%**
Under age 45	–	100.0	66.2	17.2	13.1	6.3	6.9	3.4
Aged 45 to 64	–	100.0	56.3	17.6	12.7	5.9	6.8	2.0
Aged 45 to 49	–	100.0	67.8	16.7	12.5	6.9	5.6	3.0
Aged 50 to 54	–	100.0	64.4	18.8	15.3	6.4	8.9	1.5
Aged 55 to 59	–	100.0	60.1	21.8	16.5	8.3	8.2	1.6
Aged 60 to 61	–	100.0	56.1	29.9	11.0	3.0	7.9	2.7
Aged 62 to 64	–	100.0	55.3	24.5	16.6	5.4	11.2	3.5
Aged 65 or older	–	100.0	56.4	23.6	16.4	7.6	8.8	3.7

Note: "–" means not applicable.
Source: Bureau of the Census, Geographic Mobility: 2007 to 2008, Detailed Tables, Internet site http://www.census.gov/population/www/socdemo/migrate/cps2008.html; calculations by New Strategist

Table 4.10 Reason for Moving among People Aged 45 to 64, 2007–08

(number and percent distribution of movers aged 45 to 64 by primary reason for move and share of total movers between March 2007 and March 2008; numbers in thousands)

	total movers	movers aged 45 to 64		
		number	percent distribution	share of total
TOTAL MOVERS	**35,167**	**4,886**	**100.0%**	**13.9%**
Family reasons	**10,738**	**1,332**	**27.3**	**12.4**
Change in marital status	1,987	323	6.6	16.3
To establish own household	3,682	298	6.1	8.1
Other family reasons	5,069	711	14.6	14.0
Employment reasons	**7,352**	**1,067**	**21.8**	**14.5**
New job or job transfer	2,940	361	7.4	12.3
To look for work or lost job	794	129	2.6	16.2
To be closer to work/easier commute	2,183	273	5.6	12.5
Retired	140	72	1.5	51.4
Other job-related reason	1,295	232	4.7	17.9
Housing reasons	**14,098**	**2,106**	**43.1**	**14.9**
Wanted own home, not rent	2,033	284	5.8	14.0
Wanted better home/apartment	4,866	730	14.9	15.0
Wanted better neighborhood	1,778	240	4.9	13.5
Wanted cheaper housing	2,872	454	9.3	15.8
Other housing reasons	2,549	398	8.1	15.6
Other reasons	**2,978**	**381**	**7.8**	**12.8**
To attend or leave college	872	22	0.5	2.5
Change of climate	212	57	1.2	26.9
Health reasons	460	119	2.4	25.9
Natural disaster	61	13	0.3	21.3
Other reasons	1,373	170	3.5	12.4

Source: Bureau of the Census, Geographic Mobility: 2007 to 2008, Detailed Tables, Internet site http://www.census.gov/population/www/socdemo/migrate/cps2008.html; calculations by New Strategistt

CHAPTER

5

Income

■ As Boomers moved into the age group, the incomes of householders aged 55 to 64 rose 6 percent between 2000 and 2007, after adjusting for inflation. Householders aged 45 to 54 lost ground during those years.

■ Median household income peaks among householders aged 50 to 54, at $66,244—far above the $50,233 national median.

■ Twenty-seven percent of householders aged 45 to 64 have incomes of $100,000 or more, accounting for 51 percent of all households with incomes that high.

■ Between 2000 and 2007, the median income of men aged 55 to 64 rose by a small 2 percent, after adjusting for inflation. The median income of men aged 45 to 54 fell by 7 percent during those years.

■ Among men aged 45 to 54, those with at least a bachelor's degree earned a median of $68,601. Their counterparts with just a high school diploma earned only $38,868.

■ The poverty rate bottoms out in the 55-to-59 age group, now entirely filled with the Baby-Boom generation. As Boomers age, the poverty rate may rise.

Median Income Is Declining for Households Headed by the Middle Aged

Householders aged 55 to 64 have made gains, however.

Between 2000 and 2007, median household income fell 0.6 percent after adjusting for inflation. Behind the small drop was the lackluster recovery following the recession of 2001. The recession of 2008 is not yet captured in these figures and but it is certain to have driven household incomes down further.

The median income of householders aged 45 to 54 fell much more than average between 2000 and 2007, down by 5.7 percent during those years. In contrast, the median income of householders aged 55 to 64 rose 6.3 percent. (Boomers were aged 43 to 61 in 2007.) Behind the rise in the median income of householders aged 55 to 64 is the end of early retirement.

Median household income in 2007 was higher than in 1990, despite the decline since 2000. The gains made by householders aged 45 to 54 were below average, however, while householders aged 55 to 64 saw above average increases during the time period.

■ The incomes of householders aged 55 to 64 are likely to continue to rise in the coming years as Boomers postpone retirement.

Householders aged 55 to 64 are the only ones with growing incomes

(percent change in median income of households headed by people aged 45 to 64, by age, 2000–07; in 2007 dollars)

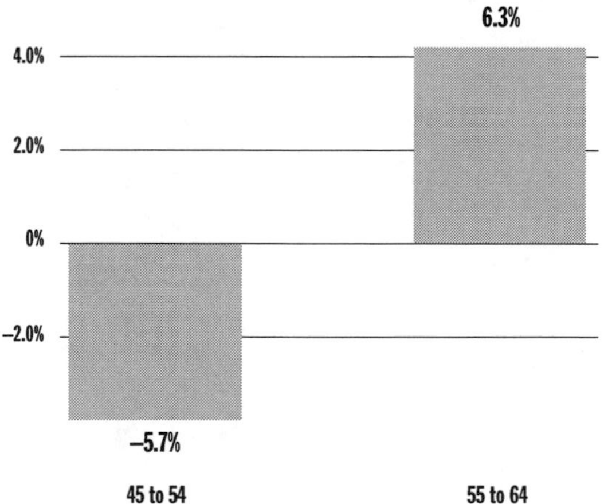

Table 5.1 Median Income of Households Headed by People Aged 45 to 64, 1990 to 2007

(median income of total households and households headed by people aged 45 to 64, and index of age group to total, 1990 to 2007; percent change for selected years; in 2007 dollars)

	total households	45 to 54	index, 45–54 to total	55 to 64	index, 55–64 to total
2007	$50,233	$65,476	130	$57,386	114
2006	49,568	66,714	135	56,141	113
2005	49,202	66,300	135	55,505	113
2004	48,665	66,989	138	55,315	114
2003	48,835	67,914	139	55,483	114
2002	48,878	68,024	139	54,403	111
2001	49,455	67,980	137	53,714	109
2000	50,557	69,403	137	54,005	107
1999	50,641	70,807	140	55,579	110
1998	49,397	68,786	139	54,837	111
1997	47,665	66,819	140	53,269	112
1996	46,704	66,416	142	52,393	112
1995	46,034	64,923	141	51,439	112
1994	44,636	65,384	146	48,742	109
1993	44,143	65,290	148	47,299	107
1992	44,359	64,340	145	49,220	111
1991	44,726	64,955	145	49,445	111
1990	46,049	64,471	140	49,773	108
Percent change					
2000 to 2007	–0.6%	–5.7%	–	6.3%	–
1990 to 2007	9.1	1.6	–	15.3	–

Note: The index is calculated by dividing the median income of the age group by the national median and multiplying by 100. "–" means not applicable.
Source: Bureau of the Census, Current Population Survey Annual Social and Economic Supplements, Internet site http://www.census.gov/hhes//www/income/histinc/inchhtoc.html; calculations by New Strategist

Household Income Peaks around Age 50

Householders aged 50 to 54 have the highest incomes.

Household income peaks in middle age because many middle-aged householders are dual-income married couples at the height of their careers. Median household income tops out at $66,244 among householders aged 50 to 54, far above the $50,233 national median.

Among the nation's most affluent households—those with incomes of $100,000 or more in 2007—the 45-to-64 age group accounts for the 51 percent majority. (Boomers were aged 43 to 61 in that year.) Nearly 30 percent of households headed by 50-to-54-year-olds have incomes of $100,000 or more.

■ The incomes of householders aged 60 to 64 are likely to rise in the next few years as the dual-income couples of the Baby-Boom generation completely fill the age group.

The middle aged have the highest incomes

(median income of households by age of householder 2007)

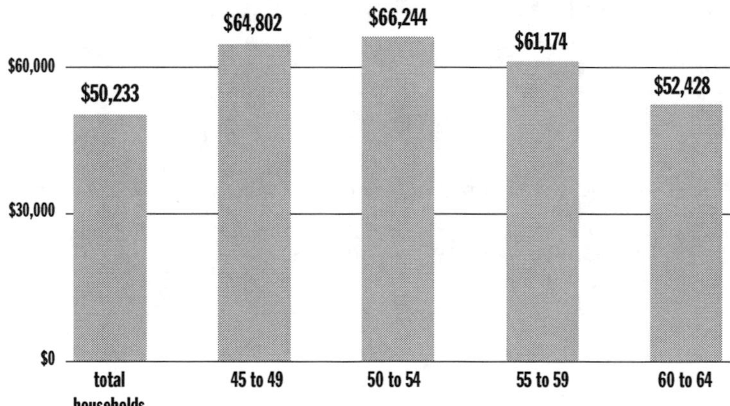

Table 5.2 Income of Households Headed by People Aged 45 to 64, 2007: Total Households

(number and percent distribution of total households and households headed by people aged 45 to 64, by income, 2007; households in thousands as of 2008)

		aged 45 to 64				
	total	total	45 to 49	50 to 54	55 to 59	60 to 64
Total households	**116,783**	**44,445**	**12,685**	**11,851**	**10,813**	**9,096**
Under $10,000	8,455	2,915	690	741	706	777
$10,000 to $19,999	13,778	3,451	806	797	855	992
$20,000 to $29,999	13,115	3,703	1,036	874	926	866
$30,000 to $39,999	12,006	3,918	1,116	952	951	898
$40,000 to $49,999	10,733	3,880	1,118	1,028	947	787
$50,000 to $59,999	9,565	3,620	1,052	940	879	750
$60,000 to $69,999	8,009	3,274	964	882	831	596
$70,000 to $79,999	7,006	2,914	906	775	697	534
$80,000 to $89,999	5,788	2,595	851	766	549	428
$90,000 to $99,999	4,741	2,201	675	607	521	398
$100,000 or more	23,586	11,975	3,471	3,488	2,950	2,067
Median income	$50,233	$61,771	$64,802	$66,244	$61,174	$52,428
Total households	**100.0%**	**100.0%**	**100.0%**	**100.0%**	**100.0%**	**100.0%**
Under $10,000	7.2	6.6	5.4	6.3	6.5	8.5
$10,000 to $19,999	11.8	7.8	6.4	6.7	7.9	10.9
$20,000 to $29,999	11.2	8.3	8.2	7.4	8.6	9.5
$30,000 to $39,999	10.3	8.8	8.8	8.0	8.8	9.9
$40,000 to $49,999	9.2	8.7	8.8	8.7	8.8	8.7
$50,000 to $59,999	8.2	8.1	8.3	7.9	8.1	8.2
$60,000 to $69,999	6.9	7.4	7.6	7.4	7.7	6.6
$70,000 to $79,999	6.0	6.6	7.1	6.5	6.4	5.9
$80,000 to $89,999	5.0	5.8	6.7	6.5	5.1	4.7
$90,000 to $99,999	4.1	5.0	5.3	5.1	4.8	4.4
$100,000 or more	20.2	26.9	27.4	29.4	27.3	22.7

Source: Bureau of the Census, 2008 Current Population Survey Annual Social and Economic Supplement, Internet site http://www.census.gov/hhes/www/macro/032008/hhinc/new02_001.htm; calculations by New Strategist

Among Boomers, Asians and Non-Hispanic Whites Have the Highest Incomes

Blacks and Hispanics have much lower household incomes.

The median income of households headed by Asians in the 45-to-64 age group easily topped $70,000 in 2007, while that of non-Hispanic whites in the age group was about $68,000. In contrast, the median household income of their black counterparts was less than $36,000, and the Hispanic median was $45,000.

About three of 10 Asian and non-Hispanic white householders in the 45-to-64 age group have a household income of $100,000 or more. Among Asians, a lofty 36 percent have incomes that high. The figure is a smaller but still substantial 31 percent among non-Hispanic whites. In contrast, only 13 percent of black householders aged 45 to 64 have incomes of $100,000 or more. The figure is 14 percent for Hispanics.

■ Black incomes are well below those of Asians and non-Hispanic whites because married couples—the most affluent household type—make up a much smaller share of black households. For Hispanics, incomes are lower because they are much less educated and, consequently, have little earning power.

Median household income varies by race and Hispanic origin

(median income of households headed b people aged 45 to 64, by race and Hispanic origin, 2007)

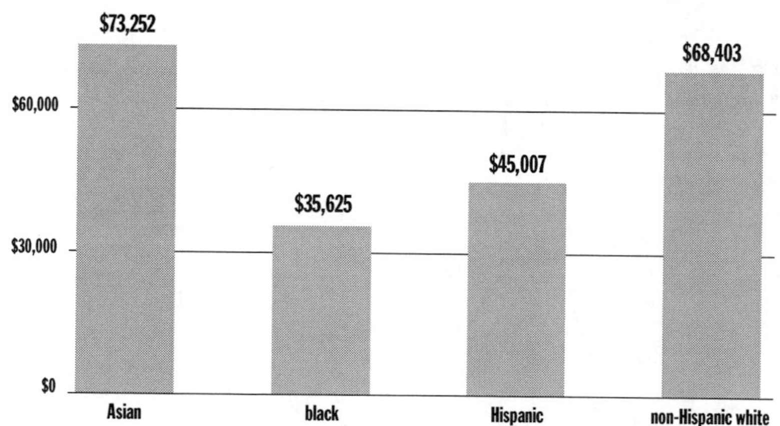

Table 5.3 Income of Households Headed by People Aged 45 to 64, 2007: Asian Households

(number and percent distribution of total Asian households and Asian households headed by people aged 45 to 64, by income, 2007; households in thousands as of 2008)

		aged 45 to 64				
	total	total	45 to 49	50 to 54	55 to 59	60 to 64
Total Asian households	**4,715**	**1647**	**509**	**475**	**385**	**278**
Under $10,000	311	85	10	26	16	33
$10,000 to $19,999	365	99	32	13	18	36
$20,000 to $29,999	388	114	40	31	30	13
$30,000 to $39,999	357	121	33	29	33	26
$40,000 to $49,999	372	146	32	48	38	28
$50,000 to $59,999	336	117	39	38	24	16
$60,000 to $69,999	327	103	41	31	21	10
$70,000 to $79,999	307	95	39	24	19	13
$80,000 to $89,999	243	96	29	25	27	15
$90,000 to $99,999	240	81	18	22	23	18
$100,000 or more	1,468	593	197	189	139	68
Median income	$65,876	$73,252	$77,813	$78,926	$76,539	$50,656
Total Asian households	**100.0%**	**100.0%**	**100.0%**	**100.0%**	**100.0%**	**100.0%**
Under $10,000	6.6	5.2	2.0	5.5	4.2	11.9
$10,000 to $19,999	7.7	6.0	6.3	2.7	4.7	12.9
$20,000 to $29,999	8.2	6.9	7.9	6.5	7.8	4.7
$30,000 to $39,999	7.6	7.3	6.5	6.1	8.6	9.4
$40,000 to $49,999	7.9	8.9	6.3	10.1	9.9	10.1
$50,000 to $59,999	7.1	7.1	7.7	8.0	6.2	5.8
$60,000 to $69,999	6.9	6.3	8.1	6.5	5.5	3.6
$70,000 to $79,999	6.5	5.8	7.7	5.1	4.9	4.7
$80,000 to $89,999	5.2	5.8	5.7	5.3	7.0	5.4
$90,000 to $99,999	5.1	4.9	3.5	4.6	6.0	6.5
$100,000 or more	31.1	36.0	38.7	39.8	36.1	24.5

Note: Asians include those who identify themselves as being of the race alone and those who identify themselves as being of the race in combination with other races.
Source: Bureau of the Census, 2008 Current Population Survey Annual Social and Economic Supplement, Internet site http://www.census.gov/hhes/www/macro/032008/hhinc/new02_001.htm; calculations by New Strategist

Table 5.4 Income of Households Headed by People Aged 45 to 64, 2007: Black Households

(number and percent distribution of total black households and black households headed by people aged 45 to 64, by income, 2007; households in thousands as of 2008)

		aged 45 to 64				
	total	total	45 to 49	50 to 54	55 to 59	60 to 64
Total black households	**14,976**	**5,563**	**1,739**	**1,516**	**1,344**	**964**
Under $10,000	2,256	746	184	208	209	145
$10,000 to $19,999	2,444	683	146	163	219	155
$20,000 to $29,999	1,988	667	221	176	144	126
$30,000 to $39,999	1,746	606	193	174	124	115
$40,000 to $49,999	1,379	560	181	165	112	102
$50,000 to $59,999	1,161	504	179	128	119	78
$60,000 to $69,999	867	386	141	112	83	50
$70,000 to $79,999	683	276	117	71	61	27
$80,000 to $89,999	549	243	88	72	48	35
$90,000 to $99,999	403	182	64	49	37	32
$100,000 or more	1,500	707	224	201	186	96
Median income	$34,091	$35,625	$46,696	$41,502	$37,447	$3,870
Total black households	**100.0%**	**100.0%**	**100.0%**	**100.0%**	**100.0%**	**100.0%**
Under $10,000	15.1	13.4	10.6	13.7	15.6	15.0
$10,000 to $19,999	16.3	12.3	8.4	10.8	16.3	16.1
$20,000 to $29,999	13.3	12.0	12.7	11.6	10.7	13.1
$30,000 to $39,999	11.7	10.9	11.1	11.5	9.2	11.9
$40,000 to $49,999	9.2	10.1	10.4	10.9	8.3	10.6
$50,000 to $59,999	7.8	9.1	10.3	8.4	8.9	8.1
$60,000 to $69,999	5.8	6.9	8.1	7.4	6.2	5.2
$70,000 to $79,999	4.6	5.0	6.7	4.7	4.5	2.8
$80,000 to $89,999	3.7	4.4	5.1	4.7	3.6	3.6
$90,000 to $99,999	2.7	3.3	3.7	3.2	2.8	3.3
$100,000 or more	10.0	12.7	12.9	13.3	13.8	10.0

Note: Blacks include those who identify themselves as being of the race alone and those who identify themselves as being of the race in combination with other races.
Source: Bureau of the Census, 2008 Current Population Survey Annual Social and Economic Supplement, Internet site http://www.census.gov/hhes/www/macro/032008/hhinc/new02_001.htm; calculations by New Strategist

Table 5.5 Income of Households Headed by People Aged 45 to 64, 2007: Hispanic Households

(number and percent distribution of total Hispanic households and Hispanic households headed by people aged 45 to 64, by income, 2007; households in thousands as of 2008)

		aged 45 to 64				
	total	total	45 to 49	50 to 54	55 to 59	60 to 64
Total Hispanic households	**13,339**	**3,977**	**1,424**	**1,056**	**868**	**629**
Under $10,000	1,184	390	125	96	89	80
$10,000 to $19,999	1,901	464	137	107	102	118
$20,000 to $29,999	1,961	473	179	131	90	73
$30,000 to $39,999	1,787	467	160	122	116	69
$40,000 to $49,999	1,387	356	124	101	79	52
$50,000 to $59,999	1,119	337	129	86	76	46
$60,000 to $69,999	921	309	128	76	72	33
$70,000 to $79,999	758	261	99	74	52	36
$80,000 to $89,999	534	195	73	61	35	26
$90,000 to $99,999	401	167	75	35	36	21
$100,000 or more	1,385	552	193	166	119	74
Median income	$38,679	$45,007	$47,887	$47,277	$44,338	$35,600
Total Hispanic households	**100.0%**	**100.0%**	**100.0%**	**100.0%**	**100.0%**	**100.0%**
Under $10,000	8.9	9.8	8.8	9.1	10.3	12.7
$10,000 to $19,999	14.3	11.7	9.6	10.1	11.8	18.8
$20,000 to $29,999	14.7	11.9	12.6	12.4	10.4	11.6
$30,000 to $39,999	13.4	11.7	11.2	11.6	13.4	11.0
$40,000 to $49,999	10.4	9.0	8.7	9.6	9.1	8.3
$50,000 to $59,999	8.4	8.5	9.1	8.1	8.8	7.3
$60,000 to $69,999	6.9	7.8	9.0	7.2	8.3	5.2
$70,000 to $79,999	5.7	6.6	7.0	7.0	6.0	5.7
$80,000 to $89,999	4.0	4.9	5.1	5.8	4.0	4.1
$90,000 to $99,999	3.0	4.2	5.3	3.3	4.1	3.3
$100,000 or more	10.4	13.9	13.6	15.7	13.7	11.8

Source: Bureau of the Census, 2008 Current Population Survey Annual Social and Economic Supplement, Internet site http://www.census.gov/hhes/www/macro/032008/hhinc/new02_001.htm; calculations by New Strategist

Table 5.6 Income of Households Headed by People Aged 45 to 64, 2007: Non-Hispanic White Households

(number and percent distribution of total non-Hispanic white households and non-Hispanic white households headed by people aged 45 to 64, by income, 2007; households in thousands as of 2008)

		aged 45 to 64				
	total	total	45 to 49	50 to 54	55 to 59	60 to 64
Total non-Hispanic white households	**82,765**	**32,815**	**8,892**	**8,685**	**8,126**	**7,112**
Under $10,000	4,607	1,647	365	399	387	496
$10,000 to $19,999	8,971	2,162	481	496	508	677
$20,000 to $29,999	8,639	2,398	591	517	651	639
$30,000 to $39,999	8,017	2,684	718	614	675	677
$40,000 to $49,999	7,479	2,774	768	703	711	592
$50,000 to $59,999	6,854	2,628	699	684	655	590
$60,000 to $69,999	5,836	2,452	649	655	646	502
$70,000 to $79,999	5,213	2,262	639	603	562	458
$80,000 to $89,999	4,419	2,033	651	603	432	347
$90,000 to $99,999	3,664	1,761	521	490	425	325
$100,000 or more	19,062	10,015	2,811	2,918	2,476	1,810
Median income	$54,920	$68,403	$72,199	$74,548	$66,874	$57,902
Total non-Hispanic white households	**100.0%**	**100.0%**	**100.0%**	**100.0%**	**100.0%**	**100.0%**
Under $10,000	5.6	5.0	4.1	4.6	4.8	7.0
$10,000 to $19,999	10.8	6.6	5.4	5.7	6.3	9.5
$20,000 to $29,999	10.4	7.3	6.6	6.0	8.0	9.0
$30,000 to $39,999	9.7	8.2	8.1	7.1	8.3	9.5
$40,000 to $49,999	9.0	8.5	8.6	8.1	8.7	8.3
$50,000 to $59,999	8.3	8.0	7.9	7.9	8.1	8.3
$60,000 to $69,999	7.1	7.5	7.3	7.5	7.9	7.1
$70,000 to $79,999	6.3	6.9	7.2	6.9	6.9	6.4
$80,000 to $89,999	5.3	6.2	7.3	6.9	5.3	4.9
$90,000 to $99,999	4.4	5.4	5.9	5.6	5.2	4.6
$100,000 or more	23.0	30.5	31.6	33.6	30.5	25.4

Note: Non-Hispanic whites are those who identify themselves as being white alone and not Hispanic.
Source: Bureau of the Census, 2008 Current Population Survey Annual Social and Economic Supplement, Internet site http://www.census.gov/hhes/www/macro/032008/hhinc/new02_001.htm; calculations by New Strategist

Married Couples Have the Highest Incomes

No other household type comes close to the affluence of married couples.

Among households headed by people aged 45 to 64 (Boomers were aged 43 to 61 in 2007), the median household income of married couples is far above the median incomes of other household types. Married-couple householders aged 45 to 64 had a median income of $84,289 in 2007. Women in the 45-to-64 age group who live alone had the lowest incomes, a median of just $29,598. The most affluent households in the nation are couples aged 50 to 54, with a median income of $90,099. Fully 43 percent of these couples have incomes of $100,000 or more.

Dual earners explain the higher incomes of married couples. The more earners in a household, the higher the income. Female-headed families have low incomes because they typically have only one earner in the home. Similarly, men and women who live alone also have relatively low incomes because there is at best one earner in the household.

■ Forty percent of married couples aged 45 to 64 have incomes of $100,000 or more.

Incomes peak among married couples aged 50 to 54

(median income of married couples, by age of householder, 2007)

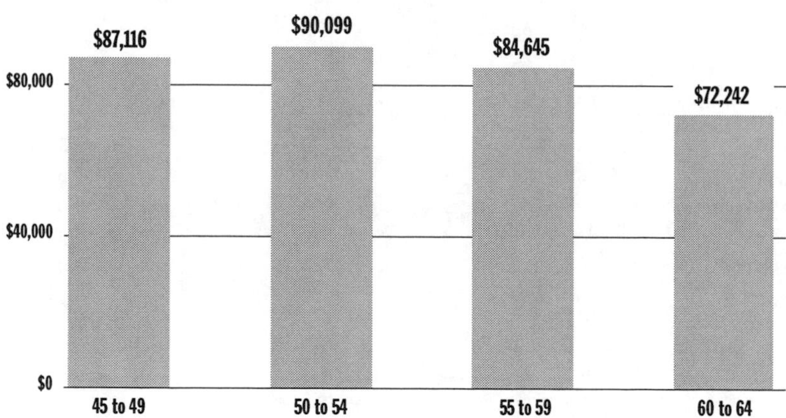

Table 5.7 Income of Households by Household Type, 2007: Aged 45 to 64

(number and percent distribution of households headed by people aged 45 to 64, by income and household type, 2007; households in thousands as of 2008)

		family households			nonfamily households			
					female householder		male householder	
	total	married couples	female hh, no spouse present	male hh, no spouse present	total	living alone	total	living alone
Total households headed by 45-to-64-year-olds	**44,445**	**24,986**	**4,605**	**1,577**	**6,871**	**6,147**	**6,407**	**5,426**
Under $10,000	2,915	433	419	87	1,114	1,081	864	834
$10,000 to $19,999	3,451	764	573	139	1,136	1,080	841	782
$20,000 to $29,999	3,703	1,196	611	151	982	905	766	688
$30,000 to $39,999	3,918	1,486	558	183	857	775	831	746
$40,000 to $49,999	3,880	1,776	489	176	796	725	642	560
$50,000 to $59,999	3,620	1,920	477	146	528	461	552	462
$60,000 to $69,999	3,274	1,925	389	133	426	352	400	305
$70,000 to $79,999	2,914	2,001	253	117	237	198	306	237
$80,000 to $89,999	2,595	1,910	208	95	169	133	213	148
$90,000 to $99,999	2,201	1,692	155	56	127	82	170	134
$100,000 or more	11,975	9,881	471	296	499	347	828	537
Median income	$61,771	$84,289	$42,640	$53,097	$32,192	$29,598	$38,108	$34,914
Total households headed by 45-to-64-year-olds	**100.0%**	**100.0%**	**100.0%**	**100.0%**	**100.0%**	**100.0%**	**100.0%**	**100.0%**
Under $10,000	6.6	1.7	9.1	5.5	16.2	17.6	13.5	15.4
$10,000 to $19,999	7.8	3.1	12.4	8.8	16.5	17.6	13.1	14.4
$20,000 to $29,999	8.3	4.8	13.3	9.6	14.3	14.7	12.0	12.7
$30,000 to $39,999	8.8	5.9	12.1	11.6	12.5	12.6	13.0	13.7
$40,000 to $49,999	8.7	7.1	10.6	11.2	11.6	11.8	10.0	10.3
$50,000 to $59,999	8.1	7.7	10.4	9.3	7.7	7.5	8.6	8.5
$60,000 to $69,999	7.4	7.7	8.4	8.4	6.2	5.7	6.2	5.6
$70,000 to $79,999	6.6	8.0	5.5	7.4	3.4	3.2	4.8	4.4
$80,000 to $89,999	5.8	7.6	4.5	6.0	2.5	2.2	3.3	2.7
$90,000 to $99,999	5.0	6.8	3.4	3.6	1.8	1.3	2.7	2.5
$100,000 or more	26.9	39.5	10.2	18.8	7.3	5.6	12.9	9.9

Note: "hh" is short for householder.
Source: Bureau of the Census, 2008 Current Population Survey Annual Social and Economic Supplement, Internet site http://www.census.gov/hhes/www/macro/032008/hhinc/new02_000.htm; calculations by New Strategist

Table 5.8 Income of Households by Household Type, 2007: Aged 45 to 49

(number and percent distribution of households headed by people aged 45 to 49, by income and household type, 2007; households in thousands as of 2008)

		family households			nonfamily households			
					female householder		male householder	
	total	married couples	female hh, no spouse present	male hh, no spouse present	total	living alone	total	living alone
Total households headed by 45-to-49-year-olds	**12,685**	**7,105**	**1,736**	**597**	**1,481**	**1,232**	**1,766**	**1,470**
Under $10,000	690	77	154	32	229	215	199	195
$10,000 to $19,999	806	159	201	48	221	204	179	154
$20,000 to $29,999	1,036	294	254	64	203	176	221	213
$30,000 to $39,999	1,116	372	220	79	205	172	240	221
$40,000 to $49,999	1,118	471	181	71	178	153	217	193
$50,000 to $59,999	1,052	520	202	47	114	90	170	126
$60,000 to $69,999	964	575	139	56	91	71	103	72
$70,000 to $79,999	906	597	93	54	63	44	97	71
$80,000 to $89,999	851	641	76	33	34	19	67	52
$90,000 to $99,999	675	515	62	15	31	20	53	42
$100,000 or more	3,471	2,885	154	99	111	65	222	132
Median income	$64,802	$87,116	$41,714	$50,899	$33,834	$30,882	$41,452	$37,338
Total households headed by 45-to-49-year-olds	**100.0%**	**100.0%**	**100.0%**	**100.0%**	**100.0%**	**100.0%**	**100.0%**	**100.0%**
Under $10,000	5.4	1.1	8.9	5.4	15.5	17.5	11.3	13.3
$10,000 to $19,999	6.4	2.2	11.6	8.0	14.9	16.6	10.1	10.5
$20,000 to $29,999	8.2	4.1	14.6	10.7	13.7	14.3	12.5	14.5
$30,000 to $39,999	8.8	5.2	12.7	13.2	13.8	14.0	13.6	15.0
$40,000 to $49,999	8.8	6.6	10.4	11.9	12.0	12.4	12.3	13.1
$50,000 to $59,999	8.3	7.3	11.6	7.9	7.7	7.3	9.6	8.6
$60,000 to $69,999	7.6	8.1	8.0	9.4	6.1	5.8	5.8	4.9
$70,000 to $79,999	7.1	8.4	5.4	9.0	4.3	3.6	5.5	4.8
$80,000 to $89,999	6.7	9.0	4.4	5.5	2.3	1.5	3.8	3.5
$90,000 to $99,999	5.3	7.2	3.6	2.5	2.1	1.6	3.0	2.9
$100,000 or more	27.4	40.6	8.9	16.6	7.5	5.3	12.6	9.0

Note: "hh" is short for householder.
Source: Bureau of the Census, 2008 Current Population Survey Annual Social and Economic Supplement, Internet site http://www.census.gov/hhes/www/macro/032008/hhinc/new02_000.htm; calculations by New Strategist

Table 5.9 Income of Households by Household Type, 2007: Aged 50 to 54

(number and percent distribution of households headed by people aged 50 to 54, by income and household type, 2007; households in thousands as of 2008)

		family households			nonfamily households			
					female householder		male householder	
	total	married couples	female hh, no spouse present	male hh, no spouse present	total	living alone	total	living alone
Total households headed by 50-to-54-year-olds	**11,851**	**6,737**	**1,307**	**467**	**1,644**	**1,481**	**1,696**	**1,396**
Under $10,000	741	119	130	28	237	225	229	221
$10,000 to $19,999	797	142	169	39	247	229	201	187
$20,000 to $29,999	874	249	161	34	228	219	202	176
$30,000 to $39,999	952	305	162	59	199	176	226	192
$40,000 to $49,999	1,028	449	140	51	221	197	166	142
$50,000 to $59,999	940	492	127	35	131	119	156	138
$60,000 to $69,999	882	490	131	31	107	92	123	90
$70,000 to $79,999	775	558	60	32	50	47	76	55
$80,000 to $89,999	766	559	55	32	61	49	59	43
$90,000 to $99,999	607	467	47	26	24	15	43	30
$100,000 or more	3,488	2,905	126	99	140	109	217	126
Median income	$66,244	$90,099	$41,775	$55,788	$34,839	$32,766	$39,364	$35,881
Total households headed by 50-to-54-year-olds	**100.0%**	**100.0%**	**100.0%**	**100.0%**	**100.0%**	**100.0%**	**100.0%**	**100.0%**
Under $10,000	6.3	1.8	9.9	6.0	14.4	15.2	13.5	15.8
$10,000 to $19,999	6.7	2.1	12.9	8.4	15.0	15.5	11.9	13.4
$20,000 to $29,999	7.4	3.7	12.3	7.3	13.9	14.8	11.9	12.6
$30,000 to $39,999	8.0	4.5	12.4	12.6	12.1	11.9	13.3	13.8
$40,000 to $49,999	8.7	6.7	10.7	10.9	13.4	13.3	9.8	10.2
$50,000 to $59,999	7.9	7.3	9.7	7.5	8.0	8.0	9.2	9.9
$60,000 to $69,999	7.4	7.3	10.0	6.6	6.5	6.2	7.3	6.4
$70,000 to $79,999	6.5	8.3	4.6	6.9	3.0	3.2	4.5	3.9
$80,000 to $89,999	6.5	8.3	4.2	6.9	3.7	3.3	3.5	3.1
$90,000 to $99,999	5.1	6.9	3.6	5.6	1.5	1.0	2.5	2.1
$100,000 or more	29.4	43.1	9.6	21.2	8.5	7.4	12.8	9.0

Note: "hh" is short for householder.
Source: Bureau of the Census, 2008 Current Population Survey Annual Social and Economic Supplement, Internet site http://www.census.gov/hhes/www/macro/032008/hhinc/new02_000.htm; calculations by New Strategist

Table 5.10 Income of Households by Household Type, 2007: Aged 55 to 59

(number and percent distribution of households headed by people aged 55 to 59, by income and household type, 2007; households in thousands as of 2008)

		family households			nonfamily households			
					female householder		male householder	
	total	married couples	female hh, no spouse present	male hh, no spouse present	total	living alone	total	living alone
Total households headed by 55-to-59-year-olds	**10,813**	**6,049**	**920**	**301**	**1,878**	**1,703**	**1,666**	**1,448**
Under $10,000	706	81	81	16	271	269	259	246
$10,000 to $19,999	855	201	127	21	265	250	240	231
$20,000 to $29,999	926	305	114	35	301	279	173	151
$30,000 to $39,999	951	368	93	28	244	227	219	206
$40,000 to $49,999	947	441	103	35	221	207	147	125
$50,000 to $59,999	879	460	82	45	160	146	131	113
$60,000 to $69,999	831	489	67	28	137	112	109	91
$70,000 to $79,999	697	469	65	15	68	58	80	68
$80,000 to $89,999	549	409	45	16	32	31	48	27
$90,000 to $99,999	521	411	29	5	42	28	33	26
$100,000 or more	2,950	2,416	112	58	137	96	227	166
Median income	$61,174	$84,645	$44,819	$51,530	$35,057	$32,105	$36,659	$34,205
Total households headed by 55-to-59-year-olds	**100.0%**	**100.0%**	**100.0%**	**100.0%**	**100.0%**	**100.0%**	**100.0%**	**100.0%**
Under $10,000	6.5	1.3	8.8	5.3	14.4	15.8	15.5	17.0
$10,000 to $19,999	7.9	3.3	13.8	7.0	14.1	14.7	14.4	16.0
$20,000 to $29,999	8.6	5.0	12.4	11.6	16.0	16.4	10.4	10.4
$30,000 to $39,999	8.8	6.1	10.1	9.3	13.0	13.3	13.1	14.2
$40,000 to $49,999	8.8	7.3	11.2	11.6	11.8	12.2	8.8	8.6
$50,000 to $59,999	8.1	7.6	8.9	15.0	8.5	8.6	7.9	7.8
$60,000 to $69,999	7.7	8.1	7.3	9.3	7.3	6.6	6.5	6.3
$70,000 to $79,999	6.4	7.8	7.1	5.0	3.6	3.4	4.8	4.7
$80,000 to $89,999	5.1	6.8	4.9	5.3	1.7	1.8	2.9	1.9
$90,000 to $99,999	4.8	6.8	3.2	1.7	2.2	1.6	2.0	1.8
$100,000 or more	27.3	39.9	12.2	19.3	7.3	5.6	13.6	11.5

Note: "hh" is short for householder.
Source: Bureau of the Census, 2008 Current Population Survey Annual Social and Economic Supplement, Internet site http://www.census.gov/hhes/www/macro/032008/hhinc/new02_000.htm; calculations by New Strategist

Table 5.11 Income of Households by Household Type, 2007: Aged 60 to 64

(number and percent distribution of households headed by people aged 60 to 64, by income and household type, 2007; households in thousands as of 2008)

		family households			nonfamily households			
					female householder		male householder	
	total	married couples	female hh, no spouse present	male hh, no spouse present	total	living alone	total	living alone
Total households headed by 60-to-64-year-olds	**9,096**	**5,095**	**642**	**212**	**1,868**	**1,731**	**1,279**	**1,112**
Under $10,000	777	156	54	11	377	372	177	172
$10,000 to $19,999	992	262	76	31	403	397	221	210
$20,000 to $29,999	866	348	82	18	250	231	170	148
$30,000 to $39,999	898	441	83	17	209	200	146	127
$40,000 to $49,999	787	415	65	19	176	168	112	100
$50,000 to $59,999	750	448	66	19	123	106	95	85
$60,000 to $69,999	596	371	52	18	91	77	65	52
$70,000 to $79,999	534	377	35	16	56	49	53	43
$80,000 to $89,999	428	301	32	14	42	34	39	26
$90,000 to $99,999	398	299	17	10	30	19	41	36
$100,000 or more	2,067	1,675	79	40	111	77	162	113
Median income	$52,428	$72,242	$43,784	$55,587	$25,681	$23,508	$33,714	$31,418
Total households headed by 60-to-64-year-olds	**100.0%**	**100.0%**	**100.0%**	**100.0%**	**100.0%**	**100.0%**	**100.0%**	**100.0%**
Under $10,000	8.5	3.1	8.4	5.2	20.2	21.5	13.8	15.5
$10,000 to $19,999	10.9	5.1	11.8	14.6	21.6	22.9	17.3	18.9
$20,000 to $29,999	9.5	6.8	12.8	8.5	13.4	13.3	13.3	13.3
$30,000 to $39,999	9.9	8.7	12.9	8.0	11.2	11.6	11.4	11.4
$40,000 to $49,999	8.7	8.1	10.1	9.0	9.4	9.7	8.8	9.0
$50,000 to $59,999	8.2	8.8	10.3	9.0	6.6	6.1	7.4	7.6
$60,000 to $69,999	6.6	7.3	8.1	8.5	4.9	4.4	5.1	4.7
$70,000 to $79,999	5.9	7.4	5.5	7.5	3.0	2.8	4.1	3.9
$80,000 to $89,999	4.7	5.9	5.0	6.6	2.2	2.0	3.0	2.3
$90,000 to $99,999	4.4	5.9	2.6	4.7	1.6	1.1	3.2	3.2
$100,000 or more	22.7	32.9	12.3	18.9	5.9	4.4	12.7	10.2

Note: "hh" is short for householder.
Source: Bureau of the Census, 2008 Current Population Survey Annual Social and Economic Supplement, Internet site http://www.census.gov/hhes/www/macro/032008/hhinc/new02_000.htm; calculations by New Strategist

Median Income of Middle-Aged Men Has Declined

Women's incomes have risen, however.

Between 2000 and 2007, the median income of men aged 45 to 54 fell 7 percent, after adjusting for inflation, while that of men aged 55 to 64 rose a small 2 percent (Boomers were aged 43 to 61 in 2007). While the slow recovery following the recession of 2001 could be blamed for the decline between 2000 and 2007, in fact men in the 45-to-54 age group have been experiencing falling incomes for more than a decade. In contrast, the incomes of women have grown since 1990, among both those aged 45 to 54 and those aged 55 to 64. The older group saw a whopping 75 percent increase in median income. Even in the 2000-to-2007 period, incomes continued to grow for these women, although more slowly. Behind women's rising income is their growing labor force participation.

The median income gains experienced by men aged 55 to 64 stand in stark contrast to the losses experienced by men aged 45 to 54. These gains are likely to continue as Boomer men postpone retirement until they reach age 65 or older.

■ With the incomes of Boomer men declining, the incomes of women are increasingly important to the financial well-being of the nation's middle-aged householders.

Among the middle aged, women are faring better than men

(percent change in median income of people aged 45 to 64 by age and sex, 2000–07; in 2007 dollars)

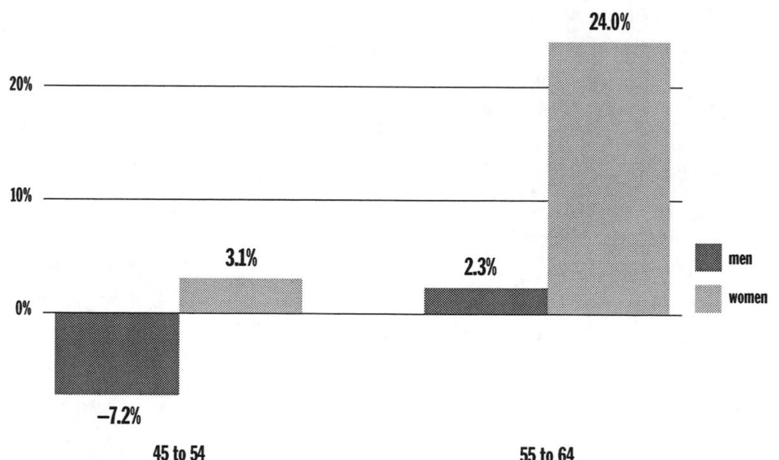

Table 5.12 Median Income of Men Aged 45 to 64, 1990 to 2007

(median income of men aged 15 or older and aged 45 to 64, and index of age group to total, 1990 to 2007; percent change for selected years; in 2007 dollars)

	total men	45 to 54	index, 45–54 to total	55 to 64	index, 55–64 to total
2007	$33,196	$45,849	138	$42,129	127
2006	33,180	46,989	142	42,654	129
2005	33,217	46,336	139	43,178	130
2004	33,497	45,955	137	43,126	129
2003	33,743	47,438	141	43,871	130
2002	33,698	47,218	140	41,811	124
2001	34,082	48,139	141	41,736	122
2000	34,126	49,412	145	41,165	121
1999	33,963	50,776	150	41,668	123
1998	33,654	49,444	147	41,637	124
1997	32,475	48,462	149	40,132	124
1996	31,363	47,678	152	38,853	124
1995	30,480	48,074	158	39,150	128
1994	30,049	48,328	161	37,457	125
1993	29,817	46,846	157	35,521	119
1992	29,617	46,596	157	37,089	125
1991	30,389	47,180	155	37,799	124
1990	31,208	47,685	153	38,146	122
Percent change					
2000 to 2007	–2.7%	–7.2%	–	2.3%	–
1990 to 2007	6.4	–3.9	–	10.4	–

Note: The index is calculated by dividing the median income of the age group by the national median and multiplying by 100. "–" means not applicable.
Source: Bureau of the Census, data from the Current Population Survey Annual Demographic Supplements, Internet site http://www.census.gov/hhes/www/income/histinc/p08AR.html; calculations by New Strategist

Table 5.13 Median Income of Women Aged 45 to 64, 1990 to 2007

(median income of women aged 15 or older and aged 45 to 64, and index of age group to total, 1990 to 2007; percent change for selected years; in 2007 dollars)

	total women	45 to 54	index, 45–54 to total	55 to 64	index, 55–64 to total
2007	$20,922	$29,453	141	$25,262	121
2006	20,582	28,634	139	24,872	121
2005	19,729	28,120	143	23,495	119
2004	19,393	28,795	148	22,834	118
2003	19,457	29,160	150	22,962	118
2002	19,376	29,004	150	22,088	114
2001	19,458	28,266	145	20,873	107
2000	19,340	28,574	148	20,372	105
1999	19,044	28,083	147	19,838	104
1998	18,331	27,424	150	18,642	102
1997	17,650	26,449	150	18,517	105
1996	16,863	25,063	149	17,523	104
1995	16,387	23,943	146	16,726	102
1994	15,863	23,589	149	15,034	95
1993	15,608	23,066	148	15,301	98
1992	15,513	22,953	148	14,672	95
1991	15,553	21,860	141	14,701	95
1990	15,486	21,884	141	14,456	93
Percent change					
2000 to 2007	8.2%	3.1%	–	24.0%	–
1990 to 2007	35.1	34.6	–	74.8	–

Note: The index is calculated by dividing the median income of the age group by the national median and multiplying by 100. "–" means not applicable.
Source: Bureau of the Census, data from the Current Population Survey Annual Demographic Supplements, Internet site http://www.census.gov/hhes/www/income/histinc/p08AR.html; calculations by New Strategist

Men Aged 50 to 54 Have the Highest Incomes

The incomes of non-Hispanic white men are higher than those of Asians, blacks, or Hispanics.

Income grows through middle age as men rise through the ranks in their career. Median income peaks among men aged 50 to 54, at $46,325 in 2007. Median income is lower for men aged 55 to 64, but only because fewer are in the labor force. Men aged 55 to 64 who work full-time have higher incomes than full-time workers aged 50 to 54.

Among men aged 45 to 64 who work full-time, non-Hispanic whites have the highest incomes, a median of $58,896 in 2007. Asian men are second, with a median income of $52,556. The median income of black men aged 45 to 64 who work full-time is a much lower $40,815, and the Hispanic median is just $35,671. The percentage of men aged 45 to 64 who work full-time ranges from a low of 59 percent among blacks to a high of 73 percent among Asians.

■ Among non-Hispanic white men aged 45 to 64, one in six has an income of $100,000 or more.

Median income tops $57,000 for men aged 60 to 64 who work full-time

(median income of men who work full-time, by age, 2007)

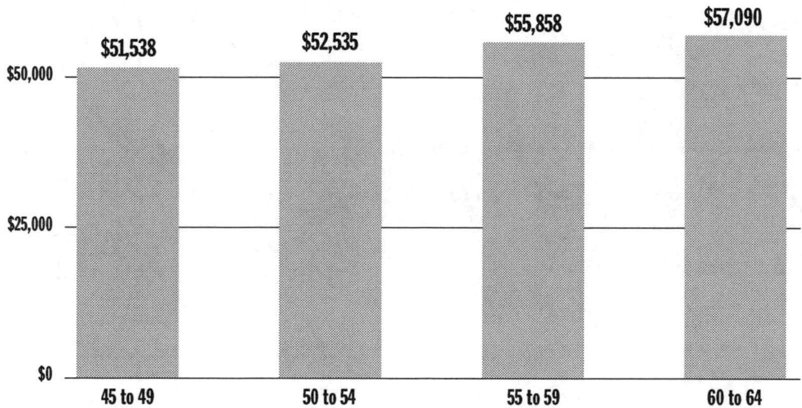

Table 5.14 Income of Men Aged 45 to 64, 2007: Total Men

(number and percent distribution of men aged 15 or older and aged 45 to 64 by income, 2007; median income by work status, and percent working year-round, full-time; men in thousands as of 2008)

		aged 45 to 64				
	total	total	45 to 49	50 to 54	55 to 59	60 to 64
TOTAL MEN	**115,678**	**37,618**	**11,165**	**10,374**	**8,929**	**7,150**
Without income	**10,889**	**1,414**	**428**	**429**	**317**	**240**
With income	**104,789**	**36,204**	**10,737**	**9,945**	**8,612**	**6,910**
Under $10,000	13,989	2,810	815	745	664	586
$10,000 to $19,999	16,953	4,072	1,038	946	1,046	1,042
$20,000 to $29,999	15,483	4,265	1,277	1,127	960	901
$30,000 to $39,999	13,877	4,787	1,433	1,381	1,100	873
$40,000 to $49,999	10,420	4,110	1,338	1,094	925	753
$50,000 to $59,999	8,291	3,455	1,081	1,005	788	581
$60,000 to $69,999	5,814	2,623	732	794	641	456
$70,000 to $79,999	4,677	2,175	712	627	502	334
$80,000 to $89,999	3,066	1,525	462	436	383	244
$90,000 to $99,999	2,273	1,066	328	298	228	212
$100,000 or more	9,949	5,312	1,520	1,493	1,371	928
Median income of men with income	$33,196	$44,675	$45,507	$46,325	$45,112	$40,435
Median income of full-time workers	46,224	53,570	51,538	52,535	55,858	57,090
Percent working full-time	54.5%	67.8%	76.1%	73.7%	65.8%	48.6%
TOTAL MEN	**100.0%**	**100.0%**	**100.0%**	**100.0%**	**100.0%**	**100.0%**
Without income	**9.4**	**3.8**	**3.8**	**4.1**	**3.6**	**3.4**
With income	**90.6**	**96.2**	**96.2**	**95.9**	**96.4**	**96.6**
Under $10,000	12.1	7.5	7.3	7.2	7.4	8.2
$10,000 to $19,999	14.7	10.8	9.3	9.1	11.7	14.6
$20,000 to $29,999	13.4	11.3	11.4	10.9	10.8	12.6
$30,000 to $39,999	12.0	12.7	12.8	13.3	12.3	12.2
$40,000 to $49,999	9.0	10.9	12.0	10.5	10.4	10.5
$50,000 to $59,999	7.2	9.2	9.7	9.7	8.8	8.1
$60,000 to $69,999	5.0	7.0	6.6	7.7	7.2	6.4
$70,000 to $79,999	4.0	5.8	6.4	6.0	5.6	4.7
$80,000 to $89,999	2.7	4.1	4.1	4.2	4.3	3.4
$90,000 to $99,999	2.0	2.8	2.9	2.9	2.6	3.0
$100,000 or more	8.6	14.1	13.6	14.4	15.4	13.0

Source: Bureau of the Census, 2008 Current Population Survey Annual Social and Economic Supplement, Internet site http://www.census.gov/hhes/www/macro/032008/perinc/new01_000.htm; calculations by New Strategist

Table 5.15 Income of Men Aged 45 to 64, 2007: Asian Men

(number and percent distribution of Asian men aged 15 or older and aged 45 to 64 by income, 2007; median income by work status, and percent working year-round, full-time; men in thousands as of 2008)

		aged 45 to 64				
	total	total	45 to 49	50 to 54	55 to 59	60 to 64
TOTAL ASIAN MEN	**5,414**	**1,538**	**508**	**426**	**356**	**248**
Without income	**705**	**76**	**22**	**13**	**20**	**21**
With income	**4,709**	**1,462**	**486**	**413**	**336**	**227**
Under $10,000	639	124	23	31	29	41
$10,000 to $19,999	645	140	50	15	32	43
$20,000 to $29,999	646	184	57	55	43	29
$30,000 to $39,999	536	191	68	60	35	28
$40,000 to $49,999	426	166	59	47	39	21
$50,000 to $59,999	338	100	37	31	22	10
$60,000 to $69,999	278	98	34	35	18	11
$70,000 to $79,999	276	82	25	16	31	10
$80,000 to $89,999	156	67	15	23	22	7
$90,000 to $99,999	144	44	18	10	10	6
$100,000 or more	625	264	102	87	53	22
Median income of men with income	$36,729	$44,257	$45,712	$49,234	$46,119	$30,056
Median income of full-time workers	51,001	52,556	50,654	55,105	57,386	45,139
Percent working full-time	58.5%	73.2%	83.3%	81.0%	68.3%	46.0%
TOTAL ASIAN MEN	**100.0%**	**100.0%**	**100.0%**	**100.0%**	**100.0%**	**100.0%**
Without income	**13.0**	**4.9**	**4.3**	**3.1**	**5.6**	**8.5**
With income	**87.0**	**95.1**	**95.7**	**96.9**	**94.4**	**91.5**
Under $10,000	11.8	8.1	4.5	7.3	8.1	16.5
$10,000 to $19,999	11.9	9.1	9.8	3.5	9.0	17.3
$20,000 to $29,999	11.9	12.0	11.2	12.9	12.1	11.7
$30,000 to $39,999	9.9	12.4	13.4	14.1	9.8	11.3
$40,000 to $49,999	7.9	10.8	11.6	11.0	11.0	8.5
$50,000 to $59,999	6.2	6.5	7.3	7.3	6.2	4.0
$60,000 to $69,999	5.1	6.4	6.7	8.2	5.1	4.4
$70,000 to $79,999	5.1	5.3	4.9	3.8	8.7	4.0
$80,000 to $89,999	2.9	4.4	3.0	5.4	6.2	2.8
$90,000 to $99,999	2.7	2.9	3.5	2.3	2.8	2.4
$100,000 or more	11.5	17.2	20.1	20.4	14.9	8.9

Note: Asians include those who identify themselves as being of the race alone and those who identify themselves as being of the race in combination with other races.
Source: Bureau of the Census, 2008 Current Population Survey Annual Social and Economic Supplement, Internet site http://www.census.gov/hhes/www/macro/032008/perinc/new01_000.htm; calculations by New Strategist

Table 5.16 Income of Men Aged 45 to 64, 2007: Black Men

(number and percent distribution of black men aged 15 or older and aged 45 to 64 by income, 2007; median income by work status, and percent working year-round, full-time; men in thousands as of 2008)

		aged 45 to 64				
	total	total	45 to 49	50 to 54	55 to 59	60 to 64
TOTAL BLACK MEN	**13,370**	**3,930**	**1,291**	**1,130**	**916**	**593**
Without income	**2,389**	**311**	**118**	**91**	**79**	**23**
With income	**10,981**	**3,619**	**1,173**	**1,039**	**837**	**570**
Under $10,000	2,307	484	150	120	117	97
$10,000 to $19,999	2,145	542	139	119	163	121
$20,000 to $29,999	1,691	553	176	181	117	79
$30,000 to $39,999	1,559	617	182	223	126	86
$40,000 to $49,999	997	393	156	107	78	52
$50,000 to $59,999	747	292	117	84	71	20
$60,000 to $69,999	482	219	77	66	33	43
$70,000 to $79,999	345	161	64	41	29	27
$80,000 to $89,999	196	94	21	31	30	12
$90,000 to $99,999	122	66	27	19	14	6
$100,000 or more	390	198	67	46	57	28
Median income of men with income	$25,792	$33,129	$36,472	$33,904	$30,882	$27,847
Median income of full-time workers	36,780	40,815	42,346	38,693	41,168	40,982
Percent working full-time	46.1%	59.1%	66.6%	65.4%	54.1%	38.8%
TOTAL BLACK MEN	**100.0%**	**100.0%**	**100.0%**	**100.0%**	**100.0%**	**100.0%**
Without income	**17.9**	**7.9**	**9.1**	**8.1**	**8.6**	**3.9**
With income	**82.1**	**92.1**	**90.9**	**91.9**	**91.4**	**96.1**
Under $10,000	17.3	12.3	11.6	10.6	12.8	16.4
$10,000 to $19,999	16.0	13.8	10.8	10.5	17.8	20.4
$20,000 to $29,999	12.6	14.1	13.6	16.0	12.8	13.3
$30,000 to $39,999	11.7	15.7	14.1	19.7	13.8	14.5
$40,000 to $49,999	7.5	10.0	12.1	9.5	8.5	8.8
$50,000 to $59,999	5.6	7.4	9.1	7.4	7.8	3.4
$60,000 to $69,999	3.6	5.6	6.0	5.8	3.6	7.3
$70,000 to $79,999	2.6	4.1	5.0	3.6	3.2	4.6
$80,000 to $89,999	1.5	2.4	1.6	2.7	3.3	2.0
$90,000 to $99,999	0.9	1.7	2.1	1.7	1.5	1.0
$100,000 or more	2.9	5.0	5.2	4.1	6.2	4.7

Note: Blacks include those who identify themselves as being of the race alone and those who identify themselves as being of the race in combination with other races.
Source: Bureau of the Census, 2008 Current Population Survey Annual Social and Economic Supplement, Internet site http://www.census.gov/hhes/www/macro/032008/perinc/new01_000.htm; calculations by New Strategist

Table 5.17 Income of Men Aged 45 to 64, 2007: Hispanic Men

(number and percent distribution of Hispanic men aged 15 or older and aged 45 to 64 by income, 2007; median income by work status, and percent working year-round, full-time; men in thousands as of 2008)

		aged 45 to 64				
	total	total	45 to 49	50 to 54	55 to 59	60 to 64
TOTAL HISPANIC MEN	**16,837**	**3,820**	**1,408**	**1,070**	**787**	**555**
Without income	**2,228**	**251**	**83**	**75**	**48**	**45**
With income	**14,609**	**3,569**	**1,325**	**995**	**739**	**510**
Under $10,000	2,135	368	118	104	72	74
$10,000 to $19,999	3,548	734	242	218	157	117
$20,000 to $29,999	3,168	675	272	190	135	78
$30,000 to $39,999	2,143	559	209	143	131	76
$40,000 to $49,999	1,209	341	144	80	64	53
$50,000 to $59,999	809	299	120	86	52	41
$60,000 to $69,999	513	180	67	69	31	13
$70,000 to $79,999	330	98	41	17	26	14
$80,000 to $89,999	201	86	28	31	14	13
$90,000 to $99,999	127	67	24	18	17	8
$100,000 or more	425	162	62	35	40	25
Median income of men with income	$24,451	$29,581	$30,762	$28,844	$30,180	$27,159
Median income of full-time workers	30,454	35,671	35,137	35,256	35,507	38,061
Percent working full-time	58.0%	65.5%	72.7%	65.3%	64.0%	49.9%
TOTAL HISPANIC MEN	**100.0%**	**100.0%**	**100.0%**	**100.0%**	**100.0%**	**100.0%**
Without income	**13.2**	**6.6**	**5.9**	**7.0**	**6.1**	**8.1**
With income	**86.8**	**93.4**	**94.1**	**93.0**	**93.9**	**91.9**
Under $10,000	12.7	9.6	8.4	9.7	9.1	13.3
$10,000 to $19,999	21.1	19.2	17.2	20.4	19.9	21.1
$20,000 to $29,999	18.8	17.7	19.3	17.8	17.2	14.1
$30,000 to $39,999	12.7	14.6	14.8	13.4	16.6	13.7
$40,000 to $49,999	7.2	8.9	10.2	7.5	8.1	9.5
$50,000 to $59,999	4.8	7.8	8.5	8.0	6.6	7.4
$60,000 to $69,999	3.0	4.7	4.8	6.4	3.9	2.3
$70,000 to $79,999	2.0	2.6	2.9	1.6	3.3	2.5
$80,000 to $89,999	1.2	2.3	2.0	2.9	1.8	2.3
$90,000 to $99,999	0.8	1.8	1.7	1.7	2.2	1.4
$100,000 or more	2.5	4.2	4.4	3.3	5.1	4.5

Source: Bureau of the Census, 2008 Current Population Survey Annual Social and Economic Supplement, Internet site http://www.census.gov/hhes/www/macro/032008/perinc/new01_000.htm; calculations by New Strategist

Table 5.18 Income of Men Aged 45 to 64, 2007: Non-Hispanic White Men

(number and percent distribution of non-Hispanic white men aged 15 or older and aged 45 to 64 by income, 2007; median income by work status, and percent working year-round, full-time; men in thousands as of 2008)

		aged 45 to 64				
	total	total	45 to 49	50 to 54	55 to 59	60 to 64
TOTAL NON-HISPANIC WHITE MEN	**79,100**	**27,957**	**7,846**	**7,659**	**6,763**	**5,689**
Without income	**5,483**	**759**	**202**	**245**	**164**	**148**
With income	**73,617**	**27,198**	**7,644**	**7,414**	**6,599**	**5,541**
Under $10,000	8,760	1,774	495	473	435	371
$10,000 to $19,999	10,470	2,613	599	588	684	742
$20,000 to $29,999	9,834	2,808	763	687	648	710
$30,000 to $39,999	9,518	3,371	963	936	797	675
$40,000 to $49,999	7,703	3,176	970	847	738	621
$50,000 to $59,999	6,323	2,721	791	800	625	505
$60,000 to $69,999	4,493	2,104	544	621	554	385
$70,000 to $79,999	3,717	1,826	581	551	412	282
$80,000 to $89,999	2,491	1,269	397	347	309	216
$90,000 to $99,999	1,871	884	259	248	185	192
$100,000 or more	8,438	4,648	1,279	1,317	1,209	843
Median income of men with income	$37,373	$48,981	$50,234	$51,261	$49,919	$43,067
Median income of full-time workers	51,465	58,896	56,273	58,373	60,570	61,226
Percent working full-time	55.0%	69.2%	78.1%	75.8%	67.6%	49.8%
TOTAL NON-HISPANIC WHITE MEN	**100.0%**	**100.0%**	**100.0%**	**100.0%**	**100.0%**	**100.0%**
Without income	**6.9**	**2.7**	**2.6**	**3.2**	**2.4**	**2.6**
With income	**93.1**	**97.3**	**97.4**	**96.8**	**97.6**	**97.4**
Under $10,000	11.1	6.3	6.3	6.2	6.4	6.5
$10,000 to $19,999	13.2	9.3	7.6	7.7	10.1	13.0
$20,000 to $29,999	12.4	10.0	9.7	9.0	9.6	12.5
$30,000 to $39,999	12.0	12.1	12.3	12.2	11.8	11.9
$40,000 to $49,999	9.7	11.4	12.4	11.1	10.9	10.9
$50,000 to $59,999	8.0	9.7	10.1	10.4	9.2	8.9
$60,000 to $69,999	5.7	7.5	6.9	8.1	8.2	6.8
$70,000 to $79,999	4.7	6.5	7.4	7.2	6.1	5.0
$80,000 to $89,999	3.1	4.5	5.1	4.5	4.6	3.8
$90,000 to $99,999	2.4	3.2	3.3	3.2	2.7	3.4
$100,000 or more	10.7	16.6	16.3	17.2	17.9	14.8

Note: Non-Hispanic whites are only those who identify themselves as being white alone and not Hispanic.
Source: Bureau of the Census, 2008 Current Population Survey Annual Social and Economic Supplement, Internet site http://www.census.gov/hhes/www/macro/032008/perinc/new01_000.htm; calculations by New Strategist

Women's Incomes Are Flat through Middle Age

Among women who work full-time, income does not vary much by age.

The median income of women aged 45 to 59 hovers just below $30,000. It then drops in the 60-to-64 age group to just $21,462, primarily because fewer of the older women are in the workforce. The median income of women who work full-time tops $40,000 among those aged 50 to 59.

Compared with men, women's incomes vary less by age and by race or Hispanic origin. The median income of non-Hispanic white women aged 45 to 64 who work full-time stood at $41,167. For their Asian counterparts, the figure was a slightly higher $42,397. Among blacks, the median income of full-time workers aged 45 to 64 was $34,407. Hispanic women have the lowest incomes. Among those working full-time, median income was just $29,870 in 2007.

■ Women's incomes do not soar in middle age because many choose lower-paying jobs that allow them to spend more time with their family.

Among women working full-time, there is little difference in income by age

(median income of women who work full-time, by age, 2007)

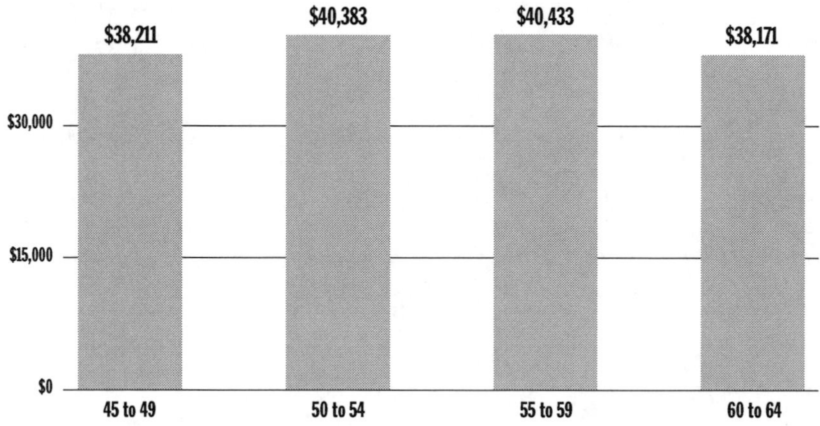

Table 5.19 Income of Women Aged 45 to 64, 2007: Total Women

(number and percent distribution of women aged 15 or older and aged 45 to 64 by income, 2007; median income by work status, and percent working year-round, full-time; women in thousands as of 2008)

		aged 45 to 64				
	total	total	45 to 49	50 to 54	55 to 59	60 to 64
TOTAL WOMEN	**122,470**	**39,619**	**11,536**	**10,860**	**9,442**	**7,781**
Without income	**17,240**	**3,775**	**1,117**	**1,036**	**928**	**694**
With income	**105,230**	**35,844**	**10,419**	**9,824**	**8,514**	**7,087**
Under $10,000	26,931	6,902	1,760	1,733	1,603	1,806
$10,000 to $19,999	23,616	6,421	1,787	1,609	1,495	1,530
$20,000 to $29,999	16,710	5,782	1,750	1,609	1,373	1,050
$30,000 to $39,999	12,457	4,807	1,550	1,363	1,100	794
$40,000 to $49,999	8,573	3,725	1,121	1,068	923	613
$50,000 to $59,999	5,461	2,508	749	710	611	438
$60,000 to $69,999	3,589	1,664	468	532	427	237
$70,000 to $79,999	2,317	1,109	325	330	286	168
$80,000 to $89,999	1,371	717	225	219	170	103
$90,000 to $99,999	958	509	174	141	128	66
$100,000 or more	3,246	1,699	511	512	395	281
Median income of women with income	$20,922	$27,510	$29,262	$29,654	$27,888	$21,462
Median income of full-time workers	36,167	39,328	38,211	40,383	40,433	38,171
Percent working full-time	37.3%	49.3%	55.4%	54.6%	49.8%	32.3%
TOTAL WOMEN	**100.0%**	**100.0%**	**100.0%**	**100.0%**	**100.0%**	**100.0%**
Without income	**14.1**	**9.5**	**9.7**	**9.5**	**9.8**	**8.9**
With income	**85.9**	**90.5**	**90.3**	**90.5**	**90.2**	**91.1**
Under $10,000	22.0	17.4	15.3	16.0	17.0	23.2
$10,000 to $19,999	19.3	16.2	15.5	14.8	15.8	19.7
$20,000 to $29,999	13.6	14.6	15.2	14.8	14.5	13.5
$30,000 to $39,999	10.2	12.1	13.4	12.6	11.7	10.2
$40,000 to $49,999	7.0	9.4	9.7	9.8	9.8	7.9
$50,000 to $59,999	4.5	6.3	6.5	6.5	6.5	5.6
$60,000 to $69,999	2.9	4.2	4.1	4.9	4.5	3.0
$70,000 to $79,999	1.9	2.8	2.8	3.0	3.0	2.2
$80,000 to $89,999	1.1	1.8	2.0	2.0	1.8	1.3
$90,000 to $99,999	0.8	1.3	1.5	1.3	1.4	0.8
$100,000 or more	2.7	4.3	4.4	4.7	4.2	3.6

Source: Bureau of the Census, 2008 Current Population Survey Annual Social and Economic Supplement, Internet site http://www.census.gov/hhes/www/macro/032008/perinc/new01_000.htm; calculations by New Strategist

Table 5.20 Income of Women Aged 45 to 64, 2007: Asian Women

(number and percent distribution of Asian women aged 15 or older and aged 45 to 64 by income, 2007; median income by work status, and percent working year-round, full-time; women in thousands as of 2008)

		aged 45 to 64				
	total	total	45 to 49	50 to 54	55 to 59	60 to 64
TOTAL ASIAN WOMEN	**6,029**	**1,783**	**546**	**504**	**417**	**316**
Without income	**1,243**	**276**	**62**	**68**	**76**	**70**
With income	**4,786**	**1,507**	**484**	**436**	**341**	**246**
Under $10,000	1,217	249	69	57	67	56
$10,000 to $19,999	866	295	79	84	75	57
$20,000 to $29,999	632	197	65	53	52	27
$30,000 to $39,999	511	181	64	51	34	32
$40,000 to $49,999	426	159	46	63	33	17
$50,000 to $59,999	289	105	35	39	14	17
$60,000 to $69,999	212	82	32	26	13	11
$70,000 to $79,999	171	64	32	16	10	6
$80,000 to $89,999	102	41	12	14	9	6
$90,000 to $99,999	94	29	12	5	10	2
$100,000 or more	265	103	38	27	25	13
Median income of women with income	$24,095	$30,013	$34,534	$34,031	$25,112	$22,259
Median income of full-time workers	41,254	42,397	45,637	42,265	39,712	40,550
Percent working full-time	40.4%	52.1%	58.4%	60.3%	48.7%	32.6%
TOTAL ASIAN WOMEN	**100.0%**	**100.0%**	**100.0%**	**100.0%**	**100.0%**	**100.0%**
Without income	**20.6**	**15.5**	**11.4**	**13.5**	**18.2**	**22.2**
With income	**79.4**	**84.5**	**88.6**	**86.5**	**81.8**	**77.8**
Under $10,000	20.2	14.0	12.6	11.3	16.1	17.7
$10,000 to $19,999	14.4	16.5	14.5	16.7	18.0	18.0
$20,000 to $29,999	10.5	11.0	11.9	10.5	12.5	8.5
$30,000 to $39,999	8.5	10.2	11.7	10.1	8.2	10.1
$40,000 to $49,999	7.1	8.9	8.4	12.5	7.9	5.4
$50,000 to $59,999	4.8	5.9	6.4	7.7	3.4	5.4
$60,000 to $69,999	3.5	4.6	5.9	5.2	3.1	3.5
$70,000 to $79,999	2.8	3.6	5.9	3.2	2.4	1.9
$80,000 to $89,999	1.7	2.3	2.2	2.8	2.2	1.9
$90,000 to $99,999	1.6	1.6	2.2	1.0	2.4	0.6
$100,000 or more	4.4	5.8	7.0	5.4	6.0	4.1

Note: Asians include those who identify themselves as being of the race alone and those who identify themselves as being of the race in combination with other races.
Source: Bureau of the Census, 2008 Current Population Survey Annual Social and Economic Supplement, Internet site http://www.census.gov/hhes/www/macro/032008/perinc/new01_000.htm; calculations by New Strategist

Table 5.21 Income of Women Aged 45 to 64, 2007: Black Women

(number and percent distribution of black women aged 15 or older and aged 45 to 64 by income, 2007; median income by work status, and percent working year-round, full-time; women in thousands as of 2008)

		aged 45 to 64				
	total	total	45 to 49	50 to 54	55 to 59	60 to 64
TOTAL BLACK WOMEN	**16,097**	**4,817**	**1,526**	**1,365**	**1,112**	**814**
Without income	**2,670**	**483**	**144**	**159**	**112**	**68**
With income	**13,427**	**4,334**	**1,382**	**1,206**	**1,000**	**746**
Under $10,000	3,628	859	236	233	210	180
$10,000 to $19,999	3,158	910	251	225	219	215
$20,000 to $29,999	2,295	821	289	232	165	135
$30,000 to $39,999	1,659	566	205	159	119	83
$40,000 to $49,999	1,016	450	167	137	98	48
$50,000 to $59,999	594	268	82	69	81	36
$60,000 to $69,999	435	172	54	53	41	24
$70,000 to $79,999	220	93	38	25	25	5
$80,000 to $89,999	139	68	18	24	21	5
$90,000 to $99,999	63	36	15	12	7	2
$100,000 or more	223	91	29	35	14	13
Median income of women with income	$19,712	$23,921	$26,396	$25,227	$22,926	$18,451
Median income of full-time workers	31,672	34,407	34,503	35,343	35,472	31,201
Percent working full-time	41.2%	52.7%	61.6%	56.8%	48.0%	35.6%
TOTAL BLACK WOMEN	**100.0%**	**100.0%**	**100.0%**	**100.0%**	**100.0%**	**100.0%**
Without income	**16.6**	**10.0**	**9.4**	**11.6**	**10.1**	**8.4**
With income	**83.4**	**90.0**	**90.6**	**88.4**	**89.9**	**91.6**
Under $10,000	22.5	17.8	15.5	17.1	18.9	22.1
$10,000 to $19,999	19.6	18.9	16.4	16.5	19.7	26.4
$20,000 to $29,999	14.3	17.0	18.9	17.0	14.8	16.6
$30,000 to $39,999	10.3	11.8	13.4	11.6	10.7	10.2
$40,000 to $49,999	6.3	9.3	10.9	10.0	8.8	5.9
$50,000 to $59,999	3.7	5.6	5.4	5.1	7.3	4.4
$60,000 to $69,999	2.7	3.6	3.5	3.9	3.7	2.9
$70,000 to $79,999	1.4	1.9	2.5	1.8	2.2	0.6
$80,000 to $89,999	0.9	1.4	1.2	1.8	1.9	0.6
$90,000 to $99,999	0.4	0.7	1.0	0.9	0.6	0.2
$100,000 or more	1.4	1.9	1.9	2.6	1.3	1.6

Note: Blacks include those who identify themselves as being of the race alone and those who identify themselves as being of the race in combination with other races.

Source: Bureau of the Census, 2008 Current Population Survey Annual Social and Economic Supplement, Internet site http://www.census.gov/hhes/www/macro/032008/perinc/new01_000.htm; calculations by New Strategist

Table 5.22 Income of Women Aged 45 to 64, 2007: Hispanic Women

(number and percent distribution of Hispanic women aged 15 or older and aged 45 to 64 by income, 2007; median income by work status, and percent working year-round, full-time; women in thousands as of 2008)

		aged 45 to 64				
	total	total	45 to 49	50 to 54	55 to 59	60 to 64
TOTAL HISPANIC WOMEN	**15,853**	**3,860**	**1,337**	**1,073**	**824**	**626**
Without income	**4,588**	**834**	**268**	**255**	**171**	**140**
With income	**11,265**	**3,026**	**1,069**	**818**	**653**	**486**
Under $10,000	3,397	756	219	178	184	175
$10,000 to $19,999	2,967	768	284	190	162	132
$20,000 to $29,999	1,973	518	202	162	91	63
$30,000 to $39,999	1,284	370	139	107	85	39
$40,000 to $49,999	675	241	92	74	53	22
$50,000 to $59,999	359	110	35	32	20	23
$60,000 to $69,999	202	73	29	18	17	9
$70,000 to $79,999	144	63	18	22	11	12
$80,000 to $89,999	66	30	11	11	7	1
$90,000 to $99,999	51	23	13	5	3	2
$100,000 or more	148	70	24	21	18	7
Median income of women with income	$16,748	$19,544	$21,031	$21,418	$18,584	$14,422
Median income of full-time workers	27,154	29,870	27,713	30,655	30,893	31,785
Percent working full-time	34.2%	42.6%	48.8%	44.9%	42.0%	26.2%
TOTAL HISPANIC WOMEN	**100.0%**	**100.0%**	**100.0%**	**100.0%**	**100.0%**	**100.0%**
Without income	**28.9**	**21.6**	**20.0**	**23.8**	**20.8**	**22.4**
With income	**71.1**	**78.4**	**80.0**	**76.2**	**79.2**	**77.6**
Under $10,000	21.4	19.6	16.4	16.6	22.3	28.0
$10,000 to $19,999	18.7	19.9	21.2	17.7	19.7	21.1
$20,000 to $29,999	12.4	13.4	15.1	15.1	11.0	10.1
$30,000 to $39,999	8.1	9.6	10.4	10.0	10.3	6.2
$40,000 to $49,999	4.3	6.2	6.9	6.9	6.4	3.5
$50,000 to $59,999	2.3	2.8	2.6	3.0	2.4	3.7
$60,000 to $69,999	1.3	1.9	2.2	1.7	2.1	1.4
$70,000 to $79,999	0.9	1.6	1.3	2.1	1.3	1.9
$80,000 to $89,999	0.4	0.8	0.8	1.0	0.8	0.2
$90,000 to $99,999	0.3	0.6	1.0	0.5	0.4	0.3
$100,000 or more	0.9	1.8	1.8	2.0	2.2	1.1

Source: Bureau of the Census, 2008 Current Population Survey Annual Social and Economic Supplement, Internet site http://www.census.gov/hhes/www/macro/032008/perinc/new01_000.htm; calculations by New Strategist

Table 5.23 Income of Women Aged 45 to 64, 2007: Non-Hispanic White Women

(number and percent distribution of non-Hispanic white women aged 15 or older and aged 45 to 64 by income, 2007; median income by work status, and percent working year-round, full-time; women in thousands as of 2008)

		aged 45 to 64				
	total	total	45 to 49	50 to 54	55 to 59	60 to 64
TOTAL NON-HISPANIC WHITE WOMEN	**83,534**	**28,783**	**8,017**	**7,809**	**7,015**	**5,942**
Without income	**8,632**	**2,161**	**630**	**551**	**566**	**414**
With income	**74,902**	**26,622**	**7,387**	**7,258**	**6,449**	**5,528**
Under $10,000	18,386	4,939	1,222	1,237	1,120	1,360
$10,000 to $19,999	16,472	4,395	1,162	1,090	1,027	1,116
$20,000 to $29,999	11,666	4,169	1,172	1,137	1,048	812
$30,000 to $39,999	8,904	3,638	1,122	1,028	858	630
$40,000 to $49,999	6,403	2,840	805	786	731	518
$50,000 to $59,999	4,185	2,006	585	568	496	357
$60,000 to $69,999	2,719	1,329	351	435	350	193
$70,000 to $79,999	1,769	882	233	265	238	146
$80,000 to $89,999	1,053	575	183	169	134	89
$90,000 to $99,999	746	414	131	116	108	59
$100,000 or more	2,596	1,427	417	429	336	245
Median income of women with income	$21,687	$29,040	$30,814	$31,021	$30,233	$22,636
Median income of full-time workers	38,678	41,167	40,738	41,776	41,489	40,564
Percent working full-time	37.0%	49.6%	55.1%	55.4%	51.1%	32.6%
TOTAL NON-HISPANIC WHITE WOMEN	**100.0%**	**100.0%**	**100.0%**	**100.0%**	**100.0%**	**100.0%**
Without income	**10.3**	**7.5**	**7.9**	**7.1**	**8.1**	**7.0**
With income	**89.7**	**92.5**	**92.1**	**92.9**	**91.9**	**93.0**
Under $10,000	22.0	17.2	15.2	15.8	16.0	22.9
$10,000 to $19,999	19.7	15.3	14.5	14.0	14.6	18.8
$20,000 to $29,999	14.0	14.5	14.6	14.6	14.9	13.7
$30,000 to $39,999	10.7	12.6	14.0	13.2	12.2	10.6
$40,000 to $49,999	7.7	9.9	10.0	10.1	10.4	8.7
$50,000 to $59,999	5.0	7.0	7.3	7.3	7.1	6.0
$60,000 to $69,999	3.3	4.6	4.4	5.6	5.0	3.2
$70,000 to $79,999	2.1	3.1	2.9	3.4	3.4	2.5
$80,000 to $89,999	1.3	2.0	2.3	2.2	1.9	1.5
$90,000 to $99,999	0.9	1.4	1.6	1.5	1.5	1.0
$100,000 or more	3.1	5.0	5.2	5.5	4.8	4.1

Note: Non-Hispanic whites are only those who identify themselves as being white alone and not Hispanic.
Source: Bureau of the Census, 2008 Current Population Survey Annual Social and Economic Supplement, Internet site http://www.census.gov/hhes/www/macro/032008/perinc/new01_000.htm; calculations by New Strategist

Earnings Rise with Education

The highest earners are men with professional degrees.

A college degree has been well worth the cost for the Baby-Boom generation. The higher their educational level, the greater their earnings. Among men ranging in age from 45 to 64 in 2007 (Boomers were aged 43 to 61 in that year), those with professional degrees (such as physicians and lawyers) had median earnings of $100,000 or more. Among women, median earnings also are highest for those with a professional degree. Median earnings peak at $85,293 among those aged 55 to 64 who work full-time.

Among men aged 45 to 64 who did not finish high school, the earnings of those working full-time range from just $31,324 to $35,735. For male full-time workers with at least a bachelor's degree, median earnings range from $77,212 to $76,155. The pattern is the same for women. Among women aged 45 to 64 with full-time jobs who did not finish high school, median annual earnings do not rise above $21,135. Among college graduates, earnings are above $52,000.

■ The steeply rising cost of a college degree, combined with competition from well-educated but lower-paid workers in other countries, may reduce the financial return of a college education in the years ahead.

College bonus is still big

(median earnings of men aged 45 to 54 who work full-time, by education, 2007)

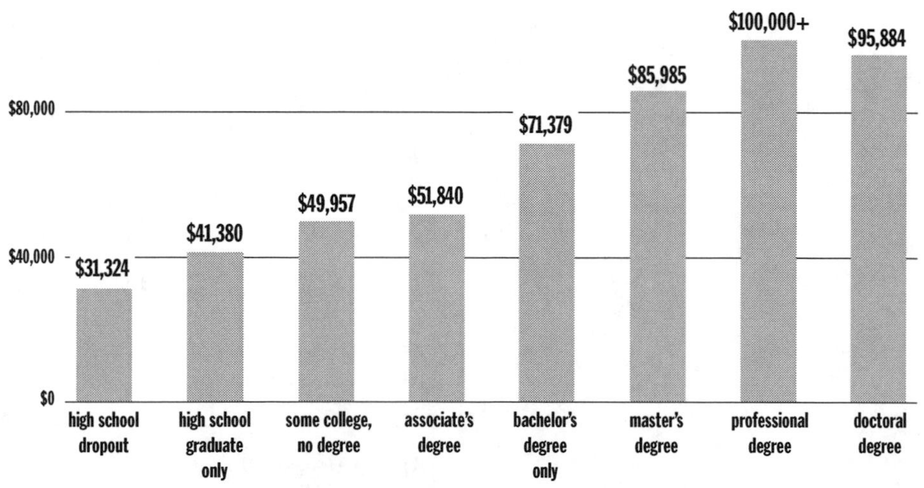

Table 5.24 Earnings of Men by Education, 2007: Aged 45 to 54

(number and percent distribution of men aged 45 to 54 by earnings and education, 2007; men in thousands as of 2008)

							bachelor's degree or more				
	total	less than 9th grade	9th to 12th grade, no degree	high school graduate, incl. GED	some college, no degree	associate's degree	total	bachelor's degree	master's degree	professional degree	doctoral degree
TOTAL MEN AGED 45 TO 54	**21,539**	**975**	**1,601**	**7,234**	**3,554**	**1,899**	**6,276**	**3,965**	**1,480**	**480**	**351**
Without earnings	**2,543**	**262**	**421**	**1,026**	**393**	**157**	**284**	**222**	**42**	**12**	**8**
With earnings	**18,996**	**713**	**1,180**	**6,208**	**3,161**	**1,742**	**5,992**	**3,743**	**1,438**	**468**	**343**
Under $10,000	894	90	128	367	153	71	88	60	21	6	2
$10,000 to $19,999	1,554	214	204	627	223	88	197	139	36	12	9
$20,000 to $29,999	2,351	171	282	989	400	201	307	224	61	9	12
$30,000 to $39,999	2,730	120	225	1,188	502	281	413	318	71	15	10
$40,000 to $49,999	2,411	37	131	1,038	448	231	524	387	110	15	14
$50,000 to $59,999	2,083	33	91	714	392	245	607	412	135	36	26
$60,000 to $69,999	1,531	26	39	447	289	197	536	355	121	22	37
$70,000 to $79,999	1,354	10	36	368	221	159	558	370	137	22	28
$80,000 to $89,999	831	2	13	150	137	102	427	275	108	26	18
$90,000 to $99,999	562	2	11	76	81	49	344	201	101	13	29
$100,000 or more	2,696	7	19	244	314	120	1,992	1,001	540	293	157
Median earnings of men with earnings	$47,156	$21,861	$28,450	$38,868	$46,210	$50,024	$75,526	$68,601	$81,443	$100,000+	$92,771
Median earnings of full-time workers	51,115	25,661	31,324	41,380	49,957	51,840	77,212	71,379	85,985	100,000+	95,884
Percent working full-time	74.9%	53.7%	56.3%	70.8%	75.8%	79.5%	85.9%	85.1%	87.5%	84.8%	89.2%
TOTAL MEN AGED 45 TO 54	**100.0%**	**100.0%**	**100.0%**	**100.0%**	**100.0%**	**100.0%**	**100.0%**	**100.0%**	**100.0%**	**100.0%**	**100.0%**
Without earnings	**11.8**	**26.9**	**26.3**	**14.2**	**11.1**	**8.3**	**4.5**	**5.6**	**2.8**	**2.5**	**2.3**
With earnings	**88.2**	**73.1**	**73.7**	**85.8**	**88.9**	**91.7**	**95.5**	**94.4**	**97.2**	**97.5**	**97.7**
Under $10,000	4.2	9.2	8.0	5.1	4.3	3.7	1.4	1.5	1.4	1.3	0.6
$10,000 to $19,999	7.2	21.9	12.7	8.7	6.3	4.6	3.1	3.5	2.4	2.5	2.6
$20,000 to $29,999	10.9	17.5	17.6	13.7	11.3	10.6	4.9	5.6	4.1	1.9	3.4
$30,000 to $39,999	12.7	12.3	14.1	16.4	14.1	14.8	6.6	8.0	4.8	3.1	2.8
$40,000 to $49,999	11.2	3.8	8.2	14.3	12.6	12.2	8.3	9.8	7.4	3.1	4.0
$50,000 to $59,999	9.7	3.4	5.7	9.9	11.0	12.9	9.7	10.4	9.1	7.5	7.4
$60,000 to $69,999	7.1	2.7	2.4	6.2	8.1	10.4	8.5	9.0	8.2	4.6	10.5
$70,000 to $79,999	6.3	1.0	2.2	5.1	6.2	8.4	8.9	9.3	9.3	4.6	8.0
$80,000 to $89,999	3.9	0.2	0.8	2.1	3.9	5.4	6.8	6.9	7.3	5.4	5.1
$90,000 to $99,999	2.6	0.2	0.7	1.1	2.3	2.6	5.5	5.1	6.8	2.7	8.3
$100,000 or more	12.5	0.7	1.2	3.4	8.8	6.3	31.7	25.2	36.5	61.0	44.7

Source: Bureau of the Census, 2008 Current Population Survey Annual Social and Economic Supplement, Internet site http://www.census.gov/hhes/www/macro/032008/perinc/new03_000.htm; calculations by New Strategist

Table 5.25 Earnings of Men by Education, 2007: Aged 55 to 64

(number and percent distribution of men aged 55 to 64 by earnings and education, 2007; men in thousands as of 2008)

							bachelor's degree or more				
	total	less than 9th grade	9th to 12th grade, no degree	high school graduate, incl. GED	some college, no degree	associate's degree	total	bachelor's degree	master's degree	professional degree	doctoral degree
TOTAL MEN AGED 55 TO 64	**16,079**	**783**	**1,046**	**4,464**	**2,869**	**1,368**	**5,549**	**3,182**	**1,532**	**429**	**405**
Without earnings	**4,184**	**374**	**477**	**1,356**	**762**	**317**	**898**	**613**	**222**	**28**	**35**
With earnings	**11,895**	**409**	**569**	**3,109**	**2,107**	**1,050**	**4,651**	**2,568**	**1,311**	**402**	**370**
Under $10,000	830	52	78	231	154	78	237	159	66	7	5
$10,000 to $19,999	1,050	104	107	355	197	73	212	127	60	17	9
$20,000 to $29,999	1,425	109	107	549	297	94	270	193	60	8	10
$30,000 to $39,999	1,555	78	98	508	372	176	321	193	94	13	21
$40,000 to $49,999	1,392	23	67	494	245	149	415	228	161	13	13
$50,000 to $59,999	1,237	18	46	337	249	142	443	262	140	13	29
$60,000 to $69,999	999	4	19	237	208	98	434	250	116	31	36
$70,000 to $79,999	714	7	15	138	115	69	369	207	101	30	30
$80,000 to $89,999	545	2	10	94	75	65	298	171	80	20	26
$90,000 to $99,999	343	1	3	23	34	17	263	128	97	18	21
$100,000 or more	1,809	11	17	141	162	89	1,388	649	335	232	172
Median earnings of men with earnings	$46,648	$22,225	$29,132	$36,768	$40,680	$46,154	$69,443	$62,094	$64,161	$100,000+	$91,399
Median earnings of full-time workers	51,962	26,468	35,735	41,477	47,061	51,058	76,155	70,776	72,326	100,000+	100,000+
Percent working full-time	58.1%	38.1%	37.3%	54.3%	56.4%	60.9%	68.2%	65.4%	69.3%	78.8%	74.1%
TOTAL MEN AGED 55 TO 64	**100.0%**	**100.0%**	**100.0%**	**100.0%**	**100.0%**	**100.0%**	**100.0%**	**100.0%**	**100.0%**	**100.0%**	**100.0%**
Without earnings	**26.0**	**47.8**	**45.6**	**30.4**	**26.6**	**23.2**	**16.2**	**19.3**	**14.5**	**6.5**	**8.6**
With earnings	**74.0**	**52.2**	**54.4**	**69.6**	**73.4**	**76.8**	**83.8**	**80.7**	**85.6**	**93.7**	**91.4**
Under $10,000	5.2	6.6	7.5	5.2	5.4	5.7	4.3	5.0	4.3	1.6	1.2
$10,000 to $19,999	6.5	13.3	10.2	8.0	6.9	5.3	3.8	4.0	3.9	4.0	2.2
$20,000 to $29,999	8.9	13.9	10.2	12.3	10.4	6.9	4.9	6.1	3.9	1.9	2.5
$30,000 to $39,999	9.7	10.0	9.4	11.4	13.0	12.9	5.8	6.1	6.1	3.0	5.2
$40,000 to $49,999	8.7	2.9	6.4	11.1	8.5	10.9	7.5	7.2	10.5	3.0	3.2
$50,000 to $59,999	7.7	2.3	4.4	7.5	8.7	10.4	8.0	8.2	9.1	3.0	7.2
$60,000 to $69,999	6.2	0.5	1.8	5.3	7.2	7.2	7.8	7.9	7.6	7.2	8.9
$70,000 to $79,999	4.4	0.9	1.4	3.1	4.0	5.0	6.6	6.5	6.6	7.0	7.4
$80,000 to $89,999	3.4	0.3	1.0	2.1	2.6	4.8	5.4	5.4	5.2	4.7	6.4
$90,000 to $99,999	2.1	0.1	0.3	0.5	1.2	1.2	4.7	4.0	6.3	4.2	5.2
$100,000 or more	11.3	1.4	1.6	3.2	5.6	6.5	25.0	20.4	21.9	54.1	42.5

Source: Bureau of the Census, 2008 Current Population Survey Annual Social and Economic Supplement, Internet site http://www.census.gov/hhes/www/macro/032008/perinc/new03_000.htm; calculations by New Strategist

Table 5.26 Earnings of Women by Education, 2007: Aged 45 to 54

(number and percent distribution of women aged 45 to 54 by earnings and education, 2007; women in thousands as of 2008)

							bachelor's degree or more				
	total	less than 9th grade	9th to 12th grade, no degree	high school graduate, incl. GED	some college, no degree	associate's degree	total	bachelor's degree	master's degree	professional degree	doctoral degree
TOTAL WOMEN AGED 45 TO 54	**22,396**	**864**	**1,297**	**6,835**	**4,128**	**2,564**	**6,707**	**4,466**	**1,801**	**265**	**176**
Without earnings	**5,195**	**453**	**631**	**1,795**	**924**	**438**	**955**	**741**	**169**	**27**	**17**
With earnings	**17,201**	**412**	**666**	**5,040**	**3,204**	**2,127**	**5,753**	**3,724**	**1,632**	**237**	**159**
Under $10,000	1,771	96	151	585	346	192	403	304	80	12	7
$10,000 to $19,999	2,843	194	240	1,090	517	314	488	373	106	7	3
$20,000 to $29,999	3,227	81	154	1,437	638	410	507	401	92	6	8
$30,000 to $39,999	2,831	23	71	905	691	391	753	563	169	10	10
$40,000 to $49,999	2,077	9	21	529	414	287	819	527	256	27	11
$50,000 to $59,999	1,459	5	11	191	268	213	774	448	269	31	24
$60,000 to $69,999	912	2	4	129	129	134	514	308	153	26	26
$70,000 to $79,999	619	0	7	77	78	66	392	227	131	21	12
$80,000 to $89,999	412	0	1	20	46	52	294	148	113	20	12
$90,000 to $99,999	233	0	0	23	18	15	177	90	67	9	12
$100,000 or more	813	2	4	58	63	53	633	335	195	68	34
Median earnings of women with earnings	$31,590	$15,761	$16,862	$25,023	$30,844	$32,203	$47,626	$42,244	$52,169	$67,456	$65,626
Median earnings of full-time workers	37,299	18,509	21,135	29,201	35,518	39,475	52,321	50,379	56,962	70,962	70,842
Percent working full-time	55.0%	30.9%	32.8%	52.7%	56.6%	59.2%	62.2%	59.2%	67.6%	68.3%	72.7%
TOTAL WOMEN AGED 45 TO 54	**100.0%**	**100.0%**	**100.0%**	**100.0%**	**100.0%**	**100.0%**	**100.0%**	**100.0%**	**100.0%**	**100.0%**	**100.0%**
Without earnings	**23.2**	**52.4**	**48.7**	**26.3**	**22.4**	**17.1**	**14.2**	**16.6**	**9.4**	**10.2**	**9.7**
With earnings	**76.8**	**47.7**	**51.3**	**73.7**	**77.6**	**83.0**	**85.8**	**83.4**	**90.6**	**89.4**	**90.3**
Under $10,000	7.9	11.1	11.6	8.6	8.4	7.5	6.0	6.8	4.4	4.5	4.0
$10,000 to $19,999	12.7	22.5	18.5	15.9	12.5	12.2	7.3	8.4	5.9	2.6	1.7
$20,000 to $29,999	14.4	9.4	11.9	21.0	15.5	16.0	7.6	9.0	5.1	2.3	4.5
$30,000 to $39,999	12.6	2.7	5.5	13.2	16.7	15.2	11.2	12.6	9.4	3.8	5.7
$40,000 to $49,999	9.3	1.0	1.6	7.7	10.0	11.2	12.2	11.8	14.2	10.2	6.3
$50,000 to $59,999	6.5	0.6	0.8	2.8	6.5	8.3	11.5	10.0	14.9	11.7	13.6
$60,000 to $69,999	4.1	0.2	0.3	1.9	3.1	5.2	7.7	6.9	8.5	9.8	14.8
$70,000 to $79,999	2.8	0.0	0.5	1.1	1.9	2.6	5.8	5.1	7.3	7.9	6.8
$80,000 to $89,999	1.8	0.0	0.1	0.3	1.1	2.0	4.4	3.3	6.3	7.5	6.8
$90,000 to $99,999	1.0	0.0	0.0	0.3	0.4	0.6	2.6	2.0	3.7	3.4	6.8
$100,000 or more	3.6	0.2	0.3	0.8	1.5	2.1	9.4	7.5	10.8	25.7	19.3

Source: Bureau of the Census, 2008 Current Population Survey Annual Social and Economic Supplement, Internet site http://www.census.gov/hhes/www/macro/032008/perinc/new03_000.htm; calculations by New Strategist

Table 5.27 Earnings of Women by Education, 2007: Aged 55 to 64

(number and percent distribution of women aged 55 to 64 by earnings and education, 2007; women in thousands as of 2008)

							bachelor's degree or more				
	total	less than 9th grade	9th to 12th grade, no degree	high school graduate, incl. GED	some college, no degree	associate's degree	total	bachelor's degree	master's degree	professional degree	doctoral degree
TOTAL WOMEN AGED 55 TO 64	**17,223**	**798**	**1,108**	**5,756**	**3,143**	**1,598**	**4,819**	**2,915**	**1,523**	**182**	**200**
Without earnings	**6,333**	**532**	**648**	**2,354**	**1,072**	**449**	**1,278**	**845**	**347**	**46**	**39**
With earnings	**10,890**	**267**	**460**	**3,403**	**2,070**	**1,149**	**3,541**	**2,069**	**1,176**	**136**	**160**
Under $10,000	1,509	104	128	531	269	107	372	234	126	8	3
$10,000 to $19,999	1,868	94	175	818	321	172	288	211	62	6	8
$20,000 to $29,999	1,989	46	69	834	442	222	376	282	74	11	9
$30,000 to $39,999	1,674	10	53	614	347	240	412	277	113	9	10
$40,000 to $49,999	1,287	7	20	297	287	166	508	333	155	9	12
$50,000 to $59,999	895	5	11	141	163	104	470	214	224	10	22
$60,000 to $69,999	537	0	0	63	100	71	302	170	95	6	30
$70,000 to $79,999	387	0	0	44	43	29	271	129	108	15	18
$80,000 to $89,999	230	0	0	21	35	22	152	63	68	13	8
$90,000 to $99,999	121	0	0	21	6	4	89	31	47	5	7
$100,000 or more	394	0	4	17	56	14	303	125	104	43	31
Median earnings of women with earnings	$30,282	$12,859	$15,606	$23,426	$30,039	$31,615	$46,216	$40,602	$51,595	$73,559	$61,887
Median earnings of full-time workers	37,042	19,730	19,440	28,828	36,222	37,159	53,239	48,895	58,249	85,293	67,397
Percent working full-time	41.9%	14.9%	22.9%	39.5%	45.5%	48.0%	49.1%	48.1%	50.2%	52.7%	52.5%
TOTAL WOMEN AGED 55 TO 64	**100.0%**	**100.0%**	**100.0%**	**100.0%**	**100.0%**	**100.0%**	**100.0%**	**100.0%**	**100.0%**	**100.0%**	**100.0%**
Without earnings	**36.8**	**66.7**	**58.5**	**40.9**	**34.1**	**28.1**	**26.5**	**29.0**	**22.8**	**25.3**	**19.5**
With earnings	**63.2**	**33.5**	**41.5**	**59.1**	**65.9**	**71.9**	**73.5**	**71.0**	**77.2**	**74.7**	**80.0**
Under $10,000	8.8	13.0	11.6	9.2	8.6	6.7	7.7	8.0	8.3	4.4	1.5
$10,000 to $19,999	10.8	11.8	15.8	14.2	10.2	10.8	6.0	7.2	4.1	3.3	4.0
$20,000 to $29,999	11.5	5.8	6.2	14.5	14.1	13.9	7.8	9.7	4.9	6.0	4.5
$30,000 to $39,999	9.7	1.3	4.8	10.7	11.0	15.0	8.5	9.5	7.4	4.9	5.0
$40,000 to $49,999	7.5	0.9	1.8	5.2	9.1	10.4	10.5	11.4	10.2	4.9	6.0
$50,000 to $59,999	5.2	0.6	1.0	2.4	5.2	6.5	9.8	7.3	14.7	5.5	11.0
$60,000 to $69,999	3.1	0.0	0.0	1.1	3.2	4.4	6.3	5.8	6.2	3.3	15.0
$70,000 to $79,999	2.2	0.0	0.0	0.8	1.4	1.8	5.6	4.4	7.1	8.2	9.0
$80,000 to $89,999	1.3	0.0	0.0	0.4	1.1	1.4	3.2	2.2	4.5	7.1	4.0
$90,000 to $99,999	0.7	0.0	0.0	0.4	0.2	0.3	1.8	1.1	3.1	2.7	3.5
$100,000 or more	2.3	0.0	0.4	0.3	1.8	0.9	6.3	4.3	6.8	23.6	15.5

Source: Bureau of the Census, 2008 Current Population Survey Annual Social and Economic Supplement, Internet site http://www.census.gov/hhes/www/macro/032008/perinc/new03_000.htm; calculations by New Strategist

Poverty Rate among Boomers Is below Average

But poverty among black and Hispanic Boomers is more than twice the level among non-Hispanic whites.

While 12 percent of all Americans were poor in 2007, the poverty rate among the Baby-Boom generation, aged 43 to 61, was a smaller 8 percent. Boomers account for only 18 percent of the nation's poor, a much smaller proportion than their share of the population.

The poverty rate for non-Hispanic white Boomers was just 6 percent in 2007, well less than half the rate among their black and Hispanic counterparts. Sixteen percent of Hispanics and blacks aged 43 to 61 are poor. Although higher than the rate for non-Hispanic whites, these figures are well below the 22 percent poverty rate for all Hispanics and the 24 percent rate for all blacks. Ten percent of Asians are poor, including 8 percent of Asians aged 43 to 61. Non-Hispanic whites account for the 53 percent majority of poor Boomers, while blacks account for 23 percent, Hispanics for 19 percent, and Asians for 4 percent.

■ The poverty rate bottoms out in the 55-to-59 age group, now entirely filled with the Baby-Boom generation. As Boomers age, the poverty rate may rise.

Black Boomers are most likely to be poor

(percent of people aged 43 to 61 below poverty level, by race and Hispanic origin, 2007)

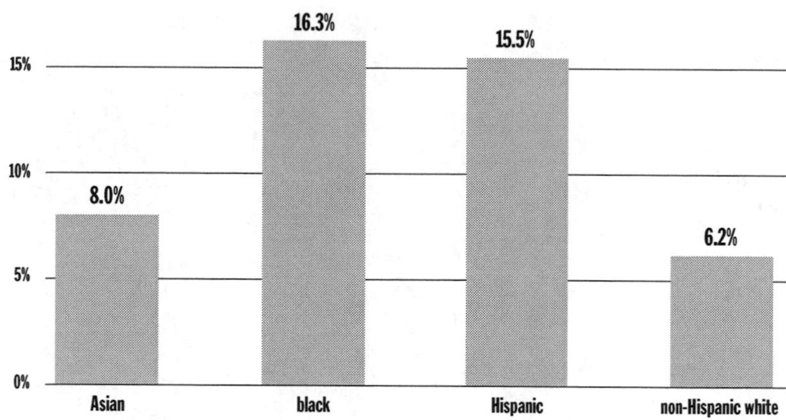

Table 5.28 People below Poverty Level by Age, Race, and Hispanic Origin, 2007

(number, percent, and percent distribution of people below poverty level by age, race, and Hispanic origin, 2007; people in thousands as of 2008)

	total	Asian	black	Hispanic	non-Hispanic white
NUMBER IN POVERTY					
Total people	**37,276**	**1,467**	**9,668**	**9,890**	**16,032**
Under age 45	27,129	1,043	7,468	8,257	10,279
Boomers (aged 43 to 61)	6,651	281	1,497	1,275	3,512
Aged 45 to 49	2,354	77	405	433	1,007
Aged 50 to 54	1,775	73	417	329	932
Aged 55 to 59	1,471	59	375	241	779
Aged 60 to 64	1,403	70	256	194	856
Aged 65 or older	3,557	145	749	437	2,180
PERCENT IN POVERTY					
Total people	**12.5%**	**10.2%**	**24.4%**	**21.5%**	**8.2%**
Under age 45	14.7	10.6	27.1	23.1	9.3
Boomers (aged 43 to 61)	8.5	8.0	16.3	15.5	6.2
Aged 45 to 49	10.4	7.3	14.4	15.8	6.3
Aged 50 to 54	8.4	7.9	16.7	15.4	6.0
Aged 55 to 59	8.0	7.6	18.5	15.0	5.7
Aged 60 to 64	9.4	12.4	18.2	16.4	7.4
Aged 65 or older	9.7	11.2	23.3	17.1	7.4
PERCENT DISTRIBUTION OF POOR BY AGE					
Total people	**100.0%**	**100.0%**	**100.0%**	**100.0%**	**100.0%**
Under age 45	72.8	71.1	77.2	83.5	64.1
Boomers (aged 43 to 61)	17.8	19.2	15.5	12.9	21.9
Aged 45 to 49	6.3	5.2	4.2	4.4	6.3
Aged 50 to 54	4.8	5.0	4.3	3.3	5.8
Aged 55 to 59	3.9	4.0	3.9	2.4	4.9
Aged 60 to 64	3.8	4.8	2.6	2.0	5.3
Aged 65 or older	9.5	9.9	7.7	4.4	13.6
PERCENT DISTRIBUTION OF POOR BY RACE AND HISPANIC ORIGIN					
Total people	**100.0%**	**3.9%**	**25.9%**	**26.5%**	**43.0%**
Under age 45	100.0	3.8	27.5	30.4	37.9
Boomers (aged 43 to 61)	100.0	4.2	22.5	19.2	52.8
Aged 45 to 49	100.0	3.3	17.2	18.4	42.8
Aged 50 to 54	100.0	4.1	23.5	18.5	52.5
Aged 55 to 59	100.0	4.0	25.5	16.4	53.0
Aged 60 to 64	100.0	5.0	18.2	13.8	61.0
Aged 65 or older	100.0	4.1	21.1	12.3	61.3

Note: Numbers do not add to total because Asians and blacks include those who identify themselves as being of the race alone and those who identify themselves as being of the race in combination with other races, because Hispanics may be of any race, and because not all races are shown. Non-Hispanic whites are those who identify themselves as being white alone and not Hispanic.

Source: Bureau of the Census, 2008 Current Population Survey Annual Social and Economic Supplement, Internet site http://www.census.gov/hhes/www/macro/032008/pov/new34_100.htm; calculations by New Strategist

CHAPTER
6

Labor Force

■ Among men aged 45 to 54, the labor force participation rate declined slightly between 2000 and 2008. Among men aged 55 to 64, the rate rose by 2 to 5 percentage points during those years as early retirement became less common.

■ Among the nation's 154 million workers in 2008, nearly 58 million were aged 45 to 64 (Boomers were aged 44 to 62 in that year), accounting for 37 percent of the labor force.

■ Seventy percent of couples aged 45 to 54 are dual earners. The dual-earner lifestyle accounts for a much smaller 49 percent of couples aged 55 to 64.

■ Boomers account for 59 percent of chief executives and 57 percent of legislators. They are also 58 percent of economists, 54 percent of clergy, and 52 percent of education administrators.

■ Between 2000 and 2008, the percentage of men aged 30 to 54 who had been with their current employer for at least 10 years fell. But long-term employment increased among men aged 55 to 59 as early retirement became less common.

■ As Boomers enter their late sixties and early seventies during the next decade, the number of workers aged 65 or older will expand by 78 percent among men and 91 percent among women.

Labor Force Participation among Older Boomers Has Risen

Men and women aged 55 to 64 are more likely to work.

Trends in the labor force participation rate of middle-aged men and women are complicated by job losses, the entry of career-oriented Baby-Boom women into the older age groups, and the end of early retirement.

Among men aged 45 to 54 (the Baby Boom generation was aged 44 to 62 in 2008), the labor force participation rate declined slightly between 2000 and 2008. (Note: the labor force participation rate includes both the employed and the unemployed.) This continues a long-term trend of falling participation among men as more women have gone to work. Among men aged 55 to 64, however, labor force participation rose by 2 to 5 percentage points between 2000 and 2008. Behind the rise is the end of early retirement. Among men aged 65 or older, the labor force participation rate increased by nearly 4 percentage points.

Among women aged 45 to 49, the labor force participation rate fell by nearly 2 percentage points between 2000 and 2008 because of the weak economy. Among women aged 55 to 64, the rate increased by 6.3 to 8.5 percentage points as Boomers filled the age group. Women aged 65 or older were also more likely to work, their labor force participation rate increasing by nearly 4 percentage points during those years.

■ Since many Boomers have experienced huge losses in their retirement accounts, expect the hlabor force participation rate in the older age groups to continue to climb.

A growing share of 60-to-64-year-olds are in the labor force

(percent of people aged 60 to 64 who are in the labor force, by sex, 2000 and 2008)

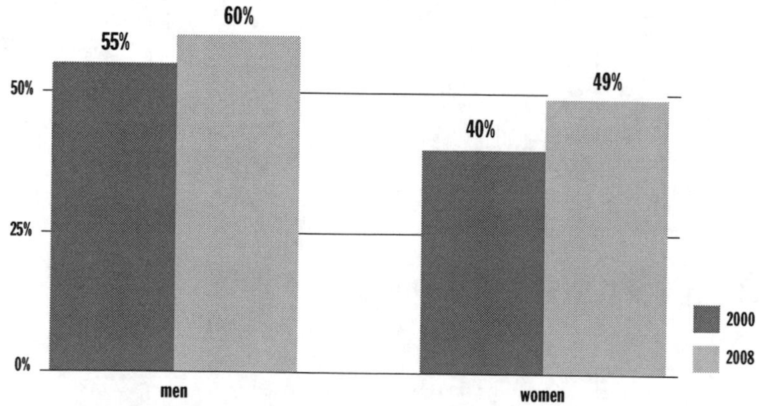

Table 6.1 Labor Force Participation Rate by Sex and Age, 2000 and 2008

(civilian labor force participation rate of people aged 16 or older, by sex and age, 2000 and 2008; percentage point change, 2000–2008)

	2008	2000	percentage point change
Men aged 16 or older	**73.0%**	**74.8%**	**–1.8**
Aged 16 to 17	26.8	40.9	–14.1
Aged 18 to 19	55.4	65.0	–9.6
Aged 20 to 24	78.7	82.6	–3.9
Aged 25 to 29	90.2	92.5	–2.3
Aged 30 to 34	92.9	94.2	–1.3
Aged 35 to 39	92.7	93.2	–0.5
Aged 40 to 44	91.8	92.1	–0.3
Aged 45 to 49	89.7	90.2	–0.5
Aged 50 to 54	86.2	86.8	–0.6
Aged 55 to 59	78.8	77.0	1.8
Aged 60 to 64	59.9	54.9	5.0
Aged 65 or older	21.5	17.7	3.8
Women aged 16 or older	**59.5**	**59.9**	**–0.4**
Aged 16 to 17	29.2	40.8	–11.6
Aged 18 to 19	53.0	61.3	–8.3
Aged 20 to 24	70.0	73.1	–3.1
Aged 25 to 29	75.9	76.7	–0.8
Aged 30 to 34	74.4	75.5	–1.1
Aged 35 to 39	75.2	75.7	–0.5
Aged 40 to 44	77.1	78.7	–1.6
Aged 45 to 49	77.2	79.1	–1.9
Aged 50 to 54	74.8	74.1	0.7
Aged 55 to 59	67.7	61.4	6.3
Aged 60 to 64	48.7	40.2	8.5
Aged 65 or older	13.3	9.4	3.9

Source: Bureau of Labor Statistics, Public Query Data Tool, Internet site http://www.bls.gov/data; and 2008 Current Population Survey, Internet site http://www.bls.gov/cps/tables.htm#empstat; calculations by New Strategist

Boomers Are a Large Share of Workers

Nearly half of Boomer workers are women.

Among the nation's 154 million workers in 2008, nearly 58 million were aged 45 to 64 (Boomers were aged 44 to 62 in that year), accounting for 37 percent of the labor force. Among workers in the 45-to-64 age group, 27 million—or 47 percent—are women.

Eighty percent of men and 69 percent of women aged 45 to 64 are in the labor force. For both men and women, the labor force participation rate falls within the age group. Among men aged 45 to 49, nearly 90 percent are in the labor force. The figure drops to just 60 percent among men aged 60 to 64 as some opt for early retirement. Among women, the labor force participation rate declines from a high of 77 percent among those in their late forties to 49 percent among those aged 60 to 64.

Because unemployment is less common among the middle aged than young adults, people aged 45 to 64 account for a smaller share of the unemployed (26 percent) than they do of the labor force as a whole. In 2008, Boomer women were slightly less likely to be unemployed than their male counterparts—3.8 versus 4.1 percent.

■ Few Boomers will retire before reaching the age of eligibility for Social Security and Medicare benefits, and many will continue to work long after.

Labor force participation rate falls with age among Boomer men

(percent of men aged 45 to 64 in the labor force, by age, 2008)

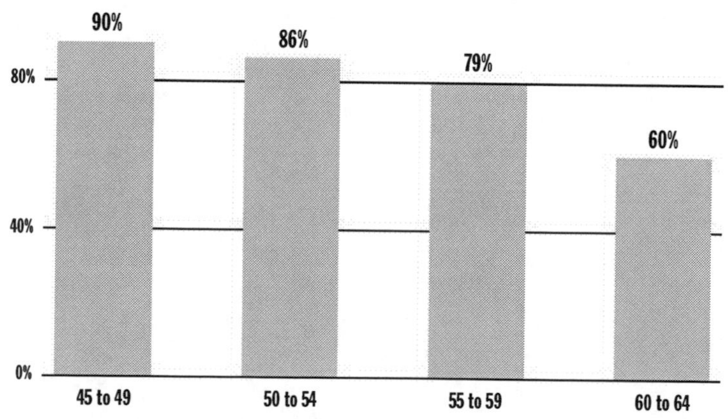

Table 6.2 Employment Status by Sex and Age, 2008

(number and percent of people aged 16 or older in the civilian labor force by sex and age, 2008; numbers in thousands)

		civilian labor force				
					unemployed	
	civilian noninstitutional population	total	percent of population	employed	number	percent of labor force
Total aged 16 or older	**233,788**	**154,287**	**66.0%**	**145,362**	**8,924**	**5.8%**
Under age 45	119,177	90,425	75.9	84,042	6,384	7.1
Aged 45 to 64	77,451	57,618	74.4	55,341	2,277	4.0
Aged 45 to 49	22,644	18,870	83.3	18,106	764	4.0
Aged 50 to 54	21,316	17,133	80.4	16,423	710	4.1
Aged 55 to 59	18,444	13,480	73.1	12,969	511	3.8
Aged 60 to 64	15,047	8,135	54.1	7,843	292	3.6
Aged 65 or older	37,161	6,243	16.8	5,979	264	4.2
Men aged 16 or older	**113,113**	**82,520**	**73.0**	**77,486**	**5,033**	**6.1**
Under age 45	59,475	48,812	82.1	45,161	3,651	7.5
Aged 45 to 64	37,635	30,273	80.4	29,042	1,229	4.1
Aged 45 to 49	11,108	9,962	89.7	9,541	420	4.2
Aged 50 to 54	10,404	8,966	86.2	8,582	384	4.3
Aged 55 to 59	8,929	7,035	78.8	6,770	265	3.8
Aged 60 to 64	7,194	4,310	59.9	4,149	160	3.7
Aged 65 or older	16,002	3,436	21.5	3,282	153	4.5
Women aged 16 or older	**120,675**	**71,767**	**59.5**	**67,876**	**3,891**	**5.4**
Under age 45	59,701	41,613	69.7	38,880	2,734	6.6
Aged 45 to 64	39,815	27,345	68.7	26,299	1,047	3.8
Aged 45 to 49	11,536	8,908	77.2	8,565	343	3.9
Aged 50 to 54	10,912	8,167	74.8	7,841	326	4
Aged 55 to 59	9,515	6,445	67.7	6,199	246	3.8
Aged 60 to 64	7,852	3,825	48.7	3,694	132	3.4
Aged 65 or older	21,160	2,808	13.3	2,697	111	3.9

Source: Bureau of Labor Statistics, 2008 Current Population Survey, Internet site http://www.bls.gov/cps/tables.htm#empstat; calculations by New Strategist

Among Boomer Men, Blacks Have the Lowest Labor Force Participation

Blacks also have the highest unemployment rate.

Among men aged 45 to 64, from 82 to 84 percent of Asians, Hispanics, and whites were in the labor force in 2008 (when Boomers were aged 44 to 62). The labor force includes both the employed and the unemployed. The lowest labor force participation rate is among black men. Only 70 percent of those aged 45 to 64 were in the labor force in 2008, with the rate dipping below 50 percent among black men aged 60 to 64.

Unemployment was significantly higher in 2008 for black men than for Asian, Hispanic, or white men. Only 3.7 percent of white men aged 45 to 64 were unemployed versus 3.8 percent of Asian men, 5.8 percent of Hispanic men, and 7.6 percent of black men in the age group.

■ Among men aged 65 or older, labor force participation ranges much more narrowly by race and Hispanic origin.

Labor force participation rate varies by race and Hispanic origin

(percent of men aged 45 to 64 in the labor force, by race and Hispanic origin, 2008)

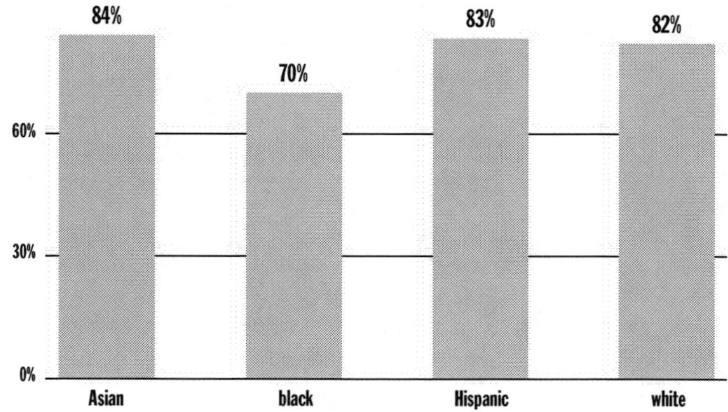

Table 6.3 Employment Status of Men by Race, Hispanic Origin, and Age, 2008

(number and percent of men aged 16 or older in the civilian labor force by race, Hispanic origin, and age, 2008; numbers in thousands)

		civilian labor force				
					unemployed	
	civilian noninstitutional population	total	percent of population	employed	number	percent of labor force
ASIAN MEN						
Total aged 16 or older	**5,112**	**3,852**	**75.3%**	**3,692**	**160**	**4.1%**
Under age 45	3,023	2,438	80.6	2,334	105	4.3
Aged 45 to 64	1,534	1,293	84.3	1,244	49	3.8
Aged 45 to 49	492	452	91.9	438	14	3.1
Aged 50 to 54	426	384	90.0	368	15	4.0
Aged 55 to 59	360	290	80.5	276	14	4.8
Aged 60 to 64	256	167	65.4	162	6	3.4
Aged 65 or older	553	120	21.8	114	6	5.1
BLACK MEN						
Total aged 16 or older	**12,516**	**8,347**	**66.7**	**7,398**	**949**	**11.4**
Under age 45	7,417	5,424	73.1	4,700	724	13.3
Aged 45 to 64	3,854	2,698	70.0	2,494	204	7.6
Aged 45 to 49	1,227	1,002	81.7	922	80	7.9
Aged 50 to 54	1,108	844	76.2	781	63	7.5
Aged 55 to 59	876	575	65.7	536	39	6.8
Aged 60 to 64	643	277	43.1	255	22	7.9
Aged 65 or older	1,245	225	18.1	204	21	9.5
HISPANIC MEN						
Total aged 16 or older	**16,524**	**13,255**	**80.2**	**12,248**	**1,007**	**7.6**
Under age 45	11,538	9,818	85.1	9,016	803	8.2
Aged 45 to 64	3,866	3,195	82.6	3,008	186	5.8
Aged 45 to 49	1,415	1,277	90.2	1,201	75	5.9
Aged 50 to 54	1,086	939	86.5	878	61	6.5
Aged 55 to 59	786	615	78.3	580	35	5.7
Aged 60 to 64	579	364	62.7	349	15	4.0
Aged 65 or older	1,121	243	21.7	224	19	7.8
WHITE MEN						
Total aged 16 or older	**92,725**	**68,351**	**73.7**	**64,624**	**3,727**	**5.5**
Under age 45	47,227	39,548	83.7	36,885	2,662	6.7
Aged 45 to 64	31,528	25,760	81.7	24,818	942	3.7
Aged 45 to 49	9,164	8,322	90.8	8,010	312	3.7
Aged 50 to 54	8,666	7,583	87.5	7,290	293	3.9
Aged 55 to 59	7,528	6,060	80.5	5,853	207	3.4
Aged 60 to 64	6,170	3,795	61.5	3,665	130	3.4
Aged 65 or older	13,972	3,046	21.8	2,922	124	4.1

Note: Race is shown only for those selecting that race group only. People who selected more than one race are not included. Hispanics may be of any race.
Source: Bureau of Labor Statistics, 2008 Current Population Survey, Internet site http://www.bls.gov/cps/tables.htm#empstat; calculations by New Strategist

Hispanic Women Have the Lowest Participation Rate

But the majority of Hispanic women are in the labor force.

Among Asian, black, and white women aged 45 to 64, from 66 to 69 percent are in the labor force. The participation rate is a smaller 61 percent for their Hispanic counterparts. Labor force participation varies within the 45 to 64 age group. While 69 percent of Hispanic women aged 45 to 49 are in the labor force, only 38 percent of those aged 60 to 64 are working or looking for work. The rates also falls with increasing age for Asian, black, and white women, but only to a low of 46 to 49 percent in the 60-to-64 age group.

Within the 45-to-64 age group, the unemployment rate is higher for black and Hispanic women than for Asian or white women. While 3.3 percent of Asian women and 3.5 percent of white women in the age group were unemployed in 2008, the figure was 6 percent among black and Hispanic women.

■ Among women aged 65 or older, labor force participation ranges much more narrowly by race and Hispanic origin.

Hispanic women are least likely to work

(percent of women aged 45 to 64 in the labor force, by race and Hispanic origin, 2008)

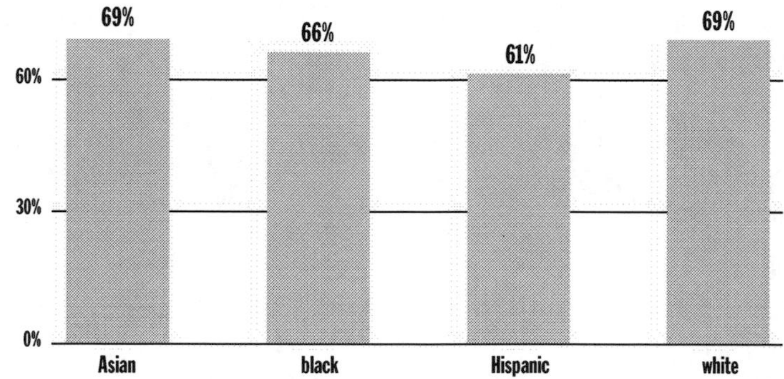

Table 6.4 Employment Status of Women by Race, Hispanic Origin, and Age, 2008

(number and percent of women aged 16 or older in the civilian labor force by race, Hispanic origin, and age, 2008; numbers in thousands)

		civilian labor force				
					unemployed	
	civilian noninstitutional population	total	percent of population	employed	number	percent of labor force
ASIAN WOMEN						
Total aged 16 or older	**5,639**	**3,350**	**59.4%**	**3,225**	**125**	**3.7%**
Under age 45	3,160	2,045	64.7	1,962	83	4.1
Aged 45 to 64	1,741	1,206	69.3	1,166	40	3.3
Aged 45 to 49	541	420	77.6	405	15	3.5
Aged 50 to 54	474	353	74.5	343	10	2.9
Aged 55 to 59	431	289	67.1	278	11	3.8
Aged 60 to 64	295	144	48.9	140	4	3.0
Aged 65 or older	738	99	13.4	97	2	2.2
BLACK WOMEN						
Total aged 16 or older	**15,328**	**9,393**	**61.3**	**8,554**	**839**	**8.9**
Under age 45	8,633	5,988	69.4	5,351	637	10.6
Aged 45 to 64	4,758	3,155	66.3	2,967	188	6.0
Aged 45 to 49	1,499	1,154	77.0	1,080	74	6.4
Aged 50 to 54	1,349	945	70.1	887	58	6.2
Aged 55 to 59	1,088	681	62.6	644	37	5.5
Aged 60 to 64	822	375	45.6	356	19	5.0
Aged 65 or older	1,937	251	13.0	236	15	5.8
HISPANIC WOMEN						
Total aged 16 or older	**15,616**	**8,769**	**56.2**	**8,098**	**672**	**7.7**
Under age 45	10,218	6,227	60.9	5,705	521	8.4
Aged 45 to 64	3,909	2,368	60.6	2,232	136	5.7
Aged 45 to 49	1,350	936	69.3	881	55	5.9
Aged 50 to 54	1,085	710	65.4	660	50	7.0
Aged 55 to 59	838	478	57.0	452	26	5.5
Aged 60 to 64	636	244	38.3	239	5	2.1
Aged 65 or older	1,488	174	11.7	161	13	7.7
WHITE WOMEN						
Total aged 16 or older	**96,814**	**57,284**	**59.2**	**54,501**	**2,782**	**4.9**
Under age 45	46,099	32,383	70.2	30,478	1,903	5.9
Aged 45 to 64	32,522	22,484	69.1	21,697	787	3.5
Aged 45 to 49	9,256	7,166	77.4	6,924	242	3.4
Aged 50 to 54	8,855	6,709	75.8	6,462	247	3.7
Aged 55 to 59	7,829	5,368	68.6	5,175	193	3.6
Aged 60 to 64	6,582	3,241	49.2	3,136	105	3.2
Aged 65 or older	18,193	2,417	13.3	2,325	92	3.8

Note: Race is shown only for those selecting that race group only. People who selected more than one race are not included. Hispanics may be of any race.
Source: Bureau of Labor Statistics, 2008 Current Population Survey, Internet site http://www.bls.gov/cps/tables.htm#empstat; calculations by New Strategist

More than Sixty Percent of Boomer Couples Are Dual Earners

In only one-fifth of couples is the husband alone in the labor force.

Dual incomes are by far the norm among married couples. Both husband and wife are in the labor force in 55 percent of all married couples. In another 22 percent, the husband is the only worker. Not far behind are the 16 percent of couples in which neither spouse is in the labor force. The wife is the sole worker in 7 percent of couples.

Seventy percent of couples aged 45 to 54 are dual earners, while the husband is the only spouse in the labor force in another 21 percent. The dual-earner lifestyle accounts for a much smaller 49 percent of couples aged 55 to 64. The wife is the only one employed in a substantial 13 percent of couples in this age group. In these homes, typically, the older husband is retired while the younger wife is still at work. For 67 percent of couples aged 65 or older, neither husband nor wife is working.

■ Only 11 percent of couples aged 65 or older have dual incomes. Expect this share to rise as aging Boomers postpone retirement.

Dual earners are the norm among Boomers aged 45 to 54

(percent of married couples in which both husband and wife are in the labor force, by age, 2008)

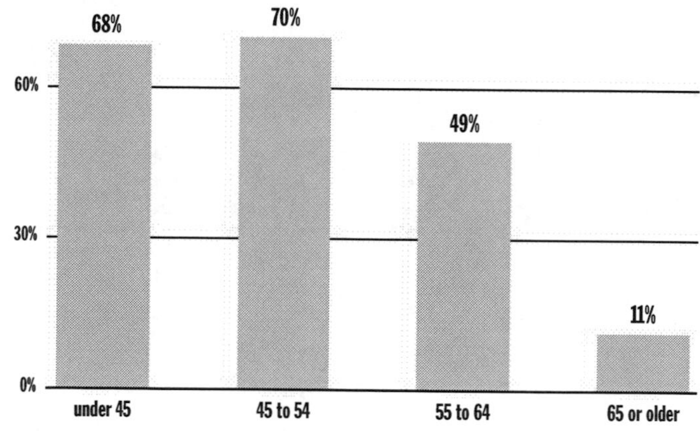

Table 6.5 Labor Force Status of Married-Couple Family Groups by Age, 2008

(number and percent distribution of married-couple family groups by age of reference person and labor force status of husband and wife, 2008; numbers in thousands)

	total	husband and wife in labor force	husband only in labor force	wife only in labor force	neither husband nor wife in labor force
Total married-couple family groups	**60,129**	**32,988**	**13,141**	**4,118**	**9,882**
Under age 45	24,074	16,290	6,539	774	469
Aged 45 to 64	25,609	15,535	5,426	2,242	2,406
Aged 45 to 54	14,210	9,922	3,000	796	491
Aged 55 to 64	11,399	5,613	2,426	1,446	1,915
Aged 65 or older	10,446	1,163	1,176	1,102	7,007
PERCENT DISTRIBUTION BY LABOR FORCE STATUS					
Total married-couple family groups	**100.0%**	**54.9%**	**21.9%**	**6.8%**	**16.4%**
Under age 45	100.0	67.7	27.2	3.2	1.9
Aged 45 to 64	100.0	60.7	21.2	8.8	9.4
Aged 45 to 54	100.0	69.8	21.1	5.6	3.5
Aged 55 to 64	100.0	49.2	21.3	12.7	16.8
Aged 65 or older	100.0	11.1	11.3	10.5	67.1
PERCENT DISTRIBUTION BY AGE					
Total married-couple family groups	**100.0%**	**100.0%**	**100.0%**	**100.0%**	**100.0%**
Under age 45	40.0	49.4	49.8	18.8	4.7
Aged 45 to 64	42.6	47.1	41.3	54.4	24.3
Aged 45 to 54	23.6	30.1	22.8	19.3	5.0
Aged 55 to 64	19.0	17.0	18.5	35.1	19.4
Aged 65 or older	17.4	3.5	8.9	26.8	70.9

Source: Bureau of the Census, America's Families and Living Arrangements: 2008, Internet site http://www.census.gov/population/www/socdemo/hh-fam/cps2008.html; calculations by New Strategist

Boomers Are Almost Half of Nation's Managers

They account for less than 20 percent of food prep workers.

Among the 145 million employed Americans in 2008, more than 55 million (or 38 percent) were in the broad 45 to 64 age group (Boomers were aged 44 to 62 in that year). In some occupations, more than 50 percent of workers are aged 45 to 64. Boomers account for 59 percent of chief executives and 57 percent of legislators. They are also 58 percent of economists, 54 percent of clergy, and 52 percent of education administrators.

At the other extreme, only 12 percent of waiters and waitresses are aged 45 to 64. Not surprisingly, aging boomers account for only 17 percent of athletes. They are also underrepresented in many computer-centered occupations. People aged 45 to 64 account for only 31 percent of computer software engineers.

■ The median age of workers ranges widely depending on the occupation. Farmers and ranchers have a median age of 55.5. Waiters and waitresses have a median age of just 24.8.

People aged 45 to 64 account for more than half of workers in some occupations

(percent of workers in the 45-to-64 age group, by selected occupation, 2008)

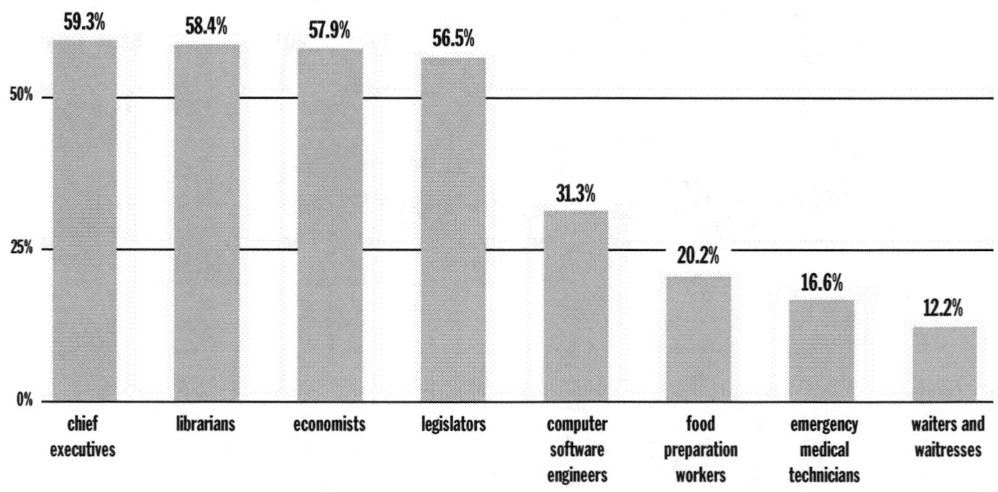

Table 6.6 Occupations of Workers Aged 45 to 64, 2008

(number of employed workers aged 16 or older, median age of workers, and number of workers aged 45 to 64, by occupation, 2008; numbers in thousands)

	total	median age	45 to 54	55 to 64
TOTAL WORKERS	**145,362**	**41.3**	**34,529**	**20,812**
Management and professional occupations	**52,761**	**43.5**	**13,824**	**8,659**
Management, business and financial operations	22,059	44.8	6,236	3,896
Management	15,852	45.6	4,684	2,910
Business and financial operations	6,207	42.8	1,552	986
Professional and related occupations	30,702	42.5	7,588	4,764
Computer and mathematical	3,676	39.9	882	345
Architecture and engineering	2,931	43.1	804	441
Life, physical, and social sciences	1,307	41.4	285	186
Community and social services	2,293	44.1	558	430
Legal	1,671	44.7	439	288
Education, training, and library	8,605	42.8	2,028	1,518
Arts, design, entertainment, sports, and media	2,820	40.5	600	382
Health care practitioner and technician	7,399	43.3	1,993	1,175
Service occupations	**24,451**	**37.1**	**4,648**	**2,730**
Health care support	3,212	38.5	672	390
Protective service	3,047	40.6	661	353
Food preparation and serving	7,824	28.9	1,007	515
Building and grounds cleaning and maintenance	5,445	42.4	1,354	829
Personal care and service	4,923	39.0	954	643
Sales and office occupations	**35,544**	**40.6**	**8,007**	**5,170**
Sales and related occupations	16,295	39.5	3,347	2,239
Office and administrative support	19,249	41.4	4,660	2,932
Natural resources, construction, maintenance occupations	**14,806**	**39.9**	**3,559**	**1,706**
Farming, fishing, and forestry	988	37.7	202	120
Construction and extraction	8,667	39.0	1,963	901
Installation, maintenance, and repair	5,152	41.7	1,393	685
Production, transportation, material-moving occupations	**17,800**	**41.9**	**4,492**	**2,546**
Production	8,973	42.3	2,385	1,322
Transportation and material moving	8,827	41.4	2,107	1,224

Source: Bureau of Labor Statistics, unpublished data from the 2008 Current Population Survey; calculations by New Strategist

Table 6.7 Share of Workers Aged 45 to 64 by Occupation, 2008

(percent distribution of employed people aged 16 or older and aged 45 to 64 by occupation, 2008)

		aged 45 to 64		
	total	total	45 to 54	55 to 64
TOTAL WORKERS	100.0%	38.1%	23.8%	14.3%
Management and professional occupations	**100.0**	**42.6**	**26.2**	**16.4**
Management, business and financial operations	100.0	45.9	28.3	17.7
Management	100.0	47.9	29.5	18.4
Business and financial operations	100.0	40.9	25.0	15.9
Professional and related occupations	100.0	40.2	24.7	15.5
Computer and mathematical	100.0	33.4	24.0	9.4
Architecture and engineering	100.0	42.5	27.4	15.0
Life, physical, and social sciences	100.0	36.0	21.8	14.2
Community and social services	100.0	43.1	24.3	18.8
Legal	100.0	43.5	26.3	17.2
Education, training, and library	100.0	41.2	23.6	17.6
Arts, design, entertainment, sports, and media	100.0	34.8	21.3	13.5
Health care practitioner and technician	100.0	42.8	26.9	15.9
Service occupations	**100.0**	**30.2**	**19.0**	**11.2**
Health care support	100.0	33.1	20.9	12.1
Protective service	100.0	33.3	21.7	11.6
Food preparation and serving	100.0	19.5	12.9	6.6
Building and grounds cleaning and maintenance	100.0	40.1	24.9	15.2
Personal care and service	100.0	32.4	19.4	13.1
Sales and office occupations	**100.0**	**37.1**	**22.5**	**14.5**
Sales and related occupations	100.0	34.3	20.5	13.7
Office and administrative support	100.0	39.4	24.2	15.2
Natural resources, construction, maintenance occupations	**100.0**	**35.6**	**24.0**	**11.5**
Farming, fishing, and forestry	100.0	32.6	20.4	12.1
Construction and extraction	100.0	33.0	22.6	10.4
Installation, maintenance, and repair	100.0	40.3	27.0	13.3
Production, transportation, material-moving occupations	**100.0**	**39.5**	**25.2**	**14.3**
Production	100.0	41.3	26.6	14.7
Transportation and material moving	100.0	37.7	23.9	13.9

Source: Calculations by New Strategist based on Bureau of Labor Statistics' unpublished data from the 2008 Current Population Survey

Table 6.8 Distribution of Workers Aged 45 to 64 by Occupation, 2008

(percent distribution of total employed people and employed people aged 45 to 64, by occupation, 2008)

	total	45 to 54	55 to 64
TOTAL WORKERS	**100.0%**	**100.0%**	**100.0%**
Management and professional occupations	**36.3**	**40.0**	**41.6**
Management, business and financial operations	15.2	18.1	18.7
Management	10.9	13.6	14.0
Business and financial operations	4.3	4.5	4.7
Professional and related occupations	21.1	22.0	22.9
Computer and mathematical	2.5	2.6	1.7
Architecture and engineering	2.0	2.3	2.1
Life, physical, and social sciences	0.9	0.8	0.9
Community and social services	1.6	1.6	2.1
Legal	1.1	1.3	1.4
Education, training, and library	5.9	5.9	7.3
Arts, design, entertainment, sports, and media	1.9	1.7	1.8
Health care practitioner and technician	5.1	5.8	5.6
Service occupations	**16.8**	**13.5**	**13.1**
Health care support	2.2	1.9	1.9
Protective service	2.1	1.9	1.7
Food preparation and serving	5.4	2.9	2.5
Building and grounds cleaning and maintenance	3.7	3.9	4.0
Personal care and service	3.4	2.8	3.1
Sales and office occupations	**24.5**	**23.2**	**24.8**
Sales and related occupations	11.2	9.7	10.8
Office and administrative support	13.2	13.5	14.1
Natural resources, construction, maintenance occupations	**10.2**	**10.3**	**8.2**
Farming, fishing, and forestry	0.7	0.6	0.6
Construction and extraction	6.0	5.7	4.3
Installation, maintenance, and repair	3.5	4.0	3.3
Production, transportation, material-moving occupations	**12.2**	**13.0**	**12.2**
Production	6.2	6.9	6.4
Transportation and material moving	6.1	6.1	5.9

Source: Calculations by New Strategist based on Bureau of Labor Statistics' unpublished 2008 Current Population Survey data

Table 6.9 Workers Aged 45 to 64 by Detailed Occupation, 2008

(number of employed workers aged 16 or older, median age, and number and percent aged 45 to 64, by selected detailed occupation, 2008; numbers in thousands)

	total workers	median age	aged 45 to 54		aged 55 to 64	
			number	percent of total	number	percent of total
Total workers	**145,362**	**41.3**	**34,529**	**23.8%**	**20,812**	**14.3%**
Chief executives	1,655	49.9	577	34.9	403	24.4
Legislators	23	54.5	6	26.1	7	30.4
Marketing and sales managers	922	41.5	248	26.9	108	11.7
Computer and information systems managers	475	42.5	144	30.3	51	10.7
Financial managers	1,168	42.9	323	27.7	180	15.4
Human resources managers	293	44.1	79	27.0	57	19.5
Farmers and ranchers	751	55.5	189	25.2	194	25.8
Construction managers	1,244	44.7	388	31.2	203	16.3
Education administrators	829	47.7	235	28.3	197	23.8
Food service managers	1,039	40.0	236	22.7	113	10.9
Medical and health services managers	561	46.8	184	32.8	118	21.0
Accountants and auditors	1,762	41.6	429	24.3	237	13.5
Computer scientists and systems analysts	837	41.0	210	25.1	100	11.9
Computer programmers	534	40.3	129	24.2	56	10.5
Computer software engineers	1,034	39.5	248	24.0	75	7.3
Architects	233	44.2	54	23.2	34	14.6
Civil engineers	346	42.9	89	25.7	55	15.9
Electrical engineers	350	44.7	107	30.6	60	17.1
Mechanical engineers	318	43.6	83	26.1	51	16.0
Medical scientists	132	39.7	28	21.2	14	10.6
Economists	19	47.3	6	31.6	5	26.3
Market researchers	134	38.8	26	19.4	10	7.5
Psychologists	176	48.9	35	19.9	46	26.1
Social workers	729	42.3	188	25.8	115	15.8
Clergy	441	51.3	125	28.3	112	25.4
Lawyers	1,014	45.8	274	27.0	177	17.5
Postsecondary teachers	1,218	43.7	263	21.6	225	18.5
Preschool and kindergarten teachers	685	39.2	161	23.5	84	12.3
Elementary and middle school teachers	2,958	42.6	694	23.5	524	17.7
Secondary school teachers	1,210	43.4	266	22.0	239	19.8
Librarians	197	51.2	54	27.4	61	31.0
Teacher assistants	1,020	43.1	277	27.2	164	16.1
Artists	213	46.2	46	21.6	45	21.1
Designers	834	40.8	203	24.3	107	12.8
Actors	30	32.6	5	16.7	2	6.7
Athletes, coaches, umpires	252	31.4	26	10.3	18	7.1
Musicians	186	44.0	47	25.3	27	14.5
Editors	171	40.9	39	22.8	23	13.5
Writers and authors	186	46.9	49	26.3	32	17.2
Dentists	152	48.2	45	29.6	32	21.1
Pharmacists	243	42.2	50	20.6	34	14.0

	total workers	median age	aged 45 to 54		aged 55 to 64	
			number	percent of total	number	percent of total
Physicians and surgeons	877	45.7	238	27.1%	161	18.4%
Registered nurses	2,778	45.0	870	31.3	480	17.3
Physical therapists	197	40.9	41	20.8	21	10.7
Emergency medical technicians and paramedics	138	32.8	17	12.3	6	4.3
Licensed practical nurses	566	43.7	149	26.3	100	17.7
Nursing, psychiatric, and home health aides	1,889	39.8	405	21.4	256	13.6
Firefighters	293	39.3	67	22.9	12	4.1
Police and sheriff's patrol officers	674	38.7	122	18.1	44	6.5
Security guards and gaming surveillance officers	867	42.0	177	20.4	140	16.1
Chefs and head cooks	351	37.3	62	17.7	28	8.0
Cooks	1,997	32.2	304	15.2	150	7.5
Food preparation workers	724	27.9	89	12.3	57	7.9
Waiters and waitresses	2,010	24.8	170	8.5	74	3.7
Janitors and building cleaners	2,125	45.5	577	27.2	405	19.1
Maids and housekeeping cleaners	1,434	43.6	375	26.2	232	16.2
Grounds maintenance workers	1,262	35.5	218	17.3	106	8.4
Hairdressers, hair stylists, and cosmetologists	773	39.0	146	18.9	96	12.4
Child care workers	1,314	36.3	258	19.6	148	11.3
Cashiers	3,031	27.1	364	12.0	257	8.5
Retail salespersons	3,416	34.9	563	16.5	425	12.4
Insurance sales agents	573	44.8	149	26.0	100	17.5
Securities, commodities, and financial services sales agents	388	40.0	87	22.4	44	11.3
Sales representatives, wholesale/manufacturing	1,343	42.8	348	25.9	193	14.4
Real estate brokers and sales agents	962	47.9	237	24.6	230	23.9
Bookkeeping, accounting, and auditing clerks	1,434	46.5	399	27.8	304	21.2
Customer service representatives	1,908	35.3	334	17.5	186	9.7
Receptionists and information clerks	1,413	37.2	241	17.1	189	13.4
Stock clerks and order fillers	1,481	33.0	271	18.3	141	9.5
Secretaries and administrative assistants	3,296	45.7	933	28.3	666	20.2
Miscellaneous agricultural workers	723	34.1	132	18.3	68	9.4
Carpenters	1,562	39.4	375	24.0	163	10.4
Construction laborers	1,651	35.9	300	18.2	125	7.6
Automotive service technicians and mechanics	852	38.8	197	23.1	89	10.4
Miscellaneous assemblers and fabricators	1,050	40.8	268	25.5	125	11.9
Machinists	409	44.8	126	30.8	67	16.4
Aircraft pilots and flight engineers	141	43.6	40	28.4	20	14.2
Driver/sales workers and truck drivers	3,388	43.5	891	26.3	524	15.5
Laborers and freight, stock, and material movers	1,889	34.3	360	19.1	163	8.6

Source: Bureau of Labor Statistics, unpublished tables from the 2008 Current Population Survey; calculations by New Strategist

Among Workers Aged 55 or Older, Few Work Part-Time

Part-time work is the rule only among teenagers aged 16 to 19.

Among employed men ranging in age from 25 to 54 in 2008, a tiny 7 percent had part-time jobs, and the 57 percent majority of those who worked part-time would have preferred full-time work. Among employed women in the broad age group, 19 percent worked part-time and only 20 percent of the part-time workers were doing so for economic reasons—meaning they could not find a full-time job.

Among workers aged 55 or older, part-time work becomes more common for both men and women but is still not the norm. Sixteen percent of employed men and 28 percent of employed women aged 55 or older had part-time jobs. Only 20 percent of the men and 12 percent of the women worked part-time because they could not find full-time work.

■ The percentage of workers who have part-time jobs because they cannot find full-time employment has been rising during the economic downturn.

Some part-time workers want full-time jobs

(percent of employed men who work part-time but would prefer a full-time job, by age, 2008)

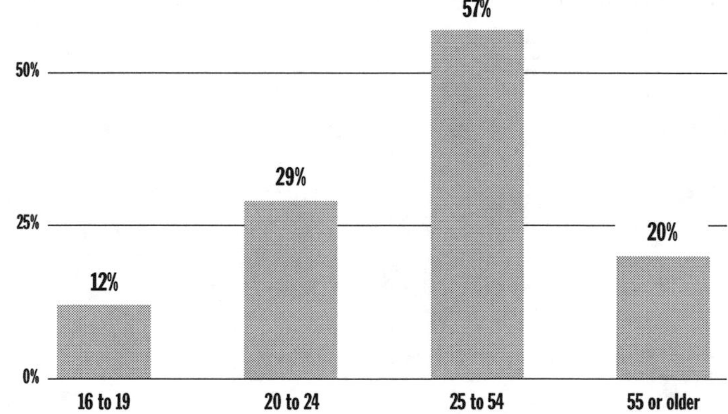

Table 6.10 Full-Time and Part-Time Workers by Age and Sex, 2008

(number and percent distribution of people aged 16 or older at work in nonagricultural industries by age, employment status, and sex, 2008; numbers in thousands)

	total			men			women		
	total	full-time	part-time	total	full-time	part-time	total	full-time	part-time
Total at work	**137,739**	**112,961**	**24,778**	**73,471**	**64,375**	**9,095**	**64,268**	**48,586**	**15,682**
Aged 16 to 19	5,252	1,526	3,727	2,556	875	1,681	2,696	650	2,046
Aged 20 to 24	13,091	9,058	4,033	6,866	5,067	1,798	6,225	3,990	2,235
Aged 25 to 54	94,577	82,960	11,617	50,972	47,468	3,504	43,605	35,492	8,112
Aged 55 or older	24,819	19,418	5,401	13,077	10,964	2,112	11,742	8,454	3,288
PERCENT DISTRIBUTION BY EMPLOYMENT STATUS									
Total at work	**100.0%**	**82.0%**	**18.0%**	**100.0%**	**87.6%**	**12.4%**	**100.0%**	**75.6%**	**24.4%**
Aged 16 to 19	100.0	29.1	71.0	100.0	34.2	65.8	100.0	24.1	75.9
Aged 20 to 24	100.0	69.2	30.8	100.0	73.8	26.2	100.0	64.1	35.9
Aged 25 to 54	100.0	87.7	12.3	100.0	93.1	6.9	100.0	81.4	18.6
Aged 55 or older	100.0	78.2	21.8	100.0	83.8	16.2	100.0	72.0	28.0
PERCENT DISTRIBUTION BY AGE									
Total at work	**100.0%**	**100.0%**	**100.0%**	**100.0%**	**100.0%**	**100.0%**	**100.0%**	**100.0%**	**100.0%**
Aged 16 to 19	3.8	1.4	15.0	3.5	1.4	18.5	4.2	1.3	13.0
Aged 20 to 24	9.5	8.0	16.3	9.3	7.9	19.8	9.7	8.2	14.3
Aged 25 to 54	68.7	73.4	46.9	69.4	73.7	38.5	67.8	73.0	51.7
Aged 55 or older	18.0	17.2	21.8	17.8	17.0	23.2	18.3	17.4	21.0

Note: Part-time work is less than 35 hours per week. Part-time workers exclude those who worked less than 35 hours in the previous week because of vacation, holidays, child care problems, weather issues, and other temporary, noneconomic reasons.
Source: Bureau of Labor Statistics, Current Population Survey, Internet site http://www.bls.gov/cps/tables.htm#empstat; calculations by New Strategist

Table 6.11 Part-Time Workers by Sex, Age, and Reason, 2008

(total number of people aged 16 or older who work in nonagricultural industries part-time, and number and percent working part-time for economic reasons, by sex and age, 2008; numbers in thousands)

		working part-time for economic reasons	
	total	number	share of total
Men working part-time	**9,095**	**3,162**	**34.8%**
Aged 16 to 19	1,681	209	12.4
Aged 20 to 24	1,798	526	29.3
Aged 25 to 54	3,504	2,014	57.5
Aged 55 or older	2,112	412	19.5
Women working part-time	**15,682**	**2,611**	**16.6**
Aged 16 to 19	2,046	173	8.5
Aged 20 to 24	2,235	412	18.4
Aged 25 to 54	8,112	1,637	20.2
Aged 55 or older	3,288	388	11.8

Note: Part-time work is less than 35 hours per week. Part-time workers exclude those who worked less than 35 hours in the previous week because of vacation, holidays, child care problems, weather issues, and other temporary, noneconomic reasons. "Economic reasons" means a worker's hours have been reduced or workers cannot find full-time employment.
Source: Bureau of Labor Statistics, Current Population Survey, Internet site http://www.bls.gov/cps/tables.htm#empstat; calculations by New Strategist

Few Boomers Are Self-Employed

Workers aged 65 or older are most likely to be self-employed.

Despite plenty of media hype about America's entrepreneurial spirit, few Americans are self-employed. Only 7 percent of the nation's workers were self-employed in 2008. Men are more likely than women to be self-employed, 8 versus 5 percent. For both men and women, the percentage who are self-employed rises with age.

The oldest workers are most likely to be self-employed. Twelve percent of working men and 8 percent of working women aged 55 to 64 work for themselves. The figure rises to 20 percent among working men and 13 percent among working women in the 65-or-older age group.

■ Many more workers would opt for self-employment if health insurance were not an obstacle.

Self-employment rises with age

(percent of workers who are self-employed, by age, 2008)

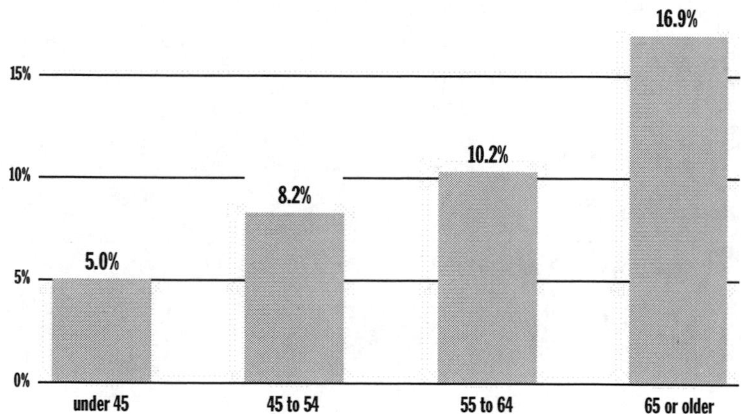

Table 6.12 Self-Employed Workers by Sex and Age, 2008

(number of employed workers aged 16 or older, number and percent who are self-employed, and percent distribution of self-employed, by age, 2008; numbers in thousands)

		self-employed		percent distribution of self-employed
	total	number	percent	by age
Total aged 16 or older	**145,362**	**10,079**	**6.9%**	**100.0%**
Under age 45	84,042	4,119	4.9	40.9
Aged 45 to 64	55,341	4,952	8.9	49.1
Aged 45 to 54	34,529	2,832	8.2	28.1
Aged 55 to 64	20,812	2,120	10.2	21.0
Aged 65 or older	5,979	1,009	16.9	10.0
Total men	**77,486**	**6,373**	**8.2**	**100.0**
Under age 45	45,161	2,592	5.7	40.7
Aged 45 to 64	29,043	3,110	10.7	48.8
Aged 45 to 54	18,124	1,769	9.8	27.8
Aged 55 to 64	10,919	1,341	12.3	21.0
Aged 65 or older	3,283	670	20.4	10.5
Total women	**67,876**	**3,707**	**5.5**	**100.0**
Under age 45	38,880	1,522	3.9	41.1
Aged 45 to 64	26,298	1,842	7.0	49.7
Aged 45 to 54	16,405	1,063	6.5	28.7
Aged 55 to 64	9,893	779	7.9	21.0
Aged 65 or older	2,697	340	12.6	9.2

Source: Bureau of Labor Statistics, Current Population Survey, Internet site http://www.bls.gov/cps/tables.htm#empstat; calculations by New Strategist

Job Tenure among Boomers Has Declined

Long-term employment is less common among middle-aged men and women.

Job tenure (the median number of years a worker has been with his current employer) has been fairly stable since 2000. But among workers aged 45 to 64, job tenure has declined. The decline has been particularly severe among men aged 45 to 54, for whom the median number of years on the job fell from 9.5 years in 2000 to 8.2 years in 2008.

As job tenure declines, so does long-term employment. Between 2000 and 2008, the percentage of men aged 30 to 54 who have been with their current employer for at least 10 years fell. But long-term employment increased among men aged 55 to 59 during those years as early retirement became less common. Among women aged 30 to 59, long-term employment fell, but it climbed among women aged 60 or older.

■ As fewer workers opt for early retirement, long-term employment among older workers may-continue to rise.

Fewer Boomer men have long-term jobs

(percent of men aged 45 to 59 who have worked for their current employer for 10 or more years, 2000 and 2008)

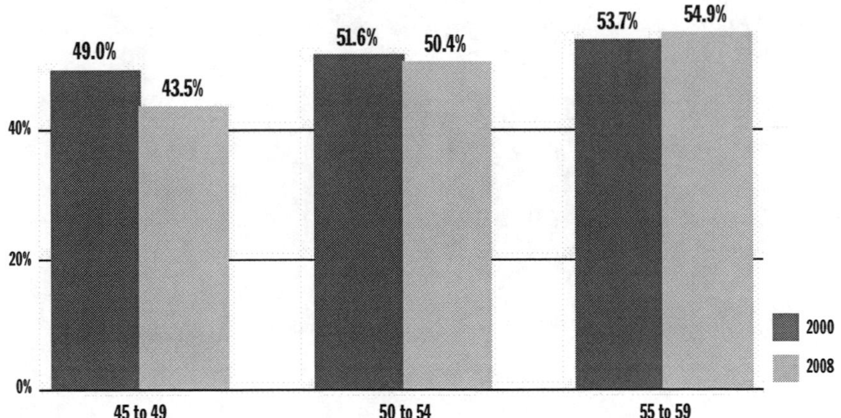

Table 6.13 Job Tenure by Sex and Age, 2000 and 2008

(median number of years workers aged 25 or older have been with their current employer by sex and age, and change in years, 2000 and 2008)

	2008	2000	change in years 2000–08
Total aged 25 or older	**5.1**	**4.7**	**0.4**
Aged 25 to 34	2.7	2.6	0.1
Aged 35 to 44	4.9	4.8	0.1
Aged 45 to 54	7.6	8.2	–0.6
Aged 55 to 64	9.9	10.0	–0.1
Aged 65 or older	10.2	9.4	0.8
Men aged 25 or older	**5.2**	**4.9**	**0.3**
Aged 25 to 34	2.8	2.7	0.1
Aged 35 to 44	5.2	5.3	–0.1
Aged 45 to 54	8.2	9.5	–1.3
Aged 55 to 64	10.1	10.2	–0.1
Aged 65 or older	10.4	9.0	1.4
Women aged 25 or older	**4.9**	**4.4**	**0.5**
Aged 25 to 34	2.6	2.5	0.1
Aged 35 to 44	4.7	4.3	0.4
Aged 45 to 54	7.0	7.3	–0.3
Aged 55 to 64	9.8	9.9	–0.1
Aged 65 or older	9.9	9.7	0.2

Source: Bureau of Labor Statistics, Employee Tenure, Internet site http://www.bls.gov/news.release/tenure.toc.htm; calculations by New Strategist

Table 6.14 Long-Term Employment by Sex and Age, 2000 and 2008

(percent of employed wage and salary workers aged 25 or older who have been with their current employer for 10 or more years, by sex and age, 2000 and 2008; percentage point change in share, 2000–08)

	2008	2000	percentage point change 2000–08
TOTAL AGED 25 OR OLDER	**31.5%**	**31.5%**	**0.0**
Men aged 25 or older	**32.9**	**33.4**	**–0.5**
Aged 25 to 29	2.4	3.0	–0.6
Aged 30 to 34	11.3	15.1	–3.8
Aged 35 to 39	25.4	29.4	–4.0
Aged 40 to 44	35.8	40.2	–4.4
Aged 45 to 49	43.5	49.0	–5.5
Aged 50 to 54	50.4	51.6	–1.2
Aged 55 to 59	54.9	53.7	1.2
Aged 60 to 64	52.4	52.4	0.0
Aged 65 or older	58.9	48.6	10.3
Women aged 25 or older	**30.0**	**29.5**	**0.5**
Aged 25 to 29	2.1	1.9	0.2
Aged 30 to 34	8.7	12.5	–3.8
Aged 35 to 39	20.3	22.3	–2.0
Aged 40 to 44	29.9	31.2	–1.3
Aged 45 to 49	36.7	41.4	–4.7
Aged 50 to 54	45.0	45.8	–0.8
Aged 55 to 59	50.0	52.5	–2.5
Aged 60 to 64	54.8	53.6	1.2
Aged 65 or older	53.8	51.0	2.8

Source: Bureau of Labor Statistics, Employee Tenure, Internet site http://www.bls.gov/news.release/tenure.toc.htm; calculations by New Strategist

Independent Contracting Appeals to Older Workers

Twenty-three percent of workers aged 65 or older have an alternative work arrangement.

Among the nation's 15 million alternative workers, most are middle-aged. But older workers are most likely to have alternative types of jobs. The Bureau of Labor Statistics defines alternative workers as independent contractors, on-call workers (such as substitute teachers), temporary-help agency workers, and people who work for contract firms (such as lawn or janitorial service companies).

The most popular alternative work arrangement is independent contracting—which includes most of the self-employed. Among the 15 million alternative workers, 10 million (or 70 percent) are independent contractors. Among all workers aged 45 to 64, a substantial 10 percent are independent contractors. Few people aged 45 to 64 choose other types of alternative work, such as temporary or on-call work.

The percentage of workers with alternative work arrangements surges in the 65-or-older age group. Nearly one in five workers aged 65 or older has an alternative work arrangement, with 18 percent being independent contractors.

■ Many older workers opt for self-employment because it gives them more control over their work schedule and their government-provided health insurance coverage allows them the freedom to strike out on their own.

Older workers are most likely to be independent contractors

(percent of employed workers who are independent contractors, by age, 2005)

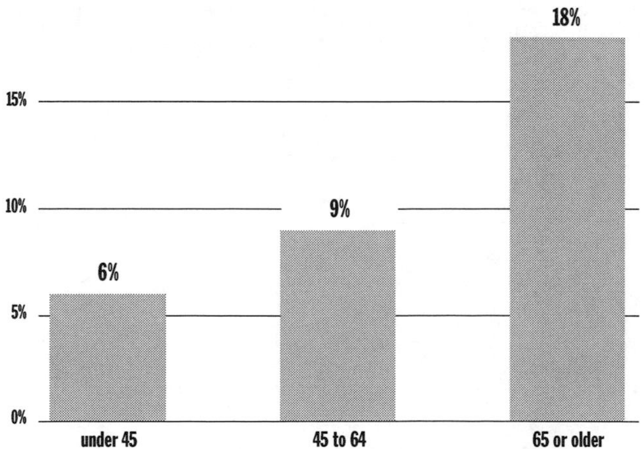

Table 6.15 Alternative Work Arrangements by Age, 2005

(number and percent distribution of employed people aged 16 or older by age and work arrangement, 2005; numbers in thousands)

			alternative workers				
	total employed	traditional arrangements	total	independent contractors	on-call workers	temporary-help agency workers	workers provided by contract firms
Total people	**138,952**	**123,843**	**14,826**	**10,342**	**2,454**	**1,217**	**813**
Under age 45	83,208	75,322	7,658	4,719	1,594	850	495
Aged 45 to 64	50,927	44,820	6,061	4,742	684	335	300
Aged 45 to 54	32,947	29,324	3,602	2,799	417	200	186
Aged 55 to 64	17,980	15,496	2,459	1,943	267	135	114
Aged 65 or older	4,817	3,701	1,107	881	175	33	18
PERCENT DISTRIBUTION BY ALTERNATIVE WORK STATUS							
Total people	**100.0%**	**89.1%**	**10.7%**	**7.4%**	**1.8%**	**0.9%**	**0.6%**
Under age 45	100.0	90.5	9.2	5.7	1.9	1.0	0.6
Aged 45 to 64	100.0	88.0	11.9	9.3	1.3	0.7	0.6
Aged 45 to 54	100.0	89.0	10.9	8.5	1.3	0.6	0.6
Aged 55 to 64	100.0	86.2	13.7	10.8	1.5	0.8	0.6
Aged 65 or older	100.0	76.8	23.0	18.3	3.6	0.7	0.4
PERCENT DISTRIBUTION BY AGE							
Total people	**100.0%**	**100.0%**	**100.0%**	**100.0%**	**100.0%**	**100.0%**	**100.0%**
Under age 45	59.9	60.8	51.7	45.6	65.0	69.8	60.9
Aged 45 to 64	36.7	36.2	40.9	45.9	27.9	27.5	36.9
Aged 45 to 54	23.7	23.7	24.3	27.1	17.0	16.4	22.9
Aged 55 to 64	12.9	12.5	16.6	18.8	10.9	11.1	14.0
Aged 65 or older	3.5	3.0	7.5	8.5	7.1	2.7	2.2

Note: Numbers may not add to total because "total employed" includes day laborers, an alternative arrangement not shown separately, and a small number of workers were both on call and provided by contract firms. Independent contractors are workers who obtain customers on their own to provide a product or service, and include the self-employed. On-call workers are in a pool of workers who are called to work only as needed, such as substitute teachers and construction workers supplied by a union hiring hall. Temporary-help agency workers are those who said they are paid by a temporary-help agency. Workers provided by contract firms are those employed by a company that provides employees or their services under contract, such as security, landscaping, and computer programming.
Source: Bureau of Labor Statistics, Contingent and Alternative Employment Arrangements, February 2005, Internet site http://www.bls.gov/news.release/conemp.t05.htm; calculations by New Strategist

Most Minimum-Wage Workers Are Young Adults

Only 14 percent are Boomers.

Among the nation's 75 million workers who are paid hourly rates, only 2 million (3 percent) made minimum wage or less in 2008, according to the Bureau of Labor Statistics. Nearly 83 percent of minimum-wage workers are under age 45. Only 14 percent are between the ages of 45 and 64 (Boomers were aged 44 to 62 in 2008). Among hourly workers in the 45-to-64 age group, only 1 percent make minimum wage or less.

The percentage of workers who make minimum wage or less rises to nearly 3 percent in the 65-or-older age group. Many are retirees working part-time jobs to supplement their retirement income.

■ Younger workers are most likely to earn minimum wage or less because many hold entry-level jobs or are part-time workers.

Boomers account for few minimum-wage workers

(percent distribution of workers who make minimum wage or less, by age, 2008)

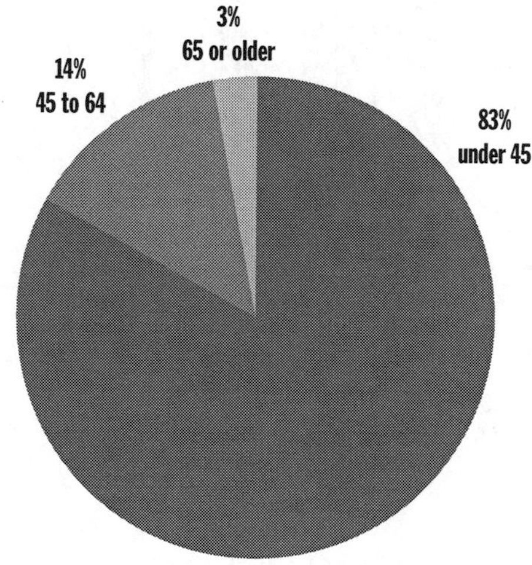

Table 6.16 Workers Earning Minimum Wage by Age, 2008

(number, percent, and percent distribution of workers aged 16 or older paid hourly rates at or below minimum wage, by age, 2008; numbers in thousands)

	total paid hourly rates	at or below minimum wage		
		number	share of total	percent distribution
Total aged 16 or older	**75,305**	**2,226**	**3.0%**	**100.0%**
Under age 45	48,051	1,846	3.8	82.9
Aged 45 to 64	24,612	309	1.3	13.9
Aged 45 to 49	8,246	126	1.5	5.7
Aged 50 to 54	7,379	76	1.0	3.4
Aged 55 to 59	5,660	67	1.2	3.0
Aged 60 to 64	3,327	40	1.2	1.8
Aged 65 or older	2,642	72	2.7	3.2

Source: Bureau of Labor Statistics, Characteristics of Minimum Wage Workers, 2008, Internet site http://www.bls.gov/cps/minwage2008.htm; calculations by New Strategist

Union Representation Peaks among Workers Aged 45 to 64

Men are more likely than women to be represented by a union.

Union representation has fallen sharply over the past few decades. In 2008, only 14 percent of wage and salary workers were represented by a union.

The percentage of workers who are represented by a union peaks in the 45-to-64 age group at 18 percent. Representation is highest among men aged 45 to 64, at 19 percent. Among women, the peak is in the 55-to-64 age group at 17 percent. Men are more likely than women to be represented by a union because men are more likely to work in manufacturing—the traditional stronghold of labor unions. In fact, the decline of labor unions is partly the result of the shift in jobs from manufacturing to services.

■ Union representation may rise along with workers' concerns about job security and the cost of health care coverage.

Few workers are represented by a union

(percent of employed wage and salary workers who are represented by unions, by age, 2008)

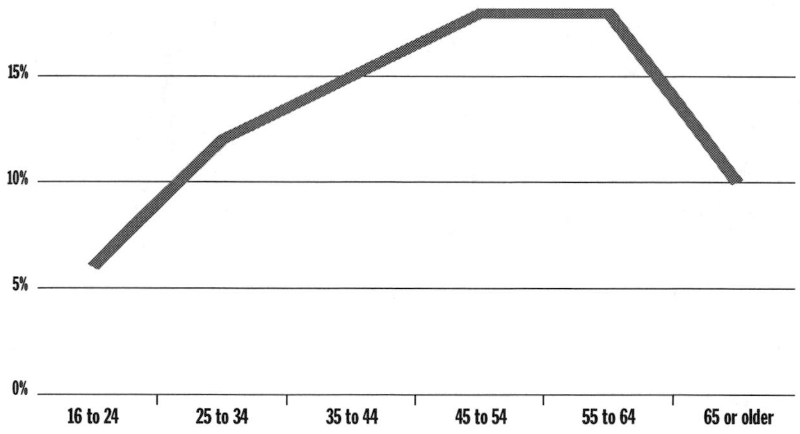

Table 6.17 Union Representation by Sex and Age, 2008

(number and percent of employed wage and salary workers aged 16 or older by union representation status, sex, and age, 2008; numbers in thousands)

		represented by unions	
	total employed	number	percent
Total aged 16 or older	**129,377**	**17,761**	**13.7%**
Aged 16 to 24	18,705	1,062	5.7
Aged 25 to 34	29,276	3,443	11.8
Aged 35 to 44	29,708	4,365	14.7
Aged 45 to 54	29,787	5,228	17.6
Aged 55 to 64	17,430	3,209	18.4
Aged 65 or older	4,471	454	10.2
Men aged 16 or older	**66,846**	**9,724**	**14.5**
Aged 16 to 24	9,537	617	6.5
Aged 25 to 34	15,780	1,909	12.1
Aged 35 to 44	15,653	2,491	15.9
Aged 45 to 54	14,988	2,812	18.8
Aged 55 to 64	8,657	1,682	19.4
Aged 65 or older	2,230	213	9.6
Women aged 16 or older	**62,532**	**8,036**	**12.9**
Aged 16 to 24	9,168	445	4.8
Aged 25 to 34	13,496	1,534	11.4
Aged 35 to 44	14,055	1,874	13.3
Aged 45 to 54	14,799	2,416	16.3
Aged 55 to 64	8,773	1,527	17.4
Aged 65 or older	2,241	241	10.7

Note: Workers represented by unions are either members of a labor union or similar employee association or workers who report no union affiliation but whose jobs are covered by a union or an employee association contract.
Source: Bureau of Labor Statistics, 2008 Current Population Survey, Internet site http://www.bls.gov/cps/tables.htm#empstat; calculations by New Strategist

Number of Workers Aged 65 or Older Will Soar during the Decade

The labor force participation rate of older workers is projected to rise.

During the next decade, the oldest members of the Baby-Boom generation will enter their late sixties. Because early retirement will be increasingly uncommon among Boomers, the labor force participation rate of people aged 65 or older is projected to rise.

Among men aged 65 or older, labor force participation will rise by 6.8 percentage points between 2006 and 2016, to 27.1 percent. The oldest women will see their labor force participation rate climb by 5.8 percentage points to 17.5 percent. The number of workers aged 65 or older will expand by 78 percent among men and 91 percent among women.

■ Millions of Baby Boomers will work well into their late sixties and early seventies because their retirement savings have been decimated by the financial crisis of 2008–09.

Expect more older workers in the labor force

(number of people aged 65 or older in the labor force, by sex, 2006 and 2016)

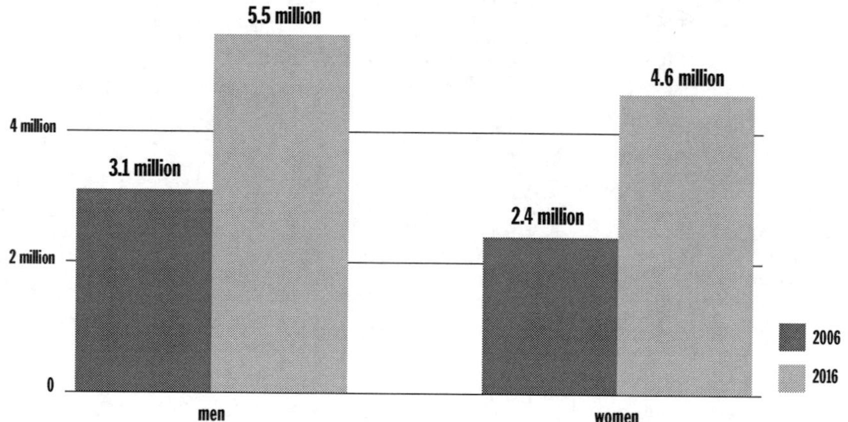

Table 6.18 Projections of the Labor Force by Sex and Age, 2006 and 2016

(number and percent of people aged 16 or older in the civilian labor force by sex and age, 2006 and 2016; percent change in number and percentage point change in participation rate, 2006–16; numbers in thousands)

	number			participation rate		
	2006	2016	percent change 2006–16	2006	2016	percentage point change 2006–16
TOTAL LABOR FORCE	**151,428**	**164,232**	**8.5%**	**66.2%**	**65.5%**	**–0.7**
Total men in labor force	**81,255**	**87,781**	**8.0**	**73.5**	**72.3**	**–1.2**
Aged 16 to 19	3,693	2,923	–20.9	43.7	36.8	–6.9
Aged 20 to 24	8,116	7,992	–1.5	79.6	76.4	–3.2
Aged 25 to 34	17,944	20,913	16.5	91.7	95.7	4.0
Aged 35 to 44	19,407	18,373	–5.3	92.1	91.7	–0.4
Aged 45 to 54	18,489	18,205	–1.5	88.1	86.6	–1.5
Aged 55 to 64	10,509	13,865	31.9	69.6	70.1	0.5
Aged 65 or older	3,096	5,511	78.0	20.3	27.1	6.8
Total women in labor force	**70,173**	**76,450**	**8.9**	**59.4**	**59.2**	**–0.2**
Aged 16 to 19	3,588	2,974	–17.1	43.7	38.3	–5.4
Aged 20 to 24	6,997	6,963	–0.5	69.5	67.2	–2.3
Aged 25 to 34	14,628	16,376	11.9	74.4	75.0	0.6
Aged 35 to 44	16,441	15,281	–7.1	75.9	75.1	–0.8
Aged 45 to 54	16,656	16,877	1.3	76.0	77.8	1.8
Aged 55 to 64	9,475	13,423	41.7	58.2	63.5	5.3
Aged 65 or older	2,388	4,556	90.8	11.7	17.5	5.8

Source: Bureau of Labor Statistics, Labor Force Projections to 2016: More Workers in Their Golden Years, Monthly Labor Review, November 2007, Internet site http://www.bls.gov/opub/mlr/2007/11/contents.htm; calculations by New Strategist

CHAPTER

7

Living Arrangements

■ Married couples account for 56 to 57 percent of households headed by people ranging in age from their late forties to their early sixties (Boomers were aged 44 to 62 in 2008).

■ Household size peaks among householders aged 35 to 39. As householders age into their forties and fifties, the nest empties.

■ Most households headed by people under age 45 include children under age 18. The proportion falls to 43 percent in the 45-to-49 age group and declines sharply with age—meaning that most Boomers are now empty-nesters.

■ Many Boomers have adult children at home. Among householders aged 55 to 64, nearly one in four has children of any age in their home—most of them adults.

■ The experience of divorce is most common among men and women aged 50 to 59. Among men in the age group, 37.5 percent had ever divorced. Among women in the age group, the percentage was an even higher 40.7 percent.

Most Boomer Households Are Headed by Married Couples

Households vary little by type among the middle aged.

In middle age, the lifestyles of the Baby-Boom generation are similar—despite the nearly 20-year span between the youngest and oldest boomers. Married couples account for 56 to 57 percent of households headed by people ranging in age from their late forties to their early sixties (Boomers were aged 44 to 62 in 2008).

There is much more variation by age in the proportion of Boomer households headed by women who live alone. The figure ranges from 10 percent in the 45-to-49 age group to 19 percent in the 60-to-64 age group as some Boomer wives become widows. Only 12 percent of Boomer households are headed by men who live alone, a figure that varies little by age.

■ Among people who live alone, women begin to outnumber men in the 50-to-54 age group.

In middle age, a growing share of households are headed by women who live alone

(single-person households headed by women as a share of total households, by age of householder, 2008)

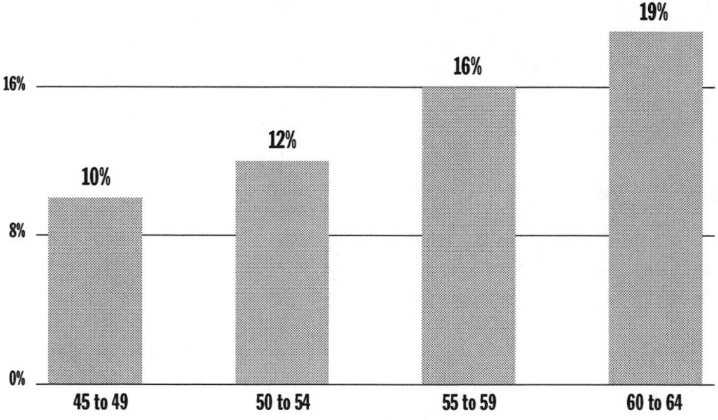

Table 7.1 Households Headed by People Aged 45 to 64 by Household Type, 2008: Total Households

(number and percent distribution of total households and households headed by people aged 45 to 64, by household type, 2008; numbers in thousands)

		aged 45 to 64				
	total	total	45 to 49	50 to 54	55 to 59	60 to 64
TOTAL HOUSEHOLDS	**116,783**	**44,445**	**12,685**	**11,851**	**10,813**	**9,096**
Family households	**77,873**	**31,167**	**9,438**	**8,511**	**7,269**	**5,949**
Married couples	58,370	24,986	7,105	6,737	6,049	5,095
Female householder, no spouse present	14,404	4,605	1,736	1,307	920	642
Male householder, no spouse present	5,100	1,577	597	467	301	212
Nonfamily households	**38,910**	**13,277**	**3,247**	**3,340**	**3,543**	**3,147**
Female householder	21,038	6,871	1,481	1,644	1,878	1,868
Living alone	18,297	6,147	1,232	1,481	1,703	1,731
Male householder	17,872	6,407	1,766	1,696	1,666	1,279
Living alone	13,870	5,426	1,470	1,396	1,448	1,112
Percent distribution by type						
TOTAL HOUSEHOLDS	**100.0%**	**100.0%**	**100.0%**	**100.0%**	**100.0%**	**100.0%**
Family households	**66.7**	**70.1**	**74.4**	**71.8**	**67.2**	**65.4**
Married couples	50.0	56.2	56.0	56.8	55.9	56.0
Female householder, no spouse present	12.3	10.4	13.7	11.0	8.5	7.1
Male householder, no spouse present	4.4	3.5	4.7	3.9	2.8	2.3
Nonfamily households	**33.3**	**29.9**	**25.6**	**28.2**	**32.8**	**34.6**
Female householder	18.0	15.5	11.7	13.9	17.4	20.5
Living alone	15.7	13.8	9.7	12.5	15.7	19.0
Male householder	15.3	14.4	13.9	14.3	15.4	14.1
Living alone	11.9	12.2	11.6	11.8	13.4	12.2
Percent distribution by age						
TOTAL HOUSEHOLDS	**100.0%**	**38.1%**	**10.9%**	**10.1%**	**9.3%**	**7.8%**
Family households	**100.0**	**40.0**	**12.1**	**10.9**	**9.3**	**7.6**
Married couples	100.0	42.8	12.2	11.5	10.4	8.7
Female householder, no spouse present	100.0	32.0	12.1	9.1	6.4	4.5
Male householder, no spouse present	100.0	30.9	11.7	9.2	5.9	4.2
Nonfamily households	**100.0**	**34.1**	**8.3**	**8.6**	**9.1**	**8.1**
Female householder	100.0	32.7	7.0	7.8	8.9	8.9
Living alone	100.0	33.6	6.7	8.1	9.3	9.5
Male householder	100.0	35.8	9.9	9.5	9.3	7.2
Living alone	100.0	39.1	10.6	10.1	10.4	8.0

Source: Bureau of the Census, 2008 Current Population Survey, Annual Social and Economic Supplement, Internet site http://www.census.gov/hhes/www/macro/032008/hhinc/new02_000.htm; calculations by New Strategist

Few Black Households Are Headed by Married Couples

Couples dominate Asian, Hispanic, and non-Hispanic white households.

In 2008, married couples accounted for the majority of Asian, Hispanic, and non-Hispanic white households headed by people aged 45 to 64 (the Baby-Boom generation was aged 44 to 62 in 2008). The married-couple share of households ranges from 55 percent among Hispanics to 69 percent among Asians. In contrast, married couples head only 36 percent of black households in the 45-to-64 age group. Female-headed families are a large share (22 percent) of black households headed by the middle aged. In contrast, among non-Hispanic whites, female-headed families account for just 8 percent of households in the 45-to-64 age group.

In the 45-to-64 age group, only 10 percent of Hispanic and Asian households are headed by women living alone. The figures are a larger 14 percent for non-Hispanic whites and 19 percent for blacks.

■ The household incomes of blacks are lower than those of non-Hispanic whites in part because married couples—the most affluent household type—are a much smaller share of households.

Married couples head a minority of households among blacks

(married couples as a percent of households headed by people aged 45 to 64, by race and Hispanic origin, 2008)

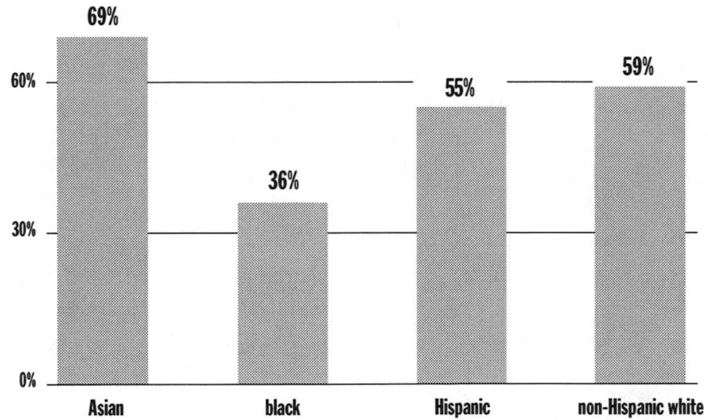

Table 7.2 Households Headed by People Aged 45 to 64 by Household Type, 2008: Asian Households

(number and percent distribution of total households headed by Asians and households headed by Asians aged 45 to 64, by household type, 2008; numbers in thousands)

		aged 45 to 64				
	total	total	45 to 49	50 to 54	55 to 59	60 to 64
TOTAL ASIAN HOUSEHOLDS	**4,715**	**1,647**	**509**	**475**	**385**	**278**
Family households	**3,451**	**1,349**	**432**	**393**	**314**	**210**
Married couples	2,757	1,143	368	321	268	186
Female householder, no spouse present	452	148	42	51	36	19
Male householder, no spouse present	242	57	22	21	9	5
Nonfamily households	**1,265**	**300**	**77**	**83**	**71**	**69**
Female householder	662	179	43	51	45	40
Living alone	545	164	38	50	39	37
Male householder	602	122	34	32	27	29
Living alone	420	105	30	27	25	23
Percent distribution by type						
TOTAL ASIAN HOUSEHOLDS	**100.0%**	**100.0%**	**100.0%**	**100.0%**	**100.0%**	**100.0%**
Family households	**73.2**	**81.9**	**84.9**	**82.7**	**81.6**	**75.5**
Married couples	58.5	69.4	72.3	67.6	69.6	66.9
Female householder, no spouse present	9.6	9.0	8.3	10.7	9.4	6.8
Male householder, no spouse present	5.1	14.7	4.3	4.6	5.5	1.8
Nonfamily households	**26.8**	**18.2**	**15.1**	**17.5**	**18.4**	**24.8**
Female householder	14.0	10.9	8.4	10.7	11.7	14.4
Living alone	11.6	10.0	7.5	10.5	10.1	13.3
Male householder	12.8	7.4	6.7	6.7	7.0	10.4
Living alone	8.9	6.4	5.9	5.7	6.5	8.3
Percent distribution by age						
TOTAL ASIAN HOUSEHOLDS	**100.0%**	**34.9%**	**10.8%**	**10.1%**	**8.2%**	**5.9%**
Family households	**100.0**	**39.1**	**12.5**	**11.4**	**9.1**	**6.1**
Married couples	100.0	41.5	13.3	11.6	9.7	6.7
Female householder, no spouse present	100.0	32.7	9.3	11.3	8.0	4.2
Male householder, no spouse present	100.0	23.6	9.1	8.7	3.7	2.1
Nonfamily households	**100.0**	**23.7**	**6.1**	**6.6**	**5.6**	**5.5**
Female householder	100.0	27.0	6.5	7.7	6.8	6.0
Living alone	100.0	30.1	7.0	9.2	7.2	6.8
Male householder	100.0	20.3	5.6	5.3	4.5	4.8
Living alone	100.0	25.0	7.1	6.4	6.0	5.5

Note: Asians include those who identify themselves as being of the race alone and those who identify themselves as being of the race in combination with other races.
Source: Bureau of the Census, 2008 Current Population Survey, Annual Social and Economic Supplement, Internet site http://www.census.gov/hhes/www/macro/032008/hhinc/new02_000.htm; calculations by New Strategist

Table 7.3 Households Headed by People Aged 45 to 64 by Household Type, 2008: Black Households

(number and percent distribution of total households headed by blacks and households headed by blacks aged 45 to 64, by household type, 2008; numbers in thousands)

		aged 45 to 64				
	total	total	45 to 49	50 to 54	55 to 59	60 to 64
TOTAL BLACK HOUSEHOLDS	**14,976**	**5,563**	**1,739**	**1,516**	**1,344**	**964**
Family households	**9,503**	**3,487**	**1,188**	**963**	**793**	**543**
Married couples	4,461	2,023	660	540	490	333
Female householder, no spouse present	4,218	1,228	447	355	256	170
Male householder, no spouse present	824	236	81	68	47	40
Nonfamily households	**5,474**	**2,075**	**551**	**552**	**551**	**421**
Female householder	3,064	1,162	283	292	308	279
Living alone	2,748	1,077	242	275	290	270
Male householder	2,410	914	268	261	243	142
Living alone	2,012	775	231	206	209	129
Percent distribution by type						
TOTAL BLACK HOUSEHOLDS	**100.0%**	**100.0%**	**100.0%**	**100.0%**	**100.0%**	**100.0%**
Family households	**63.5**	**62.7**	**68.3**	**63.5**	**59.0**	**56.3**
Married couples	29.8	36.4	38.0	35.6	36.5	34.5
Female householder, no spouse present	28.2	22.1	25.7	23.4	19.0	17.6
Male householder, no spouse present	5.5	4.2	4.7	4.5	3.5	4.1
Nonfamily households	**36.6**	**37.3**	**31.7**	**36.4**	**41.0**	**43.7**
Female householder	20.5	20.9	16.3	19.3	22.9	28.9
Living alone	18.3	19.4	13.9	18.1	21.6	28.0
Male householder	16.1	16.4	15.4	17.2	18.1	14.7
Living alone	13.4	13.9	13.3	13.6	15.6	13.4
Percent distribution by age						
TOTAL BLACK HOUSEHOLDS	**100.0%**	**37.1%**	**11.6%**	**10.1%**	**9.0%**	**6.4%**
Family households	**100.0**	**36.7**	**12.5**	**10.1**	**8.3**	**5.7**
Married couples	100.0	45.3	14.8	12.1	11.0	7.5
Female householder, no spouse present	100.0	29.1	10.6	8.4	6.1	4.0
Male householder, no spouse present	100.0	28.6	9.8	8.3	5.7	4.9
Nonfamily households	**100.0**	**37.9**	**10.1**	**10.1**	**10.1**	**7.7**
Female householder	100.0	37.9	9.2	9.5	10.1	9.1
Living alone	100.0	39.2	8.8	10.0	10.6	9.8
Male householder	100.0	37.9	11.1	10.8	10.1	5.9
Living alone	100.0	38.5	11.5	10.2	10.4	6.4

Note: Blacks include those who identify themselves as being of the race alone and those who identify themselves as being of the race in combination with other races.
Source: Bureau of the Census, 2008 Current Population Survey, Annual Social and Economic Supplement, Internet site http://www.census.gov/hhes/www/macro/032008/hhinc/new02_000.htm; calculations by New Strategist

Table 7.4 Households Headed by People Aged 45 to 64 by Household Type, 2008: Hispanic Households

(number and percent distribution of total households headed by Hispanics and households headed by Hispanics aged 45 to 64, by household type, 2008; numbers in thousands)

		aged 45 to 64				
	total	total	45 to 49	50 to 54	55 to 59	60 to 64
TOTAL HISPANIC HOUSEHOLDS	**13,339**	**3,977**	**1,424**	**1,056**	**868**	**629**
Family households	**10,394**	**3,051**	**1,153**	**819**	**624**	**455**
Married couples	6,888	2,172	780	611	446	335
Female householder, no spouse present	2,522	693	298	154	139	102
Male householder, no spouse present	983	186	75	54	39	18
Nonfamily households	**2,945**	**927**	**271**	**237**	**245**	**174**
Female householder	1,291	443	111	118	110	104
Living alone	1,065	399	87	107	104	101
Male householder	1,654	485	160	120	135	70
Living alone	1,138	393	134	94	112	53
Percent distribution by type						
TOTAL HISPANIC HOUSEHOLDS	**100.0%**	**100.0%**	**100.0%**	**100.0%**	**100.0%**	**100.0%**
Family households	**77.9**	**76.7**	**81.0**	**77.6**	**71.9**	**72.3**
Married couples	51.6	54.6	54.8	57.9	51.4	53.3
Female householder, no spouse present	18.9	17.4	20.9	14.6	16.0	16.2
Male householder, no spouse present	7.4	4.7	5.3	5.1	4.5	2.9
Nonfamily households	**22.1**	**23.3**	**19.0**	**22.4**	**28.2**	**27.7**
Female householder	9.7	11.1	7.8	11.2	12.7	16.5
Living alone	8.0	10.0	6.1	10.1	12.0	16.1
Male householder	12.4	12.2	11.2	11.4	15.6	11.1
Living alone	8.5	9.9	9.4	8.9	12.9	8.4
Percent distribution by age						
TOTAL HISPANIC HOUSEHOLDS	**100.0%**	**29.8%**	**10.7%**	**7.9%**	**6.5%**	**4.7%**
Family households	**100.0**	**29.4**	**11.1**	**7.9**	**6.0**	**4.4**
Married couples	100.0	31.5	11.3	8.9	6.5	4.9
Female householder, no spouse present	100.0	27.5	11.8	6.1	5.5	4.0
Male householder, no spouse present	100.0	18.9	7.6	5.5	4.0	1.8
Nonfamily households	**100.0**	**31.5**	**9.2**	**8.0**	**8.3**	**5.9**
Female householder	100.0	34.3	8.6	9.1	8.5	8.1
Living alone	100.0	37.5	8.2	10.0	9.8	9.5
Male householder	100.0	29.3	9.7	7.3	8.2	4.2
Living alone	100.0	34.5	11.8	8.3	9.8	4.7

Source: Bureau of the Census, 2008 Current Population Survey, Annual Social and Economic Supplement, Internet site http://www.census.gov/hhes/www/macro/032008/hhinc/new02_000.htm; calculations by New Strategist

Table 7.5 Households Headed by People Aged 45 to 64 by Household Type, 2008: Non-Hispanic White Households

(number and percent distribution of total households headed by non-Hispanic whites and households headed by non-Hispanic whites aged 45 to 64, by household type, 2008; numbers in thousands)

		aged 45 to 64				
	total	total	45 to 49	50 to 54	55 to 59	60 to 64
TOTAL NON-HISPANIC WHITE HOUSEHOLDS	82,765	32,815	8,892	8,685	8,126	7,112
Family households	**53,902**	**23,002**	**6,575**	**6,276**	**5,478**	**4,673**
Married couples	43,739	19,412	5,221	5,215	4,791	4,185
Female householder, no spouse present	7,171	2,519	943	744	488	344
Male householder, no spouse present	2,991	1,070	411	317	199	143
Nonfamily households	**28,863**	**9,813**	**2,317**	**2,409**	**2,648**	**2,439**
Female householder	15,844	5,002	1,022	1,155	1,408	1,417
Living alone	13,771	4,438	852	1,023	1,265	1,298
Male householder	13,019	4,814	1,296	1,255	1,240	1,023
Living alone	10,151	4,089	1,075	1,043	1,079	892
Percent distribution by type						
TOTAL NON-HISPANIC WHITE HOUSEHOLDS	100.0%	100.0%	100.0%	100.0%	100.0%	100.0%
Family households	**65.1**	**70.1**	**73.9**	**72.3**	**67.4**	**65.7**
Married couples	52.8	59.2	58.7	60.0	59.0	58.8
Female householder, no spouse present	8.7	7.7	10.6	8.6	6.0	4.8
Male householder, no spouse present	3.6	3.3	4.6	3.6	2.4	2.0
Nonfamily households	**34.9**	**29.9**	**26.1**	**27.7**	**32.6**	**34.3**
Female householder	19.1	15.2	11.5	13.3	17.3	19.9
Living alone	16.6	13.5	9.6	11.8	15.6	18.3
Male householder	15.7	14.7	14.6	14.5	15.3	14.4
Living alone	12.3	12.5	12.1	12.0	13.3	12.5
Percent distribution by age						
TOTAL NON-HISPANIC WHITE HOUSEHOLDS	100.0%	39.6%	10.7%	10.5%	9.8%	8.6%
Family households	**100.0**	**42.7**	**12.2**	**11.6**	**10.2**	**8.7**
Married couples	100.0	44.4	11.9	11.9	11.0	9.6
Female householder, no spouse present	100.0	35.1	13.2	10.4	6.8	4.8
Male householder, no spouse present	100.0	35.8	13.7	10.6	6.7	4.8
Nonfamily households	**100.0**	**34.0**	**8.0**	**8.3**	**9.2**	**8.5**
Female householder	100.0	31.6	6.5	7.3	8.9	8.9
Living alone	100.0	32.2	6.2	7.4	9.2	9.4
Male householder	100.0	37.0	10.0	9.6	9.5	7.9
Living alone	100.0	40.3	10.6	10.3	10.6	8.8

Note: Non-Hispanic whites are only those who identify themselves as being white alone and not Hispanic.
Source: Bureau of the Census, 2008 Current Population Survey, Annual Social and Economic Supplement, Internet site http://www.census.gov/hhes/www/macro/032008/hhinc/new02_000.htm; calculations by New Strategist

Boomer Households Are Shrinking

Household size peaks in the 35-to-39 age group.

The average American household was home to 2.56 people in 2008. Household size peaks among householders aged 35 to 39, who are most likely to have more than one child at home. As householders age into their forties and fifties, the nest empties. The average number of children per household falls below one in the 45-to-49 age group.

Boomer households are shrinking as a growing proportion become empty nesters. The youngest Boomers are exiting the crowded nest stage, with an average of 2.95 people per household in the 45-to-49 age group. The oldest Boomer age group (60 to 64) has only 2.05 people, on average, in their homes.

■ Some Boomers may see their household size rise in the next few years as the economic downturn forces many young adults to return to the family home.

The nest is emptying for householders in their forties and fifties

(average household size by age of householder, 2008)

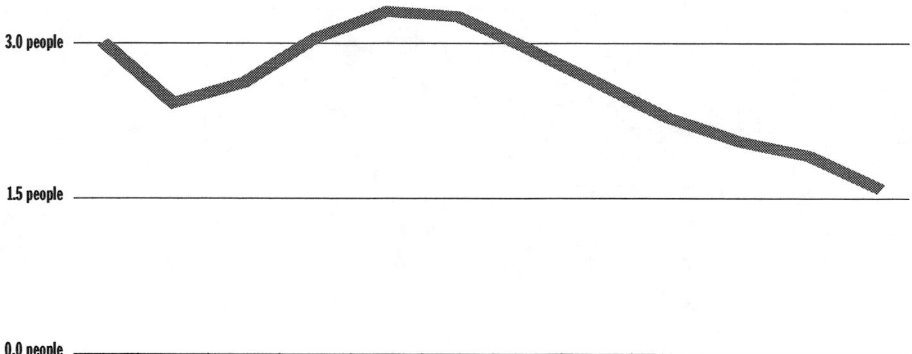

Table 7.6 Average Size of Household by Age of Householder, 2008

(number of households, average number of people per household, and average number of people under age 18 per household, by age of householder, 2008; number of households in thousands)

	number	average number of people	average number of people under age 18
Total households	**116,783**	**2.56**	**0.64**
Under age 20	862	3.01	0.84
Aged 20 to 24	5,691	2.42	0.51
Aged 25 to 29	9,400	2.62	0.80
Aged 30 to 34	9,825	3.05	1.25
Aged 35 to 39	10,900	3.31	1.43
Aged 40 to 44	11,548	3.26	1.25
Aged 45 to 49	12,685	2.95	0.81
Aged 50 to 54	11,851	2.62	0.44
Aged 55 to 59	10,813	2.28	0.23
Aged 60 to 64	9,096	2.05	0.14
Aged 65 to 74	12,284	1.91	0.09
Aged 75 or older	11,829	1.59	0.04

Source: Bureau of the Census, Current Population Survey Annual Social and Economic Supplement, America's Families and Living Arrangements: 2008, detailed tables, Internet site http://www.census.gov/population/www/socdemo/hh-fam/cps2008.html

Most Boomers Are Now Empty-Nesters

Few still have children under age 18 at home.

The 54 percent majority of households headed by people under age 45 include children under age 18. The proportion falls to 43 percent in the 45-to-49 age group and declines sharply with age—meaning that most Boomers are now empty-nesters. Only 24 percent of householders aged 50 to 54 have children under age 18 in their home, and among 55-to 64-year-olds the figure is just 7 percent.

By race and Hispanic origin, Asian Boomers are most likely to have children under age 18 at home. Among Asians householders aged 45 to 49, for example, 61 percent include children under age 18. This compares with only 41 percent of black, 43 percent of non-Hispanic white, and 51 percent of Hispanic households in the age group. Behind the higher figure among Asian Boomers is their postponed childbearing, with most Asians babies born to women aged 30 or older.

■ Although few Boomer households include dependent children, many Boomers have adult children in their home.

Few Boomer households still include children under age 18

(percent of households with children under age 18, by age of householder, 2008)

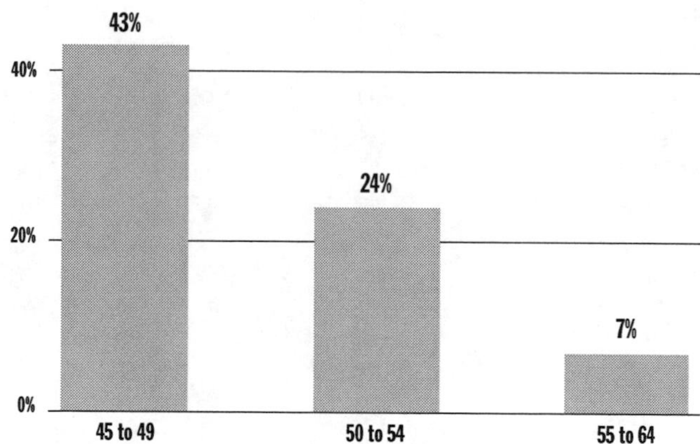

Table 7.7 Households by Type, Age of Householder, and Presence of Children, 2008: Total Households

(total number of households and number and percent with own children under age 18 at home, by household type and age of householder, 2008; numbers in thousands)

		with own children under age 18	
	total	number	percent
TOTAL HOUSEHOLDS	**116,783**	**35,709**	**30.6%**
Under age 45	48,227	25,816	53.5
Aged 45 to 49	12,685	5,489	43.3
Aged 50 to 54	11,851	2,817	23.8
Aged 55 to 64	19,909	1,316	6.6
Aged 65 or older	24,113	272	1.1
Married couples	**58,370**	**25,173**	**43.1**
Under age 45	23,206	17,619	75.9
Aged 45 to 49	7,105	4,175	58.8
Aged 50 to 54	6,737	2,165	32.1
Aged 55 to 64	11,144	1,034	9.3
Aged 65 or older	10,178	179	1.8
Female family householder, no spouse present	**14,404**	**8,374**	**58.1**
Under age 45	7,934	6,654	83.9
Aged 45 to 49	1,736	991	57.1
Aged 50 to 54	1,307	480	36.7
Aged 55 to 64	1,562	191	12.2
Aged 65 or older	1,865	58	3.1
Male family householder, no spouse present	**5,100**	**2,162**	**42.4**
Under age 45	3,074	1,543	50.2
Aged 45 to 49	597	323	54.1
Aged 50 to 54	467	172	36.8
Aged 55 to 64	513	90	17.5
Aged 65 or older	499	35	7.0

Source: Bureau of the Census, Current Population Survey Annual Social and Economic Supplement, America's Families and Living Arrangements: 2008, detailed tables, Internet site http://www.census.gov/population/www/socdemo/hh-fam/cps2008 .html; calculations by New Strategist

Table 7.8 Households by Type, Age of Householder, and Presence of Children, 2008: Asian Households

(total number of Asian households and number and percent with own children under age 18 at home, by household type and age of householder, 2008; numbers in thousands)

	total	with own children under age 18	
		number	percent
TOTAL ASIAN HOUSEHOLDS	**4,715**	**1,743**	**37.0%**
Under age 45	2,463	1,161	47.1
Aged 45 to 49	509	310	60.9
Aged 50 to 54	475	182	38.3
Aged 55 to 64	663	73	11.0
Aged 65 or older	604	16	2.6
Married couples	**2,757**	**1,482**	**53.8**
Under age 45	1,307	961	73.5
Aged 45 to 49	368	284	77.2
Aged 50 to 54	321	155	48.3
Aged 55 to 64	454	68	15.0
Aged 65 or older	305	12	3.9
Female family householder, no spouse present	**452**	**202**	**44.7**
Under age 45	256	156	60.9
Aged 45 to 49	42	22	52.4
Aged 50 to 54	51	20	39.2
Aged 55 to 64	55	5	9.1
Aged 65 or older	49	1	2.0
Male family householder, no spouse present	**242**	**60**	**24.8**
Under age 45	168	45	26.8
Aged 45 to 49	22	4	18.2
Aged 50 to 54	21	7	33.3
Aged 55 to 64	14	1	7.1
Aged 65 or older	16	3	18.8

Note: Asians include those who identify themselves as being of the race alone and those who identify themselves as being of the race in combination with other races.
Source: Bureau of the Census, Current Population Survey Annual Social and Economic Supplement, America's Families and Living Arrangements: 2008, detailed tables, Internet site http://www.census.gov/population/www/socdemo/hh-fam/cps2008.html; calculations by New Strategist

Table 7.9 Households by Type, Age of Householder, and Presence of Children, 2008: Black Households

(total number of black households and number and percent with own children under age 18 at home, by household type and age of householder, 2008; numbers in thousands)

		with own children under age 18	
	total	number	percent
TOTAL BLACK HOUSEHOLDS	**14,976**	**5,078**	**33.9**
Under age 45	8,881	3,901	43.9
Aged 45 to 49	1,516	619	40.8
Aged 50 to 54	1,344	293	21.8
Aged 55 to 64	964	204	21.2
Aged 65 or older	2,272	62	2.7
Married couples	**4,461**	**2,070**	**46.4**
Under age 45	1,854	1,407	75.9
Aged 45 to 49	660	351	53.2
Aged 50 to 54	540	160	29.6
Aged 55 to 64	823	124	15.1
Aged 65 or older	584	29	5.0
Female family householder, no spouse present	**4,218**	**2,694**	**63.9**
Under age 45	2,609	2,260	86.6
Aged 45 to 49	447	235	52.6
Aged 50 to 54	355	114	32.1
Aged 55 to 64	426	64	15.0
Aged 65 or older	381	21	5.5
Male family householder, no spouse present	**824**	**314**	**38.1**
Under age 45	521	234	44.9
Aged 45 to 49	81	32	39.5
Aged 50 to 54	68	20	29.4
Aged 55 to 64	87	16	18.4
Aged 65 or older	67	11	16.4

Note: Blacks include those who identify themselves as being of the race alone and those who identify themselves as being of the race in combination with other races.
Source: Bureau of the Census, Current Population Survey Annual Social and Economic Supplement, America's Families and Living Arrangements: 2008, detailed tables, Internet site http://www.census.gov/population/www/socdemo/hh-fam/cps2008.html; calculations by New Strategist

Table 7.10 Households by Type, Age of Householder, and Presence of Children, 2008: Hispanic Households

(total number of Hispanic households and number and percent with own children under age 18 at home, by household type and age of householder, 2008; numbers in thousands)

	total	with own children under age 18	
		number	percent
TOTAL HISPANIC HOUSEHOLDS	**13,339**	**6,431**	**48.2%**
Under age 45	7,968	5,144	64.6
Aged 45 to 49	1,424	732	51.4
Aged 50 to 54	1,056	321	30.4
Aged 55 to 64	1,497	189	12.6
Aged 65 or older	1,394	46	3.3
Married couples	**6,888**	**4,425**	**64.2**
Under age 45	4,115	3,468	84.3
Aged 45 to 49	780	538	69.0
Aged 50 to 54	611	242	39.6
Aged 55 to 64	781	145	18.6
Aged 65 or older	603	34	5.6
Female family householder, no spouse present	**2,522**	**1,642**	**65.1**
Under age 45	1,652	1,378	83.4
Aged 45 to 49	298	154	51.7
Aged 50 to 54	154	66	42.9
Aged 55 to 64	241	34	14.1
Aged 65 or older	179	11	6.1
Male family householder, no spouse present	**983**	**365**	**37.1**
Under age 45	752	301	40.0
Aged 45 to 49	75	40	53.3
Aged 50 to 54	54	13	24.1
Aged 55 to 64	57	10	17.5
Aged 65 or older	44	1	2.3

Source: Bureau of the Census, Current Population Survey Annual Social and Economic Supplement, America's Families and Living Arrangements: 2008, detailed tables, Internet site http://www.census.gov/population/www/socdemo/hh-fam/cps2008.html; calculations by New Strategist

Table 7.11 Households by Type, Age of Householder, and Presence of Children, 2008: Non-Hispanic White Households

(total number of non-Hispanic white households and number and percent with own children under age 18 at home, by household type and age of householder, 2008; numbers in thousands)

		with own children under age 18	
	total	number	percent
TOTAL NON-HISPANIC WHITE HOUSEHOLDS	**82,765**	**22,221**	**26.8%**
Under age 45	30,325	15,443	50.9
Aged 45 to 49	8,892	3,781	42.5
Aged 50 to 54	8,685	2,002	23.1
Aged 55 to 64	15,238	850	5.6
Aged 65 or older	19,625	145	0.7
Married couples	**43,739**	**16,998**	**38.9**
Under age 45	15,728	11,632	74.0
Aged 45 to 49	5,221	2,970	56.9
Aged 50 to 54	5,215	1,596	30.6
Aged 55 to 64	8,976	698	7.8
Aged 65 or older	8,599	102	1.2
Female family householder, no spouse present	**7,171**	**3,830**	**53.4**
Under age 45	3,417	2,868	83.9
Aged 45 to 49	943	568	60.2
Aged 50 to 54	744	280	37.6
Aged 55 to 64	832	90	10.8
Aged 65 or older	1,235	24	1.9
Male family householder, no spouse present	**2,991**	**1,393**	**46.6**
Under age 45	1,609	942	58.5
Aged 45 to 49	411	243	59.1
Aged 50 to 54	317	127	40.1
Aged 55 to 64	342	61	17.8
Aged 65 or older	312	19	6.1

Note: Non-Hispanic whites are those who identify themselves as being white alone and not Hispanic.
Source: Bureau of the Census, Current Population Survey Annual Social and Economic Supplement, America's Families and Living Arrangements: 2008, detailed tables, Internet site http://www.census.gov/population/www/socdemo/hh-fam/cps2008.html; calculations by New Strategist

Many Boomers Have Adult Children at Home

Nearly one-fourth of householders aged 55 to 64 have children living in their home—most of them adults.

Not only can the nest be slow to empty, but in these economically difficult times it can also refill. Many Boomer households include adult children.

Among householders aged 45 to 49, only 43 percent have children under age 18 at home but the 58 percent majority have children of any age living with them. In the 50-to-54 age group, a still substantial 45 percent have children of any age at home. The figure is 23 percent among householders aged 55 to 64.

■ Boomers head 25 percent of the nation's 17 million households with teenagers aged 12 to 17.

A large share of households headed by Boomers include children of any age

(percent of households with children of any age in the home, by age of householder, 2008)

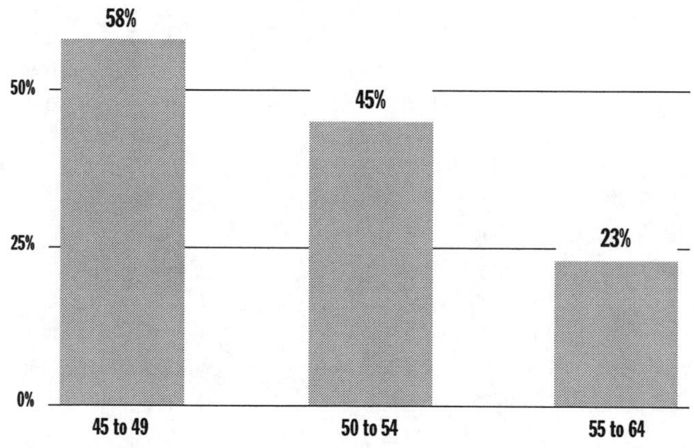

Table 7.12 Households by Presence and Age of Children and Age of Householder, 2008

(number and percent distribution of households by presence of own children at home, by age of children and age of householder, 2008; numbers in thousands)

	total	under 45	45 to 49	50 to 54	55 to 64	65 or older
Total households	**116,783**	**48,227**	**12,685**	**11,851**	**19,909**	**24,113**
With children of any age	46,995	26,716	7,318	5,351	4,643	2,966
Under age 25	41,647	26,670	7,080	4,658	2,765	473
Under age 18	35,709	25,816	5,489	2,817	1,316	272
Under age 12	26,125	22,019	2,582	925	461	138
Under age 6	15,733	14,565	739	219	164	47
Under age 3	9,192	8,748	268	81	75	20
Under age 1	3,401	3,270	76	13	30	12
Aged 12 to 17	16,907	9,329	4,169	2,237	1,001	169
PERCENT DISTRIBUTION BY AGE OF CHILD						
Total households	**100.0%**	**100.0%**	**100.0%**	**100.0%**	**100.0%**	**100.0%**
With children of any age	40.2	55.4	57.7	45.2	23.3	12.3
Under age 25	35.7	55.3	55.8	39.3	13.9	2.0
Under age 18	30.6	53.5	43.3	23.8	6.6	1.1
Under age 12	22.4	45.7	20.4	7.8	2.3	0.6
Under age 6	13.5	30.2	5.8	1.8	0.8	0.2
Under age 3	7.9	18.1	2.1	0.7	0.4	0.1
Under age 1	2.9	6.8	0.6	0.1	0.2	0.0
Aged 12 to 17	14.5	19.3	32.9	18.9	5.0	0.7
PERCENT DISTRIBUTION BY AGE OF HOUSEHOLDER						
Total households	**100.0%**	**41.3%**	**10.9%**	**10.1%**	**17.0%**	**20.6%**
With children of any age	100.0	56.8	15.6	11.4	9.9	6.3
Under age 25	100.0	64.0	17.0	11.2	6.6	1.1
Under age 18	100.0	72.3	15.4	7.9	3.7	0.8
Under age 12	100.0	84.3	9.9	3.5	1.8	0.5
Under age 6	100.0	92.6	4.7	1.4	1.0	0.3
Under age 3	100.0	95.2	2.9	0.9	0.8	0.2
Under age 1	100.0	96.1	2.2	0.4	0.9	0.4
Aged 12 to 17	100.0	55.2	24.7	13.2	5.9	1.0

Source: Bureau of the Census, Current Population Survey Annual Social and Economic Supplement, America's Families and Living Arrangements: 2008, detailed tables, Internet site http://www.census.gov/population/www/socdemo/hh-fam/cps2008.html; calculations by New Strategist

Boomers Account for More than One-Third of People Who Live Alone

The percentage of women who live alone rises steadily as they age.

Among the 32 million Americans who live alone, Boomers account for a substantial 36 percent. In 2008, 15 percent of 45-to-64-year-olds (Boomers were aged 44 to 62 in that year) lived by themselves, about double the percentage among people under age 45.

Boomer women are slightly more likely than Boomer men to live alone, and this becomes increasingly so with age. Among 45-to-49-year-olds, 13 percent of men and 11 percent of women live alone. In the 60-to-64 age group, 16 percent of men and a larger 22 percent of women head single-person households.

■ Because of the higher mortality rate of men, a growing share of Boomer women will become widows and live by themselves in the years ahead.

Women are increasingly likely to live alone as they age

(percent of women aged 45 to 64 who live alone, by age, 2008)

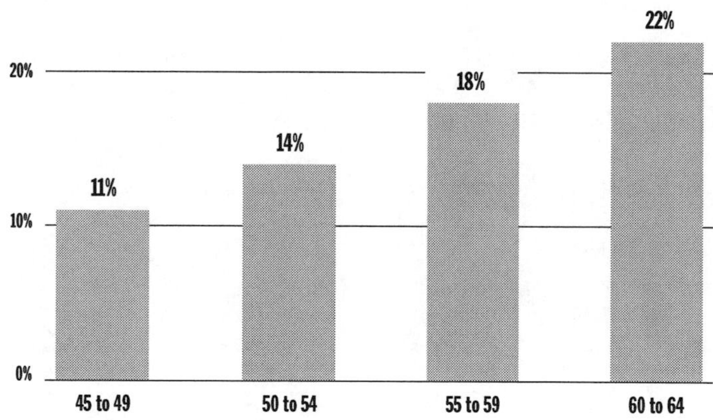

Table 7.13 People Who Live Alone by Sex and Age, 2008

(number of people aged 15 or older and number, percent, and percent distribution of people who live alone by sex and age, 2008; numbers in thousands)

		living alone		
	total	number	percent	percent distribution
Total people	**238,148**	**32,167**	**13.5%**	**100.0%**
Under age 45	124,122	9,379	7.6	29.2
Aged 45 to 64	77,237	11,574	15.0	36.0
Aged 45 to 49	22,701	2,702	11.9	8.4
Aged 50 to 54	21,234	2,877	13.5	8.9
Aged 55 to 59	18,371	3,151	17.2	9.8
Aged 60 to 64	14,931	2,843	19.0	8.8
Aged 65 or older	36,790	11,214	30.5	34.9
Total men	**115,678**	**13,870**	**12.0**	**100.0**
Under age 45	62,298	5,526	8.9	39.8
Aged 45 to 64	37,618	5,427	14.4	39.1
Aged 45 to 49	11,165	1,470	13.2	10.6
Aged 50 to 54	10,374	1,396	13.5	10.1
Aged 55 to 59	8,929	1,448	16.2	10.4
Aged 60 to 64	7,150	1,112	15.6	8.0
Aged 65 or older	15,762	2,917	18.5	21.0
Total women	**122,470**	**18,297**	**14.9**	**100.0**
Under age 45	61,824	3,853	6.2	21.1
Aged 45 to 64	39,619	6,147	15.5	33.6
Aged 45 to 49	11,536	1,232	10.7	6.7
Aged 50 to 54	10,860	1,481	13.6	8.1
Aged 55 to 59	9,442	1,703	18.0	9.3
Aged 60 to 64	7,781	1,731	22.2	9.5
Aged 65 or older	21,028	8,297	39.5	45.3

Source: Bureau of the Census, 2008 Current Population Survey, Annual Social and Economic Supplement, Internet sites http://www.census.gov/hhes/www/macro/032008/perinc/new01_000.htm and http://www.census.gov/hhes/www/macro/032008/hhinc/new02_000.htm; calculations by New Strategist

The Divorced Population Peaks in Middle Age

Most of the divorced eventually remarry.

The proportion of people who are currently divorced peaks among Baby Boomers. Seventeen to 19 percent of women aged 45 to 64 are currently divorced. Among their male counterparts, the figure ranges from 14 to 15 percent. The percentage of Boomers who have ever divorced is much higher than these figures, since many of the divorced have remarried. Despite high rates of divorce, from 63 to 65 percent of women and 65 to 73 percent of men aged 45 to 64 are currently married and living with their spouse.

Older Americans are much less likely than the middle aged to be currently divorced, but they are far more likely to be widowed. Among women age 65 or older, 42 percent are widows.

■ The lifestyles of Baby-Boom men and women will diverge as they enter their late sixties and a growing proportion of women become widows and live alone.

Most Boomers are married

(percent of people aged 45 to 64 who are currently married and living with their spouse, by sex and age, 2008)

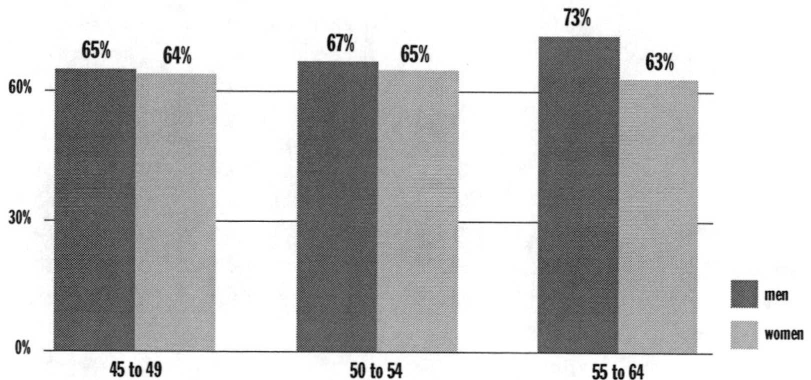

Table 7.14 Marital Status by Sex and Age, 2008: Total People

(number and percent distribution of people aged 15 or older by sex, age, and current marital status, 2008; numbers in thousands)

			married				
	total	never married	spouse present	spouse absent	separated	divorced	widowed
NUMBER							
Total men	**115,599**	**38,685**	**60,129**	**1,944**	**2,144**	**9,782**	**2,916**
Under age 45	62,244	33,731	22,915	1,164	1,104	3,209	122
Aged 45 to 49	11,158	1,822	7,226	191	267	1,580	72
Aged 50 to 54	10,372	1,265	6,991	162	242	1,556	156
Aged 55 to 64	16,072	1,213	11,663	215	333	2,250	398
Aged 65 or older	15,754	653	11,334	212	199	1,189	2,168
Total women	**122,394**	**32,794**	**60,129**	**1,470**	**3,039**	**13,564**	**11,398**
Under age 45	61,777	28,480	26,207	743	1,701	4,259	389
Aged 45 to 49	11,529	1,290	7,345	182	413	2,015	283
Aged 50 to 54	10,860	1,008	7,011	118	346	1,915	462
Aged 55 to 64	17,215	1,181	10,812	179	355	3,225	1,464
Aged 65 or older	21,013	836	8,756	248	224	2,150	8,799
PERCENT DISTRIBUTION							
Total men	**100.0%**	**33.5%**	**52.0%**	**1.7%**	**1.9%**	**8.5%**	**2.5%**
Under age 45	100.0	54.2	36.8	1.9	1.8	5.2	0.2
Aged 45 to 49	100.0	16.3	64.8	1.7	2.4	14.2	0.6
Aged 50 to 54	100.0	12.2	67.4	1.6	2.3	15.0	1.5
Aged 55 to 64	100.0	7.5	72.6	1.3	2.1	14.0	2.5
Aged 65 or older	100.0	4.1	71.9	1.3	1.3	7.5	13.8
Total women	**100.0**	**26.8**	**49.1**	**1.2**	**2.5**	**11.1**	**9.3**
Under age 45	100.0	46.1	42.4	1.2	2.8	6.9	0.6
Aged 45 to 49	100.0	11.2	63.7	1.6	3.6	17.5	2.5
Aged 50 to 54	100.0	9.3	64.6	1.1	3.2	17.6	4.3
Aged 55 to 64	100.0	6.9	62.8	1.0	2.1	18.7	8.5
Aged 65 or older	100.0	4.0	41.7	1.2	1.1	10.2	41.9

Source: Bureau of the Census, Current Population Survey Annual Social and Economic Supplement, America's Families and Living Arrangements: 2008, detailed tables, Internet site http://www.census.gov/population/www/socdemo/hh-fam/cps2008.html; calculations by New Strategist

Regardless of Race, the Middle Aged Are Most Likely to Be Married

At every age, black men and women are least likely to be married.

In the first half of the 20th century, blacks and whites were about equally likely to be married. But as the marriage rate fell, it dropped faster for blacks. Consequently, blacks today are far less likely to be married than Asians, Hispanics, or non-Hispanic whites.

Among black women ranging in age from 45 to 64, only 39 to 41 percent are currently married and living with their spouse. The figure is a higher 55 to 62 percent among Hispanics, 67 to 69 percent among non-Hispanic whites, and peaks at 71 to 77 percent among Asian women in the age group.

Among men in the 45-to-64 age group, blacks and Hispanics are least likely to be married and living with their spouse. Many Hispanic men are married and living apart from their spouse—possibly because they are immigrants who are separated from their wives. Asian men aged 45 to 64 are most likely to be married and living with their wives, with the figure peaking at 82 percent among Asian men aged 50 to 64.

■ The differences in marital status by age, race, and Hispanic origin are a major reason for the diversity of incomes and lifestyles in America today.

Middle-aged black women are least likely to be married

(percent of people aged 50 to 54 who are currrently married and living with their spouse, by race, Hispanic origin, and sex, 2008)

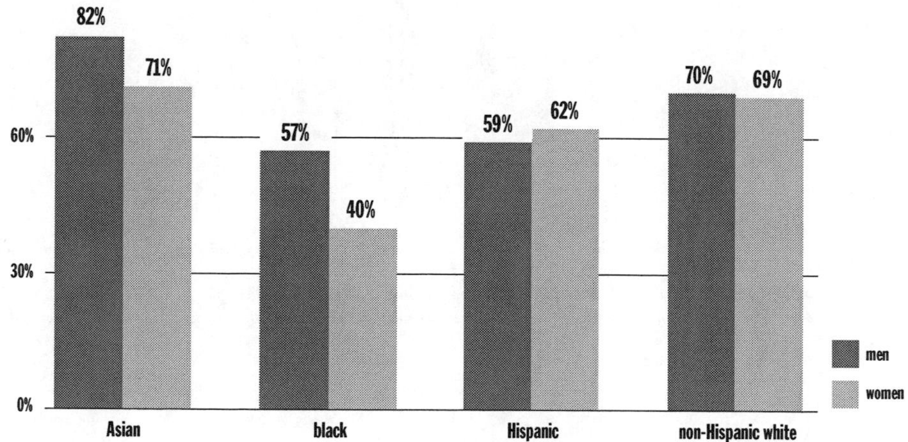

Table 7.15 Marital Status by Sex and Age, 2008: Asians

(number and percent distribution of Asians aged 15 or older by sex, age, and current marital status, 2008; numbers in thousands)

			married				
	total	never married	spouse present	spouse absent	separated	divorced	widowed
NUMBER							
Total Asian men	**5,408**	**1,922**	**2,968**	**202**	**79**	**155**	**83**
Under age 45	3,311	1,768	1,299	125	46	70	5
Aged 45 to 49	508	66	397	20	10	11	4
Aged 50 to 54	426	22	348	18	4	27	5
Aged 55 to 64	604	34	494	24	13	30	9
Aged 65 or older	558	31	430	14	7	16	60
Total Asian women	**6,022**	**1,596**	**3,413**	**158**	**105**	**325**	**424**
Under age 45	3,504	1,447	1,789	88	53	113	16
Aged 45 to 49	546	44	419	13	13	44	13
Aged 50 to 54	504	46	357	18	8	54	21
Aged 55 to 64	732	35	523	24	16	75	60
Aged 65 or older	735	25	326	14	16	41	313
PERCENT DISTRIBUTION							
Total Asian men	**100.0%**	**35.5%**	**54.9%**	**3.7%**	**1.5%**	**2.9%**	**1.5%**
Under age 45	100.0	53.4	39.2	3.8	1.4	2.1	0.2
Aged 45 to 49	100.0	13.0	78.1	3.9	2.0	2.2	0.8
Aged 50 to 54	100.0	5.2	81.7	4.2	0.9	6.3	1.2
Aged 55 to 64	100.0	5.6	81.8	4.0	2.2	5.0	1.5
Aged 65 or older	100.0	77.1	2.5	1.3	2.9	10.8	10.8
Total Asian women	**100.0**	**26.5**	**56.7**	**2.6**	**1.7**	**5.4**	**7.0**
Under age 45	100.0	41.3	51.1	2.5	1.5	3.2	0.5
Aged 45 to 49	100.0	8.1	76.7	2.4	2.4	8.1	2.4
Aged 50 to 54	100.0	9.1	70.8	3.6	1.6	10.7	4.2
Aged 55 to 64	100.0	4.8	71.4	3.3	2.2	10.2	8.2
Aged 65 or older	100.0	3.4	44.4	1.9	2.2	5.6	42.6

Note: Asians include those who identify themselves as being of the race alone and those who identify themselves as being of the race in combination with other races.
Source: Bureau of the Census, Current Population Survey Annual Social and Economic Supplement, America's Families and Living Arrangements: 2008, detailed tables, Internet site http://www.census.gov/population/www/socdemo/hh-fam/cps2008.html; calculations by New Strategist

Table 7.16 Marital Status by Sex and Age, 2008: Blacks

(number and percent distribution of blacks aged 15 or older by sex, age, and current marital status, 2008; numbers in thousands)

			married				
	total	never married	spouse present	spouse absent	separated	divorced	widowed
NUMBER							
Total black men	**13,360**	**6,412**	**4,636**	**241**	**517**	**1,219**	**335**
Under age 45	8,171	5,534	1,798	147	238	427	24
Aged 45 to 49	1,291	349	633	24	69	208	9
Aged 50 to 54	1,130	223	641	20	54	180	13
Aged 55 to 64	1,509	213	873	19	88	242	74
Aged 65 or older	1,258	93	689	32	68	162	214
Total black women	**16,094**	**7,136**	**4,439**	**261**	**820**	**2,034**	**1,404**
Under age 45	9,323	5,980	2,040	147	409	670	78
Aged 45 to 49	1,524	391	623	29	138	298	45
Aged 50 to 54	1,365	310	543	17	112	301	82
Aged 55 to 64	1,926	311	752	29	102	476	254
Aged 65 or older	1,957	144	481	38	58	290	945
PERCENT DISTRIBUTION							
Total black men	**100.0%**	**48.0%**	**34.7%**	**1.8%**	**3.9%**	**9.1%**	**2.5%**
Under age 45	100.0	67.7	22.0	1.8	2.9	5.2	0.3
Aged 45 to 49	100.0	27.0	49.0	1.9	5.3	16.1	0.7
Aged 50 to 54	100.0	19.7	56.7	1.8	4.8	15.9	1.2
Aged 55 to 64	100.0	14.1	57.9	1.3	5.8	16.0	4.9
Aged 65 or older	100.0	7.4	54.8	2.5	5.4	12.9	17.0
Total black women	**100.0**	**44.3**	**27.6**	**1.6**	**5.1**	**12.6**	**8.7**
Under age 45	100.0	64.1	21.9	1.6	4.4	7.2	0.8
Aged 45 to 49	100.0	25.7	40.9	1.9	9.1	19.6	3.0
Aged 50 to 54	100.0	22.7	39.8	1.2	8.2	22.1	6.0
Aged 55 to 64	100.0	16.1	39.0	1.5	5.3	24.7	13.2
Aged 65 or older	100.0	7.4	24.6	1.9	3.0	14.8	48.3

Note: Blacks include those who identify themselves as being of the race alone and those who identify themselves as being of the race in combination with other races.
Source: Bureau of the Census, Current Population Survey Annual Social and Economic Supplement, America's Families and Living Arrangements: 2008, detailed tables, Internet site http://www.census.gov/population/www/socdemo/hh-fam/cps2008.html; calculations by New Strategist

Table 7.17 Marital Status by Sex and Age, 2008: Hispanics

(number and percent distribution of Hispanics aged 15 or older by sex, age, and current marital status, 2008; numbers in thousands)

			married				
	total	never married	spouse present	spouse absent	separated	divorced	widowed
NUMBER							
Total Hispanic men	**16,832**	**6,955**	**7,445**	**820**	**438**	**945**	**228**
Under age 45	11,919	6,307	4,310	591	264	430	19
Aged 45 to 49	1,408	270	843	91	49	143	11
Aged 50 to 54	1,070	195	627	61	45	136	6
Aged 55 to 64	1,341	123	929	43	54	168	23
Aged 65 or older	1,094	60	737	34	27	67	168
Total Hispanic women	**15,845**	**5,066**	**7,557**	**288**	**709**	**1,385**	**839**
Under age 45	10,529	4,585	4,724	182	420	565	53
Aged 45 to 49	1,334	172	781	41	83	208	49
Aged 50 to 54	1,073	98	668	16	76	157	58
Aged 55 to 64	1,448	126	792	31	68	272	158
Aged 65 or older	1,461	85	593	18	61	182	521
PERCENT DISTRIBUTION							
Total Hispanic men	**100.0%**	**41.3%**	**44.2%**	**4.9%**	**2.6%**	**5.6%**	**1.4%**
Under age 45	100.0	52.9	36.2	5.0	2.2	3.6	0.2
Aged 45 to 49	100.0	19.2	59.9	6.5	3.5	10.2	0.8
Aged 50 to 54	100.0	18.2	58.6	5.7	4.2	12.7	0.6
Aged 55 to 64	100.0	9.2	69.3	3.2	4.0	12.5	1.7
Aged 65 or older	100.0	5.5	67.4	3.1	2.5	6.1	15.4
Total Hispanic women	**100.0**	**32.0**	**47.7**	**1.8**	**4.5**	**8.7**	**5.3**
Under age 45	100.0	43.5	44.9	1.7	4.0	5.4	0.5
Aged 45 to 49	100.0	12.9	58.5	3.1	6.2	15.6	3.7
Aged 50 to 54	100.0	9.1	62.3	1.5	7.1	14.6	5.4
Aged 55 to 64	100.0	8.7	54.7	2.1	4.7	18.8	10.9
Aged 65 or older	100.0	5.8	40.6	1.2	4.2	12.5	35.7

Source: Bureau of the Census, Current Population Survey Annual Social and Economic Supplement, America's Families and Living Arrangements: 2008, detailed tables, Internet site http://www.census.gov/population/www/socdemo/hh-fam/cps2008 .html; calculations by New Strategist

Table 7.18 Marital Status by Sex and Age, 2008: Non-Hispanic Whites

(number and percent distribution of non-Hispanic whites aged 15 or older by sex, age, and current marital status, 2008; numbers in thousands)

			married				
	total	never married	spouse present	spouse absent	separated	divorced	widowed
NUMBER							
Total non-Hispanic white men	**79,043**	**23,142**	**44,570**	**681**	**1,099**	**7,309**	**2,242**
Under age 45	38,395	19,904	15,330	300	551	2,239	72
Aged 45 to 49	7,839	1,126	5,271	62	143	1,189	48
Aged 50 to 54	7,657	815	5,325	62	132	1,197	126
Aged 55 to 64	12,446	832	9,260	125	177	1,764	289
Aged 65 or older	12,706	466	9,384	132	96	920	1,707
Total non-Hispanic white women	**83,479**	**18,794**	**44,246**	**757**	**1,401**	**9,642**	**8,639**
Under age 45	37,993	16,281	17,482	325	823	2,845	238
Aged 45 to 49	8,014	680	5,450	98	175	1,433	178
Aged 50 to 54	7,809	546	5,381	65	151	1,374	292
Aged 55 to 64	12,950	711	8,641	95	161	2,371	971
Aged 65 or older	16,714	577	7,293	175	91	1,618	6,959
PERCENT DISTRIBUTION							
Total non-Hispanic white men	**100.0%**	**29.3%**	**56.4%**	**0.9%**	**1.4%**	**9.2%**	**2.8%**
Under age 45	100.0	51.8	39.9	0.8	1.4	5.8	0.2
Aged 45 to 49	100.0	14.4	67.2	0.8	1.8	15.2	0.6
Aged 50 to 54	100.0	10.6	69.5	0.8	1.7	15.6	1.6
Aged 55 to 64	100.0	6.7	74.4	1.0	1.4	14.2	2.3
Aged 65 or older	100.0	3.7	73.9	1.0	0.8	7.2	13.4
Total non-Hispanic white women	**100.0**	**22.5**	**53.0**	**0.9**	**1.7**	**11.6**	**10.3**
Under age 45	100.0	42.9	46.0	0.9	2.2	7.5	0.6
Aged 45 to 49	100.0	8.5	68.0	1.2	2.2	17.9	2.2
Aged 50 to 54	100.0	7.0	68.9	0.8	1.9	17.6	3.7
Aged 55 to 64	100.0	5.5	66.7	0.7	1.2	18.3	7.5
Aged 65 or older	100.0	3.5	43.6	1.0	0.5	9.7	41.6

Note: Non-Hispanic whites are those who identify themselves as being white alone and not Hispanic.
Source: Bureau of the Census, Current Population Survey Annual Social and Economic Supplement, America's Families and Living Arrangements: 2008, detailed tables, Internet site http://www.census.gov/population/www/socdemo/hh-fam/cps2008.html; calculations by New Strategist

Divorce Is Highest among Men and Women in Their Fifties

The oldest boomers are most likely to have gone through a divorce.

The experience of divorce is most common among men and women aged 50 to 59. Among men in the age group in 2004, 37.5 percent had ever divorced, according to a Census Bureau study of marriage and divorce. The percentage of women in the age group, who had ever divorced was an even higher 40.7 percent.

Among all Americans aged 15 or older, 41 percent of women and 44 percent of men had married once and were still married. The figure topped 50 percent for men aged 30 or older and for women aged 30 to 39.

■ Government studies have suggested that the Vietnam War and women's changing roles are factors in the higher divorce rates of boomers.

More than one in five adults have experienced divorce

(percent of people aged 15 or older, by selected marital history and sex, 2004)

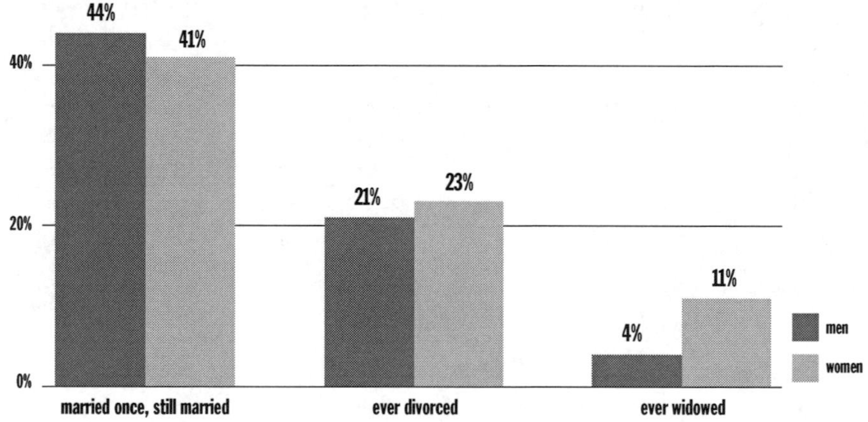

Table 7.19 Marital History of Men by Age, 2004

(number of men aged 15 or older and percent distribution by marital history and age, 2004; numbers in thousands)

	total	15–19	20–24	25–29	30–34	35–39	40–49	50–59	60–69	70+
TOTAL MEN, NUMBER	**109,830**	**10,473**	**10,022**	**9,511**	**9,848**	**10,121**	**21,857**	**17,352**	**10,571**	**10,075**
TOTAL MEN, PERCENT	**100.0%**	**100.0%**	**100.0%**	**100.0%**	**100.0%**	**100.0%**	**100.0%**	**100.0%**	**100.0%**	**100.0%**
Never married	**31.2**	**98.1**	**84.0**	**53.6**	**30.3**	**20.2**	**14.1**	**8.7**	**4.8**	**3.2**
Ever married	**68.8**	**1.9**	**16.0**	**46.4**	**69.7**	**79.8**	**85.9**	**91.3**	**95.2**	**96.8**
Married once	54.0	1.9	15.9	44.3	62.4	68.1	66.8	63.4	66.8	74.9
Still married	43.8	1.5	14.4	39.7	54.4	56.6	52.8	50.3	54.7	55.1
Married twice	11.8	0.0	0.1	2.0	6.7	10.3	15.7	21.3	20.6	17.0
Still married	9.2	0.0	0.1	1.9	6.0	8.5	12.5	16.1	16.1	12.6
Married three or more times	3.1	0.0	0.0	0.1	0.6	1.4	3.3	6.6	7.7	4.9
Still married	2.3	0.0	0.0	0.0	0.4	1.2	2.7	5.1	5.6	3.1
Ever divorced	20.7	0.1	0.8	5.1	13.1	20.7	30.3	37.5	34.1	20.6
Currently divorced	9.3	0.1	0.7	3.2	6.6	10.9	14.7	16.2	13.0	6.2
Ever widowed	3.6	0.2	0.0	0.1	0.1	0.6	1.1	2.8	7.1	23.8
Currently widowed	2.5	0.2	0.0	0.0	0.1	0.4	0.6	1.4	4.2	18.9

Source: Bureau of the Census, Number, Timing, and Duration of Marriages and Divorces: 2004, Detailed Tables, Internet site http://www.census.gov/population/www/socdemo/marr-div/2004detailed_tables.html

Table 7.20 Marital History of Women by Age, 2004

(number of women aged 15 or older and percent distribution by marital history and age, 2004; numbers in thousands)

	total	15–19	20–24	25–29	30–34	35–39	40–49	50–59	60–69	70+
TOTAL WOMEN, NUMBER	**117,677**	**10,082**	**10,027**	**9,484**	**10,097**	**10,319**	**22,818**	**18,412**	**11,852**	**14,586**
TOTAL WOMEN, PERCENT	**100.0%**	**100.0%**	**100.0%**	**100.0%**	**100.0%**	**100.0%**	**100.0%**	**100.0%**	**100.0%**	**100.0%**
Never married	**25.8**	**97.3**	**73.3**	**41.3**	**22.3**	**16.2**	**11.9**	**7.6**	**4.3**	**4.9**
Ever married	**74.2**	**2.7**	**26.7**	**58.7**	**77.7**	**83.8**	**88.1**	**92.4**	**95.7**	**95.1**
Married once	57.9	2.7	25.8	55.5	68.4	67.5	65.3	62.8	71.1	77.4
Still married	40.6	2.4	23.0	48.6	57.6	54.6	49.7	44.4	46.2	29.0
Married twice	13.2	0.1	0.8	3.1	8.2	14.1	18.9	22.6	18.7	14.9
Still married	8.8	0.0	0.7	2.8	6.6	11.3	14.0	15.5	11.3	5.3
Married three or more times	3.1	0.0	0.0	0.1	1.2	2.2	3.9	7.0	5.9	2.8
Still married	1.9	0.0	0.0	0.1	0.8	1.6	2.8	4.4	3.6	1.0
Ever divorced	22.9	0.2	2.5	7.0	17.1	25.6	33.9	40.7	32.3	17.8
Currently divorced	10.9	0.1	1.7	4.1	9.1	11.7	16.4	19.4	15.0	7.2
Ever widowed	10.8	0.1	0.1	0.3	0.7	1.1	2.5	7.8	21.2	54.5
Currently widowed	9.6	0.1	0.1	0.2	0.5	0.9	1.6	5.7	18.0	51.6

Source: Bureau of the Census, Number, Timing, and Duration of Marriages and Divorces: 2004, Detailed Tables, Internet site http://www.census.gov/population/www/socdemo/marr-div/2004detailed_tables.html

CHAPTER
8

Population

■ The nation's 76 million Baby Boomers (born between 1946 and 1964) account for 25 percent of the U.S. population. They are the largest generation of Americans.

■ Between 2008 and 2025, the number of people aged 65 or older (Boomers will be aged 61 to 79 in 2025) will expand by an enormous 64 percent—a gain of more than 25 million people.

■ Seventy-two percent of the Baby-Boom generation is non-Hispanic white, greater than the 66 percent share among the population as a whole. But Boomers are much less diverse than younger Americans.

■ Among the 11 million foreign-born in the 45-to-64 age group, 48 percent were born in Latin America—including the 23 percent who were born in Mexico.

■ Millennials outnumber Boomers in a number of states, many of them with large Hispanic populations such as Arizona, California, and Texas.

Boomers Are the Largest Generation

But Millennials are not far behind.

The Baby-Boom generation numbers 76 million, a figure that includes everyone born between 1946 and 1964 (aged 44 to 62 in 2008). Boomers account for 25 percent of the total population, making them the largest generation—but not by much. Millennials, most of them children of Boomers, are in second place. They numbered just under 76 million in 2008 and accounted for slightly less than 25 percent of the population.

Between 2000 and 2008, the oldest Boomers entered the 55-to-64 age group. During those years, the number of 55-to-59-year-olds grew by 38 percent and the number of 60-to-64-year-olds grew by 40 percent—making them the two fastest-growing age groups. In contrast, as Boomers began to exit the 40-to-44 age group, it shrank by 4 percent.

Between 2008 and 2025, the number of people aged 65 or older (Boomers will be aged 61 to 79 in 2025) will expand by an enormous 25 million. As it ages, the Boomer population will shrink, falling from the 76 million of 2008 to 66 million in 2025. Boomers will no longer be the largest generation, falling behind Millennials.

■ Although the oldest Boomers are already eligible for (early) Social Security and will soon be eligible for Medicare, many will postpone retirement because of the economic downturn.

The number of older Americans will expand rapidly

(number of people aged 65 or older, 2008 and 2025)

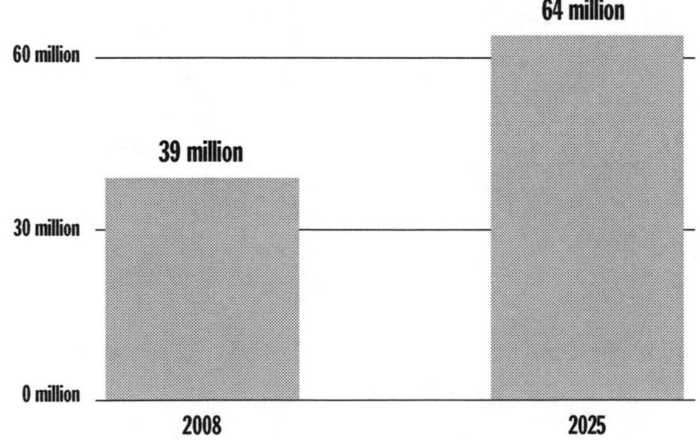

Table 8.1 Population by Age and Generation, 2008

(number and percent distribution of people by age and generation, 2008; numbers in thousands)

	number	percent distribution
Total people	**304,060**	**100.0%**
Under age 5	21,006	6.9
Aged 5 to 9	20,065	6.6
Aged 10 to 14	20,055	6.6
Aged 15 to 19	21,514	7.1
Aged 20 to 24	21,059	6.9
Aged 25 to 29	21,334	7.0
Aged 30 to 34	19,598	6.4
Aged 35 to 39	20,994	6.9
Aged 40 to 44	21,507	7.1
Aged 45 to 64	78,058	25.7
Aged 45 to 49	22,880	7.5
Aged 50 to 54	21,492	7.1
Aged 55 to 59	18,583	6.1
Aged 60 to 64	15,103	5.0
Aged 65 to 69	11,349	3.7
Aged 70 to 74	8,774	2.9
Aged 75 to 79	7,275	2.4
Aged 80 to 84	5,750	1.9
Aged 85 or older	5,722	1.9
Total people	**304,060**	**100.0**
iGeneration (under age 14)	57,115	18.8
Millennial (aged 14 to 31)	75,757	24.9
Generation X (aged 32 to 43)	49,958	16.4
Baby Boom (aged 44 to 62)	76,319	25.1
Older Americans (aged 63 or older)	44,911	14.8

Source: Bureau of the Census, Population Estimates, Internet site http://www.census.gov/popest/national/asrh/NC-EST2008-sa.html; calculations by New Strategist

Table 8.2 Population by Age and Sex, 2008

(number of people by age and sex, and sex ratio by age, 2008; numbers in thousands)

	total	female	male	sex ratio
Total people	**304,060**	**154,135**	**149,925**	**97**
Under age 5	21,006	10,258	10,748	105
Aged 5 to 9	20,065	9,806	10,259	105
Aged 10 to 14	20,055	9,792	10,262	105
Aged 15 to 19	21,514	10,487	11,027	105
Aged 20 to 24	21,059	10,214	10,845	106
Aged 25 to 29	21,334	10,393	10,941	105
Aged 30 to 34	19,598	9,639	9,959	103
Aged 35 to 39	20,994	10,425	10,569	101
Aged 40 to 44	21,507	10,762	10,746	100
Aged 45 to 64	78,058	39,955	38,103	95
Aged 45 to 49	22,880	11,566	11,314	98
Aged 50 to 54	21,492	10,954	10,539	96
Aged 55 to 59	18,583	9,569	9,015	94
Aged 60 to 64	15,103	7,867	7,236	92
Aged 65 to 69	11,349	6,042	5,306	88
Aged 70 to 74	8,774	4,816	3,959	82
Aged 75 to 79	7,275	4,178	3,097	74
Aged 80 to 84	5,750	3,510	2,239	64
Aged 85 or older	5,722	3,858	1,864	48

Note: The sex ratio is the number of males per 100 females.
Source: Bureau of the Census, Population Estimates, Internet site http://www.census.gov/popest/national/asrh/NC-EST2008-sa.html; calculations by New Strategist

Table 8.3 Population by Age, 2000 and 2008

(number of people by age, 2000 and 2008; percent change, 2000–08)

	2008	2000	percent change 2000–08
Total people	**304,060**	**281,422**	**8.0%**
Under age 5	21,006	19,176	9.5
Aged 5 to 9	20,065	20,550	–2.4
Aged 10 to 14	20,055	20,528	–2.3
Aged 15 to 19	21,514	20,220	6.4
Aged 20 to 24	21,059	18,964	11.0
Aged 25 to 29	21,334	19,381	10.1
Aged 30 to 34	19,598	20,510	–4.4
Aged 35 to 39	20,994	22,707	–7.5
Aged 40 to 44	21,507	22,442	–4.2
Aged 45 to 49	22,880	20,092	13.9
Aged 50 to 54	21,492	17,586	22.2
Aged 55 to 59	18,583	13,469	38.0
Aged 60 to 64	15,103	10,805	39.8
Aged 65 to 69	11,349	9,534	19.0
Aged 70 to 74	8,774	8,857	–0.9
Aged 75 to 79	7,275	7,416	–1.9
Aged 80 to 84	5,750	4,945	16.3
Aged 85 or older	5,722	4,240	35.0
Aged 18 to 24	29,757	27,143	9.6
Aged 18 or older	230,118	209,128	10.0
Aged 65 or older	38,870	34,992	11.1

Source: Bureau of the Census, National Population Estimates, Internet site http://www.census.gov/popest/national/asrh/ NC-EST2008-asrh.html; calculations by New Strategist

Table 8.4 Population by Age, 2008 to 2025

(number of people by age, 2008 to 2025; percent change for selected years; numbers in thousands)

	2008	2010	2015	2025	percent change 2008–10	2008–15	2008–25
Total people	**304,060**	**310,233**	**325,540**	**357,452**	**2.0%**	**7.1%**	**17.6%**
Under age 5	21,006	21,100	22,076	23,484	0.4	5.1	11.8
Aged 5 to 9	20,065	20,886	21,707	23,548	4.1	8.2	17.4
Aged 10 to 14	20,055	20,395	21,658	23,677	1.7	8.0	18.1
Aged 15 to 19	21,514	21,770	21,209	23,545	1.2	–1.4	9.4
Aged 20 to 24	21,059	21,779	22,342	23,168	3.4	6.1	10.0
Aged 25 to 29	21,334	21,418	22,400	22,417	0.4	5.0	5.1
Aged 30 to 34	19,598	20,400	22,099	23,699	4.1	12.8	20.9
Aged 35 to 39	20,994	20,267	20,841	23,645	–3.5	–0.7	12.6
Aged 40 to 44	21,507	21,010	20,460	22,851	–2.3	–4.9	6.2
Aged 45 to 49	22,880	22,596	21,001	21,154	–1.2	–8.2	–7.5
Aged 50 to 54	21,492	22,109	22,367	20,404	2.9	4.1	–5.1
Aged 55 to 59	18,583	19,517	21,682	20,575	5.0	16.7	10.7
Aged 60 to 64	15,103	16,758	18,861	21,377	11.0	24.9	41.5
Aged 65 or older	38,870	40,229	46,837	63,907	3.5	20.5	64.4
Aged 65 to 69	11,349	12,261	15,812	19,957	8.0	39.3	75.9
Aged 70 to 74	8,774	9,202	11,155	16,399	4.9	27.1	86.9
Aged 75 to 79	7,275	7,282	7,901	12,598	0.1	8.6	73.2
Aged 80 to 84	5,750	5,733	5,676	7,715	–0.3	–1.3	34.2
Aged 85 or older	5,722	5,751	6,292	7,239	0.5	10.0	26.5

Source: Bureau of the Census, 2008 National Population Projections, Internet site http://www.census.gov/population/www/projections/2008projections.html; calculations by New Strategist

Table 8.5 Population by Generation, 2008 to 2025

(number and percent distribution of people by generation, 2008 to 2025; numbers in thousands)

	number	percent distribution
2008		
Total people	**304,060**	**100.0%**
iGeneration (under age 14)	57,115	18.8
Millennial (aged 14 to 31)	75,757	24.9
Generation X (aged 32 to 43)	49,958	16.4
Baby Boom (aged 44 to 62)	76,319	25.1
Older Americans (aged 63 or older)	44,911	14.8
2010		
Total people	**310,233**	**100.0**
iGeneration (under age 16)	66,594	21.5
Millennial (aged 16 to 33)	77,248	24.9
Generation X (aged 34 to 45)	49,651	16.0
Baby Boom (aged 46 to 64)	76,511	24.7
Older Americans (aged 65 or older)	40,229	13.0
2015		
Total people	**325,540**	**100.0**
iGeneration (under age 21)	91,002	28.0
Millennial (aged 21 to 38)	79,357	24.4
Generation X (aged 39 to 50)	49,872	15.3
Baby Boom (aged 51 to 69)	74,284	22.8
Older Americans (aged 70 or older)	31,025	9.5
2025		
Total people	**357,452**	**100.0**
iGeneration (under age 31)	144,444	40.4
Millennial (aged 31 to 48)	82,736	23.1
Generation X (aged 49 to 60)	49,278	13.8
Baby Boom (aged 61 to 79)	66,041	18.5
Older Americans (aged 80 or older)	14,953	4.2

Source: Bureau of the Census, 2008 National Population Projections, Internet site http://www.census.gov/population/www/projections/2008projections.html; calculations by New Strategist"

Boomers Are Less Diverse than Younger Americans

They are more diverse than older generations, however.

Seventy-two percent of the Baby-Boom generation is non-Hispanic white, according to the Census Bureau. This figure is greater than the 66 percent for the population as a whole and far surpasses the share among the youngest Americans—only 53 percent of children under age 5 are non-Hispanic white. The Baby-Boom generation is more diverse than older Americans, however. Among people aged 85 or older in 2008, fully 84 percent were non-Hispanic white.

Boomers are the largest generation only among non-Hispanic whites, accounting for 28 percent of the non-Hispanic white total. Among Asians, Millennials outnumber Boomers. Among blacks, both the iGeneration and Millennials outnumber Boomers. Among Hispanics, even Generation X outnumbers Boomers.

■ The differing racial and ethnic makeup of Boomers versus younger generations of Americans may create political problems in the years ahead.

Nearly three out of four Baby Boomers are non-Hispanic white

(non-Hispanic white share of population by generation, 2008)

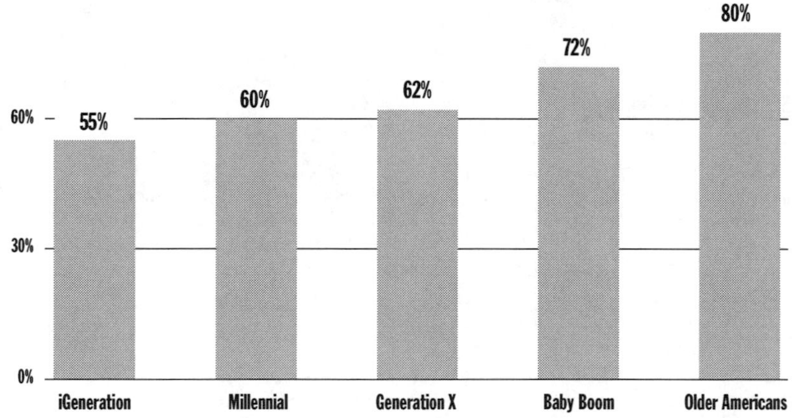

Table 8.6 Population by Age, Race, and Hispanic Origin, 2008

(number and percent distribution of people by age, race, and Hispanic origin, 2008; numbers in thousands)

	total	Asian	black	Hispanic	non-Hispanic white
Total people	**304,060**	**15,480**	**41,127**	**46,944**	**199,491**
Under age 5	21,006	1,242	3,573	5,288	11,065
Aged 5 to 9	20,065	1,107	3,298	4,464	11,222
Aged 10 to 14	20,055	1,033	3,363	3,989	11,660
Aged 15 to 19	21,514	1,018	3,667	3,850	12,903
Aged 20 to 24	21,059	1,027	3,307	3,663	12,949
Aged 25 to 29	21,334	1,206	3,166	4,141	12,740
Aged 30 to 34	19,598	1,334	2,724	4,041	11,456
Aged 35 to 39	20,994	1,404	2,823	3,730	12,981
Aged 40 to 44	21,507	1,210	2,847	3,279	14,085
Aged 45 to 64	78,058	3,534	8,984	7,836	57,192
Aged 45 to 49	22,880	1,107	2,882	2,795	15,964
Aged 50 to 54	21,492	986	2,563	2,187	15,615
Aged 55 to 59	18,583	829	2,068	1,650	13,907
Aged 60 to 64	15,103	612	1,471	1,204	11,706
Aged 65 to 69	11,349	443	1,075	853	8,899
Aged 70 to 74	8,774	339	829	653	6,899
Aged 75 to 79	7,275	255	614	496	5,871
Aged 80 to 84	5,750	176	438	346	4,763
Aged 85 or older	5,722	154	419	313	4,807
PERCENT DISTRIBUTION BY RACE AND HISPANIC ORIGIN					
Total people	**100.0%**	**5.1%**	**13.5%**	**15.4%**	**65.6%**
Under age 5	100.0	5.9	17.0	25.2	52.7
Aged 5 to 9	100.0	5.5	16.4	22.2	55.9
Aged 10 to 14	100.0	5.1	16.8	19.9	58.1
Aged 15 to 19	100.0	4.7	17.0	17.9	60.0
Aged 20 to 24	100.0	4.9	15.7	17.4	61.5
Aged 25 to 29	100.0	5.7	14.8	19.4	59.7
Aged 30 to 34	100.0	6.8	13.9	20.6	58.5
Aged 35 to 39	100.0	6.7	13.4	17.8	61.8
Aged 40 to 44	100.0	5.6	13.2	15.2	65.5
Aged 45 to 64	100.0	4.5	11.5	10.0	73.3
Aged 45 to 49	100.0	4.8	12.6	12.2	69.8
Aged 50 to 54	100.0	4.6	11.9	10.2	72.7
Aged 55 to 59	100.0	4.5	11.1	8.9	74.8
Aged 60 to 64	100.0	4.1	9.7	8.0	77.5
Aged 65 to 69	100.0	3.9	9.5	7.5	78.4
Aged 70 to 74	100.0	3.9	9.5	7.4	78.6
Aged 75 to 79	100.0	3.5	8.4	6.8	80.7
Aged 80 to 84	100.0	3.1	7.6	6.0	82.8
Aged 85 or older	100.0	2.7	7.3	5.5	84.0

Note: Numbers do not add to total because Asians and blacks include those who identified themselves as being of the race alone and those who identified themselves as being of the race in combination with other races, and because Hispanics may be of any race. Non-Hispanic whites are those who identified themselves as being white alone and not Hispanic.
Source: Bureau of the Census, Population Estimates, Internet site http://www.census.gov/popest/national/asrh/NC-EST2008-sa.html; calculations by New Strategist

Table 8.7 Population by Generation, Race, and Hispanic Origin, 2008

(number and percent distribution of people by generation, race, and Hispanic origin, 2008; numbers in thousands)

	total	Asian	black	Hispanic	non-Hispanic white
Total people	**304,060**	**15,480**	**41,127**	**46,944**	**199,491**
iGeneration (under age 14)	57,115	3,174	9,562	12,944	31,615
Millennial (aged 14 to 31)	75,757	3,991	11,902	14,068	45,506
Generation X (aged 32 to 43)	49,958	3,172	6,735	8,778	31,123
Baby Boom (aged 44 to 62)	76,319	3,531	8,965	8,011	55,326
Older Americans (aged 63 or older)	44,911	1,612	3,964	3,143	35,920
PERCENT DISTRIBUTION BY RACE AND HISPANIC ORIGIN					
Total people	**100.0%**	**5.1%**	**13.5%**	**15.4%**	**65.6%**
iGeneration (under age 14)	100.0	5.6	16.7	22.7	55.4
Millennial (aged 14 to 31)	100.0	5.3	15.7	18.6	60.1
Generation X (aged 32 to 43)	100.0	6.3	13.5	17.6	62.3
Baby Boom (aged 44 to 62)	100.0	4.6	11.7	10.5	72.5
Older Americans (aged 63 or older)	100.0	3.6	8.8	7.0	80.0
PERCENT DISTRIBUTION BY GENERATION					
Total people	**100.0%**	**100.0%**	**100.0%**	**100.0%**	**100.0%**
iGeneration (under age 14)	18.8	20.5	23.2	27.6	15.8
Millennial (aged 14 to 31)	24.9	25.8	28.9	30.0	22.8
Generation X (aged 32 to 43)	16.4	20.5	16.4	18.7	15.6
Baby Boom (aged 44 to 62)	25.1	22.8	21.8	17.1	27.7
Older Americans (aged 63 or older)	14.8	10.4	9.6	6.7	18.0

Note: Numbers do not add to total because Asians and blacks include those who identified themselves as being of the race alone and those who identified themselves as being of the race in combination with other races, and because Hispanics may be of any race. Non-Hispanic whites are those who identified themselves as being white alone and not Hispanic.
Source: Bureau of the Census, Population Estimates, Internet site http://www.census.gov/popest/national/asrh/NC-EST2008-sa.html; calculations by New Strategist

Many Boomers Live in Their State of Birth

One in seven is foreign-born.

According to the 2007 American Community Survey, 50 percent of people aged 45 to 64 (Boomers were aged 43 to 61 in that year) were born in their state of current residence—a figure nearly identical to the one among U.S. residents aged 65 or older. Thirty-five percent of Boomers were born in the United States, but in a different state. Fourteen percent were born in another country—a slightly greater share than the 13 percent of all U.S. residents who are foreign-born.

Among the foreign-born in the 45-to-64 age group, 48 percent were born in Latin America—including 23 percent who were born in Mexico. Thirty percent were born in Asia, and only 15 percent are from Europe. Within the 45-to-64 age group, the figures vary considerably, with those in the younger half more likely to be from Latin America and those in the older half more likely to be from Europe.

■ The foreign-born population adds to the multicultural mix, which is becoming a significant factor in American business and politics.

Nearly half of the foreign-born in the 45-to-64 age group are from Latin America

(percent distribution of the foreign-born aged 45 to 64, by region of birth, 2008)

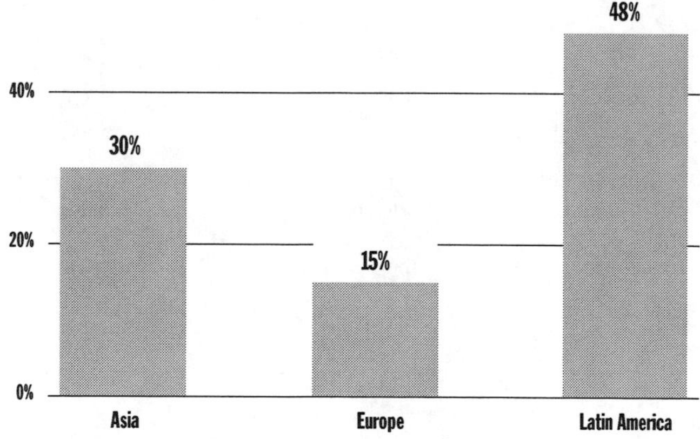

Table 8.8 Population by Age and Place of Birth, 2007

(number and percent distribution of people by age and place of birth, 2007; numbers in thousands)

		born in the United States			
	total	in state of current residence	outside state of current residence	citizen born outside United states	foreign-born
Total people	**301,621**	**177,509**	**82,253**	**3,799**	**38,060**
Under age 18	73,908	59,667	10,643	625	2,973
Aged 18 to 24	29,821	18,880	7,062	395	3,484
Aged 25 to 34	39,987	20,889	10,532	611	7,955
Aged 35 to 44	43,410	21,083	13,067	692	8,569
Aged 45 to 64	76,654	38,406	26,565	1,082	10,601
Aged 45 to 54	43,925	22,275	14,527	669	6,455
Aged 55 to 59	18,115	9,091	6,455	233	2,335
Aged 60 to 61	6,495	3,138	2,442	87	828
Aged 62 to 64	8,119	3,902	3,140	94	983
Aged 65 or older	37,841	18,584	14,385	394	4,478
PERCENT DISTRIBUTION BY PLACE OF BIRTH					
Total people	**100.0%**	**58.9%**	**27.3%**	**1.3%**	**12.6%**
Under age 18	100.0	80.7	14.4	0.8	4.0
Aged 18 to 24	100.0	63.3	23.7	1.3	11.7
Aged 25 to 34	100.0	52.2	26.3	1.5	19.9
Aged 35 to 44	100.0	48.6	30.1	1.6	19.7
Aged 45 to 64	100.0	50.1	34.7	1.4	13.8
Aged 45 to 54	100.0	50.7	33.1	1.5	14.7
Aged 55 to 59	100.0	50.2	35.6	1.3	12.9
Aged 60 to 61	100.0	48.3	37.6	1.3	12.8
Aged 62 to 64	100.0	48.1	38.7	1.2	12.1
Aged 65 or older	100.0	49.1	38.0	1.0	11.8
PERCENT DISTRIBUTION BY AGE					
Total people	**100.0%**	**100.0%**	**100.0%**	**100.0%**	**100.0%**
Under age 18	24.5	33.6	12.9	16.4	7.8
Aged 18 to 24	9.9	10.6	8.6	10.4	9.2
Aged 25 to 34	13.3	11.8	12.8	16.1	20.9
Aged 35 to 44	14.4	11.9	15.9	18.2	22.5
Aged 45 to 64	25.4	21.6	32.3	28.5	27.9
Aged 45 to 54	14.6	12.5	17.7	17.6	17.0
Aged 55 to 59	6.0	5.1	7.8	6.1	6.1
Aged 60 to 61	2.2	1.8	3.0	2.3	2.2
Aged 62 to 64	2.7	2.2	3.8	2.5	2.6
Aged 65 or older	12.5	10.5	17.5	10.4	11.8

Source: Bureau of the Census, 2007 American Community Survey, Internet site http://factfinder.census.gov/home/saff/main.html?_lang=en; calculations by New Strategist

Table 8.9 Foreign-Born Population by Age and World Region of Birth, 2007

(number and percent distribution of foreign-born by age and world region of birth, 2007; numbers in thousands)

				Latin America	
	total	Asia	Europe	total	Mexico
Total people	**38,060**	**10,185**	**4,990**	**20,410**	**11,739**
Under age 18	2,973	713	329	1,694	1,103
Aged 18 to 24	3,484	744	284	2,225	1,456
Aged 25 to 44	16,524	4,308	1,382	9,858	6,104
Aged 45 to 64	10,601	3,208	1,607	5,082	2,453
Aged 45 to 54	6,455	1,915	808	3,286	1,655
Aged 55 to 64	4,147	1,293	798	1,796	798
Aged 65 or older	4,478	1,212	1,382	1,572	610
Median age (years)	40.2	42.0	50.8	37.4	35.1
PERCENT DISTRIBUTION OF FOREIGN-BORN BY REGION OF BIRTH					
Total people	**100.0%**	**26.8%**	**13.1%**	**53.6%**	**30.8%**
Under age 18	100.0	24.0	11.1	57.0	37.1
Aged 18 to 24	100.0	21.3	8.2	63.9	41.8
Aged 25 to 44	100.0	26.1	8.4	59.7	36.9
Aged 45 to 64	100.0	30.3	15.2	47.9	23.1
Aged 45 to 54	100.0	29.7	12.5	50.9	25.6
Aged 55 to 64	100.0	31.2	19.3	43.3	19.2
Aged 65 or older	100.0	27.1	30.9	35.1	13.6
PERCENT DISTRIBUTION BY AGE					
Total people	**100.0%**	**100.0%**	**100.0%**	**100.0%**	**100.0%**
Under age 18	7.8	7.0	6.6	8.3	9.4
Aged 18 to 24	9.2	7.3	5.7	10.9	12.4
Aged 25 to 44	43.4	42.3	27.7	48.3	52.0
Aged 45 to 64	27.9	31.5	32.2	24.9	20.9
Aged 45 to 54	17.0	18.8	16.2	16.1	14.1
Aged 55 to 64	10.9	12.7	16.0	8.8	6.8
Aged 65 or older	11.8	11.9	27.7	7.7	5.2

Note: Numbers do not add to total because "other" is not shown.
Source: Bureau of the Census, 2007 American Community Survey, Internet site http://factfinder.census.gov/home/saff/main.html?_lang=en; calculations by New Strategist

The Middle-Aged Are a Substantial Share of Immigrants

Nearly one in five immigrants arriving in 2008 was aged 45 to 64.

The number of legal immigrants admitted to the United States in 2008 was over 1 million. More than 200,000 were aged 45 to 64, accounting for 18 percent of the total.

Within the 45-to-64 age group, the immigrant share declines steadily with age. Six percent of immigrants admitted to the United States in 2008 were aged 45 to 49. Only 3 percent were aged 60 to 64.

■ Because most immigrants are young adults, immigration has a much greater impact on the diversity of younger Americans than on the middle-aged or older population.

Immigrants aged 45 to 64 account for 18 percent of the 2008 total

(percent distribution of immigrants admitted in 2008, by age)

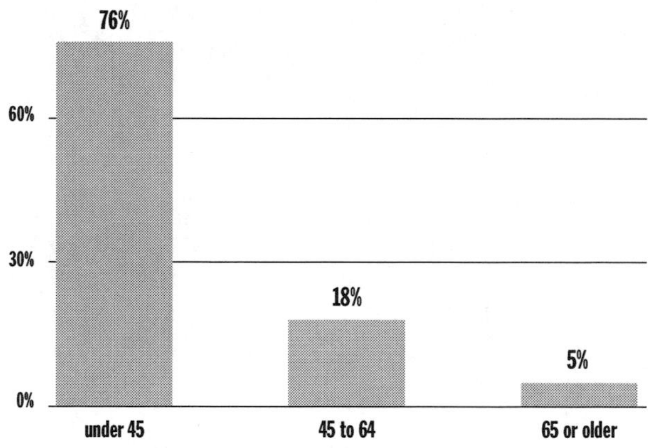

Table 8.10 Newly Arrived Immigrants by Age, 2008

(number and percent distribution of immigrants admitted in 2008, by age)

	number	percent distribution
Total immigrants	**1,107,126**	**100.0%**
Under age 1	8,280	0.7
Aged 1 to 4	29,998	2.7
Aged 5 to 9	52,993	4.8
Aged 10 to 14	74,608	6.7
Aged 15 to 19	94,697	8.6
Aged 20 to 24	104,332	9.4
Aged 25 to 29	121,416	11.0
Aged 30 to 34	140,132	12.7
Aged 35 to 39	124,341	11.2
Aged 40 to 44	92,627	8.4
Aged 45 to 64	203,091	18.3
Aged 45 to 49	69,868	6.3
Aged 50 to 54	53,848	4.9
Aged 55 to 59	43,789	4.0
Aged 60 to 64	35,586	3.2
Aged 65 to 74	45,399	4.1
Aged 75 or older	15,205	1.4

Note: Immigrants are those granted legal permanent residence in the United States. They either arrive in the United States with immigrant visas issued abroad or adjust their status in the United States from temporary to permanent residence. Numbers may not sum to total because "age not stated" is not shown.
Source: Department of Homeland Security, 2008 Yearbook of Immigration Statistics, Internet site http://www.uscis.gov/graphics/shared/statistics/yearbook/index.htm

Many Working-Age Adults Do Not Speak English at Home

Most are Spanish speakers, and most have trouble speaking English.

Fifty-five million residents of the United States speak a language other than English at home, according to the Census Bureau's 2007 American Community Survey—20 percent of the population aged 5 or older. The 62 percent majority of those who do not speak English at home are Spanish speakers.

Among working-age adults (aged 18 to 64), 21 percent do not speak English at home, and 62 percent of those who do not speak English at home are Spanish speakers. Among the Spanish speakers, 53 percent say they speak English less than "very well."

■ The language barrier is a problem for many working-age adults.

Most adults who speak Spanish at home cannot speak English very well

(percent of people aged 18 to 64 who speak a language other than English at home who speak English less than "very well," by language spoken at home, 2007)

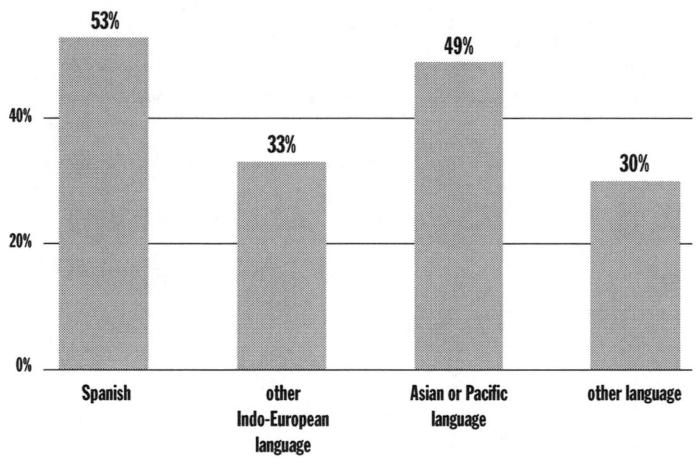

Table 8.11 Language Spoken at Home by People Aged 18 to 64, 2007

(number and percent distribution of people aged 5 or older and aged 18 to 64 who speak a language other than English at home by language spoken at home and ability to speak English very well, by age, 2007; numbers in thousands)

	total		aged 18 to 64	
	number	percent distribution	number	percent distribution
Total, aged 5 or older	**280,950**	**100.0%**	**189,873**	**100.0%**
Speak only English at home	225,506	80.3	150,635	79.3
Speak a language other than English at home	55,444	19.7	39,238	20.7
Speak English less than very well	24,469	8.7	18,624	9.8
Total who speak a language other than English at home	**55,444**	**100.0**	**39,238**	**100.0**
Speak Spanish at home	34,547	62.3	24,333	62.0
Speak other Indo-European language at home	10,321	18.6	7,034	17.9
Speak Asian or Pacific Island language at home	8,316	15.0	6,202	15.8
Speak other language at home	2,260	4.1	1,669	4.3
Speak Spanish at home	34,547	100.0	24,333	100.0
Speak English less than very well	16,368	47.4	12,791	52.6
Speak other Indo-European language at home	10,321	100.0	7,034	100.0
Speak English less than very well	3,384	32.8	2,291	32.6
Speak Asian or Pacific Island language at home	8,316	100.0	6,202	100.0
Speak English less than very well	4,042	48.6	3,034	48.9
Speak other language at home	2,260	100.0	1,669	100.0
Speak English less than very well	676	29.9	508	30.4

Source: Bureau of the Census, 2007 American Community Survey, Internet site http://factfinder.census.gov/servlet/DatasetMainPageServlet?_program=ACS&_submenuId=&_lang=en&_ts=; calculations by New Strategist

The Largest Share of Baby Boomers Lives in the South

Millennials outnumber Boomers in many states.

The South is home to the largest share of the population, and consequently to the largest share of the Baby-Boom generation. According to the Census Bureau's 2008 population estimates, 36 percent of Boomers live in the South, where they account for 25 percent of the population.

Among non-Hispanic whites aged 45 to 64 in 2007 (Boomers were aged 43 to 61 in that year), the largest share (34 percent) lived in the South, followed by 26 percent in the Midwest. Among Asians aged 45 to 64, half live in the West. Fully 56 percent of blacks aged 45 to 64 live in the South. The largest share of Hispanics aged 45 to 64 lives in the West (41 percent), followed closely by the South (36 percent).

By state, the smallest proportion of Boomers is found in Utah, at 19 percent. Millennials outnumber Boomers in a number of states, many of them with large Hispanic populations such as Arizona, California, and Texas. In Vermont, Boomers account for 29 percent of the population, the highest share among the states.

■ As younger generations enter middle age, the diversity of the population will grow in every state and region.

The Northeast is home to just 19 percent of Boomers

(percent distribution of the Baby Boom generation by region, 2008)

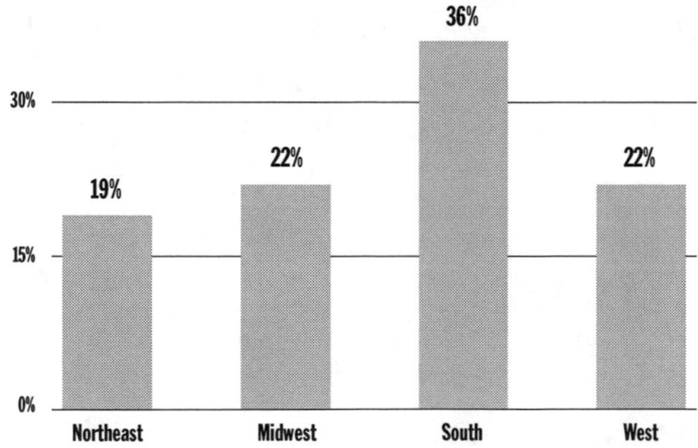

Table 8.12 Population by Age and Region, 2008

(number and percent distribution of people by age and region, 2008; numbers in thousands)

	total	Northeast	Midwest	South	West
Total people	**304,060**	**54,925**	**66,561**	**111,719**	**70,855**
Under age 45	187,132	32,456	40,352	69,115	45,209
Aged 45 to 64	78,058	14,847	17,476	28,293	17,442
Aged 45 to 49	22,880	4,374	5,112	8,238	5,156
Aged 50 to 54	21,492	4,094	4,877	7,702	4,819
Aged 55 to 59	18,583	3,514	4,186	6,729	4,155
Aged 60 to 64	15,103	2,865	3,302	5,624	3,312
Aged 65 or older	38,870	7,622	8,733	14,311	8,204
PERCENT DISTRIBUTION BY AGE					
Total people	**100.0%**	**100.0%**	**100.0%**	**100.0%**	**100.0%**
Under age 45	61.5	59.1	60.6	61.9	63.8
Aged 45 to 64	25.7	27.0	26.3	25.3	24.6
Aged 45 to 49	7.5	8.0	7.7	7.4	7.3
Aged 50 to 54	7.1	7.5	7.3	6.9	6.8
Aged 55 to 59	6.1	6.4	6.3	6.0	5.9
Aged 60 to 64	5.0	5.2	5.0	5.0	4.7
Aged 65 or older	12.8	13.9	13.1	12.8	11.6
PERCENT DISTRIBUTION BY REGION					
Total people	**100.0%**	**18.1%**	**21.9%**	**36.7%**	**23.3%**
Under age 45	100.0	17.3	21.6	36.9	24.2
Aged 45 to 64	100.0	19.0	22.4	36.2	22.3
Aged 45 to 49	100.0	19.1	22.3	36.0	22.5
Aged 50 to 54	100.0	19.0	22.7	35.8	22.4
Aged 55 to 59	100.0	18.9	22.5	36.2	22.4
Aged 60 to 64	100.0	19.0	21.9	37.2	21.9
Aged 65 or older	100.0	19.6	22.5	36.8	21.1

Source: Bureau of the Census, State Population Estimates, Internet site http://www.census.gov/popest/states/asrh/; calculations by New Strategist

Table 8.13 Population by Generation and Region, 2008

(number and percent distribution of people by generation and region, 2008; numbers in thousands)

	total	Northeast	Midwest	South	West
Total people	**304,060**	**54,925**	**66,561**	**111,719**	**70,855**
iGeneration (under age 14)	57,115	9,422	12,350	21,429	13,914
Millennial (aged 14 to 31)	75,757	13,150	16,497	27,709	18,401
Generation X (aged 32 to 43)	49,958	9,063	10,583	18,408	11,905
Baby Boom (aged 44 to 62)	76,319	14,522	17,078	27,612	17,106
Older Americans (aged 63 or older)	44,911	8,768	10,054	16,560	9,529
PERCENT DISTRIBUTION BY GENERATION					
Total people	**100.0%**	**100.0%**	**100.0%**	**100.0%**	**100.0%**
iGeneration (under age 14)	18.8	17.2	18.6	19.2	19.6
Millennial (aged 14 to 31)	24.9	23.9	24.8	24.8	26.0
Generation X (aged 32 to 43)	16.4	16.5	15.9	16.5	16.8
Baby Boom (aged 44 to 62)	25.1	26.4	25.7	24.7	24.1
Older Americans (aged 63 or older)	14.8	16.0	15.1	14.8	13.4
PERCENT DISTRIBUTION BY REGION					
Total people	**100.0%**	**18.1%**	**21.9%**	**36.7%**	**23.3%**
iGeneration (under age 14)	100.0	16.5	21.6	37.5	24.4
Millennial (aged 14 to 31)	100.0	17.4	21.8	36.6	24.3
Generation X (aged 32 to 43)	100.0	18.1	21.2	36.8	23.8
Baby Boom (aged 44 to 62)	100.0	19.0	22.4	36.2	22.4
Older Americans (aged 63 or older)	100.0	19.5	22.4	36.9	21.2

Source: Bureau of the Census, State Population Estimates, Internet site http://www.census.gov/popest/states/asrh/; calculations by New Strategist

Table 8.14 People Aged 45 to 64 by Region, Race, and Hispanic Origin, 2007

(number and percent distribution of people aged 45 to 64 by region, race, and Hispanic origin, 2007; numbers in thousands)

	total 45 to 64	Asian	black	Hispanic	non-Hispanic white
United States	**76,654**	**3,188**	**8,405**	**7,399**	**56,391**
Northeast	14,596	650	1,428	1,154	11,242
Midwest	17,246	325	1,492	582	14,633
South	27,684	630	4,741	2,631	19,298
West	17,128	1,582	744	3,032	11,218
PERCENT DISTRIBUTION BY RACE AND HISPANIC ORIGIN					
United States	**100.0%**	**4.2%**	**11.0%**	**9.7%**	**73.6%**
Northeast	100.0	4.5	9.8	7.9	77.0
Midwest	100.0	1.9	8.7	3.4	84.8
South	100.0	2.3	17.1	9.5	69.7
West	100.0	9.2	4.3	17.7	65.5
PERCENT DISTRIBUTION BY REGION					
United States	**100.0%**	**100.0%**	**100.0%**	**100.0%**	**100.0%**
Northeast	19.0	20.4	17.0	15.6	19.9
Midwest	22.5	10.2	17.7	7.9	25.9
South	36.1	19.8	56.4	35.6	34.2
West	22.3	49.6	8.9	41.0	19.9

Note: Numbers do not add to total because Asians and blacks are those who identified themselves as being of the race alone and because Hispanics may be of any race. Non-Hispanic whites are those who identified themselves as being white alone and not Hispanic.
Source: Bureau of the Census, 2007 American Community Survey, Internet site http://factfinder.census.gov/home/saff/main.html?_lang=en; calculations by New Strategist

Table 8.15 State Populations by Age, 2008

(total number of people and number aged 45 to 64 by state, 2008; numbers in thousands)

	total population	aged 45 to 64 total	45 to 49	50 to 54	55 to 59	60 to 64
United States	**304,060**	**78,058**	**22,880**	**21,492**	**18,583**	**15,103**
Alabama	4,662	1,216	342	332	295	247
Alaska	686	183	54	54	45	30
Arizona	6,500	1,524	440	406	364	314
Arkansas	2,855	727	202	194	176	155
California	36,757	8,819	2,699	2,453	2,054	1,614
Colorado	4,939	1,290	382	360	310	237
Connecticut	3,501	969	291	270	223	186
Delaware	873	231	66	62	54	48
District of Columbia	592	140	39	38	35	28
Florida	18,328	4,747	1,355	1,254	1,125	1,013
Georgia	9,686	2,389	725	654	558	452
Hawaii	1,288	332	90	89	83	69
Idaho	1,524	375	106	103	92	75
Illinois	12,902	3,239	971	902	766	601
Indiana	6,377	1,648	479	460	395	314
Iowa	3,003	788	224	220	193	152
Kansas	2,802	714	207	201	171	135
Kentucky	4,269	1,134	321	311	276	226
Louisiana	4,411	1,129	324	315	272	217
Maine	1,316	398	111	109	98	81
Maryland	5,634	1,514	456	419	354	285
Massachusetts	6,498	1,752	522	481	412	336
Michigan	10,003	2,706	780	757	651	518
Minnesota	5,220	1,392	423	390	328	252
Mississippi	2,939	730	208	202	176	145
Missouri	5,912	1,555	454	427	368	305
Montana	967	278	74	78	71	55
Nebraska	1,783	452	131	126	110	85
Nevada	2,600	653	187	174	156	135
New Hampshire	1,316	388	116	107	91	74
New Jersey	8,683	2,335	713	646	536	441
New Mexico	1,984	502	142	136	124	100
New York	19,490	5,120	1,513	1,399	1,219	990
North Carolina	9,222	2,381	685	641	571	484
North Dakota	641	167	47	48	41	31
Ohio	11,486	3,084	886	865	745	588
Oklahoma	3,642	919	260	251	220	187
Oregon	3,790	1,036	277	283	264	212
Pennsylvania	12,448	3,414	974	952	822	666
Rhode Island	1,051	282	83	79	67	54
South Carolina	4,480	1,186	326	316	292	253

	total population	aged 45 to 64				
		total	45 to 49	50 to 54	55 to 59	60 to 64
South Dakota	804	210	59	58	52	41
Tennessee	6,215	1,647	465	447	398	336
Texas	24,327	5,657	1,728	1,571	1,314	1,043
Utah	2,736	539	162	152	127	99
Vermont	621	189	52	52	47	37
Virginia	7,769	2,034	601	556	480	396
Washington	6,549	1,763	502	489	429	343
West Virginia	1,814	515	134	140	133	108
Wisconsin	5,628	1,522	451	424	365	282
Wyoming	533	147	40	42	37	28

Source: Bureau of the Census, State Population Estimates, Internet site http://www.census.gov/popest/states/asrh/; calculations by New Strategist

Table 8.16 Distribution of State Populations by Age, 2008

(percent distribution of people aged 45 to 64 by state and age, 2008)

	total population	aged 45 to 64 total	45 to 49	50 to 54	55 to 59	60 to 64
United States	**100.0%**	**25.7%**	**7.5%**	**7.1%**	**6.1%**	**5.0%**
Alabama	100.0	26.1	7.3	7.1	6.3	5.3
Alaska	100.0	26.7	7.9	7.9	6.5	4.4
Arizona	100.0	23.4	6.8	6.2	5.6	4.8
Arkansas	100.0	25.5	7.1	6.8	6.2	5.4
California	100.0	24.0	7.3	6.7	5.6	4.4
Colorado	100.0	26.1	7.7	7.3	6.3	4.8
Connecticut	100.0	27.7	8.3	7.7	6.4	5.3
Delaware	100.0	26.4	7.6	7.1	6.2	5.5
District of Columbia	100.0	23.7	6.7	6.3	5.9	4.8
Florida	100.0	25.9	7.4	6.8	6.1	5.5
Georgia	100.0	24.7	7.5	6.7	5.8	4.7
Hawaii	100.0	25.8	7.0	6.9	6.5	5.3
Idaho	100.0	24.6	6.9	6.7	6.0	4.9
Illinois	100.0	25.1	7.5	7.0	5.9	4.7
Indiana	100.0	25.8	7.5	7.2	6.2	4.9
Iowa	100.0	26.3	7.5	7.3	6.4	5.0
Kansas	100.0	25.5	7.4	7.2	6.1	4.8
Kentucky	100.0	26.6	7.5	7.3	6.5	5.3
Louisiana	100.0	25.6	7.3	7.1	6.2	4.9
Maine	100.0	30.2	8.4	8.3	7.4	6.1
Maryland	100.0	26.9	8.1	7.4	6.3	5.1
Massachusetts	100.0	27.0	8.0	7.4	6.3	5.2
Michigan	100.0	27.1	7.8	7.6	6.5	5.2
Minnesota	100.0	26.7	8.1	7.5	6.3	4.8
Mississippi	100.0	24.8	7.1	6.9	6.0	4.9
Missouri	100.0	26.3	7.7	7.2	6.2	5.2
Montana	100.0	28.8	7.7	8.1	7.3	5.7
Nebraska	100.0	25.3	7.3	7.1	6.2	4.7
Nevada	100.0	25.1	7.2	6.7	6.0	5.2
New Hampshire	100.0	29.5	8.8	8.1	6.9	5.6
New Jersey	100.0	26.9	8.2	7.4	6.2	5.1
New Mexico	100.0	25.3	7.2	6.9	6.2	5.0
New York	100.0	26.3	7.8	7.2	6.3	5.1
North Carolina	100.0	25.8	7.4	6.9	6.2	5.3
North Dakota	100.0	26.0	7.3	7.4	6.4	4.9
Ohio	100.0	26.8	7.7	7.5	6.5	5.1
Oklahoma	100.0	25.2	7.1	6.9	6.0	5.1
Oregon	100.0	27.3	7.3	7.5	7.0	5.6
Pennsylvania	100.0	27.4	7.8	7.6	6.6	5.4
Rhode Island	100.0	26.9	7.9	7.5	6.3	5.2
South Carolina	100.0	26.5	7.3	7.0	6.5	5.6

	total population	aged 45 to 64 total	45 to 49	50 to 54	55 to 59	60 to 64
South Dakota	100.0%	26.1%	7.4%	7.3%	6.4%	5.1%
Tennessee	100.0	26.5	7.5	7.2	6.4	5.4
Texas	100.0	23.3	7.1	6.5	5.4	4.3
Utah	100.0	19.7	5.9	5.5	4.6	3.6
Vermont	100.0	30.4	8.4	8.4	7.6	6.0
Virginia	100.0	26.2	7.7	7.2	6.2	5.1
Washington	100.0	26.9	7.7	7.5	6.6	5.2
West Virginia	100.0	28.4	7.4	7.7	7.3	6.0
Wisconsin	100.0	27.0	8.0	7.5	6.5	5.0
Wyoming	100.0	27.6	7.6	7.9	6.9	5.3

Source: Bureau of the Census, State Population Estimates, Internet site http://www.census.gov/popest/states/asrh/; calculations by New Strategist

Table 8.17 State Populations by Generation, 2008

(number of people by state and generation, 2008; numbers in thousands)

	total population	iGeneration (under 14)	Millennial (14 to 31)	Generation X (32 to 43)	Baby Boom (44 to 62)	Older Americans (63 or older)
United States	**304,060**	**57,115**	**75,757**	**49,958**	**76,319**	**44,911**
Alabama	4,662	864	1,145	732	1,180	741
Alaska	686	138	192	113	181	62
Arizona	6,500	1,344	1,631	1,053	1,484	988
Arkansas	2,855	545	695	443	703	469
California	36,757	7,224	9,724	6,342	8,706	4,760
Colorado	4,939	946	1,258	863	1,266	606
Connecticut	3,501	617	806	577	949	552
Delaware	873	159	209	140	224	141
District of Columbia	592	87	180	106	137	82
Florida	18,328	3,087	4,164	2,887	4,597	3,593
Georgia	9,686	1,993	2,459	1,719	2,353	1,162
Hawaii	1,288	222	319	208	321	218
Idaho	1,524	323	391	233	364	212
Illinois	12,902	2,458	3,300	2,148	3,180	1,816
Indiana	6,377	1,225	1,574	1,028	1,610	940
Iowa	3,003	548	735	447	767	505
Kansas	2,802	545	714	426	696	421
Kentucky	4,269	779	1,031	699	1,104	656
Louisiana	4,411	855	1,160	669	1,100	627
Maine	1,316	206	287	207	385	231
Maryland	5,634	1,026	1,378	950	1,486	793
Massachusetts	6,498	1,088	1,595	1,093	1,717	1,006
Michigan	10,003	1,810	2,442	1,598	2,641	1,511
Minnesota	5,220	967	1,294	842	1,366	751
Mississippi	2,939	593	756	449	710	429
Missouri	5,912	1,092	1,455	924	1,513	927
Montana	967	168	235	137	268	159
Nebraska	1,783	348	453	267	441	275
Nevada	2,600	525	631	457	637	351
New Hampshire	1,316	220	299	218	379	200
New Jersey	8,683	1,572	1,985	1,502	2,296	1,327
New Mexico	1,984	391	509	298	487	300
New York	19,490	3,360	4,857	3,257	5,013	3,004
North Carolina	9,222	1,752	2,241	1,577	2,320	1,333
North Dakota	641	110	176	88	162	107
Ohio	11,486	2,088	2,774	1,810	3,008	1,806
Oklahoma	3,642	706	934	547	890	565
Oregon	3,790	668	918	614	1,002	589
Pennsylvania	12,448	2,091	2,913	1,943	3,324	2,177
Rhode Island	1,051	173	262	170	276	169
South Carolina	4,480	822	1,096	717	1,147	697

	total population	iGeneration (under 14)	Millennial (14 to 31)	Generation X (32 to 43)	Baby Boom (44 to 62)	Older Americans (63 or older)
South Dakota	804	153	201	114	204	132
Tennessee	6,215	1,143	1,489	1,028	1,600	954
Texas	24,327	5,307	6,426	4,130	5,575	2,890
Utah	2,736	680	828	413	530	286
Vermont	621	96	145	96	183	102
Virginia	7,769	1,413	1,935	1,332	1,990	1,099
Washington	6,549	1,185	1,630	1,096	1,718	921
West Virginia	1,814	296	412	283	496	328
Wisconsin	5,628	1,005	1,379	891	1,490	863
Wyoming	533	99	136	78	143	77

Source: Bureau of the Census, State Population Estimates, Internet site http://www.census.gov/popest/states/asrh/; calculations by New Strategist

Table 8.18 Distribution of State Populations by Generation, 2008

(percent distribution of people by state and generation, 2008)

	total population	iGeneration (under 14)	Millennial (14 to 31)	Generation X (32 to 43)	Baby Boom (44 to 62)	Older Americans (63 or older)
United States	**100.0%**	**18.8%**	**24.9%**	**16.4%**	**25.1%**	**14.8%**
Alabama	100.0	18.5	24.6	15.7	25.3	15.9
Alaska	100.0	20.1	28.0	16.5	26.3	9.1
Arizona	100.0	20.7	25.1	16.2	22.8	15.2
Arkansas	100.0	19.1	24.4	15.5	24.6	16.4
California	100.0	19.7	26.5	17.3	23.7	12.9
Colorado	100.0	19.2	25.5	17.5	25.6	12.3
Connecticut	100.0	17.6	23.0	16.5	27.1	15.8
Delaware	100.0	18.2	23.9	16.1	25.6	16.1
District of Columbia	100.0	14.7	30.4	17.8	23.1	13.9
Florida	100.0	16.8	22.7	15.8	25.1	19.6
Georgia	100.0	20.6	25.4	17.7	24.3	12.0
Hawaii	100.0	17.2	24.8	16.1	25.0	16.9
Idaho	100.0	21.2	25.7	15.3	23.9	13.9
Illinois	100.0	19.0	25.6	16.6	24.7	14.1
Indiana	100.0	19.2	24.7	16.1	25.3	14.7
Iowa	100.0	18.3	24.5	14.9	25.5	16.8
Kansas	100.0	19.5	25.5	15.2	24.8	15.0
Kentucky	100.0	18.2	24.1	16.4	25.9	15.4
Louisiana	100.0	19.4	26.3	15.2	24.9	14.2
Maine	100.0	15.6	21.8	15.7	29.3	17.6
Maryland	100.0	18.2	24.5	16.9	26.4	14.1
Massachusetts	100.0	16.7	24.5	16.8	26.4	15.5
Michigan	100.0	18.1	24.4	16.0	26.4	15.1
Minnesota	100.0	18.5	24.8	16.1	26.2	14.4
Mississippi	100.0	20.2	25.7	15.3	24.2	14.6
Missouri	100.0	18.5	24.6	15.6	25.6	15.7
Montana	100.0	17.3	24.3	14.1	27.7	16.5
Nebraska	100.0	19.5	25.4	15.0	24.7	15.4
Nevada	100.0	20.2	24.2	17.6	24.5	13.5
New Hampshire	100.0	16.7	22.7	16.5	28.8	15.2
New Jersey	100.0	18.1	22.9	17.3	26.4	15.3
New Mexico	100.0	19.7	25.6	15.0	24.5	15.1
New York	100.0	17.2	24.9	16.7	25.7	15.4
North Carolina	100.0	19.0	24.3	17.1	25.2	14.5
North Dakota	100.0	17.1	27.4	13.7	25.2	16.6
Ohio	100.0	18.2	24.1	15.8	26.2	15.7
Oklahoma	100.0	19.4	25.6	15.0	24.4	15.5
Oregon	100.0	17.6	24.2	16.2	26.4	15.5
Pennsylvania	100.0	16.8	23.4	15.6	26.7	17.5
Rhode Island	100.0	16.5	25.0	16.2	26.3	16.1
South Carolina	100.0	18.4	24.5	16.0	25.6	15.6

	total population	iGeneration (under 14)	Millennial (14 to 31)	Generation X (32 to 43)	Baby Boom (44 to 62)	Older Americans (63 or older)
South Dakota	100.0%	19.1%	25.0%	14.1%	25.3%	16.5%
Tennessee	100.0	18.4	24.0	16.5	25.7	15.4
Texas	100.0	21.8	26.4	17.0	22.9	11.9
Utah	100.0	24.9	30.2	15.1	19.4	10.4
Vermont	100.0	15.4	23.4	15.5	29.4	16.4
Virginia	100.0	18.2	24.9	17.1	25.6	14.1
Washington	100.0	18.1	24.9	16.7	26.2	14.1
West Virginia	100.0	16.3	22.7	15.6	27.3	18.1
Wisconsin	100.0	17.9	24.5	15.8	26.5	15.3
Wyoming	100.0	18.7	25.5	14.7	26.8	14.4

Source: Bureau of the Census, State Population Estimates, Internet site http://www.census.gov/popest/states/asrh/; calculations by New Strategist

CHAPTER
9

Spending

■ Average household spending increased in every age group between 2000 and 2007, after adjusting for inflation. Householders aged 55 to 64 boosted their spending by 14 percent during those years, while those aged 45 to 54 spent 5 percent more.

■ Households headed by people aged 45 to 54 spent $58,331 on average in 2007, second only to the $58,934 spent by householders aged 35 to 44.

■ Households headed by people aged 55 to 64 spent $53,786 on average in 2007. The age group's spending grew rapidly between 2000 and 2007 because two-earner couples head a growing proportion of households in the age group and fewer 55-to-64-year-olds are opting for early retirement.

Spending Is Climbing for Householders Aged 55 to 64

Boomers are changing the spending patterns of the older age groups.

Spanning the ages of 43 to 61 in 2007, the Baby-Boom generation is in the peak-spending age groups. Householders aged 45 to 54 rank among the nation's biggest spenders. The average household headed by a 45-to-54-year-old spent $58,331 in 2007—18 percent more than the average household and only $600 less than 35-to-44-year-olds. Behind the slightly higher spending of householders aged 35 to 44 is their much greater spending on mortgage interest because many are recent homebuyers. The average household headed by a 35-to-44-year-old spent $6,239 on mortgage interest in 2007 compared with the $5,093 spent by householders aged 45 to 54.

Householders aged 55 to 64, an age group that includes the oldest Boomers, are not far behind in spending. In 2007, the average household headed by a 55-to-64-year-old spent $53,786 (and only $3,421 on mortgage interest)—14 percent more than in 2000 after adjusting for inflation. In contrast, householders aged 45 to 54 increased their spending by a much smaller 5 percent during those years. Behind the surge in spending by householders aged 55 to 64 is their greater labor force participation as Boomers move into the age group. Not only does the age group include more two-income couples, but early retirement is becoming less common. The number of earners in households headed by 55-to-64-year-olds increased from 1.3 to 1.4 between 2000 and 2007.

Householders aged 45 to 64 spend more than $50,000 a year

(average annual household spending, by age of householder, 2007)

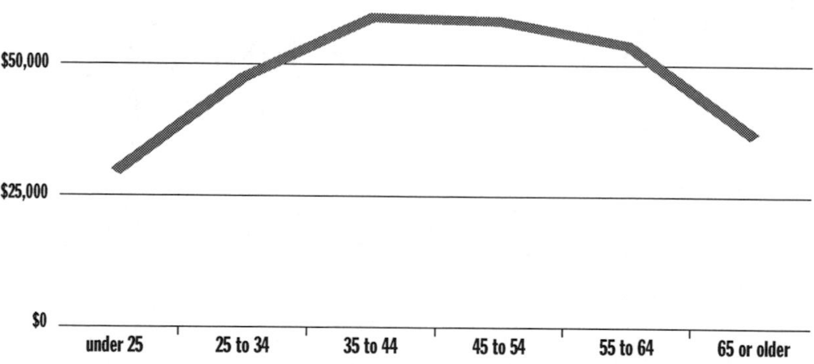

Householders aged 55 to 64 are spending more not only on necessities, but also on discretionary items. Between 2000 and 2007, they spent 10 percent more on food away from home, 19 percent more on alcoholic beverages, and 16 percent more on entertainment. Householders aged 45 to 54 boosted their discretionary spending on only a few items, but their entertainment spending rose by 18 percent.

The middle aged are devoting more dollars to nondiscretionary expenses. Spending on out-of-pocket health insurance costs rose 18 to 29 percent for householders spanning the ages of 45 to 64, after adjusting for inflation. Property taxes increased 21 to 23 percent. Vehicle insurance rose 15 to 27 percent.

■ The spending of householders aged 55 to 64 should continue to climb as Boomers completely fill the age group.

Table 9.1 Average Spending of Total Households, 2000 and 2007

(average annual spending of consumer units, 2000 and 2007; percent change, 2000–07; in 2007 dollars)

	2007	2000	percent change 2000–07
Number of consumer units (in 000s)	**120,171**	**109,367**	**9.9%**
Average annual spending	**$49,638**	**$45,809**	**8.4**
FOOD	**6,133**	**6,211**	**–1.2**
Food at home	**3,465**	**3,638**	**–4.7**
Cereals and bakery products	460	545	–15.7
Cereals and cereal products	143	188	–23.9
Bakery products	317	358	–11.4
Meats, poultry, fish, and eggs	777	957	–18.8
Beef	216	287	–24.6
Pork	150	201	–25.4
Other meats	104	122	–14.5
Poultry	142	175	–18.7
Fish and seafood	122	132	–7.9
Eggs	43	41	5.0
Dairy products	387	391	–1.1
Fresh milk and cream	154	158	–2.4
Other dairy products	234	232	0.7
Fruits and vegetables	600	627	–4.4
Fresh fruits	202	196	2.9
Fresh vegetables	190	191	–0.8
Processed fruits	112	138	–19.1
Processed vegetables	96	101	–5.1
Other food at home	1,241	1,116	11.2
Sugar and other sweets	124	141	–12.0
Fats and oils	91	100	–8.9
Miscellaneous foods	650	526	23.5
Nonalcoholic beverages	333	301	10.6
Food prepared by household on trips	43	48	–10.7
Food away from home	**2,668**	**2,573**	**3.7**
ALCOHOLIC BEVERAGES	**457**	**448**	**2.0**
HOUSING	**16,920**	**14,833**	**14.1**
Shelter	**10,023**	**8,566**	**17.0**
Owned dwellings	6,730	5,541	21.5
Mortgage interest and charges	3,890	3,178	22.4
Property taxes	1,709	1,371	24.6
Maintenance, repairs, insurance, other expenses	1,131	993	13.9
Rented dwellings	2,602	2,449	6.2
Other lodging	691	576	20.1

	2007	2000	percent change 2000–07
Utilities, fuels, public services	**$3,477**	**$2,997**	**16.0%**
Natural gas	480	370	29.9
Electricity	1,303	1,097	18.8
Fuel oil and other fuels	151	117	29.3
Telephone services	1,110	1,056	5.1
Water and other public services	434	356	21.8
Household services	**984**	**824**	**19.5**
Personal services	415	393	5.7
Other household services	569	431	32.0
Housekeeping supplies	**639**	**580**	**10.1**
Laundry and cleaning supplies	140	158	–11.2
Other household products	347	272	27.5
Postage and stationery	152	152	0.2
Household furnishings and equipment	**1,797**	**1,865**	**–3.7**
Household textiles	133	128	4.2
Furniture	446	471	–5.3
Floor coverings	46	53	–13.2
Major appliances	231	228	1.5
Small appliances, miscellaneous housewares	101	105	–3.6
Miscellaneous household equipment	840	880	–4.6
APPAREL AND SERVICES	**1,881**	**2,235**	**–15.8**
Men and boys	**435**	**530**	**–17.9**
Men, aged 16 or older	351	414	–15.3
Boys, aged 2 to 15	84	116	–27.3
Women and girls	**749**	**873**	**–14.2**
Women, aged 16 or older	627	731	–14.2
Girls, aged 2 to 15	122	142	–14.1
Children under age 2	**93**	**99**	**–5.8**
Footwear	**327**	**413**	**–20.8**
Other apparel products and services	**276**	**320**	**–13.8**
TRANSPORTATION	**8,758**	**8,931**	**–1.9**
Vehicle purchases	**3,244**	**4,116**	**–21.2**
Cars and trucks, new	1,572	1,933	–18.7
Cars and trucks, used	1,567	2,131	–26.5
Other vehicles	105	52	102.8
Gasoline and motor oil	**2,384**	**1,554**	**53.4**
Other vehicle expenses	**2,592**	**2,746**	**–5.6**
Vehicle finance charges	305	395	–22.8
Maintenance and repairs	738	751	–1.8
Vehicle insurance	1,071	937	14.3
Vehicle rental, leases, licenses, other charges	478	663	–28.0
Public transportation	**538**	**514**	**4.6**

	2007	2000	percent change 2000–07
HEALTH CARE	**$2,853**	**$2,488**	**14.7%**
Health insurance	1,545	1,184	30.5
Medical services	709	684	3.7
Drugs	481	501	–4.0
Medical supplies	118	119	–1.0
ENTERTAINMENT	**2,698**	**2,243**	**20.3**
Fees and admissions	658	620	6.1
Audio and visual equipment and services	987	749	31.8
Pets, toys, hobbies, and playground equipment	560	402	39.2
Other entertainment supplies, services	493	473	4.2
PERSONAL CARE PRODUCTS, SERVICES	**588**	**679**	**–13.4**
READING	**118**	**176**	**–32.9**
EDUCATION	**945**	**761**	**24.2**
TOBACCO PRODUCTS, SMOKING SUPPLIES	**323**	**384**	**–15.9**
MISCELLANEOUS	**808**	**934**	**–13.5**
CASH CONTRIBUTIONS	**1,821**	**1,435**	**26.9**
PERSONAL INSURANCE AND PENSIONS	**5,336**	**4,052**	**31.7**
Life and other personal insurance	309	480	–35.7
Pensions and Social Security	5,027	–	–
PERSONAL TAXES	**2,233**	**3,753**	**–40.5**
Federal income taxes	1,569	2,901	–45.9
State and local income taxes	468	677	–30.8
Other taxes	196	176	11.5
GIFTS FOR PEOPLE IN OTHER HOUSEHOLDS	**1,198**	**1,304**	**–8.1**

Note: The Bureau of Labor Statistics uses consumer unit rather than household as the sampling unit in the Consumer Expenditure Survey. For the definition of consumer unit, see the glossary. Spending on gifts is also included in the preceding product and service categories. Average spending is rounded to the nearest dollar, but the percent change calculation is based on unrounded figures. "–" means comparable data are not available.

Source: Bureau of Labor Statistics, 2000 and 2007 Consumer Expenditure Survey, Internet site http://www.bls.gov/cex/; calculations by New Strategist

Table 9.2 Average Spending of Householders Aged 45 to 54, 2000 and 2007

(average annual spending of consumer units headed by people aged 45 to 54, 2000 and 2007; percent change, 2000–07; in 2007 dollars)

	2007	2000	percent change 2000–07
Number of consumer units (in 000s)	**25,245**	**21,874**	**15.4%**
Average annual spending	**$58,331**	**$55,580**	**4.9**
FOOD	**7,181**	**7,580**	**–5.3**
Food at home	**4,003**	**4,403**	**–9.1**
Cereals and bakery products	522	674	–22.6
Cereals and cereal products	161	217	–25.7
Bakery products	361	458	–21.1
Meats, poultry, fish, and eggs	907	1,168	–22.3
Beef	243	356	–31.8
Pork	173	238	–27.4
Other meats	125	146	–14.2
Poultry	173	203	–15.0
Fish and seafood	146	176	–16.9
Eggs	47	48	–2.4
Dairy products	442	454	–2.6
Fresh milk and cream	172	176	–2.2
Other dairy products	271	279	–3.0
Fruits and vegetables	684	754	–9.3
Fresh fruits	232	225	3.0
Fresh vegetables	217	242	–10.3
Processed fruits	123	160	–23.2
Processed vegetables	112	126	–11.4
Other food at home	1,447	1,353	6.9
Sugar and other sweets	150	172	–12.9
Fats and oils	107	123	–12.9
Miscellaneous foods	729	636	14.7
Nonalcoholic beverages	411	361	13.8
Food prepared by household on trips	50	63	–20.1
Food away from home	**3,178**	**3,176**	**0.1**
ALCOHOLIC BEVERAGES	**498**	**502**	**–0.8**
HOUSING	**19,195**	**17,073**	**12.4**
Shelter	**11,617**	**9,990**	**16.3**
Owned dwellings	8,626	7,181	20.1
Mortgage interest and charges	5,093	4,284	18.9
Property taxes	2,178	1,771	23.0
Maintenance, repairs, insurance, other expenses	1,356	1,126	20.4
Rented dwellings	2,055	1,943	5.7
Other lodging	936	866	8.1

	2007	2000	percent change 2000–07
Utilities, fuels, public services	**$4,053**	**$3,440**	**17.8%**
Natural gas	539	414	30.1
Electricity	1,499	1,258	19.1
Fuel oil and other fuels	192	131	46.3
Telephone services	1,330	1,213	9.7
Water and other public services	493	424	16.3
Household services	**867**	**702**	**23.5**
Personal services	193	177	9.0
Other household services	674	524	28.7
Housekeeping supplies	**724**	**641**	**13.0**
Laundry and cleaning supplies	161	165	–2.4
Other household products	365	297	22.7
Postage and stationery	198	177	11.9
Household furnishings and equipment	**1,933**	**2,301**	**–16.0**
Household textiles	120	151	–20.3
Furniture	461	567	–18.7
Floor coverings	54	61	–12.1
Major appliances	285	269	6.1
Small appliances, miscellaneous housewares	115	152	–24.2
Miscellaneous household equipment	898	1,102	–18.5
APPAREL AND SERVICES	**2,191**	**2,855**	**–23.3**
Men and boys	**514**	**695**	**–26.0**
Men, aged 16 or older	428	580	–26.3
Boys, aged 2 to 15	87	114	–23.9
Women and girls	**952**	**1,176**	**–19.1**
Women, aged 16 or older	822	1,023	–19.7
Girls, aged 2 to 15	130	152	–14.3
Children under age 2	**54**	**65**	**–16.9**
Footwear	**383**	**527**	**–27.4**
Other apparel products and services	**287**	**391**	**–26.7**
TRANSPORTATION	**9,943**	**10,628**	**–6.4**
Vehicle purchases	**3,223**	**4,651**	**–30.7**
Cars and trucks, new	1,645	2,035	–19.2
Cars and trucks, used	1,404	2,562	–45.2
Other vehicles	174	54	221.1
Gasoline and motor oil	**2,846**	**1,917**	**48.5**
Other vehicle expenses	**3,213**	**3,453**	**–7.0**
Vehicle finance charges	335	471	–28.8
Maintenance and repairs	941	964	–2.4
Vehicle insurance	1,382	1,206	14.5
Vehicle rental, leases, licenses, other charges	555	812	–31.6
Public transportation	**661**	**608**	**8.7**

	2007	2000	percent change 2000–07
HEALTH CARE	**$2,792**	**$2,649**	**5.4%**
Health insurance	1,386	1,175	17.9
Medical services	772	842	–8.3
Drugs	498	490	1.6
Medical supplies	135	142	–5.0
ENTERTAINMENT	**3,163**	**2,686**	**17.7**
Fees and admissions	823	767	7.3
Audio and visual equipment and services	1,126	838	34.4
Pets, toys, hobbies, and playground equipment	711	462	53.8
Other entertainment supplies, services	504	619	–18.6
PERSONAL CARE PRODUCTS, SERVICES	**686**	**821**	**–16.5**
READING	**137**	**214**	**–36.1**
EDUCATION	**1,687**	**1,380**	**22.3**
TOBACCO PRODUCTS, SMOKING SUPPLIES	**388**	**453**	**–14.3**
MISCELLANEOUS	**1,008**	**1,116**	**–9.7**
CASH CONTRIBUTIONS	**1,972**	**1,851**	**6.6**
PERSONAL INSURANCE AND PENSIONS	**7,489**	**5,774**	**29.7**
Life and other personal insurance	402	661	–39.2
Pensions and Social Security	7,087	–	–
PERSONAL TAXES	**3,485**	**5,707**	**–38.9**
Federal income taxes	2,490	4,464	–44.2
State and local income taxes	754	1,021	–26.2
Other taxes	241	223	8.2
GIFTS FOR PEOPLE IN OTHER HOUSEHOLDS	**1,847**	**2,076**	**–11.0**

Note: The Bureau of Labor Statistics uses consumer unit rather than household as the sampling unit in the Consumer Expenditure Survey. For the definition of consumer unit, see the glossary. Spending on gifts is also included in the preceding product and service categories. Average spending is rounded to the nearest dollar, but the percent change calculation is based on unrounded figures. "–" means comparable data are not available.
Source: Bureau of Labor Statistics, 2000 and 2007 Consumer Expenditure Survey, Internet site http://www.bls.gov/cex/; calculations by New Strategist

Table 9.3 Average Spending of Householders Aged 55 to 64, 2000 and 2007

(average annual spending of consumer units headed by people aged 55 to 64, 2000 and 2007; percent change, 2000–07; in 2007 dollars)

	2007	2000	percent change 2000–07
Number of consumer units (in 000s)	**19,462**	**14,161**	**37.4%**
Average annual spending	**$53,786**	**$47,368**	**13.5**
FOOD	**6,241**	**6,223**	**0.3**
Food at home	**3,457**	**3,698**	**–6.5**
Cereals and bakery products	456	531	–14.1
Cereals and cereal products	129	169	–23.5
Bakery products	327	362	–9.8
Meats, poultry, fish, and eggs	758	1,002	–24.3
Beef	200	293	–31.6
Pork	147	224	–34.4
Other meats	107	119	–10.2
Poultry	134	176	–23.8
Fish and seafood	127	138	–8.3
Eggs	44	52	–15.0
Dairy products	384	387	–0.6
Fresh milk and cream	142	152	–6.4
Other dairy products	242	235	3.1
Fruits and vegetables	640	672	–4.7
Fresh fruits	219	223	–1.7
Fresh vegetables	207	208	–0.6
Processed fruits	113	138	–18.4
Processed vegetables	102	105	–2.6
Other food at home	1,219	1,105	10.3
Sugar and other sweets	119	138	–14.1
Fats and oils	95	108	–12.3
Miscellaneous foods	599	479	25.0
Nonalcoholic beverages	343	317	8.3
Food prepared by household on trips	63	63	0.6
Food away from home	**2,784**	**2,525**	**10.3**
ALCOHOLIC BEVERAGES	**533**	**447**	**19.3**
HOUSING	**17,223**	**14,885**	**15.7**
Shelter	**9,763**	**7,931**	**23.1**
Owned dwellings	7,063	5,755	22.7
Mortgage interest and charges	3,421	2,743	24.7
Property taxes	2,127	1,760	20.8
Maintenance, repairs, insurance, other expenses	1,515	1,252	21.0
Rented dwellings	1,539	1,352	13.8
Other lodging	1,161	825	40.8

	2007	2000	percent change 2000–07
Utilities, fuels, public services	**$3,754**	**$3,318**	**13.1%**
Natural gas	557	411	35.7
Electricity	1,403	1,262	11.2
Fuel oil and other fuels	171	136	25.7
Telephone services	1,135	1,095	3.7
Water and other public services	488	415	17.5
Household services	**860**	**653**	**31.8**
Personal services	159	112	42.0
Other household services	701	541	29.7
Housekeeping supplies	**902**	**704**	**28.1**
Laundry and cleaning supplies	134	222	–39.5
Other household products	572	315	81.3
Postage and stationery	197	167	17.7
Household furnishings and equipment	**1,944**	**2,277**	**–14.6**
Household textiles	170	151	12.9
Furniture	437	435	0.5
Floor coverings	48	67	–28.8
Major appliances	266	266	0.0
Small appliances, miscellaneous housewares	92	128	–27.9
Miscellaneous household equipment	931	1,231	–24.3
APPAREL AND SERVICES	**1,888**	**2,040**	**–7.4**
Men and boys	**402**	**476**	**–15.5**
Men, aged 16 or older	367	424	–13.4
Boys, aged 2 to 15	35	51	–30.8
Women and girls	**793**	**827**	**–4.1**
Women, aged 16 or older	723	759	–4.7
Girls, aged 2 to 15	70	69	2.0
Children under age 2	**55**	**64**	**–13.8**
Footwear	**351**	**361**	**–2.8**
Other apparel products and services	**286**	**312**	**–8.3**
TRANSPORTATION	**9,608**	**9,442**	**1.8**
Vehicle purchases	3,348	4,362	–23.3
Cars and trucks, new	1,700	2,525	–32.7
Cars and trucks, used	1,582	1,816	–12.9
Other vehicles	66	22	204.5
Gasoline and motor oil	**2,504**	**1,624**	**54.2**
Other vehicle expenses	**2,993**	**2,860**	**4.7**
Vehicle finance charges	325	420	–22.7
Maintenance and repairs	885	809	9.4
Vehicle insurance	1,214	958	26.7
Vehicle rental, leases, licenses, other charges	569	673	–15.5
Public transportation	**763**	**596**	**28.0**

	2007	2000	percent change 2000–07
HEALTH CARE	**$3,476**	**$3,020**	**15.1%**
Health insurance	1,751	1,363	28.5
Medical services	883	868	1.7
Drugs	674	648	4.0
Medical supplies	168	141	19.3
ENTERTAINMENT	**2,730**	**2,354**	**16.0**
Fees and admissions	645	613	5.2
Audio and visual equipment and services	965	700	37.9
Pets, toys, hobbies, and playground equipment	653	431	51.5
Other entertainment supplies, services	468	610	–23.3
PERSONAL CARE PRODUCTS, SERVICES	**632**	**685**	**–7.8**
READING	**151**	**216**	**–29.9**
EDUCATION	**929**	**458**	**103.0**
TOBACCO PRODUCTS, SMOKING SUPPLIES	**353**	**420**	**–16.0**
MISCELLANEOUS	**1,084**	**992**	**9.3**
CASH CONTRIBUTIONS	**2,746**	**1,567**	**75.3**
PERSONAL INSURANCE AND PENSIONS	**6,193**	**4,621**	**34.0**
Life and other personal insurance	461	707	–34.8
Pensions and Social Security	5,732	–	–
PERSONAL TAXES	**3,083**	**4,815**	**–36.0**
Federal income taxes	2,234	3,687	–39.4
State and local income taxes	551	845	–34.8
Other taxes	298	283	5.3
GIFTS FOR PEOPLE IN OTHER HOUSEHOLDS	**1,948**	**1,619**	**20.3**

Note: The Bureau of Labor Statistics uses consumer unit rather than household as the sampling unit in the Consumer Expenditure Survey. For the definition of consumer unit, see the glossary. Spending on gifts is also included in the preceding product and service categories. Average spending is rounded to the nearest dollar, but the percent change calculation is based on unrounded figures. "–" means comparable data are not available.
Source: Bureau of Labor Statistics, 2000 and 2007 Consumer Expenditure Survey, Internet site http://www.bls.gov/cex/; calculations by New Strategist

Householders Aged 45 to 54 Are among the Biggest Spenders

Their spending patterns reflect the fact that many are empty-nesters.

Householders aged 45 to 54 spent $58,331 on average in 2007, more than any other age group except those aged 35 to 44 and 18 percent more than the $49,638 spent by the average household. The age group controls 25 percent of household spending, a larger share than any other age group.

Because most householders aged 45 to 54 are either empty-nesters or have older children at home, their spending patterns differ considerably from householders aged 35 to 44. They spend less than average, for example, on household personal services (day care expenses). But they spend 35 percent more than average on other lodging (hotels, motels, and college dorms). They spend 22 to 31 percent more than average on men's and women's clothes, 54 percent more on gifts for people in other households, and 79 percent more on education. The 45-to-54 age group controls more than one-third of household spending on education. Surprisingly, however, they spend only an average amount on furniture, new cars and trucks, and out-of-pocket health insurance costs.

■ As Boomers filled the 45-to-54 age group, they proved to be cautious spenders. The spending of households in this age group increased by just 5 percent between 2000 and 2007, well below the 8 percent spending increase posted by the average household.

Householders aged 45 to 54 spend 79 percent more than the average household on education

(indexed spending of householders aged 45 to 54 on selected items, 2007)

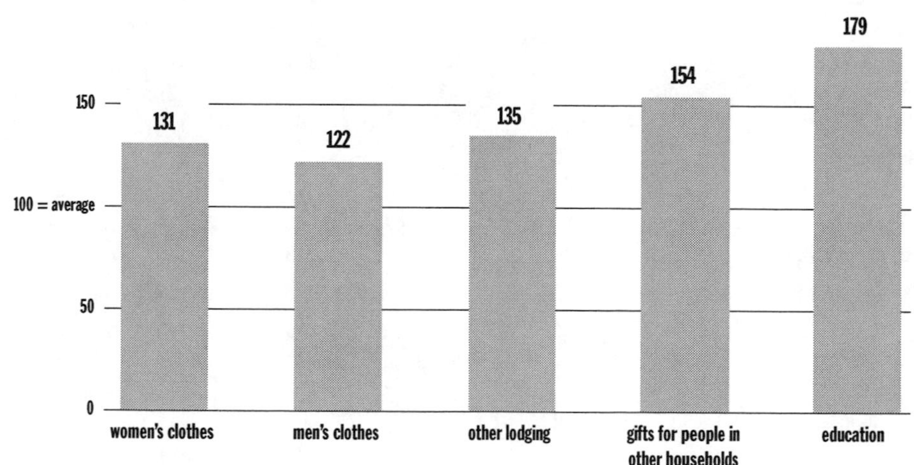

Table 9.4 Average, Indexed, and Market Share of Spending by Householders Aged 45 to 54, 2007

(average annual spending of total consumer units and average annual, indexed, and market share of spending by consumer units headed by 45-to-54-year-olds, 2007)

	total consumer units	consumer units headed by 45-to-54-year-olds		
		average spending	indexed spending	market share
Number of consumer units (in 000s)	**120,171**	**25,245**	**–**	**21.0%**
Average annual spending	**$49,638**	**$58,331**	**118**	**24.7**
FOOD	**6,133**	**7,181**	**117**	**24.6**
Food at home	**3,465**	**4,003**	**116**	**24.3**
Cereals and bakery products	460	522	113	23.8
Cereals and cereal products	143	161	113	23.7
Bakery products	317	361	114	23.9
Meats, poultry, fish, and eggs	777	907	117	24.5
Beef	216	243	113	23.6
Pork	150	173	115	24.2
Other meats	104	125	120	25.2
Poultry	142	173	122	25.6
Fish and seafood	122	146	120	25.1
Eggs	43	47	109	23.0
Dairy products	387	442	114	24.0
Fresh milk and cream	154	172	112	23.5
Other dairy products	234	271	116	24.3
Fruits and vegetables	600	684	114	23.9
Fresh fruits	202	232	115	24.1
Fresh vegetables	190	217	114	24.0
Processed fruits	112	123	110	23.1
Processed vegetables	96	112	117	24.5
Other food at home	1,241	1,447	117	24.5
Sugar and other sweets	124	150	121	25.4
Fats and oils	91	107	118	24.7
Miscellaneous foods	650	729	112	23.6
Nonalcoholic beverages	333	411	123	25.9
Food prepared by household on trips	43	50	116	24.4
Food away from home	**2,668**	**3,178**	**119**	**25.0**
ALCOHOLIC BEVERAGES	**457**	**498**	**109**	**22.9**
HOUSING	**16,920**	**19,195**	**113**	**23.8**
Shelter	**10,023**	**11,617**	**116**	**24.3**
Owned dwellings	6,730	8,626	128	26.9
Mortgage interest and charges	3,890	5,093	131	27.5
Property taxes	1,709	2,178	127	26.8
Maintenance, repairs, insurance, other expenses	1,131	1,356	120	25.2
Rented dwellings	2,602	2,055	79	16.6
Other lodging	691	936	135	28.5

	total consumer units	consumer units headed by 45-to-54-year-olds average spending	indexed spending	market share
Utilities, fuels, public services	**$3,477**	**$4,053**	**117**	**24.5%**
Natural gas	480	539	112	23.6
Electricity	1,303	1,499	115	24.2
Fuel oil and other fuels	151	192	127	26.7
Telephone services	1,110	1,330	120	25.2
Water and other public services	434	493	114	23.9
Household services	**984**	**867**	**88**	**18.5**
Personal services	415	193	47	9.8
Other household services	569	674	118	24.9
Housekeeping supplies	**639**	**724**	**113**	**23.8**
Laundry and cleaning supplies	140	161	115	24.2
Other household products	347	365	105	22.1
Postage and stationery	152	198	130	27.4
Household furnishings and equipment	**1,797**	**1,933**	**108**	**22.6**
Household textiles	133	120	90	19.0
Furniture	446	461	103	21.7
Floor coverings	46	54	117	24.7
Major appliances	231	285	123	25.9
Small appliances, miscellaneous housewares	101	115	114	23.9
Miscellaneous household equipment	840	898	107	22.5
APPAREL AND SERVICES	**1,881**	**2,191**	**116**	**24.5**
Men and boys	**435**	**514**	**118**	**24.8**
Men, aged 16 or older	351	428	122	25.6
Boys, aged 2 to 15	84	87	104	21.8
Women and girls	**749**	**952**	**127**	**26.7**
Women, aged 16 or older	627	822	131	27.5
Girls, aged 2 to 15	122	130	107	22.4
Children under age 2	**93**	**54**	**58**	**12.2**
Footwear	**327**	**383**	**117**	**24.6**
Other apparel products and services	**276**	**287**	**104**	**21.8**
TRANSPORTATION	**8,758**	**9,943**	**114**	**23.8**
Vehicle purchases	**3,244**	**3,223**	**99**	**20.9**
Cars and trucks, new	1,572	1,645	105	22.0
Cars and trucks, used	1,567	1,404	90	18.8
Other vehicles	105	174	166	34.8
Gasoline and motor oil	**2,384**	**2,846**	**119**	**25.1**
Other vehicle expenses	**2,592**	**3,213**	**124**	**26.0**
Vehicle finance charges	305	335	110	23.1
Maintenance and repairs	738	941	128	26.8
Vehicle insurance	1,071	1,382	129	27.1
Vehicle rental, leases, licenses, other charges	478	555	116	24.4
Public transportation	**538**	**661**	**123**	**25.8**

	total consumer units	consumer units headed by 45-to-54-year-olds average spending	indexed spending	market share
HEALTH CARE	**$2,853**	**$2,792**	**98**	**20.6%**
Health insurance	1,545	1,386	90	18.8
Medical services	709	772	109	22.9
Drugs	481	498	104	21.8
Medical supplies	118	135	114	24.0
ENTERTAINMENT	**2,698**	**3,163**	**117**	**24.6**
Fees and admissions	658	823	125	26.3
Audio and visual equipment and services	987	1,126	114	24.0
Pets, toys, hobbies, and playground equipment	560	711	127	26.7
Other entertainment supplies, services	493	504	102	21.5
PERSONAL CARE PRODUCTS, SERVICES	**588**	**686**	**117**	**24.5**
READING	**118**	**137**	**116**	**24.4**
EDUCATION	**945**	**1,687**	**179**	**37.5**
TOBACCO PRODUCTS, SMOKING SUPPLIES	**323**	**388**	**120**	**25.2**
MISCELLANEOUS	**808**	**1,008**	**125**	**26.2**
CASH CONTRIBUTIONS	**1,821**	**1,972**	**108**	**22.7**
PERSONAL INSURANCE AND PENSIONS	**5,336**	**7,489**	**140**	**29.5**
Life and other personal insurance	309	402	130	27.3
Pensions and Social Security	5,027	7,087	141	29.6
PERSONAL TAXES	**2,233**	**3,485**	**156**	**32.8**
Federal income taxes	1,569	2,490	159	33.3
State and local income taxes	468	754	161	33.8
Other taxes	196	241	123	25.8
GIFTS FOR PEOPLE IN OTHER HOUSEHOLDS	**1,198**	**1,847**	**154**	**32.4**

Note: The Bureau of Labor Statistics uses consumer unit rather than household as the sampling unit in the Consumer Expenditure Survey. For the definition of consumer unit, see the glossary. Spending on gifts is also included in the preceding product and service categories. "–" means not applicable.
Source: Bureau of Labor Statistics, 2007 Consumer Expenditure Survey, Internet site http://www.bls.gov/cex/; calculations by New Strategist

Spending of Householders Aged 55 to 64 Is above Average

As Boomers fill the age group, spending patterns are changing.

The spending of householders aged 55 to 64 grew 14 percent between 2000 and 2007 after adjusting for inflation—a bigger increase than any other age group. Households headed by 55-to-64-year-olds spent $53,786 in 2007—or 8 percent more than the average household. The age group's spending is growing because lifestyles are changing. Two-earner couples are heading a growing proportion of households, and most of those couples are postponing retirement as early retirement options diminish. Rather than coping with reduced incomes in retirement, many are continuing to enjoy peak earnings well into their sixties.

On many discretionary items, householders aged 55 to 64 spend well above average. People in this age group are ardent travelers, which is reflected in their spending. Householders aged 55 to 64 spend 68 percent more than average on other lodging (mostly hotels and motels) and 42 percent more than average on public transportation (mostly airfares). They spend 63 percent more than average on gifts for people living in other households, 40 percent more on drugs, 17 percent more on alcoholic beverages, and 15 percent more on women's clothes.

■ The spending patterns of householders aged 55 to 64 will continue to change as Boomers completely fill the age group.

Householders aged 55 to 64 spend 68 percent more than average on other lodging, which is mostly hotel and motel expenses

(indexed spending of householders aged 55 to 64 on selected items, 2007)

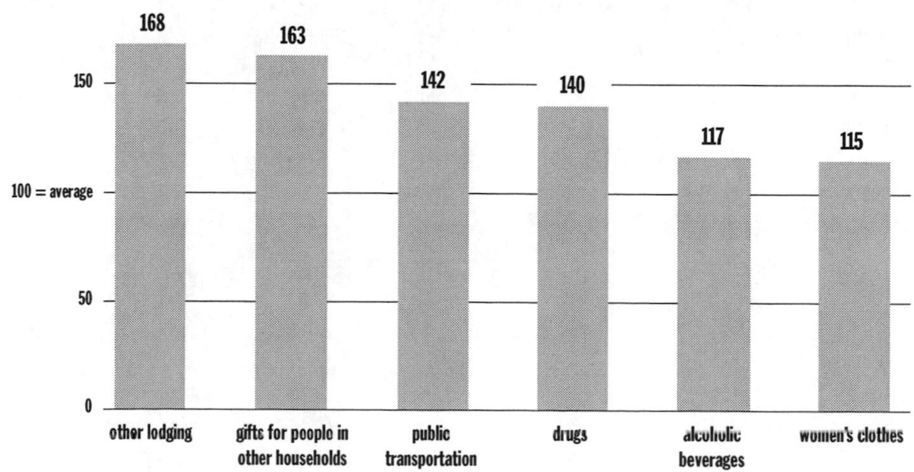

Table 9.5 Average, Indexed, and Market Share of Spending by Householders Aged 55 to 64, 2007

(average annual spending of total consumer units and average annual, indexed, and market share of spending by consumer units headed by 55-to-64-year-olds, 2007)

		consumer units headed by 55-to-64-year-olds		
	total consumer units	average spending	indexed spending	market share
Number of consumer units (in 000s)	**120,171**	**19,462**	**–**	**16.2%**
Average annual spending	**$49,638**	**$53,786**	**108**	**17.5**
FOOD	**6,133**	**6,241**	**102**	**16.5**
Food at home	**3,465**	**3,457**	**100**	**16.2**
Cereals and bakery products	460	456	99	16.1
Cereals and cereal products	143	129	90	14.6
Bakery products	317	327	103	16.7
Meats, poultry, fish, and eggs	777	758	98	15.8
Beef	216	200	93	15.0
Pork	150	147	98	15.9
Other meats	104	107	103	16.7
Poultry	142	134	94	15.3
Fish and seafood	122	127	104	16.9
Eggs	43	44	102	16.6
Dairy products	387	384	99	16.1
Fresh milk and cream	154	142	92	14.9
Other dairy products	234	242	103	16.7
Fruits and vegetables	600	640	107	17.3
Fresh fruits	202	219	108	17.6
Fresh vegetables	190	207	109	17.6
Processed fruits	112	113	101	16.3
Processed vegetables	96	102	106	17.2
Other food at home	1,241	1,219	98	15.9
Sugar and other sweets	124	119	96	15.5
Fats and oils	91	95	104	16.9
Miscellaneous foods	650	599	92	14.9
Nonalcoholic beverages	333	343	103	16.7
Food prepared by household on trips	43	63	147	23.7
Food away from home	**2,668**	**2,784**	**104**	**16.9**
ALCOHOLIC BEVERAGES	**457**	**533**	**117**	**18.9**
HOUSING	**16,920**	**17,223**	**102**	**16.5**
Shelter	**10,023**	**9,763**	**97**	**15.8**
Owned dwellings	6,730	7,063	105	17.0
Mortgage interest and charges	3,890	3,421	88	14.2
Property taxes	1,709	2,127	124	20.2
Maintenance, repairs, insurance, other expenses	1,131	1,515	134	21.7
Rented dwellings	2,602	1,539	59	9.6
Other lodging	691	1,161	168	27.2

	total consumer units	consumer units headed by 55-to-64-year-olds		
		average spending	indexed spending	market share
Utilities, fuels, public services	**$3,477**	**$3,754**	**108**	**17.5%**
Natural gas	480	557	116	18.8
Electricity	1,303	1,403	108	17.4
Fuel oil and other fuels	151	171	113	18.3
Telephone services	1,110	1,135	102	16.6
Water and other public services	434	488	112	18.2
Household services	**984**	**860**	**87**	**14.2**
Personal services	415	159	38	6.2
Other household services	569	701	123	20.0
Housekeeping services	**639**	**902**	**141**	**22.9**
Laundry and cleaning supplies	140	134	96	15.5
Other household products	347	572	165	26.7
Postage and stationery	152	197	130	21.0
Household furnishings and equipment	**1,797**	**1,944**	**108**	**17.5**
Household textiles	133	170	128	20.7
Furniture	446	437	98	15.9
Floor coverings	46	48	104	16.9
Major appliances	231	266	115	18.6
Small appliances, miscellaneous housewares	101	92	91	14.8
Miscellaneous household equipment	840	931	111	17.9
APPAREL AND SERVICES	**1,881**	**1,888**	**100**	**16.3**
Men and boys	**435**	**402**	**92**	**15.0**
Men, aged 16 or older	351	367	105	16.9
Boys, aged 2 to 15	84	35	42	6.7
Women and girls	**749**	**793**	**106**	**17.1**
Women, aged 16 or older	627	723	115	18.7
Girls, aged 2 to 15	122	70	57	9.3
Children under age 2	**93**	**55**	**59**	**9.6**
Footwear	**327**	**351**	**107**	**17.4**
Other apparel products and services	**276**	**286**	**104**	**16.8**
TRANSPORTATION	**8,758**	**9,608**	**110**	**17.8**
Vehicle purchases	**3,244**	**3,348**	**103**	**16.7**
Cars and trucks, new	1,572	1,700	108	17.5
Cars and trucks, used	1,567	1,582	101	16.4
Other vehicles	105	66	63	10.2
Gasoline and motor oil	**2,384**	**2,504**	**105**	**17.0**
Other vehicle expenses	**2,592**	**2,993**	**115**	**18.7**
Vehicle finance charges	305	325	107	17.3
Maintenance and repairs	738	885	120	19.4
Vehicle insurance	1,071	1,214	113	18.4
Vehicle rental, leases, licenses, other charges	478	569	119	19.3
Public transportation	**538**	**763**	**142**	**23.0**

	total consumer units	consumer units headed by 55-to-64-year-olds average spending	indexed spending	market share
HEALTH CARE	**$2,853**	**$3,476**	**122**	**19.7%**
Health insurance	1,545	1,751	113	18.4
Medical services	709	883	125	20.2
Drugs	481	674	140	22.7
Medical supplies	118	168	142	23.1
ENTERTAINMENT	**2,698**	**2,730**	**101**	**16.4**
Fees and admissions	658	645	98	15.9
Audio and visual equipment and services	987	965	98	15.8
Pets, toys, hobbies, and playground equipment	560	653	117	18.9
Other entertainment supplies, services	493	468	95	15.4
PERSONAL CARE PRODUCTS, SERVICES	**588**	**632**	**107**	**17.4**
READING	**118**	**151**	**128**	**20.7**
EDUCATION	**945**	**929**	**98**	**15.9**
TOBACCO PRODUCTS, SMOKING SUPPLIES	**323**	**353**	**109**	**17.7**
MISCELLANEOUS	**808**	**1,084**	**134**	**21.7**
CASH CONTRIBUTIONS	**1,821**	**2,746**	**151**	**24.4**
PERSONAL INSURANCE AND PENSIONS	**5,336**	**6,193**	**116**	**18.8**
Life and other personal insurance	309	461	149	24.2
Pensions and Social Security	5,027	5,732	114	18.5
PERSONAL TAXES	**2,233**	**3,083**	**138**	**22.4**
Federal income taxes	1,569	2,234	142	23.1
State and local income taxes	468	551	118	19.1
Other taxes	196	298	152	24.6
GIFTS FOR PEOPLE IN OTHER HOUSEHOLDS	**1,198**	**1,948**	**163**	**26.3**

Note: The Bureau of Labor Statistics uses consumer unit rather than household as the sampling unit in the Consumer Expenditure Survey. For the definition of consumer unit, see the glossary. Spending on gifts is also included in the preceding product and service categories. "–" means not applicable.
Source: Bureau of Labor Statistics, 2007 Consumer Expenditure Survey, Internet site http://www.bls.gov/cex/; calculations by New Strategist

CHAPTER

10

Time Use

■ The middle aged spend the most time at work. Men aged 45 to 54 spend an average of 5.22 hours per day at work versus the 4.16 hours per day spent at work by the average man.

■ Women aged 45 to 54 spend 3.92 hours per day in leisure activities, 9 percent less than the average woman. They spend a larger 4.01 hours per day at work.

■ People aged 55 to 64 spend 56 percent more time than the average person caring for animals and pets.

■ People aged 55 to 64 spend twice as much time as the average person caring for adults in other households—primarily their elderly parents.

The Middle Aged Spend More Time at Work than at Play

Men aged 45 to 54 spend 25 percent more time than the average man at work.

Time use varies sharply by age. The middle aged are the ones who spend the most time at work and the least time at play, according to the Bureau of Labor Statistics' American Time Use Survey. Men aged 45 to 54 spend 5.22 hours per day at work versus the 4.16 hours per day spent at work by the average man. Time at work declines in the 55-to-64 age group, with men of that age spending 8 percent less time than the average man at work because some are retired.

Women aged 45 to 54 spend 37 percent more time than the average woman at work, while those aged 55 to 64 spend about an average amount of time at work. Women aged 55 to 64 spend much more time than the average woman caring for adults in other households—often their elderly parents.

■ As Boomers age, they will have less leisure time than today's elderly because many will have to postpone retirement.

Time at work peaks in middle age

(average number of hours per day spent working, by age, 2007)

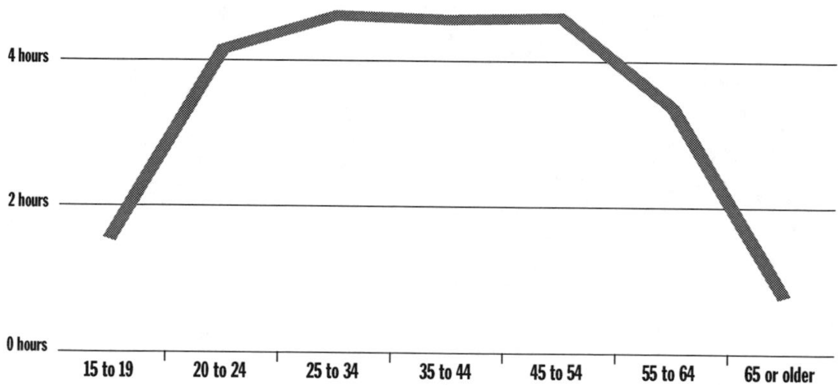

Table 10.1 Detailed Time Use of People Aged 45 to 54, 2007

(hours per day spent in primary activities by total people aged 15 or older and people aged 45 to 54, and index of age group to total, 2007)

	hours per day for total people	hours per day for people aged 45 to 54	index, 45 to 54 to total
TOTAL, ALL ACTIVITIES	**24.00**	**24.00**	**100**
Personal care activities	**9.31**	**9.01**	**97**
Sleeping	8.57	8.24	96
Grooming	0.67	0.68	101
Health-related self-care	0.07	0.08	114
Household activities	**1.87**	**2.09**	**112**
Housework	0.64	0.72	113
Food preparation and cleanup	0.52	0.57	110
Lawn, garden, and houseplants	0.21	0.22	105
Animals and pets	0.09	0.12	133
Vehicles	0.04	0.03	75
Household management	0.22	0.21	95
Household and personal mail and messages (except email)	0.02	0.02	100
Household and personal email and messages	0.05	0.04	80
Caring for and helping household members	**0.45**	**0.29**	**64**
Caring for and helping household children	0.38	0.21	55
Caring for household adults	0.03	0.03	100
Helping household adults	0.01	0.01	100
Caring for and helping people in other households	**0.14**	**0.13**	**93**
Caring for and helping children in other households	0.06	0.07	117
Caring for adults in other households	0.01	0.01	100
Helping adults in other households	0.06	0.05	83
Working and work-related activities	**3.53**	**4.60**	**130**
Working	3.47	4.56	131
Educational activities	**0.40**	**0.07**	**18**
Attending class	0.26	0.03	12
Homework and research	0.14	0.05	36
Consumer purchases	**0.39**	**0.40**	**103**
Shopping (store, telephone, Internet)	0.39	0.40	103
Grocery shopping	0.10	0.11	110
Shopping (except groceries, food, and gas)	0.27	0.26	96
Professional and personal care services	**0.09**	**0.09**	**100**
Medical and care services	0.05	0.05	100
Eating and drinking	**1.11**	**1.10**	**99**
Socializing, relaxing, and leisure	**4.52**	**4.09**	**90**
Socializing and communicating	0.64	0.57	89
Attending or hosting social events	0.09	0.10	111
Relaxing and leisure	3.70	3.33	90
Television and movies	2.62	2.47	94
Playing games	0.19	0.07	37
Computer use for leisure (except games)	0.14	0.13	93
Reading for personal interest	0.35	0.31	89
Arts and entertainment (other than sports)	0.09	0.09	100
Attending movies	0.03	0.02	67

	hours per day for total people	hours per day for people aged 45 to 54	index, 45 to 54 to total
Sports, exercise, and recreation	**0.35**	**0.28**	**80**
Participating in sports, exercise, and recreation	0.32	0.24	75
Attending sporting or recreational events	0.03	0.04	133
Religious and spiritual activities	**0.15**	**0.15**	**100**
Volunteer activities	**0.16**	**0.16**	**100**
Telephone calls	**0.11**	**0.09**	**82**
Traveling	**1.23**	**1.27**	**103**

Note: Primary activities are those respondents identified as their main activity. Other activities done simultaneously are not included. Travel related to activities is reported separately. Numbers do not sum to total because not all activities are shown. The index is calculated by dividing time spent by age group by time spent by average person and multiplying by 100.
Source: Bureau of Labor Statistics, unpublished tables from the 2007 American Time Use Survey, Internet site http://www.bls.gov/tus/home.htm

Table 10.2 Detailed Time Use of Men Aged 45 to 54, 2007

(hours per day spent in primary activities by total men aged 15 or older and men aged 45 to 54, and index of age group to total, 2007)

	hours per day for total men	hours per day for men aged 45 to 54	index, 45 to 54 to total
TOTAL, ALL ACTIVITIES	**24.00**	**24.00**	**100**
Personal care activities	**9.12**	**8.81**	**97**
Sleeping	8.52	8.18	96
Grooming	0.54	0.57	106
Health-related self-care	0.05	0.06	120
Household activities	**1.45**	**1.60**	**110**
Housework	0.29	0.32	110
Food preparation and cleanup	0.28	0.31	111
Lawn, garden, and houseplants	0.30	0.31	103
Animals and pets	0.09	0.11	122
Vehicles	0.07	0.05	71
Household management	0.19	0.17	89
Household and personal mail and messages (except email)	0.02	0.01	50
Household and personal email and messages	0.05	0.03	60
Caring for and helping household members	**0.27**	**0.23**	**85**
Caring for and helping household children	0.22	0.17	77
Caring for household adults	0.02	0.02	100
Helping household adults	0.01	0.01	100
Caring for and helping people in other households	**0.11**	**0.12**	**109**
Caring for and helping children in other households	0.04	0.05	125
Caring for adults in other households	0.01	0.01	100
Helping adults in other households	0.06	0.06	100
Working and work-related activities	**4.16**	**5.22**	**125**
Working	4.09	5.17	126
Educational activities	**0.38**	**0.07**	**18**
Attending class	0.26	0.01	4
Homework and research	0.12	0.06	50
Consumer purchases	**0.31**	**0.32**	**103**
Shopping (store, telephone, Internet)	0.31	0.32	103
Grocery shopping	0.07	0.09	129
Shopping (except groceries, food, and gas)	0.21	0.21	100
Professional and personal care services	**0.06**	**0.06**	**100**
Medical and care services	0.04	0.04	100
Eating and drinking	**1.14**	**1.17**	**103**
Socializing, relaxing, and leisure	**4.77**	**4.27**	**90**
Socializing and communicating	0.59	0.51	86
Attending or hosting social events	0.08	0.10	125
Relaxing and leisure	4.02	3.60	90
Television and movies	2.88	2.78	97
Playing games	0.24	0.06	25
Computer use for leisure (except games)	0.17	0.16	94
Reading for personal interest	0.28	0.22	79
Arts and entertainment (other than sports)	0.09	0.07	78
Attending movies	0.03	0.02	67

	hours per day for total men	hours per day for men aged 45 to 54	index, 45 to 54 to total
Sports, exercise, and recreation	**0.45**	**0.36**	**80**
Participating in sports, exercise, and recreation	0.42	0.31	74
Attending sporting or recreational events	0.03	0.04	133
Religious and spiritual activities	**0.11**	**0.10**	**91**
Volunteer activities	**0.13**	**0.15**	**115**
Telephone calls	**0.06**	**0.04**	**67**
Traveling	**1.28**	**1.31**	**102**

Note: Primary activities are those respondents identified as their main activity. Other activities done simultaneously are not included. Travel related to activities is reported separately. Numbers do not sum to total because not all activities are shown. The index is calculated by dividing time spent by age group by time spent by average man and multiplying by 100.
Source: Bureau of Labor Statistics, unpublished tables from the 2007 American Time Use Survey, Internet site http://www.bls.gov/tus/home.htm

Table 10.3 Detailed Time Use of Women Aged 45 to 54, 2007

(hours per day spent in primary activities by total women aged 15 or older and women aged 45 to 54, and index of age group to total, 2007)

	hours per day for total women	hours per day for women aged 45 to 54	index, 45 to 54 to total
TOTAL, ALL ACTIVITIES	**24.00**	**24.00**	**100**
Personal care activities	**9.50**	**9.20**	**97**
Sleeping	8.63	8.29	96
Grooming	0.79	0.80	101
Health-related self-care	0.08	0.10	125
Household activities	**2.27**	**2.56**	**113**
Housework	0.97	1.09	112
Food preparation and cleanup	0.74	0.82	111
Lawn, garden, and houseplants	0.12	0.13	108
Animals and pets	0.10	0.13	130
Vehicles	0.01	0.01	100
Household management	0.24	0.25	104
Household and personal mail and messages (except email)	0.03	0.03	100
Household and personal email and messages	0.05	0.05	100
Caring for and helping household members	**0.62**	**0.34**	**55**
Caring for and helping household children	0.52	0.24	46
Caring for household adults	0.03	0.04	133
Helping household adults	0.01	0.01	100
Caring for and helping people in other households	**0.16**	**0.14**	**88**
Caring for and helping children in other households	0.09	0.09	100
Caring for adults in other households	0.02	0.01	50
Helping adults in other households	0.05	0.04	80
Working and work-related activities	**2.93**	**4.01**	**137**
Working	2.89	3.98	138
Educational activities	**0.42**	**0.07**	**17**
Attending class	0.25	0.04	16
Homework and research	0.15	0.03	20
Consumer purchases	**0.48**	**0.47**	**98**
Shopping (store, telephone, Internet)	0.48	0.47	98
Grocery shopping	0.12	0.14	117
Shopping (except groceries, food, and gas)	0.33	0.30	91
Professional and personal care services	**0.12**	**0.12**	**100**
Medical and care services	0.06	0.06	100
Eating and drinking	**1.09**	**1.02**	**94**
Socializing, relaxing, and leisure	**4.29**	**3.92**	**91**
Socializing and communicating	0.69	0.63	91
Attending or hosting social events	0.10	0.10	100
Relaxing and leisure	3.40	3.08	91
Television and movies	2.38	2.17	91
Playing games	0.14	0.08	57
Computer use for leisure (except games)	0.11	0.10	91
Reading for personal interest	0.42	0.41	98
Arts and entertainment (other than sports)	0.10	0.11	110
Attending movies	0.03	0.03	100

	hours per day for total women	hours per day for women aged 45 to 54	index, 45 to 54 to total
Sports, exercise, and recreation	**0.25**	**0.21**	**84**
Participating in sports, exercise, and recreation	0.22	0.18	82
Attending sporting or recreational events	0.03	0.03	100
Religious and spiritual activities	**0.18**	**0.20**	**111**
Volunteer activities	**0.18**	**0.16**	**89**
Telephone calls	**0.15**	**0.14**	**93**
Traveling	**1.18**	**1.24**	**105**

Note: Primary activities are those respondents identified as their main activity. Other activities done simultaneously are not included. Travel related to activities is reported separately. Numbers do not sum to total because not all activities are shown. The index is calculated by dividing time spent by age group by time spent by average woman and multiplying by 100.
Source: Bureau of Labor Statistics, unpublished tables from the 2007 American Time Use Survey, Internet site http://www.bls.gov/tus/home.htm

Table 10.4 Detailed Time Use of People Aged 55 to 64, 2007

(hours per day spent in primary activities by total people aged 15 or older and people aged 55 to 64, and index of age group to total, 2007)

	hours per day for total people	hours per day for people aged 55 to 64	index, 55 to 64 to total
TOTAL, ALL ACTIVITIES	**24.00**	**24.00**	**100**
Personal care activities	**9.31**	**9.02**	**97**
Sleeping	8.57	8.26	96
Grooming	0.67	0.65	97
Health-related self-care	0.07	0.11	157
Household activities	**1.87**	**2.41**	**129**
Housework	0.64	0.77	120
Food preparation and cleanup	0.52	0.59	113
Lawn, garden, and houseplants	0.21	0.34	162
Animals and pets	0.09	0.14	156
Vehicles	0.04	0.05	125
Household management	0.22	0.28	127
Household and personal mail and messages (except email)	0.02	0.03	150
Household and personal email and messages	0.05	0.06	120
Caring for and helping household members	**0.45**	**0.13**	**29**
Caring for and helping household children	0.38	0.05	13
Caring for household adults	0.03	0.06	200
Helping household adults	0.01	0.01	100
Caring for and helping people in other households	**0.14**	**0.24**	**171**
Caring for and helping children in other households	0.06	0.13	217
Caring for adults in other households	0.01	0.04	400
Helping adults in other households	0.06	0.08	133
Working and work-related activities	**3.53**	**3.37**	**95**
Working	3.47	3.33	96
Educational activities	**0.40**	**0.03**	**8**
Attending class	0.26	0.01	4
Homework and research	0.14	0.01	7
Consumer purchases	**0.39**	**0.49**	**126**
Shopping (store, telephone, Internet)	0.39	0.49	126
Grocery shopping	0.10	0.11	110
Shopping (except groceries, food, and gas)	0.27	0.35	130
Professional and personal care services	**0.09**	**0.11**	**122**
Medical and care services	0.05	0.07	140
Eating and drinking	**1.11**	**1.19**	**107**
Socializing, relaxing, and leisure	**4.52**	**4.83**	**107**
Socializing and communicating	0.64	0.55	86
Attending or hosting social events	0.09	0.05	56
Relaxing and leisure	3.70	4.14	112
Television and movies	2.62	2.91	111
Playing games	0.19	0.12	63
Computer use for leisure (except games)	0.14	0.12	86
Reading for personal interest	0.35	0.54	154
Arts and entertainment (other than sports)	0.09	0.09	100
Attending movies	0.03	0.02	67

	hours per day for total people	hours per day for people aged 55 to 64	index, 55 to 64 to total
Sports, exercise, and recreation	**0.35**	**0.28**	**80**
Participating in sports, exercise, and recreation	0.32	0.26	81
Attending sporting or recreational events	0.03	0.02	67
Religious and spiritual activities	**0.15**	**0.18**	**120**
Volunteer activities	**0.16**	**0.21**	**131**
Telephone calls	**0.11**	**0.10**	**91**
Traveling	**1.23**	**1.21**	**98**

Note: Primary activities are those respondents identified as their main activity. Other activities done simultaneously are not included. Travel related to activities is reported separately. Numbers do not sum to total because not all activities are shown. The index is calculated by dividing time spent by age group by time spent by average person and multiplying by 100.
Source: Bureau of Labor Statistics, unpublished tables from the 2007 American Time Use Survey, Internet site http://www.bls .gov/tus/home.htm

Table 10.5 Detailed Time Use of Men Aged 55 to 64, 2007

(hours per day spent in primary activities by total men aged 15 or older and men aged 55 to 64, and index of age group to total, 2007)

	hours per day for total men	hours per day for men aged 55 to 64	index, 55 to 64 to total
TOTAL, ALL ACTIVITIES	**24.00**	**24.00**	**100**
Personal care activities	**9.12**	**8.96**	**98**
Sleeping	8.52	8.32	98
Grooming	0.54	0.51	94
Health-related self-care	0.05	0.13	260
Household activities	**1.45**	**2.02**	**139**
Housework	0.29	0.30	103
Food preparation and cleanup	0.28	0.38	136
Lawn, garden, and houseplants	0.30	0.51	170
Animals and pets	0.09	0.14	156
Vehicles	0.07	0.09	129
Household management	0.19	0.27	142
Household and personal mail and messages (except email)	0.02	0.02	100
Household and personal email and messages	0.05	0.06	120
Caring for and helping household members	**0.27**	**0.10**	**37**
Caring for and helping household children	0.22	0.03	14
Caring for household adults	0.02	0.04	200
Helping household adults	0.01	0.01	100
Caring for and helping people in other households	**0.11**	**0.14**	**127**
Caring for and helping children in other households	0.04	0.06	150
Caring for adults in other households	0.01	0.01	100
Helping adults in other households	0.06	0.08	133
Working and work-related activities	**4.16**	**3.82**	**92**
Working	4.09	3.77	92
Educational activities	**0.38**	**0.03**	**8**
Attending class	0.26	0.02	8
Homework and research	0.12	0.01	8
Consumer purchases	**0.31**	**0.35**	**113**
Shopping (store, telephone, Internet)	0.31	0.35	113
Grocery shopping	0.07	0.08	114
Shopping (except groceries, food, and gas)	0.21	0.24	114
Professional and personal care services	**0.06**	**0.06**	**100**
Medical and care services	0.04	0.05	125
Eating and drinking	**1.14**	**1.23**	**108**
Socializing, relaxing, and leisure	**4.77**	**5.13**	**108**
Socializing and communicating	0.59	0.54	92
Attending or hosting social events	0.08	0.04	50
Relaxing and leisure	4.02	4.48	111
Television and movies	2.88	3.22	112
Playing games	0.24	0.14	58
Computer use for leisure (except games)	0.17	0.14	82
Reading for personal interest	0.28	0.51	182
Arts and entertainment (other than sports)	0.09	0.07	78
Attending movies	0.03	0.01	33

	hours per day for total men	hours per day for men aged 55 to 64	index, 55 to 64 to total
Sports, exercise, and recreation	**0.45**	**0.39**	**87**
Participating in sports, exercise, and recreation	0.42	0.36	86
Attending sporting or recreational events	0.03	0.03	100
Religious and spiritual activities	**0.11**	**0.16**	**145**
Volunteer activities	**0.13**	**0.18**	**138**
Telephone calls	**0.06**	**0.05**	**83**
Traveling	**1.28**	**1.18**	**92**

Note: Primary activities are those respondents identified as their main activity. Other activities done simultaneously are not included. Travel related to activities is reported separately. Numbers do not sum to total because not all activities are shown. The index is calculated by dividing time spent by age group by time spent by average man and multiplying by 100.
Source: Bureau of Labor Statistics, unpublished tables from the 2007 American Time Use Survey, Internet site http://www.bls .gov/tus/home.htm

Table 10.6 Detailed Time Use of Women Aged 55 to 64, 2007

(hours per day spent in primary activities by total women aged 15 or older and women aged 55 to 64, and index of age group to total, 2007)

	hours per day for total women	hours per day for women aged 55 to 64	index, 55 to 64 to total
TOTAL, ALL ACTIVITIES	**24.00**	**24.00**	**100**
Personal care activities	**9.50**	**9.08**	**96**
Sleeping	8.63	8.20	95
Grooming	0.79	0.78	99
Health-related self-care	0.08	0.09	113
Household activities	**2.27**	**2.77**	**122**
Housework	0.97	1.21	125
Food preparation and cleanup	0.74	0.80	108
Lawn, garden, and houseplants	0.12	0.18	150
Animals and pets	0.10	0.14	140
Vehicles	0.01	0.01	100
Household management	0.24	0.28	117
Household and personal mail and messages (except email)	0.03	0.05	167
Household and personal email and messages	0.05	0.06	120
Caring for and helping household members	**0.62**	**0.15**	**24**
Caring for and helping household children	0.52	0.06	12
Caring for household adults	0.03	0.07	233
Helping household adults	0.01	0.01	100
Caring for and helping people in other households	**0.16**	**0.34**	**213**
Caring for and helping children in other households	0.09	0.19	211
Caring for adults in other households	0.02	0.06	300
Helping adults in other households	0.05	0.08	160
Working and work-related activities	**2.93**	**2.95**	**101**
Working	2.89	2.92	101
Educational activities	**0.42**	**0.02**	**5**
Attending class	0.25	0.01	4
Homework and research	0.15	0.01	7
Consumer purchases	**0.48**	**0.63**	**131**
Shopping (store, telephone, Internet)	0.48	0.63	131
Grocery shopping	0.12	0.13	108
Shopping (except groceries, food, and gas)	0.33	0.46	139
Professional and personal care services	**0.12**	**0.16**	**133**
Medical and care services	0.06	0.09	150
Eating and drinking	**1.09**	**1.16**	**106**
Socializing, relaxing, and leisure	**4.29**	**4.54**	**106**
Socializing and communicating	0.69	0.56	81
Attending or hosting social events	0.10	0.05	50
Relaxing and leisure	3.40	3.81	112
Television and movies	2.38	2.61	110
Playing games	0.14	0.10	71
Computer use for leisure (except games)	0.11	0.10	91
Reading for personal interest	0.42	0.58	138
Arts and entertainment (other than sports)	0.10	0.11	110
Attending movies	0.03	0.03	100

	hours per day for total women	hours per day for women aged 55 to 64	index, 55 to 64 to total
Sports, exercise, and recreation	**0.25**	**0.19**	**76**
Participating in sports, exercise, and recreation	0.22	0.17	77
Attending sporting or recreational events	0.03	0.01	33
Religious and spiritual activities	**0.18**	**0.20**	**111**
Volunteer activities	**0.18**	**0.24**	**133**
Telephone calls	**0.15**	**0.15**	**100**
Traveling	**1.18**	**1.24**	**105**

Note: Primary activities are those respondents identified as their main activity. Other activities done simultaneously are not included. Travel related to activities is reported separately. Numbers do not sum to total because not all activities are shown. The index is calculated by dividing time spent by age group by time spent by average womanand multiplying by 100.
Source: Bureau of Labor Statistics, unpublished tables from the 2007 American Time Use Survey, Internet site http://www.bls.gov/tus/home.htm

CHAPTER

11

Wealth

■ Financial problems were emerging among Boomers even before the financial turmoil of 2008. The median net worth of householders aged 45 to 54 rose 15 percent between 2004 and 2007, but that of householders aged 55 to 64 fell 7 percent during those years. (Boomers were aged 43 to 61 in 2007.)

■ The median financial assets of householders aged 45 to 54 grew by a substantial 27 percent between 2004 and 2007 (to $54,000). In contrast, the median financial assets of 55-to-64-year-olds fell by 15 percent during those years (to $72,400).

■ The median value of the nonfinancial assets owned by householders aged 45 to 54 rose 11 percent between 2004 and 2007 (to $224,900). The nonfinancial assets owned by householders aged 55 to 64 declined by 6 percent to $233,100.

■ Debt has been mounting for Boomers. Householders aged 45 to 64 saw their median debt rise 5 to 14 percent between 2004 and 2007, after adjusting for inflation.

■ Boomers are worried about retirement. In 2009, only 10 percent of workers aged 45 to 54 were "very confident" they would have enough money to live comfortably throughout retirement, down from 21 percent in 1999.

Younger Boomers Saw Their Net Worth Increase during the Housing Bubble

Even before the financial meltdown of 2008–09, the net worth of older Boomers was declining.

Net worth is one of the most important measures of wealth. It is the amount that remains after a household's debts are subtracted from its assets. During this decade's housing bubble, housing values rose faster than mortgage debt. Consequently, net worth grew substantially—up 18 percent for the average household between 2004 and 2007, after adjusting for inflation. The gain did not last, however. The Federal Reserve Board estimates that by October 2008, median net worth for the average household had fallen to $99,000—3 percent less than in 2004.

The net worth of householders aged 45 to 64 (Boomers were aged 43 to 61 in 2007) grew 15 percent between 2004 and 2007, to $182,500. The net worth of this age group is probably much lower today because of the ongoing decline in housing values and stock prices. Householders aged 55 to 64 saw their net worth decline even before the financial meltdown, the median falling by 7 percent between 2004 and 2007—to $253,700. The figure is probably much lower today.

■ Although the net worth of 55-to-64-year-olds fell between 2004 and 2007, the age group continues to have a greater net worth than any other.

The net worth of householders aged 55 to 64 fell between 2004 and 2007

(percent change in net worth of households by age of householder, 2004 to 2007; in 2007 dollars)

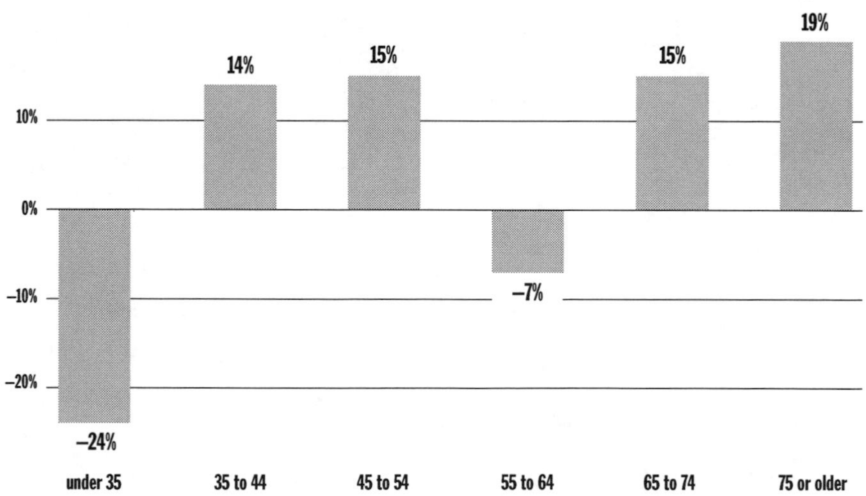

Table 11.1 Net Worth of Households by Age of Householder, 2004 to 2007

(median net worth of households by age of householder, 2004 to 2007; percent change, 2004–07; in 2007 dollars)

	2007	2004	percent change 2004–07
Total households	**$120,300**	**$102,200**	**17.7%**
Under age 35	11,800	15,600	–24.4
Aged 35 to 44	86,600	76,200	13.6
Aged 45 to 54	182,500	158,900	14.9
Aged 55 to 64	253,700	273,100	–7.1
Aged 65 to 74	239,400	208,800	14.7
Aged 75 or older	213,500	179,100	19.2

Source: Federal Reserve Board, Changes in U.S. Family Finances from 2004 to 2007: Evidence from the Survey of Consumer Finances, Federal Reserve Bulletin, February 2009, Internet site http://www.federalreserve.gov/pubs/oss/oss2/2007/scf2007home.html; calculations by New Strategist

Fewer Older Boomers Own Stock

They saw the value of their financial assets plunge between 2004 and 2007.

Between 2004 and 2007, the value of the financial assets of the average American household rose 14 percent after adjusting for inflation—to a median of $28,800, according to the Federal Reserve Board's Survey of Consumer Finances. The median financial assets of householders aged 45 to 54 grew by a substantial 27 percent during those years (to $54,000). At the same time, the median value of the financial assets owned by 55-to-64-year-olds fell 16 percent (to $72,400). Householders aged 55 to 64 have more financial assets than any other age group.

Slightly more than half of all households (51 percent) owned stocks directly or indirectly in 2007, up slightly from the 50 percent of 2004. Stock ownership among householders aged 45 to 54 grew by 4 percentage points (to 60 percent), while ownership among householders aged 55 to 64 declined by 4 percentage points (to 59 percent). The median value of stock holdings fell by 18 percent among those aged 45 to 54, while it did not change for the older group.

Only 53 percent of households owned a retirement account in 2007, but among householders aged 45 to 64 the figure ranges from 61 to 65 percent. The median value of the retirement accounts owned by householders aged 45 to 54 is $67,000, while that of householders aged 55 to 64 is $98,000.

■ The value of retirement accounts has plunged since these figures were collected by the Survey of Consumer Finances.

Financial assets of Boomers are modest

(median value of financial assets of households, by age of householder, 2007)

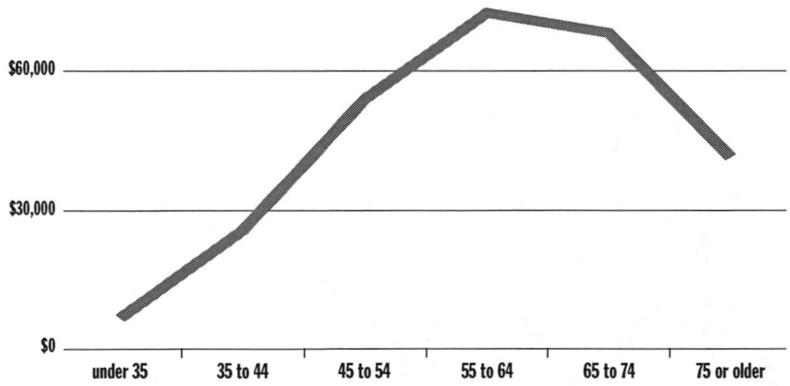

Table 11.2 Financial Assets of Households by Age of Householder, 2004 and 2007

(percentage of households owning financial assets and median value of assets for owners, by age of householder, 2004 and 2007; percentage point change in ownership and percent change in value of asset, 2004–07; in 2007 dollars)

	2007	2004	percentage point change
PERCENT OWNING ANY FINANCIAL ASSET			
Total households	**93.9%**	**93.8%**	**0.1**
Under age 35	89.2	90.1	–0.9
Aged 35 to 44	93.1	93.6	–0.5
Aged 45 to 54	93.3	93.6	–0.3
Aged 55 to 64	97.8	95.2	2.6
Aged 65 to 74	96.1	96.5	–0.4
Aged 75 or older	97.4	97.6	–0.2

	2007	2004	percent change
MEDIAN VALUE OF FINANCIAL ASSETS			
Total households	**$28,800**	**$25,300**	**13.8%**
Under age 35	6,800	5,700	19.3
Aged 35 to 44	25,800	20,900	23.4
Aged 45 to 54	54,000	42,400	27.4
Aged 55 to 64	72,400	85,700	–15.5
Aged 65 to 74	68,100	39,600	72.0
Aged 75 or older	41,500	42,600	–2.6

Source: Federal Reserve Board, Changes in U.S. Family Finances from 2004 to 2007: Evidence from the Survey of Consumer Finances, Federal Reserve Bulletin, February 2009, Internet site http://www.federalreserve.gov/pubs/oss/oss2/2007/scf2007home.html; calculations by New Strategist

Table 11.3 Financial Assets of Households by Type of Asset and Age of Householder, 2007

(percentage of households owning financial assets, and median value of asset for owners, by type of asset and age of householder, 2007)

	total	under 35	35 to 44	45 to 54	55 to 64	65 to 74	75 or older
PERCENT OWNING ASSET							
Any financial asset	**93.9%**	**89.2%**	**93.1%**	**93.3%**	**97.8%**	**96.1%**	**97.4%**
Transaction accounts	92.1	87.3	91.2	91.7	96.4	94.6	95.3
Certificates of deposit	16.1	6.7	9.0	14.3	20.5	24.2	37.0
Savings bonds	14.9	13.7	16.8	19.0	16.2	10.3	7.9
Bonds	1.6	–	0.7	1.1	2.1	4.2	3.5
Stocks	17.9	13.7	17.0	18.6	21.3	19.1	30.2
Pooled investment funds	11.4	5.3	11.6	12.6	14.3	14.6	13.2
Retirement accounts	52.6	41.6	57.5	64.7	60.9	51.7	30.0
Cash value life insurance	23.0	11.4	17.5	22.3	35.2	34.3	27.6
Other managed assets	5.8	–	2.2	5.1	7.7	13.2	14.0
Other financial assets	9.3	10.0	9.6	10.5	9.2	9.4	5.3
MEDIAN VALUE OF ASSET							
Any financial asset	**$28,800**	**$6,800**	**$25,800**	**$54,000**	**$72,400**	**$68,100**	**$41,500**
Transaction accounts	4,000	2,400	3,400	5,000	5,200	7,700	6,100
Certificates of deposit	20,000	5,000	5,000	15,000	23,000	23,200	30,000
Savings bonds	1,000	700	1,000	1,000	1,900	1,000	20,000
Bonds	80,000	–	9,700	200,000	90,800	50,000	100,000
Stocks	17,000	3,000	15,000	18,500	24,000	38,000	40,000
Pooled investment funds	56,000	18,000	22,500	50,000	112,000	86,000	75,000
Retirement accounts	45,000	10,000	36,000	67,000	98,000	77,000	35,000
Cash value life insurance	8,000	2,800	8,300	10,000	10,000	10,000	5,000
Other managed assets	70,000	–	24,000	45,000	59,000	70,000	100,000
Other financial assets	6,000	1,500	8,000	6,000	20,000	10,000	15,000

Note: "–" means sample is too small to make a reliable estimate.
Source: Federal Reserve Board, Changes in U.S. Family Finances from 2004 to 2007: Evidence from the Survey of Consumer Finances, Federal Reserve Bulletin, February 2009, Internet site http://www.federalreserve.gov/pubs/oss/oss2/2007/scf2007home.html; calculations by New Strategist

Table 11.4 Stock Ownership of Households by Age of Householder, 2004 and 2007

(percentage of households owning stock directly or indirectly, median value of stock for owners, and share of total household financial assets accounted for by stock holdings, by age of householder, 2004 and 2007; percent and percentage point change, 2004–07; in 2007 dollars)

	2007	2004	percentage point change
PERCENT OWNING STOCK			
Total households	**51.1%**	**50.2%**	**0.9**
Under age 35	38.6	40.8	–2.2
Aged 35 to 44	53.5	54.5	–1.0
Aged 45 to 54	60.4	56.5	3.9
Aged 55 to 64	58.9	62.8	–3.9
Aged 65 to 74	52.1	46.9	5.2
Aged 75 or older	40.1	34.8	5.3

	2007	2004	percent change
MEDIAN VALUE OF STOCK			
Total households	**$35,000**	**$35,700**	**–2.0%**
Under age 35	7,000	8,800	–20.5
Aged 35 to 44	26,000	22,000	18.2
Aged 45 to 54	45,000	54,900	–18.0
Aged 55 to 64	78,000	78,000	0.0
Aged 65 to 74	57,000	76,900	–25.9
Aged 75 or older	41,000	94,300	–56.5

	2007	2004	percentage point change
STOCK AS SHARE OF FINANCIAL ASSETS			
Total households	**53.3%**	**51.3%**	**2.0**
Under age 35	44.3	40.3	4.0
Aged 35 to 44	53.7	53.5	0.2
Aged 45 to 54	53.0	53.8	–0.8
Aged 55 to 64	55.0	55.0	0.0
Aged 65 to 74	55.3	51.5	3.8
Aged 75 or older	48.1	39.3	8.8

Source: Federal Reserve Board, Changes in U.S. Family Finances from 2004 to 2007: Evidence from the Survey of Consumer Finances, Federal Reserve Bulletin, February 2009, Internet site http://www.federalreserve.gov/pubs/oss/oss2/2007/scf2007home.html; calculations by New Strategist

Nonfinancial Assets of Younger Boomers Grew between 2004 and 2007

Their older counterparts lost ground during those years.

The median value of the nonfinancial assets owned by the average American household stood at $177,400 in 2007—9 percent more than in 2004, after adjusting for inflation. All age groups did not see gains, however. Whereas the median value of the nonfinancial assets owned by householders aged 45 to 54 rose 11 percent during those years, the value of the nonfinancial assets owned by householders aged 55 to 64 declined 6 percent, to $233,100.

Because housing equity accounts for the largest share of nonfinancial assets, the rise in home values was the biggest contributor to gains in this category. Among homeowners aged 45 to 54, median home value rose to $230,000—23 percent more than in 2004, after adjusting for inflation. Among householders aged 55 to 64, median home value fell by 4 percent during those years, to $210,000.

Since 2007, housing values have plunged and the decline is ongoing. The Federal Reserve Board has estimated that the median value of the average home fell from $200,000 in 2007 to $181,600 in October 2008—a 9 percent decline. Housing values have continued to fall since then and are likely lower today than they were in 2004, after adjusting for inflation.

■ The drop in housing values since 2007 has greatly reduced household net worth.

Median housing value peaks in the 45-to-54 age group

(median value of the primary residence among homeowners, by age of householder, 2007)

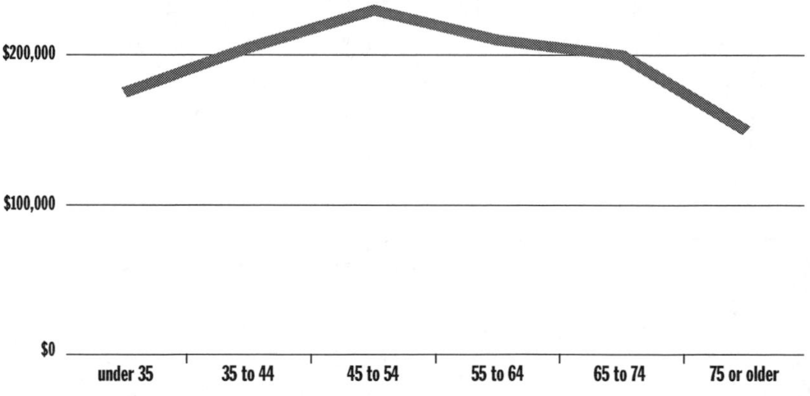

Table 11.5 Nonfinancial Assets of Households by Age of Householder, 2004 and 2007

(percentage of households owning nonfinancial assets and median value of assets for owners, by age of householder, 2004 and 2007; percentage point change in ownership and percent change in value of asset, 2004–07; in 2007 dollars)

	2007	2004	percentage point change
PERCENT OWNING ANY NONFINANCIAL ASSET			
Total households	**92.0%**	**92.5%**	**–0.5**
Under age 35	88.2	88.6	–0.4
Aged 35 to 44	91.3	93.0	–1.7
Aged 45 to 54	95.0	94.7	0.3
Aged 55 to 64	95.6	92.6	3.0
Aged 65 to 74	94.5	95.6	–1.1
Aged 75 or older	87.3	92.5	–5.2
	2007	**2004**	**percent change**
MEDIAN VALUE OF NONFINANCIAL ASSETS			
Total households	**$177,400**	**$162,300**	**9.3%**
Under age 35	30,900	35,500	–13.0
Aged 35 to 44	182,600	166,200	9.9
Aged 45 to 54	224,900	202,600	11.0
Aged 55 to 64	233,100	248,600	–6.2
Aged 65 to 74	212,200	177,000	19.9
Aged 75 or older	157,100	150,600	4.3

Source: Federal Reserve Board, Changes in U.S. Family Finances from 2004 to 2007: Evidence from the Survey of Consumer Finances, Federal Reserve Bulletin, February 2009, Internet site http://www.federalreserve.gov/pubs/oss/oss2/2007/scf2007home.html; calculations by New Strategist

Table 11.6 Nonfinancial Assets of Households by Type of Asset and Age of Householder, 2007

(percentage of households owning nonfinancial assets, and median value of asset for owners, by type of asset and age of householder, 2007)

	total	under 35	35 to 44	45 to 54	55 to 64	65 to 74	75 or older
PERCENT OWNING ASSET							
Any nonfinancial asset	**92.0%**	**88.2%**	**91.3%**	**95.0%**	**95.6%**	**94.5%**	**87.3%**
Vehicles	87.0	85.4	87.5	90.3	92.2	90.6	71.5
Primary residence	68.6	40.7	66.1	77.3	81.0	85.5	77.0
Other residential property	13.7	5.6	12.0	15.7	20.9	18.9	13.4
Equity in nonresidential property	8.1	3.2	7.5	9.5	11.5	12.3	6.8
Business equity	12.0	6.8	16.0	15.2	16.3	10.1	3.8
Other nonfinancial assets	7.2	5.9	5.5	8.7	8.5	9.1	5.8
MEDIAN VALUE OF ASSET							
Total nonfinancial assets	**$177,400**	**$30,900**	**$182,600**	**$224,900**	**$233,100**	**$212,200**	**$157,100**
Vehicles	15,500	13,300	17,400	18,700	17,400	14,600	9,400
Primary residence	200,000	175,000	205,000	230,000	210,000	200,000	150,000
Other residential property	146,000	85,000	150,000	150,000	157,000	150,000	100,000
Equity in nonresidential property	75,000	50,000	50,000	80,000	90,000	75,000	110,000
Business equity	100,500	59,900	86,000	100,000	116,300	415,000	250,000
Other nonfinancial assets	14,000	8,000	10,000	15,000	20,000	20,000	25,000

Source: Federal Reserve Board, Changes in U.S. Family Finances from 2004 to 2007: Evidence from the Survey of Consumer Finances, Federal Reserve Bulletin, February 2009, Internet site http://www.federalreserve.gov/pubs/oss/oss2/2007/scf2007home.html; calculations by New Strategist

Table 11.7 Household Ownership of Primary Residence by Age of Householder, 2004 and 2007

(percentage of households owning their primary residence, median value of asset for owners, and median value of home-secured debt for owners, by age of householder, 2004 and 2007; percentage point change in ownership and percent change in value of asset, 2004–07; in 2007 dollars)

	2007	2004	percentage point change
PERCENT OWNING PRIMARY RESIDENCE			
Total households	**68.6%**	**69.1%**	**–0.5**
Under age 35	40.7	41.6	–0.9
Aged 35 to 44	66.1	68.3	–2.2
Aged 45 to 54	77.3	77.3	0.0
Aged 55 to 64	81.0	79.1	1.9
Aged 65 to 74	85.5	81.3	4.2
Aged 75 or older	77.0	85.2	–8.2

	2007	2004	percent change
MEDIAN VALUE OF PRIMARY RESIDENCE			
Total households	**$200,000**	**$175,700**	**13.8%**
Under age 35	175,000	148,300	18.0
Aged 35 to 44	205,000	175,700	16.7
Aged 45 to 54	230,000	186,700	23.2
Aged 55 to 64	210,000	218,700	–4.0
Aged 65 to 74	200,000	164,700	21.4
Aged 75 or older	150,000	137,300	9.2

	2007	2004	percent change
MEDIAN VALUE OF HOME-SECURED DEBT			
Total households	**$100,000**	**$95,600**	**4.6%**
Under age 35	78,000	68,600	13.7
Aged 35 to 44	101,600	82,400	23.3
Aged 45 to 54	82,000	95,600	–14.2
Aged 55 to 64	130,000	119,500	8.8
Aged 65 to 74	125,000	109,800	13.8
Aged 75 or older	50,000	42,800	16.8

Source: Federal Reserve Board, Changes in U.S. Family Finances from 2004 to 2007: Evidence from the Survey of Consumer Finances, Federal Reserve Bulletin, February 2009, Internet site http://www.federalreserve.gov/pubs/oss/oss2/2007/scf2007home.html; calculations by New Strategist

Debt Increased for Boomers

The increase is higher among older Boomers.

The median debt of the average American household grew 11 percent between 2004 and 2007 after adjusting for inflation—to $67,300. Among householders aged 45 to 54, median debt rose just 5 percent during those years, while those aged 55 to 64 experienced a 14 percent increase. But the younger group owes a substantially larger amount, a median of $95,500. This compares with a median of $60,300 owed by the older householders.

Home-secured debt accounts for the largest share of debt by far. Forty-nine percent of households have debt secured by their primary residence, and they owe a median of $107,000. Naturally such debt declines with age as householders pay off their mortgages. Householders aged 45 to 54 have a median home-secured debt of $110,000, while those aged 55 to 64 owe a smaller $85,000. Slightly more than half the Boomers carry a credit card balance, with a median balance of $3,600. They also owe a median of between $10,900 and $12,900 in installment loan debt (such as car loans).

■ Unless Boomers pay down their mortgage debt, they will not see growth in their net worth.

Debt declines with age

(median amount of debt owed by households, by age of householder, 2007)

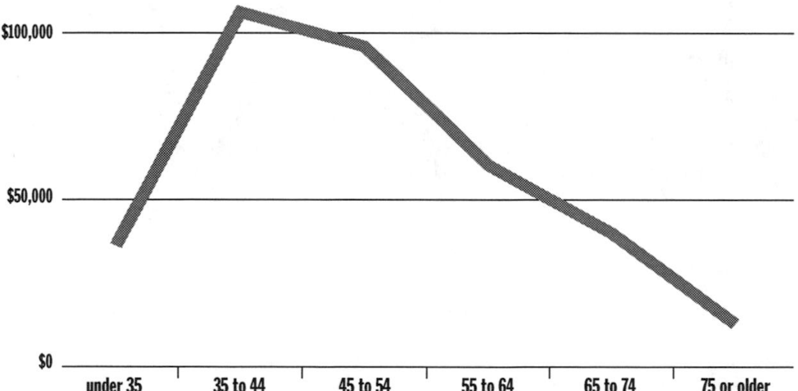

Table 11.8 Debt of Households by Age of Householder, 2004 and 2007

(percentage of households with debt and median amount of debt for debtors, by age of householder, 2004 and 2007; percentage point change in households with debt and percent change in amount of debt, 2004–07; in 2007 dollars)

	2007	2004	percentage point change
PERCENT WITH DEBT			
Total households	**77.0%**	**76.4%**	**0.6**
Under age 35	83.5	79.8	3.7
Aged 35 to 44	86.2	88.6	–2.4
Aged 45 to 54	86.8	88.4	–1.6
Aged 55 to 64	81.8	76.3	5.5
Aged 65 to 74	65.5	58.8	6.7
Aged 75 or older	31.4	40.3	–8.9

	2007	2004	percent change
MEDIAN AMOUNT OF DEBT			
Total households	**$67,300**	**$60,700**	**10.9%**
Under age 35	36,200	36,900	–1.9
Aged 35 to 44	106,200	95,800	10.9
Aged 45 to 54	95,900	91,400	4.9
Aged 55 to 64	60,300	52,700	14.4
Aged 65 to 74	40,100	27,500	45.8
Aged 75 or older	13,000	16,900	–23.1

Source: Federal Reserve Board, Changes in U.S. Family Finances from 2004 to 2007: Evidence from the Survey of Consumer Finances, Federal Reserve Bulletin, February 2009, Internet site http://www.federalreserve.gov/pubs/oss/oss2/2007/scf2007home.html; calculations by New Strategist

Table 11.9 Debt of Households by Type of Debt and Age of Householder, 2007

(percentage of households with debt, and median value of debt for those with debt, by type of debt and age of householder, 2007)

	total	under 35	35 to 44	45 to 54	55 to 64	65 to 74	75 or older
PERCENT WITH DEBT							
Any debt	**77.0%**	**83.5%**	**86.2%**	**86.8%**	**81.8%**	**65.5%**	**31.4%**
Secured by residential property							
Primary residence	48.7	37.3	59.5	65.5	55.3	42.9	13.9
Other	5.5	3.3	6.5	8.0	7.8	5.0	0.6
Lines of credit not secured by residential property	1.7	2.1	2.2	1.9	1.2	1.5	–
Installment loans	46.9	65.2	56.2	51.9	44.6	26.1	7.0
Credit card balances	46.1	48.5	51.7	53.6	49.9	37.0	18.8
Other debt	6.8	5.9	7.5	9.8	8.7	4.4	1.3
MEDIAN AMOUNT OF DEBT							
Any debt	**$67,300**	**$36,200**	**$106,200**	**$95,900**	**$60,300**	**$40,100**	**$13,000**
Secured by residential property							
Primary residence	107,000	135,300	128,000	110,000	85,000	69,000	40,000
Other	100,000	78,000	101,600	82,000	130,000	125,000	50,000
Lines of credit not secured by residential property	3,800	1,000	4,600	6,000	10,000	30,000	–
Installment loans	13,000	15,000	13,500	12,900	10,900	10,300	8,000
Credit card balances	3,000	1,800	3,500	3,600	3,600	3,000	800
Other debt	5,000	4,500	5,000	4,500	6,000	5,000	4,500

Note: "–" means sample is too small to make a reliable estimate.
Source: Federal Reserve Board, Changes in U.S. Family Finances from 2004 to 2007: Evidence from the Survey of Consumer Finances, Federal Reserve Bulletin, February 2009, Internet site http://www.federalreserve.gov/pubs/oss/oss2/2007/scf2007home.html; calculations by New Strategist

Retirement Coverage Peaks in the 45-to-64 Age Group

Boomers are worried about their economic security in retirement.

Fifty-two percent of American workers were offered an employer-sponsored retirement plan in 2007, but only 41.5 percent took advantage of the opportunity, according to an analysis by the Employee Benefit Research Institute (EBRI). Retirement coverage is highest among workers aged 45 to 64, 59 percent of whom are offered, and 52 to 53 percent of whom participate in, an employer-sponsored retirement plan.

Another EBRI study shows that only 51 to 52 percent of workers aged 45 to 64 own an IRA or participate in a 401(k)-type retirement plan. Among those aged 45 to 64 who participate in a 401(k)-type plan, only 10 to 13 percent made the maximum contribution in 2005.

Just one-third of workers aged 45 to 64 has savings of $100,000 or more. With little savings and a steep decline in stock values, it is no surprise that Boomers are worried about retirement. In 2009, only 10 percent of workers aged 45 to 54 were "very confident" they would have enough money to live comfortably throughout retirement, down from 21 percent in 1999.

■ With the value of 401(k)s plummeting, many Boomers will have to postpone retirement.

Workers aged 45 to 54 expect to work for many more years

(percent distribution of workers aged 45 to 54 by expected age of retirement, 2009)

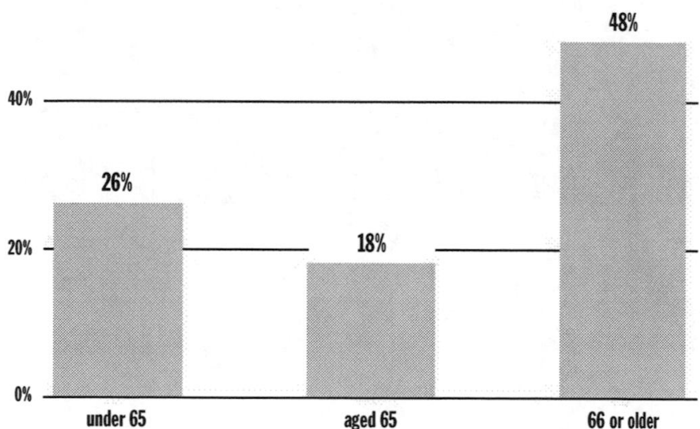

Table 11.10 Retirement Plan Coverage by Age, 2007

(total number of workers, percent whose employer offers a retirement plan, and percent participating in plan, by type of employment and age of worker, 2007; numbers in thousands)

	number of workers	percent with an employer who sponsors a retirement plan	percent participating in employer's retirement plan
Total workers	**158,099**	**51.8%**	**41.5%**
Under age 21	10,450	24.0	4.9
Aged 21 to 24	12,695	38.5	19.3
Aged 25 to 34	33,485	51.1	38.7
Aged 35 to 44	35,299	55.8	47.5
Aged 45 to 54	36,139	59.3	52.6
Aged 55 to 64	22,782	59.2	52.0
Aged 65 or older	7,249	39.1	28.7
PRIVATE WAGE AND SALARY WORKERS AGED 21 TO 64			
Total workers	**110,148**	**52.7**	**42.0**
Aged 21 to 24	11,397	37.3	17.9
Aged 25 to 34	27,816	48.9	35.7
Aged 35 to 44	27,788	54.5	45.3
Aged 45 to 54	27,068	58.1	50.7
Aged 55 to 64	16,079	57.7	49.9
PUBLIC WAGE AND SALARY WORKERS AGED 21 TO 64			
Total workers	**21,106**	**83.3**	**75.4**
Aged 21 to 24	1,035	58.5	38.9
Aged 25 to 34	4,250	80.1	69.5
Aged 35 to 44	5,183	84.3	77.7
Aged 45 to 54	6,179	85.7	79.9
Aged 55 to 64	4,459	87.9	80.7

Source: Employee Benefit Research Institute, Employment-Based Retirement Plan Participation: Geographic Differences and Trends, 2007, Issue Brief 322, October 2008, Internet site http://www.ebri.org/publications/ib/index.cfm?fa=ibDisp&content_id=3989

Table 11.11 Ownership of IRAs and 401(k)s by Age, 2005

(percentage of workers aged 21 to 64 owning IRAs and/or participating in a 401(k)-type plan, by age, 2005)

	IRA and/or 401(k)-type plan	IRA only	401(k)-type plan only	both IRA and 401(k)-type plan	neither IRA nor 401(k)-type plan
Total workers	**43.8%**	**10.7%**	**20.9%**	**12.2%**	**56.2%**
Aged 21 to 24	11.4	2.1	8.3	1.0	88.6
Aged 25 to 34	35.4	6.6	20.4	8.4	64.6
Aged 35 to 44	47.4	10.2	24.4	12.8	52.6
Aged 45 to 54	51.2	12.4	22.7	16.1	48.8
Aged 55 to 64	52.1	18.5	18.2	15.4	47.9

Source: Employee Benefit Research Institute, Ownership of Individual Retirement Accounts (IRAs) and 401(k)-Type Plans, by Craig Copeland, Notes, Vol. 29, No. 5, May 2008, Internet site http://www.ebri.org/publications/notes/index.cfm?fa=main&doc_type=2

Table 11.12 Participation in IRAs and 401(k)s by Age, 2005

(percent of workers aged 21 to 64 owning an IRA or participating in 401(k)-type plan, percent making a contribution to the IRA, and mean amount contributed and percent making maximum contribution among contributors, by age, 2005)

	has IRA in own name	made tax-deductible contribution to IRA	among IRA contributors: mean contribution	among IRA contributors: percent making maximum contribution
Total workers	**22.9%**	**6.2%**	**$2,540**	**26.8%**
Aged 21 to 24	3.2	0.6	1,149	0.0
Aged 25 to 34	15.0	4.3	2,089	20.5
Aged 35 to 44	23.0	6.4	2,497	31.3
Aged 45 to 54	28.5	7.4	2,527	25.0
Aged 55 to 64	33.9	9.2	2,943	29.3

	percent participating in 401(k)	among 401(k) contributors: mean contribution	among 401(k) contributors: percent making maximum contribution
Total workers	**33.1%**	**$4,274**	**8.9%**
Aged 21 to 24	9.3	1,597	0.0
Aged 25 to 34	28.8	3,353	5.0
Aged 35 to 44	37.2	4,226	8.4
Aged 45 to 54	38.8	1,695	10.3
Aged 55 to 64	33.5	4,993	13.2

Source: Employee Benefit Research Institute, Ownership of Individual Retirement Accounts (IRAs) and 401(k)-Type Plans, by Craig Copeland, Notes, Vol. 29, No. 5, May 2008, Internet site http://www.ebri.org/publications/notes/index.cfm?fa=main&doc_type=2

Table 11.13 Retirement Planning by Age, 2009

(percentage of workers aged 25 or older responding by age, 2009)

	total	25 to 34	35 to 44	45 to 54	55 or older
Very confident in having enough money to live comfortably throughout retirement	13%	18%	12%	10%	13%
Very confident in having enough money to take care of medical expenses in retirement	13	16	13	11	14
Worker and/or spouse have saved for retirement	75	66	78	78	79
Worker and/or spouse are currently saving for retirement	65	57	68	68	66
Contribute to a workplace retirement savings plan	64	52	72	65	64
Expected retirement age					
Before age 60	9	17	8	9	1
Aged 60 to 64	17	14	16	17	22
Aged 65	23	29	29	18	15
Aged 66 or older	31	22	33	35	34
Never retire	10	9	6	13	11
Don't know/refused	7	8	3	6	12
Total savings and investments (not including value of primary residence)					
Less than $25,000	53	73	53	43	36
$25,000 to $49,999	11	12	8	11	13
$50,000 to $99,999	12	9	14	14	10
$100,000 to $249,999	12	5	16	15	15
$250,000 or more	12	2	9	17	26

Source: Employee Benefit Research Institute, Retirement Confidence Surveys, Internet site http://www.ebri.org/surveys/rcs/2009/

Table 11.14 Changes in Retirement Confidence by Age, 1999 and 2009

(percentage of workers aged 25 or older responding by age, 1999 and 2009)

	total	25 to 34	35 to 44	45 to 54	55 or older
Very confident in having enough money to live comfortably throughout retirement					
2009	13%	18%	12%	10%	13%
1999	22	27	20	21	18
Very confident in having enough money to take care of medical expenses in retirement					
2009	13	16	13	11	14
1999	16	16	15	13	22
Say they are doing a good job of preparing financially for retirement					
2009	20	23	21	18	16
1999	23	22	22	24	29

Source: Employee Benefit Research Institute, Retirement Confidence Surveys, Internet site http://www.ebri.org/surveys/rcs/2009/

Glossary

adjusted for inflation Income or a change in income that has been adjusted for the rise in the cost of living, or the consumer price index (CPI-U-RS).

age Classification by age is based on the age of the person at his/her last birthday.

American Housing Survey The AHS collects national and metropolitan-level data on the nation's housing, including apartments, single-family homes, and mobile homes. The nationally representative survey, with a sample of 55,000 homes, is conducted by the Census Bureau for the Department of Housing and Urban Development every other year.

American Indians In this book, American Indians include Alaska Natives (Eskimos and Aleuts) unless those groups are shown separately.

American Time Use Survey Under contract with the Bureau of Labor Statistics, the Census Bureau collects ATUS information, which reveals how people spend their time. The ATUS sample is drawn from U.S. households that have completed their final month of interviews for the Current Population Survey. One individual from each selected household is chosen to participate in the ATUS. Respondents are interviewed by telephone only once about their time use on the previous day.

Asian Includes Native Hawaiians and other Pacific Islanders unless those groups are shown separately.

Baby Boom Americans born between 1946 and 1964.

Baby Bust Americans born between 1965 and 1976, also known as Generation X.

Behavioral Risk Factor Surveillance System A collaborative project of the Centers for Disease Control and Prevention and U.S. states and territories. It is an ongoing data collection program designed to measure behavioral risk factors in the adult population aged 18 or older. All 50 states, three territories, and the District of Columbia take part in the survey, making the BRFSS the primary source of information on the health-related behaviors of Americans.

black A racial category that includes those who identified themselves as "black" or "African American."

central cities The largest city in a metropolitan area. The balance of the metropolitan area outside the central city is regarded as the "suburbs."

Consumer Expenditure Survey An ongoing study of the day-to-day spending of American households administered by the Bureau of Labor Statistics. The CEX includes an interview survey and a diary survey. The average spending figures shown in this book are the integrated data from both the diary and interview components of the survey. Two separate, nationally representative samples are used for the interview and diary surveys. For the interview survey, about 7,500 consumer units are interviewed on a rotating panel basis each quarter for five consecutive quarters. For the diary survey, 7,500 consumer units keep weekly diaries of spending for two consecutive weeks.

consumer unit *(on spending tables only)* For convenience, the term consumer unit and households are used interchangeably in the spending section of this book, although consumer units are somewhat different from the Census Bureau's households. Consumer units are all related members of a household, or financially independent members of a household. A household may include more than one consumer unit.

Current Population Survey A nationally representative survey of the civilian noninstitutional population aged 15 or older. It is taken monthly by the Census Bureau for the Bureau of Labor Statistics, collecting information from more than 50,000 households on employment and unemployment. In March of each year, the survey includes the Annual Social and Economic Supplement (formerly called the Annual Demographic Survey), which is the source of most national data on the characteristics of Americans, such as educational attainment, living arrangements, and incomes.

disability As defined by the National Health Interview Survey, respondents aged 18 or older are asked whether they have difficulty in physical functioning, probing whether respondents can perform nine activities by themselves without using special equipment. The categories are walking a quarter mile; standing for two hours; sitting for two hours; walking up 10 steps without resting; stooping, bending, kneeling; reaching over one's head; grasping or handling small objects; carrying a 10-pound object; and pushing/pulling a large object. Adults who report that any of these activities is very difficult or they cannot do it at all are defined as having physical difficulties.

dual-earner couple A married couple in which both the householder and the householder's spouse are in the labor force.

earnings The amount of money a person receives from his or her job. *See also* Income.

employed All civilians who did any work as a paid employee or farmer/self-employed worker, or who worked 15 hours or more as an unpaid farm worker or in a family-owned business, during the reference period. All those who have jobs but who are temporarily absent from their jobs due to illness, bad weather, vacation, labor management dispute, or personal reasons are considered employed.

expenditure The transaction cost including excise and sales taxes of goods and services acquired during the survey period. The full cost of each purchase is recorded even though full payment may not have been made at the date of purchase. Average expenditure figures may be artificially low for infrequently purchased items such as cars because figures are calculated using all consumer units within a demographic segment rather than just purchasers. Expenditure estimates include money spent on gifts for others.

family A group of two or more people (one of whom is the householder) related by birth, marriage, or adoption and living in the same household.

family household A household maintained by a householder who lives with one or more people related to him or her by blood, marriage, or adoption.

female/male householder A woman or man who maintains a household without a spouse present. May head family or nonfamily households.

foreign-born population People who are not U.S. citizens at birth.

full-time employment Thirty-five or more hours of work per week during a majority of the weeks worked.

full-time, year-round Fifty or more weeks of full-time employment during the previous calendar year.

Generation X Americans born between 1965 and 1976, also known as the baby-bust generation.

Hispanic Because Hispanic is an ethnic origin rather than a race, Hispanics may be of any race. While most Hispanics are white, there are black, Asian, and American Indian Hispanics.

household All the persons who occupy a housing unit. A household includes the related family members and all the unrelated persons, if any, such as lodgers, foster children, wards, or employees who share the housing unit. A person living alone is counted as a household. A group of unrelated people who share a housing unit as roommates or unmarried partners is also counted as a household. Households do not include group quarters such as college dormitories, prisons, or nursing homes.

household, race/ethnicity of Households are categorized according to the race or ethnicity of the householder only.

householder The person (or one of the persons) in whose name the housing unit is owned or rented or, if there is no such person, any adult member. With married couples, the householder may be either the husband or wife. The householder is the reference person for the household.

householder, age of The age of the householder is used to categorize households into age groups such as those used in this book. Married couples, for example, are classified according to the age of either the husband or wife, depending on which one identified him or herself as the householder.

housing unit A house, an apartment, a group of rooms, or a single room occupied or intended for occupancy as separate living quarters. Separate living quarters are those in which the occupants do not live and eat with any other persons in the structure and that have direct access from the outside of the building or through a common hall that is used or intended for use by the occupants of another unit or by the general public. The occupants may be a single family, one person living alone, two or more families living together, or any other group of related or unrelated persons who share living arrangements.

Housing Vacancy Survey A supplement to the Current Population Survey, which provides quarterly and annual data on rental and homeowner vacancy rates, characteristics of units available for occupancy, and homeownership rates by age, household type, region, state, and metropolitan area. The Current Population Survey sample includes 51,000 occupied housing units and 9,000 vacant units.

housing value The respondent's estimate of how much his or her house and lot would sell for if it were for sale.

iGeneration Americans born from 1995 to the present.

immigration The relatively permanent movement (change of residence) of people into the country of reference.

income Money received in the preceding calendar year by each person aged 15 or older from each of the following sources: (1) earnings from longest job (or self-employment), (2) earnings from jobs other than longest job, (3) unemployment compensation, (4) workers' compensation, (5) Social Security, (6) Supplemental Security income, (7) public assistance, (8) veterans' payments, (9) survivor benefits, (10) disability benefits, (11) retirement pensions, (12) interest, (13) dividends, (14) rents and royalties or estates and trusts, (15) educational assistance, (16) alimony, (17) child support, (18) financial assistance from outside the household, and other periodic income. Income is reported in several ways in this book. Household income is the combined income of all household members. Income of persons is all income accruing to a person from all sources. Earnings are the money a person receives from his or her job.

industry The industry in which a person worked longest in the preceding calendar year.

job tenure The length of time a person has been employed continuously by the same employer.

labor force The labor force tables in this book show the civilian labor force only. The labor force includes both the employed and the unemployed (people who are looking for work). People are counted as in the labor force if they were working or looking for work during the reference week in which the Census Bureau fields the Current Population Survey.

labor force participation rate The percent of the civilian noninstitutional population that is in the civilian labor force, which includes both the employed and the unemployed.

married couples with or without children under age 18 Refers to married couples with or without own children under age 18 living in the same household. Couples without children under age 18 may be parents of grown children who live elsewhere, or they could be childless couples.

median The amount that divides the population or households into two equal portions: one below and one above the median. Medians can be calculated for income, age, and many other characteristics.

median income The amount that divides the income distribution into two equal groups, half having incomes above the median, half having incomes below the median. The medians for households or families are based on all households or families. The median for persons are based on all persons aged 15 or older with income.

Medical Expenditure Panel Survey A nationally representative survey that collects detailed information on the health status, access to care, health care use and expenses and health insurance coverage of the civilian noninstitutionalized population of the U.S. and nursing home residents. MEPS comprises four component surveys: the Household Component, the Medical Provider Component, the Insurance Component, and the Nursing Home Component. The Household Component is the core survey, is conducted each year, and includes 15,000 households and 37,000 people.

metropolitan statistical area A city with 50,000 or more inhabitants, or a Census Bureau-defined urbanized area of at least 50,000 inhabitants and a total metropolitan population of at least 100,000 (75,000 in New England). The county (or counties) that contains the largest city becomes the "central county" (counties), along with any adjacent counties that have at least 50 percent of their population in the urbanized area surrounding the largest city. Additional "outlying counties" are included in the MSA if they meet specified requirements of commuting to the central counties and other selected requirements of metropolitan character (such as population density and percent urban). In New England, MSAs are defined in terms of cities and towns rather than counties. For this reason, the concept of NECMA is used to define metropolitan areas in the New England division.

Millennial generation Americans born between 1977 and 1994.

mobility status People are classified according to their mobility status on the basis of a comparison between their place of residence at the time of the March Current Population Survey and their place of residence in March of the previous year. Nonmovers are people living in the same house at the end of the period as at the beginning of the period. Movers are people living in a different house at the end of the period than at the beginning of the period. Movers from abroad are either citizens or aliens whose place of residence is outside the United States at the beginning of the period, that is, in an outlying area under the jurisdiction of the United States or in a foreign country. The mobility status for children is fully allocated from the mother if she is in the household; otherwise it is allocated from the householder.

National Ambulatory Medical Care Survey An annual survey of visits to nonfederally employed office-based physicians who are primarily engaged in direct patient care. Data are collected from physicians rather than patients, with each physician assigned a one-week reporting period. During that week, a systematic random sample of visit characteristics are recorded by the physician or office staff.

National Health and Nutrition Examination Survey A continuous survey of a representative sample of the U.S. civilian noninstitutionalized population. Respondents are interviewed at home about their health and nutrition, and the interview is followed up by a physical examination that measures such things as height and weight in mobile examination centers.

National Health Interview Survey A continuing nationwide sample survey of the civilian noninstitutional population of the U.S. conducted by the Census

Bureau for the National Center for Health Statistics. Each year, data are collected from more than 100,000 people about their illnesses, injuries, impairments, chronic and acute conditions, activity limitations, and the use of health services.

National Hospital Ambulatory Medical Care Survey The NHAMCS, sponsored by the National Center for Health Statistics, is an annual national probability sample survey of visits to emergency departments and outpatient departments at non-Federal, short stay and general hospitals. Data are collected by hospital staff from patient records.

National Hospital Discharge Survey This survey has been conducted annually since 1965, sponsored by the National Center for Health Statistics, to collect nationally representative information on the characteristics of inpatients discharged from nonfederal, short-stay hospitals in the U.S. The survey collects data from a sample of approximately 270,000 inpatient records acquired from a national sample of about 500 hospitals.

National Household Education Survey The NHES, sponsored by the National Center for Education Statistics, provides descriptive data on the educational activities of the U.S. population, including after-school care and adult education. The NHES is a system of telephone surveys of a representative sample of 45,000 to 60,000 households in the U.S.

National Nursing Home Survey This is a series of national sample surveys of nursing homes, their residents, and staff conducted at various intervals since 1973-74 and sponsored by the National Center for Health Statistics. Data for the survey are obtained through personal interviews with administrators and staff, and occasionally with self-administered questionnaires, in a sample of about 1,500 facilities.

National Survey of Family Growth The 2002 NSFG, sponsored by the National Center for Health Statistics, is a nationally representative survey of the civilian noninstitutional population aged 15 to 44. In-person interviews were completed with 12,571 men and women, collecting data on marriage, divorce, contraception, and infertility. The 2002 survey updates previous NSFG surveys taken in 1973, 1976, 1988, and 1995.

National Survey on Drug Use and Health Formerly called the National Household Survey on Drug Abuse, this survey, sponsored by the Substance Abuse and Mental Health Services Administration, has been conducted since 1971. It is the primary source of information on the use of illegal drugs by the U.S. population. Each year, a nationally representative sample of about 70,000 individuals aged 12 or older are surveyed in the 50 states and the District of Columbia.

net worth The amount of money left over after a household's debts are subtracted from its assets.

nonfamily household A household maintained by a householder who lives alone or who lives with people to whom he or she is not related.

nonfamily householder A householder who lives alone or with nonrelatives.

non-Hispanic People who do not identify themselves as Hispanic are classified as non-Hispanic. Non-Hispanics may be of any race.

non-Hispanic white People who identify their race as white and who do not indicate a Hispanic origin.

nonmetropolitan area Counties that are not classified as metropolitan areas.

occupation Occupational classification is based on the kind of work a person did at his or her job during the previous calendar year. If a person changed jobs during the year, the data refer to the occupation of the job held the longest during that year.

occupied housing units A housing unit is classified as occupied if a person or group of people is living in it or if the occupants are only temporarily absent—on vacation, example. By definition, the count of occupied housing units is the same as the count of households.

outside central city The portion of a metropolitan county or counties that falls outside of the central city or cities; generally regarded as the suburbs.

own children Sons and daughters, including stepchildren and adopted children, of the householder. The totals include never-married children living away from home in college dormitories.

owner occupied A housing unit is "owner occupied" if the owner lives in the unit, even if it is mortgaged or not fully paid for. A cooperative or condominium unit is "owner occupied" only if the owner lives in it. All other occupied units are classified as "renter occupied."

part-time employment Less than 35 hours of work per week in a majority of the weeks worked during the year.

percent change The change (either positive or negative) in a measure that is expressed as a proportion of the starting measure. When median income changes from $20,000 to $25,000, for example, this is a 25 percent increase.

percentage point change The change (either positive or negative) in a value which is already expressed as a percentage. When a labor force participation rate changes from 70 percent of 75 percent, for example, this is a 5 percentage point increase.

poverty level The official income threshold below which families and people are classified as living in poverty. The threshold rises each year with inflation and varies depending on family size and age of householder.

primary activity In the time use tables, those activities that respondents identify as their main activity. Other activities done simultaneously are not included.

proportion or share The value of a part expressed as a percentage of the whole. If there are 4 million people aged 25 and 3 million of them are white, then the white proportion is 75 percent.

race Race is self-reported and can be defined in three ways. The "race alone" population comprises people who identify themselves as only one race. The "race in combination" population comprises people who identify themselves as more than one race, such as white and black. The "race, alone or in combination" population includes both those who identify themselves as one race and those who identify themselves as more than one race.

regions The four major regions and nine census divisions of the United States are the state groupings as shown below:

Northeast:
—New England: Connecticut, Maine, Massachusetts, New Hampshire, Rhode Island, and Vermont
—Middle Atlantic: New Jersey, New York, and Pennsylvania

Midwest:
—East North Central: Illinois, Indiana, Michigan, Ohio, and Wisconsin
—West North Central: Iowa, Kansas, Minnesota, Missouri, Nebraska, North Dakota, and South Dakota

South:
—South Atlantic: Delaware, District of Columbia, Florida, Georgia, Maryland, North Carolina, South Carolina, Virginia, and West Virginia
—East South Central: Alabama, Kentucky, Mississippi, and Tennessee
—West South Central: Arkansas, Louisiana, Oklahoma, and Texas

West:
—Mountain: Arizona, Colorado, Idaho, Montana, Nevada, New Mexico, Utah, and Wyoming
—Pacific: Alaska, California, Hawaii, Oregon, and Washington

renter occupied *See* Owner Occupied.

Retirement Confidence Survey An annual survey, sponsored by the Employee Benefit Research Institute, the American Savings Education Council, and Mathew Greenwald & Associates, of a nationally representative sample of 1,000 people aged 25 or older. Respondents are asked a core set of questions that have been asked since 1996, measuring attitudes and behavior towards retirement.

rounding Percentages are rounded to the nearest tenth of a percent; therefore, the percentages in a distribution do not always add exactly to 100.0 percent. The totals, however, are always shown as 100.0. Moreover, individual figures are rounded to the nearest thousand without being adjusted to group totals, which are independently rounded; percentages are based on the unrounded numbers.

self-employment A person is categorized as self-employed if he or she was self-employed in the job held longest during the reference period. Persons who report self-employment from a second job are excluded, but those who report wage-and-salary income from a second job are included. Unpaid workers in family businesses are excluded. Self-employment statistics include only nonagricultural workers and exclude people who work for themselves in incorporated business.

sex ratio The number of men per 100 women.

suburbs *See* Outside Central City.

Survey of Consumer Finances A triennial survey taken by the Federal Reserve Board. It collects data on the assets, debts, and net worth of American households. For the 2007 survey, the Federal Reserve Board interviewed more than 4,000 households.

unemployed Those who, during the survey period, had no employment but were available and looking for work. Those who were laid off from their jobs and were waiting to be recalled are also classified as unemployed.

white A racial category that includes many Hispanics (who may be of any race) unless the term "non-Hispanic white" is used.

Youth Risk Behavior Surveillance System Created by the Centers for Disease Control to monitor health risks being taken by young people at the national, state, and local level. The national survey is taken every two years based on a nationally representative sample of 16,000 students in 9th through 12th grade in public and private schools.

Bibliography

Agency for Healthcare Research and Quality

Internet site http://www.ahrq.gov/

—Medical Expenditure Panel Survey, Internet site http://www.meps.ahrq.gov/mepsweb/survey_comp/household.jsp

Bureau of Labor Statistics

Internet site http://www.bls.gov

—2000 and 2007 Consumer Expenditure Surveys, Internet site http://www.bls.gov/cex/

—2007 American Time Use Survey, Internet site http://www.bls.gov/tus/home.htm

—2007 American Time Use Survey, Summary Table 2. Number of persons and average hours per day by detailed activity classification (travel reported separately), 2007 annual averages, unpublished tables received upon special request

—Characteristics of Minimum Wage Workers, 2008, Internet site http://www.bls.gov/cps/minwage2008tbls.htm

—College Enrollment and Work Activity of 2008 High School Graduates, Internet site http://www.bls.gov/news.release/hsgec.toc.htm

—Contingent and Alternative Employment Arrangements, Internet site http://www.bls.gov/news.release/conemp.toc.htm

—Economic and Employment Projections, Internet site http://www.bls.gov/news.release/ecopro.toc.htm

—Employee Benefits Survey, Internet site http://www.bls.gov/ncs/ebs/benefits/2008/ownership_civilian.htm

—Employee Tenure, Internet site http://www.bls.gov/news.release/tenure.toc.htm

—Employment Characteristics of Families, Internet site http://www.bls.gov/news.release/famee.toc.htm

—Labor Force Statistics from the Current Population Survey, Internet site http://www.bls.gov/cps/tables.htm#empstat

—*Monthly Labor Review*, "Labor Force Projections to 2016: More Workers in Their Golden Years," November 2007, Internet site http://www.bls.gov/opub/mlr/2007/11/contents.htm

—*Monthly Labor Review*, "Youth enrollment and employment during the school year," February 2008, Internet site http://www.bls.gov/opub/mlr/2008/02/contents.htm

—Table 15. Employed persons by detailed occupation, sex, and age, Annual Average 2008 (Source: Current Population Survey), unpublished table received upon special request

Bureau of the Census

Internet site http://www.census.gov

—2007 American Community Survey, Internet site http://factfinder.census.gov/servlet/DatasetMainPageServlet?_program=ACS&_submenuId=&_lang=en&_ts=l

—2008 Current Population Survey Annual Social and Economic Supplement, Internet site http://www.census.gov/hhes/www/income/dinctabs.html

—2008 National Population Projections, Internet site http://www.census.gov/population/www/projections/2008projections.html

—A Child's Day: 2006 (Selected Indicators of Child Well-Being), Detailed Tables, Internet site http://www.census.gov/population/www/socdemo/2006_detailedtables.html

—American Housing Survey for the United States in 2007, Internet site http://www.census.gov/hhes/www/housing/ahs/ahs07/ahs07.html

—America's Families and Living Arrangements, 2008 Current Population Survey Annual Social and Economic Supplement, Internet site http://www.census.gov/population/www/socdemo/hh-fam/cps2008.html

—Educational Attainment, Historical Tables, Internet site http://www.census.gov/population/www/socdemo/educ-attn.html

—Educational Attainment in the United States: 2008, Detailed Tables, Current Population Survey Annual Social and Economic Supplement, Internet site http://www.census.gov/population/www/socdemo/education/cps2008.html

—Families and Living Arrangements, Historical Time Series, Current Population Survey Annual Social and Economic Supplements, Internet site http://www.census.gov/population/www/socdemo/hh-fam.html

—Fertility of American Women, Current Population Survey—June 2006, Detailed Tables, Internet site http://www.census.gov/population/www/socdemo/fertility/cps2006.html

—Geographic Mobility: 2007 to 2008, Detailed Tables, Current Population Survey Annual Social and Economic Supplement, Internet site http://www.census.gov/population/www/socdemo/migrate/cps2008.html

—Geographical Mobility/Migration, Current Population Survey Annual Social and Economic Supplements, Internet site http://www.census.gov/population/www/socdemo/migrate.html

—Health Insurance, Internet site http://pubdb3.census.gov/macro/032008/health/toc.htm

—Historical Health Insurance Tables, Internet site http://www.census.gov/hhes/www/hlthins/historic/index.html

—Historical Income Tables, Current Population Survey Annual Social and Economic Supplements, Internet site http://www.census.gov/hhes/www/income/histinc/histinctb.html

—Housing Vacancy Surveys, Internet site http://www.census.gov/hhes/www/housing/hvs/hvs.html

—National Population Estimates, Internet site http://www.census.gov/popest/national/asrh/NC-EST2008-sa.html

—Number, Timing, and Duration of Marriages and Divorces: 2004, Detailed Tables, Internet site http://www.census.gov/population/www/socdemo/marr-div/2004detailed_tables.html

—School Enrollment, Historical Tables, Internet site http://www.census.gov/population/www/socdemo/school.html

—School Enrollment—Social and Economic Characteristics of Students: October 2007, detailed tables, Internet site http://www.census.gov/population/www/socdemo/school/cps2007.html

—State Population Estimates, Internet site http://www.census.gov/popest/states/asrh/

Centers for Disease Control and Prevention

Internet site http://www.cdc.gov

—Behavioral Risk Factor Surveillance System, Prevalence Data, Internet site http://apps.nccd.cdc.gov/brfss/

—Cases of HIV/AIDS and AIDS, Internet site http://www.cdc.gov/hiv/topics/surveillance/resources/reports/2006report/table3.htm

—"Youth Risk Behavior Surveillance–United States, 2007," *Mortality and Morbidity Weekly Report*, Vol. 57/SS-4, June 6, 2008; Internet site http://www.cdc.gov/HealthyYouth/yrbs/index.htm

Department of Homeland Security

Internet site http://www.dhs.gov/index.shtm

—Immigration, 2008 Yearbook of Immigration Statistics, Internet site http://www.uscis.gov/graphics/shared/statistics/yearbook/index.htm

Employee Benefit Research Institute

Internet site http://www.ebri.org/

—Retirement Confidence Surveys, Internet site http://www.ebri.org/surveys/rcs/

—"Employment-Based Retirement Plan Participation: Geographic Differences and Trends, 2007," *Issue Brief* 322, October 2008, Internet site http://www.ebri.org/publications/ib/index.cfm?fa=ibDisp&content_id=3989

—"Ownership of Individual Accounts (IRAs) and 401(k)-Type Plans," by Craig Copeland, *Notes*, Vol. 29, No. 5, May 2008; Internet site http://www.ebri.org/publications/notes/index.cfm?fa=main&doc_type=2

Federal Interagency Forum on Child and Family Statistics

Internet site http://childstats.gov

—America's Children in Brief: Key National Indicators of Well-Being, 2008, Internet site http://childstats.gov/americaschildren/tables.asp

Federal Reserve Board

Internet site http://www.federalreserve.gov/pubs/oss/oss2/scfindex.html

—"Changes in U.S. Family Finance from 2004 to 2007: Evidence from the Survey of Consumer Finances," *Federal Reserve Bulletin*, February 2009, Internet site http://www.federalreserve.gov/pubs/oss/oss2/2007/scf2007home.html

National Center for Education Statistics

Internet site http://nces.ed.gov

—The Condition of Education, Internet site http://nces.ed.gov/programs/coe/

—Digest of Education Statistics: 2008, Internet site http://nces.ed.gov/programs/digest/

— National Household Education Surveys Program, Parent and Family Involvement in Education, 2006–07 School Year, Internet site http://nces.ed.gov/pubsearch/pubsinfo.asp?pubid=2008050

National Center for Health Statistics

Internet site http://www.cdc.gov/nchs

—*2006 National Hospital Discharge Survey,* National Health Statistics Report, No. 5, 2008, Internet site http://www.cdc.gov/nchs/about/major/hdasd/listpubs.htm

—*Ambulatory Medical Care Utilization Estimates for 2006*, National Health Statistics Reports, No. 8, 2008, Internet site http://www.cdc.gov/nchs/about/major/ahcd/adata.htm#CombinedReports

—*Anthropometric Reference Data for Children and Adults: United States, 2003–2006*, National Health Statistics Reports, Number 10, 2008, Internet site http://www.cdc.gov/nchs/products/pubs/pubd/nhsr/nhsr.htm

—*Births: Final Data for 2006*, National Vital Statistics Reports, Vol. 57, No. 7, 2009, Internet site http://www.cdc.gov/nchs/products/nvsr.htm#57_12

—*Births: Preliminary Data for 2007*, National Vital Statistics Reports, Vol. 57, No. 12, 2009, Internet site http://www.cdc.gov/nchs/products/nvsr.htm#57_12

—*Complementary and Alternative Medicine Use Among Adults and Children: United States, 2007*, National Health Statistics Report, No. 12, 2008, Internet site http://nccam.nih.gov/news/camstats/2007/index.htm

—*Deaths: Final Data for 2006*, National Vital Statistics Reports, Vol. 57, No. 14, 2009, Internet site http://www.cdc.gov/nchs/products/nvsr.htm#vol57

—*Fertility, Contraception, and Fatherhood: Data on Men and Women from Cycle 6 of the 2002 National Survey of Family Growth*, Vital and Health Statistics, Series 23, No. 26, 2006; Internet site http://www.cdc.gov/nchs/nsfg.htm

—*Fertility, Family Planning, and Reproductive Health of U.S. Women: Data from the 2002 National Survey of Family Growth*, Vital and Health Statistics, Series 23, No. 25, 2005; Internet site http://www.cdc.gov/nchs/nsfg.htm

—*Health Characteristics of Adults 55 Years of Age and Over: United States, 2000-2003, Advance Data, No. 370,* 2006, Internet site http://www.cdc.gov/nchs/nhis.htm

—*National Ambulatory Medical Care Survey: 2006 Summary,* National Health Statistics Report, No. 3, 2008, Internet site http://www.cdc.gov/nchs/about/major/ahcd/adata.htm

—National Center for Chronic Disease Prevention and Health Promotion, Prevalence Data, Internet site http://apps.nccd.cdc.gov/HRQOL/

—*National Hospital Ambulatory Medical Care Survey: 2006 Emergency Department Summary,* National Health Statistics Report, No. 4, 2007, Internet site http://www.cdc.gov/nchs/about/major/ahcd/adata.htm

—*National Hospital Ambulatory Medical Care Survey: 2006 Outpatient Department Summary,* National Health Statistics Report, No. 4, 2008, Internet site http://www.cdc.gov/nchs/about/major/ahcd/adata.htm

—*Health United States 2008,* Internet site http://www.cdc.gov/nchs/hus.htm

—*Sexual Behavior and Selected Health Measures: Men and Women 15-44 Years of Age, United States, 2002*, Advance Data, No. 362, 2005; Internet site http://www.cdc.gov/nchs/nsfg.htm

—*Summary Health Statistics for U.S. Adults: National Health Interview Survey, 2007*, Series 10, No. 240, 2008, Internet site http://www.cdc.gov/nchs/nhis.htm
—*Summary Health Statistics for U.S. Children: National Health Interview Survey, 2007*, Series 10, No. 239, 2008, Internet site http://www.cdc.gov/nchs/nhis.htm
—*Summary Health Statistics for the U.S. Population: National Health Interview Survey, 2007*, Series 10, No. 238, 2008, Internet site http://www.cdc.gov/nchs/nhis.htm

National Sporting Goods Association
Internet site http://www.nsga.org
—Sports Participation, Internet site http://www.nsga.org

Substance Abuse and Mental Health Services Administration
Internet site http://www.samhsa.gov
—National Survey on Drug Use and Health, 2007, Internet site http://www.oas.samhsa.gov/nsduh.htm

Survey Documentation and Analysis, Computer-assisted Survey Methods Program, University of California, Berkeley
Internet site http://sda.berkeley.edu/
—General Social Surveys, 1972-2008 Cumulative Data Files, Internet site http://sda.berkeley.edu/cgi-bin32/hsda?harcsda+gss08

Index